BEHIND THE BOARDS

BEHIND THE BOARDS

The Making of Rock 'n' Roll's Greatest Records Revealed

Jake Brown

HAL LEONARD BOOKS

An Imprint of Hal Leonard Corporation

Published in 2012 by Hal Leonard Books
An Imprint of Hal Leonard Corporation
7777 West Bluemound Road
Milwaukee, WI 53213

Trade Book Division Editorial Offices
33 Plymouth St., Montclair, NJ 07042

Cover photograph by Curtis Wayne Millard
Interior photographs provided by the interviewed producers

Printed in the United States of America

Book design by Leslie Goldman

Library of Congress Cataloging-in-Publication Data

Brown, Jake.
Behind the boards : the making of rock 'n' roll's greatest records revealed / Jake Brown.
pages cm
1. Sound recording executives and producers—Interviews.
2. Sound recordings—Production and direction.
3. Popular music—History and criticism. I. Title.
ML3790.B776 2012
781.66'149--dc23

2012025417

ISBN 978-1-4584-1972-9

www.halleonardbooks.com

This book is dedicated to my beloved parents, James and Christina Brown—my father, James, for teaching me never to fear the ambition he gave me, and my mom for the creative DNA to have the chance to do just that in the form of dreams-come-true like this one . . .

CONTENTS

CONTENTS

CONTENTS

ACKNOWLEDGMENTS

Project Thank-You(s): I would first and foremost like to thank the amazing galaxy of su-perstar producers who have joined me over the last nine years as their schedules permitted in rounding out a roster I couldn't be prouder to define myself by first and foremost as a music fan in the context of the records they produced, so a toast to all of you: *Jack Douglas, Daniel Lanois, Mario Caldato Jr., Dave Jerden, Bob Rock, Linda Perry, Mike Fraser, Butch Vig, Gil Norton, Tom Werman, Kevin Elson, Eddie Kramer, Al Jourgensen, Michael Beinhorn, Bob Ezrin, Scott Humphrey and "The" Tommy Lee (thanks for sitting in, my man, a real honor as a lifelong Crüe fan!), J. Mascis, Bones Howe, Don Gehman, Butch Walker, Hugh Padgham, Flemming Rasmussen, Tony Platt, Don Was, Richie Zito, Keith Olsen, "Col." Tom Allom, Ron Nevison, Matt Wallace, Andy Johns,* and *Stephen Hague.* In concert with this amazing list of talent, I'd like to thank its shepherd to stores, Hal Leonard, and specifically group publisher John Cerullo, copy editor Gary Mor-ris, Matt Cerullo, et al., for taking a chance on this FIRST of its kind book. . . . Thanks to Lee Foster, photographer Curtis Wayne Millard, et al., at Electric Lady Studios (www.elec-tricladystudios.com) for the dream come true of allowing us to star the beloved Studio A as this book's cover photo—it captures the true visual essence of this anthology, thank you.

Personal Thanks: First and foremost, along with my aforementioned parents James and Christina, and dear brother Joshua, thank you to my beautiful Carriedoll for the way you tirelessly love and inspire me. To my lifelong best friends: Alex and Jackson Schuchard;

AKNOWLEDGMENTS

Andrew and Sarah McDermott; "The" Sean Fillinich; Adam Perri; Chris "See" Ellauri; Matt, Eileen, and the kids; the HANDSOME Hanaman, Bill and Susan, et al.; Richard, Lisa, and Regan Kendrick; Paul and Helen Watts; Bob O'Brien and Cayenne Engel; Lexi "Clown" Federov and Larry; MVD Distribution/Big Daddy Music; Aaron "Whippit" Harmon for continuing to have my back musically week in and week out; Joe Viers/Sonic Lounge Studios for twelve years of great ears; Andrew McNeice at Melodic Rock; Keavin Wiggins at Antimusic.com; Cheryl Hoahing at Metal Edge; Andrew, Metal Tim, et al., at Brave Words/Bloody Knuckles; Rock and Roll Report; Blabbermouth.net; John Cerullo et al. at Hal Leonard for giving this opus a home after nine years in the making; John Blake Publishing; Aaron, Gabriel, Victor, John, and everyone at SCB Distribution/Rock N Roll Books; Cherry Red Books Co.; ECW Press; and Tony/Yvonne Rose at Amber Books for giving me my start ten years ago and continuing to believe in me; my agents Nicole, Frank Wiemann, Elyse Tanzillo, and the Literary Group; and anyone else who has played a role in getting me thirty-plus books into a career I would never have envisioned back as a kid growing up on the amazing bands/albums/hits chronicled in this book, my In the Studio series, etc.!

BEHIND THE BOARDS

CHAPTER 1

January 28th, 2012 . . .

"This book is called *Behind the Boards?*"

"That's exactly where I'm sitting!" replies a producer who—five years before returning to the studio for Aerosmith's last studio outing, the blues-covers album *Honkin' on Bobo*—had taken a dramatic step out of the spotlight at the height of his career to recover from the death of John Lennon, his last legendary studio collaboration prior thereto. Having spent the last night before Lennon's death with the singer, the producer recalled the wind had been fully at Lennon's back following the release three weeks prior of *Double Fantasy*. Lennon's first new studio album in five years, the *New York Times* reported the collaboration had been so prolific that "Mr. Lennon and Miss Ono had recorded enough material for two albums during the summer and fall of 1980." As Douglas elaborated more intimately on that evening, "we were talking about making records with Paul and Ringo, and a tour, and a bunch of cool stuff, and to be with him on that last night before his death . . . and then all the media pressure after his death—it was something I wanted to back out of for a while, and I did."

For a producer of Douglas's historic renown, to have reclaimed his crown as one of the biggest rock producers in the business is rare indeed. With his role as lead producer on Aerosmith's first studio in almost a decade, and arguably their most anticipated since *Permanent Vacation*, Douglas has done just that, declaring excitedly that with the band's new LP,

> I was looking to get back to the truth, both in sound and in the songs themselves. Breaking it down to the raw sound that we used to get, which is: two guitars, bass and drums, vocals, an occasional keyboard, an occasional lead over the two rhythms going. And then truth in sound, I mean we recorded to tape; the processing is all old analog 2 inch, so we're really looking to get back to where we were in the '70s in feel. We're trying to make a true album. Some of the albums during the 1990s, some were very successful and were made that feel like they were trying to sell to a young audience.

Seeking to channel both his and the band's revitalized energies collectively into a sound that allowed the band to bridge one generation of fans with another, Douglas revealed that

> on this record, we wanted to do two things: we want to go to the fan base and really the hard-core fans who let us know all over the world what kind of record they want to hear—so that's what we're doing. Then, Steven has created so many new fans with *Idol*, and so many people have gone back to listen to the early stuff that even the kids want to hear that kind of thing again. So we're just having a blast, and when you make a record that's about the truth and true, it's always more fun, because you don't have the pressure of trying to be something you're not on the record.

That authenticity on the part of the band was first cemented via their mid-1970s collaborations with Douglas, who *Billboard* argued "either helped the band ease into the studio or captured their sound in a way their debut never did." Though the pair's teaming began in 1974 on the band's second LP, *Get Your Wings*, it was in the songs that rocked their seminal third studio album, *Toys in the Attic*, where MTV would later conclude that

> by the time it was recorded, the band's sound had developed into a sleek, hard-driving hard rock powered by simple, almost brutal, blues-based riffs. Many critics at the time labeled the group as punk rockers, and it's easy to see why—instead of adhering to the world-music pretensions of Led Zeppelin or the prolonged gloomy mysticism of Black Sabbath, Aerosmith stripped heavy metal to its basic core, spitting out spare riffs that not only rocked, but rolled. Steven Tyler's lyrics were filled with double-entendres and clever jokes, and the entire band had a streetwise charisma that separated them from the heavy, lumbering arena rockers of the era.

Rolling Stone magazine added their highly regarded opinion that with *Toys*, "Aerosmith perfected their raunchy blues-rock sound," adding the spotlight compliment to the band's producer that the fact that the album "stood the test of time is testimony to the band's raw abilities and some outstanding production on the part of Jack Douglas."

As the group plugged in this time around to begin working with their classic producer, Douglas takes readers behind the scenes of that process by addressing briefly the controversy that surrounded the band prior to their entering the studio together, reasoning that it was only natural because

it's hard for any family to be together for 40 years, so they've become the symbol of something more than just a band. When you see them up onstage, it's a family playing together and having fun together and living together, and that goes beyond music. Not many of those people around, so that's a very cool thing. Last night, we went to a screening—Steven, Joe, and I—of a concert film about Aerosmith in Japan. What was really interesting was, the band went there to play right after the radiation, when no one else wanted to go, but they love the Japanese people and the Japanese people love them. So they asked some Japanese fans in the film what it is about Aerosmith they really liked, and they said, "They seem like a family." And we loved that, because as a family for 40 years, they love that.

Proceeding in that spirit down a very familiar path as he and the band began writing for the new LP, Douglas recalled that "back in the *Toys in the Attic* days, the band wrote a lot live in the studio, and we're still doing it exactly the same way." Delving into the heart of that creative process, the producer shares that

the way it works is: we come up with a lick, and then we develop the lick into a feel, and a feel is something that Steven can hold in his hands and bite into. And as soon as he's got that, and feels he can bite into it, we sit in the rehearsal room and we work it up so it's something that he can start singing over—even if it's not lyrics, he starts to get a feel for what the lyrics might be, and he starts singing syllables. Then we go right in to record it while the idea's fresh. Then we listen back to it a few times, make some changes, and go on to another tune. We might come back to that tune later with some fresh ideas that may just be changing a couple of chords in a chorus, but slowly these things develop until we end up at the point where we are right now, which is: we have 15 songs that feel like they're almost complete. But now maybe a couple of chords change here or there, maybe the corner notes on the bass turn to eighth notes, things like that.

As the band jams out new musical ideas for their first album of new material in a decade, Douglas next shared that "all the while Steven is singing along, and he's in the control room right next to me. Sometimes I'll give him a 57, and I can be doing an overdub, and Steven is singing right into everybody's headphones, and it starts to take shape. So then he'll take it home, or in the case of Swing House, we have a writing nest which is over the studio, and he can go up into the nest and has everything he needs up there to get some lyrics done." While much of Tyler's writing for the new album happened in real time with the band's jams, the producer added that the front man at times also finds inspiration in the moment of a particular song's vocal tracking, wherein "I recognize when he's come up with something that's hooky or catchy, and I'll encourage him sometimes, but he's pretty pro-active with that, even when he's jamming: he'll come in and say, 'Let me put a harmony on that right now, just so I can take it home,' and he'll do it. He was doing it yesterday as a matter of fact."

Taking readers back to the band's '70s heyday and into the studio for a look at how classics like the aforementioned *Toys in the Attic*, *Rocks*, and *Draw the Line* were created, Douglas shared his memory that "the way it was done when we would do it in New York in the '70s at the Record Plant, we would do the same process as now and Steven would end up in the stairwell writing the lyrics. So he would go in the stairwell at the point where the syllables were just about to turn into lyrics."

Once Tyler was rocking before the microphone live recording a lead vocal track, the producer says, "the mics I used with Steven depended on the song. A lot of the times—because he's got a great big voice—I would stick him in front of a 57, then use a Sennheiser Shotgun mic about eight to ten feet away from it and point it right at him to get all of the snarl and everything else that was going on—get his chest, and his head and his mouth. Otherwise, I'd use 57s and 87s."

Turning the dial back to Tyler's modern-day vocal recording technique, in contrast to the '70s, Douglas shares that "right now, I'm using a 48 on him—that's the classic Beatles mic. It's a 47 that has a figure-eight or cardioid, just an amazing sounding capsule. We have old 67s, a Peluso 67, which sounds like a 67 with a little extra top on it—again it's all song dependent. I've even used an Altec 'Saltshaker' mic, which is instant low-fi, and all of a sudden you've got the attitude you want and you don't have to process it. He sings because he hears that sound in his headphones as it's coming right out of his mouth." As Tyler built each of the new album's vocal tracks, once he was happy with a lead, the singer dove right into building harmonies, with Douglas explaining that "after Steven's done his comp, he'll try every harmony known to man. He's a walking Polyphonic keyboard, because he grew up under a piano with his father—he just knows every kind of harmonic, even if it's dissonant, he'll go for it."

As an extension of Tyler's universal knowledge of the musical side of composition, Douglas throughout the making of Aerosmith's new album has been tapping into the singer's equally thorough knowledge of the catalog of composers spanning a range of eras and genres:

> Steven has pretty much the same catalog in his head as I do—I carry a *huge* catalog in my head of classical music. I'm a big fan of Debussy and Sergey Prokofiev. I don't know how many times I've stolen licks from Prokofiev's *Romeo and Juliet (Complete Ballet)*. Chord structures and things like that, I don't mean direct lines, but chord structure, so I have a *vast* classic catalog in my head. I also have a *vast* standards catalog in my head, and so does Steven, so if we hear something that Bing Crosby did in 1937, we both understand that that harmonic structure can be used in rock. That things don't have to sound like nursery rhymes—you can be very sophisticated and still be really cool. So my arrangement chops, with Aerosmith, is very 50/50—with Steven, Joe, and the band.

Offering an exclusive look inside that catalog come to life in the studio, the producer remarked it had been an exciting process because, after forty-plus years as a rockologist, "Steven's got the book in his head of every lick that was ever played by any musician, from Beethoven or Bach to Philip Glass, to Satchmo, Jimi Hendrix, and John Coltrane—they're all in there, that catalog. And Joe's got that 'Fuck-all, if this chord sounds weird because it's dissonant, I don't care, I like the way it feels.' And when Steven hears that, he thinks: 'You know what, I know that same chord, Stravinsky played it, it's totally cool. Go with it, let's see where this goes. . . . ' And because of that, they come up with very novel and original-sounding licks and lyrics and melody lines."

Elaborating on Perry's half of the hit-making team at the heart of hits like "Walk This Way," "Sweet Emotion," "Back in the Saddle," "Same Old Song and Dance," and "Last Child," Douglas picked up with his latter point that

> Joe is a feel guy, and totally goes by feel. I do too, but I have a book first. I have a book in my head, I make suggestions from the book in my head, Steven does the same, and then Joe goes by gut feeling. After that, it's all what feels good. With Joe, I like to dig out weirdness and then drop it back in places, because he plays some very weird stuff. And sometimes that weirdness will be in the middle of something that we're gonna throw away, so "Naw, I didn't like it, but I'll save it." Then that will show its head somewhere during a solo, and I like that, I like that a lot because nobody plays weirder than him. Well, Jeff Beck plays pretty weird, but Joe plays in a really extraordinary unorthodox style.

Turning to any audiophile Aerosmith fans itching for a look inside the technical world of bringing Perry's signature brand of hard-rock riffage live to tape, Douglas revealed that in capturing the guitarist's sound, "I take it direct off of his pedals; I mic multiple cabinets. I use a Voyer 121 with the tube in it, 57s and 421s—both of which are right above the speakers. The ribbon mics are some distance away, sometimes I'll put one of those vocal blockers on the other side of the ribbon to contain the figure-eight sound. Then I always use at least four room mics, so that you get the sensation of space in the sound." Reviewing some of the effects that he'd kept stationary in the course of crafting a sound that *Billboard* would later argue was "responsible for inspiring thousands of teenagers to pick up guitars and start rocking & rolling in the 1970s and beyond," the producer shared that

> I still like reel tape delay, and I have two mono Ampex 300 decks, which are Elvis decks from '62 and '63. I still use very, very old mic-Pres, or I use 1073s, but I use Ampex 601s that are modified. I use mic-Pres from Crown—DC800s from the '50s that are modified to sound like they're brand new. I like the Crowns because they have a really primitive EQ in them, treble and bass is basically what it is. And the Ampex 601 were remote recorders from the '50s, so with those mic-Pres, you could run a tank over them and they're gonna work they're so solid. So that kind of stuff I've always had and I like it.

On the subject of tracking Steven Tyler's moving piano work on the ballad "You See Me Crying" that brought *Toys in the Attic* to its close, Douglas proudly recalled that "that was recorded with piano and an orchestra, and I used KM-84s on Steven's piano, which I also used on John Lennon's piano during the recording of 'Imagine.' I also like Earthworks mics as well." For acoustic guitars, the producer stated his preference for "a 56 mic, and you have to put your ear to the guitar to find the sweet spot, there's no rule on that one because everybody plays different. And the key of the song, it just depends on everything, and your ear will tell you. You have to put your ear down and listen to it, you have to do that on almost any instrument—because the players vary—but particularly on an acoustic guitar."

When his ears were focused on drummer Joey Kramer, Douglas quipped that not much had changed in his approach to capturing the legendary drummer's power playing, such that

> it's pretty much the same technique on this album, except I use a parade drum in front of his real bass drum as a resonator. The old way was no front head, and a D-112 in there, and I never miced the hi-hat back in the old days. Now you mic the hi-hat. You always got plenty of hi-hat in the overheads, and back on the '70s records, I miced the overheads with RCA ribbon mics, 77s, something warm because Joey really hits hard

so it's nice to level that out a little bit. I would place the overheads an equal distance from the snare drum left and right, and a foot or two—depending on the ceiling of the studio—above the drum kit. I like to have one mono-mic high over him and just super-compressed. I used to mic just the top of the snare, but now I like—because of the Telefunken M80 dynamic—to mic the underside of the snare with that. I also like some condenser mics on the bottom. For the top of the snare, I like a 57 or when available, an RCA BK5B—that's a cardioid ribbon mic from the '50s that was built to record gunshots for film. For the toms, I always liked an 87 or 87s—depending on how many floor toms—with a 10 DP pad on it and no rolloff on floor toms, and then 421s on racks so you get that percussion. But with those 87s on the floor toms, you get the attack because it's an 87, but you also get the bottom because it likes it, it's just wonderful.

Throwing readers a bonus technical treat, the producer added that "the effect on the start of 'Walk This Way,' when the drums come in, was an old Eventide DDL effect."

While much of the drum recording for Aerosmith's new LP remained the same, one departure the producer volunteered came with the fact that "for the first time, Steven's playing drums on this album, on one song. Joe came up with a riff, and Steven always has an idea, and Joey said, 'Why don't you just play drums on it man, it will sound really cool, and will be really different on the record, have a totally different feel.'" Drummer Joey Kramer underscored his respect for the singer's skin-hitting chops when he revealed to the band's official website in an interview in 2011, "Steven nursed me along the way when we first started the band, making me hipper to what drumming is really all about." Joey now recalls, "When I met Steven I had a lot more chops rather than knowledge about what I wanted to do, and he helped to steer me in a direction that enabled me to use what talent I had."

Critics have marveled for years over the revolution for hard rock that Aerosmith started rolling with its pioneering brand of rock 'n' roll, reinforced with a poignant confirmation coming courtesy of *Rolling Stone*, who would conclude that "after the twin triumphs of *Toys in the Attic* and *Rocks*, hard-rock landmarks that bring the melody without stinting on the toughness . . . Aerosmith were the top American hard-rock band of the mid-Seventies; if you set foot in a high school parking lot back then, the verbose back-alley numbers on 1975's *Toys in the Attic* and 1976's *Rocks* were inescapable." Because of the success Douglas achieved with the band, the *L.A. Times* would later add that "rock 'n' roll intellectuals hated Aerosmith in the '70s because the band wrote tight, commercial, radio songs in an era when 'pop' was a dirty word. The sound created more or less the template for contemporary hard rock, and today's American hard-rock bands mine Aerosmith the way the Stones used to plunder the Delta blues."

With hopes understandably high all around and fingers crossed for a similar success—for fans and critics musically, and for an industry desperate for a big-selling record—Douglas conceded that "going into a record like this new Aerosmith album, the expectations are very high, the label pressure is relatively high, the band is putting pressure on itself, then you have to mediate that pressure. You have to get in between that pressure and the artist and take the air out of it." An important part of Douglas's approach to making the studio atmosphere breathe as free of commerciality as possible comes with his avoiding conscious focus on the consideration of hits, with the producer volunteering that "I don't know how to make a hit. I really don't, if you ask me, with so many records that I've done. . . . Yeah, I knew 'Starting Over' was gonna be a hit, because it sounded like a classic hit. With everything else, all I ever do is my best, and what I think feels right for the song, and too many times after that, it's in the hands of a marketing department. So I'm not a guy who sits down and says, 'I'm going to make a single.' There's so many guys that do that, but I'm not your hit-maker. But you know what, I make a good record, and sometimes they just turn out to be hits."

Offering a surprisingly candid look inside the pressure the producer manages within his own head throughout managing that of everyone around him, Douglas shared that

> I tell you, when I walk into the studio, I'm a different person, and some nights when I leave to go home, I'm still thinking, "Oh Geez, okay, you better think this out, I want to wring all this out before I lay my head on the pillow, so let's take a look at it," and I do it in an organized way. I write out to-do lists, whether I get them all done or not, I can look at physically what has to happen here for this record to go forward. What do I have to do? Do I have to get involved with the marketing dept.? Who do I have to call? How do I make sure there's the right food in the studio to keep everybody happy? How do I make sure we're not going over budget so there's no budgetary pressure from the label? You have to look at all those things, so that when you walk into the studio, you don't bring a thing in there except your big happy face and the energy to be part of a team that's moving the project forward. And absolutely having a blast and sincerely loving what you're doing.

Journeying deeper into the making of a milestone moment touched on earlier with John Lennon's *Double Fantasy*, the final album Lennon would ever record, was an affair that in spite of the height of its commercial expectation, from the artistic side held almost none on the part of the legendary former Beatle going into the Record Plant to begin work on the album, such that—as Douglas recounted—"his expectations heading into that record were that he probably wasn't going to be able to pull it off, which was a great challenge for me because first of all, I had to make sure that what he was doing we really were pulling off and that it really was cool. And then I had to convince him in very subtle ways that he still had an amazing voice and could still write amazing songs. So his expectations going into the project were rather low; his excitement level was high, but his expectations were low."

As he began putting his strategy in play as tape began rolling, Douglas kept a tight ship, working overtime alongside his studio staff heading into production to ensure that

> with John, because with some insecurity comes a lack of patience, I had to make sure that things happened quickly. So everything had to move quickly, and I made sure that that happened—with the band that I put together to back him up; with the crew that I brought into the studio to engineer; with the studio I used—I made sure all those things were in order. Then I did the arrangements on the songs when he wasn't there, because John wasn't at the rehearsals. He gave me these raw demo tapes he'd made in Bermuda, and I would go to the studio, do the arrangements, and then come back to the Dakota after the rehearsals, and play him the rehearsal tapes, and he would make a few suggestions. Then the next day I would put those into motion in rehearsal, because the band didn't know whose album they were making, it was total secrecy. And the fact that he was making a new album was kept secret, so there was no public pressure and no label pressure, none at all.

With the latter bases covered, from a purely production vantage point, the producer next recalled that "from there, it was a matter of making sure that his vocals were really good." To help accomplish that end, Douglas recalled, "I used a 67 on John when we were recording. I liked that one because it was easy for him to work that mic, he liked to work a mic, and he didn't like a pop filter, so we didn't have to use a pop filter on him." Sharing the behind-the-board secret to Lennon's signature chorusy, slap-back vocal sound, rather than owing its creation to an effect, the producer instead revealed that it came naturally via the singer and

> this technique he had which he called "catch the pop" or "catch the S," where he would wave his hand in front of his mouth right at just the moment when the P was gonna pop, he would catch that pop in his hand and throw it away, or an S. And he liked to work the front of the mic, and the side of the mic, and get different sounds. When you hear his vocals—even on the older records—and you wonder, "Oh, I wonder how they're getting that great Lennon sound?" It's him! His expertise in working a mic was just wonderful, and a 67—he had some nasal tone in his voice—so that mic made him sound really nice and broad.

Where Douglas did make use of effects in the course of recording Lennon's leads, he shared that it was limited to "just some tape slap. I always had some tape slap running. He liked this thing that he called 'Automatic Track Doubling,' or ATD, so what we did at Record Plant to get that sound was to take a 350 deck, and the motors on those things were tremendous, and so we ran it at 30, and put a doubling cat-stand on it so it ran at 60. With the 14-inch reels on it, we could give him almost tape-doubling with the 60 IPS." Reflecting the true mastery of his instinct as a recording artist no matter how many years he'd been out of the studio, rather than laboring for hours in front of the mic crafting hits-to-be like "Woman," "I'm Losing You," "Beautiful Boy," and the timeless "(Just Like) Starting Over," the producer volunteered that, in fact, "when we were tracking, he gave me four takes and he left the room and said, 'I'll come back when you comp it. After you comp it, I'll double it.'"

Using the occasion to elaborate more broadly on general advice for recording and producing vocals, Douglas says that a producer and his/her band should "never over-rehearse anything and think that what you have planned out is going to be the perfect thing. You have to stay open, you have to improvise, no success comes without failure. If you go safe, you end up with a safe piece of music. People buy safe music, and we're suffering through an era of safe music—aside from hip-hop. It's been very safe, where sounds are homogenated, and pitched and tuned and put perfectly in time, with just very little surprise."

In spite of the tragedy that followed its release, with *Double Fantasy*, Douglas and Lennon had successfully answered the question of whether domesticity had ruined the rocker for anything else, inspiring the BBC to conclude the album delivered "powerful rock which incongruously celebrates his househusband status." Creating a collection of songs so tangible that another of Lennon's homeland mainstay papers, London's *Examiner*, would write that "Lennon's voice sends chills up your spine the minute that '*(Just Like) Starting Over*' begins," while *Rolling Stone* magazine would rank the album #29 in their "100 Best Albums of the 1980s" list, further reporting that "on November 15 they released *Double Fantasy* (Number One, 1980) . . . "Just Like Starting Over" hit Number One, and there was talk of a possible world tour . . . Two other singles from *Double Fantasy* were hits: 'Woman' (Number Two, 1981) and 'Watching the Wheels' (Number 10, 1981) . . . (culminating with its winning) the 1981 Grammy for Album of the Year."

Having come full circle with his recovery from the tragedy, along with his role as producer on Aerosmith's new studio LP—arguably the most coveted rock producer gig of the decade so far—Douglas has been keeping company behind the console with another rock legend in Bob Dylan, coproducing *First Blues*, with *Billboard* nodding to the producer with their report that the record was "engineered by no less a studio persona than Jack Douglas." Using the collaboration as an opportunity to show up-and-coming engineers some of his techniques for keeping a steady hand on the fader while working alongside legends like the aforementioned, Douglas said:

I recently coproduced a record with Bob Dylan for Allen Ginsberg, and the thing was: so Bob Dylan's an icon, right? And we're producing Allen Ginsberg, who as a poet is an icon, right? Yeah, okay. The thing is: if you go into that project knowing that what you have to do is what you have to do, and what he has to do is what he has to do. And that you have to meet on a common ground to make this thing happen—with every one that you work with. As soon as an iconic artist gets that feel that they don't have to be with you what they have to be with the public, everything changes, and then when you're working, it becomes: you're all part of the same project, and things change drastically. So you have to come in knowing that you guys are all in the same place doing the same thing, and that will cause an artist to drop all the pretense and the walls. It may take a couple of hours, or may take a few days, but you have to stay at it, and then it's gone. I had to do it with Lennon, I had to do it with Dylan, the Who, whatever artist I was working with.

Through their seminal '70s collaboration with Douglas over the course of five studio LPs, the Rock and Roll Hall of Fame recently concluded that Aerosmith became "America's feisty retort to hard-rocking British groups like the Rolling Stones, the Yardbirds, the Who, Cream, Deep Purple and Led Zeppelin. Almost alone among American bands, Aerosmith matched those British legends in power, intensity, and notoriety. Moreover, they've long since surpassed many of their influences in terms of longevity and popularity," while Bloomberg added that the group through albums like *Toys* and *Rocks* became "America's most beloved and legendary rock and roll band." With that popularity rockin' harder than ever, the producer beams with healthy optimism at the band's chances for giving fans what they want, revealing as a final detail of the album's content that "I can't tell you the title of the record, but we went into recording already having the title and concept and knowing what the album is about. And so having those things—and knowing what it's about—also drives everything, because it's again—like *Rocks* or *Toys in the Attic*—while it's not a concept album, it has a feel for what the whole is."

Underscoring in closing what he feels is, was, and always will be the key to any record producer's success—regardless of commercial considerations—in making an album that has the shelf life of many sitting in Douglas's platinum record collection, he describes his current collaboration with Aerosmith: "I know there'll be singles that come off it—we like there to be a beginning, an arch in the middle and an ending—so that's the way we're doing this one as well. We like to make albums . . ." Looking ahead, the producer seems to take great comfort in his feeling that the tide is finally turning back toward the fundamentals that first made hard rock the most beloved of rock's many subgenres: "With Aerosmith going in this direction, and the Foo Fighters going in a really cool direction, and a few other people, we're finally getting as a genre back to making real music." Arguing it's a gamble worth taking for any rock band, new or veteran, Douglas predicts that, if rock bands take that chance, "people will buy it, people are buying stuff that they're being sold, and also are discovering really cool stuff because there's so much of it, so if we can lead by being one of those big voices that says, 'Hey look, we're improvising, we're going for it, we're not afraid to fall on our faces, this stuff is rough, raw and improvised,' that keeps it fresh for the listener."

CHAPTER 2

Mario Caldato Jr.—Puttin' It on Wax!

The Beastie Boys have made an art form out of clowning around on wax for twenty-five years, but for anyone who has for a moment doubted their genius, the joke has been on the haters from day one. The Beasties loosened up a burgeoning scene of fans who were opening up to hip-hop as a culture and music like a horny pair of ears had to the white rock establishment's reinvention of rhythm and blues thirty years before via superstars like Elvis, the Rolling Stones, and the Beatles. Without much debate, the Beastie Boys are the Beatles of hip-hop, the first group to fuse the classic B-Boy audience with that of alternative rock, even though— as the Beasties' live concert audiences would prove— those two cliques had been shopping stylistically in the same aisles of vinyl sensibility for years. The Beastie Boys without argument or competition would be historically hailed as the pioneers of pushing fans to take chances with their ears that defied conventional categorization; the "Scientists of sound, mathematically putting it down," as they'd rightfully boast in 1998, following a decade of LPs that— along with Dr. Dre—would translate for a white hip-hop audience a depth of musical roots that ran far deeper than the superficial lyrical surface.

Taking readers down the rabbit hole and into the heart of hip-hop's potential to create a subgenre that would in time become hip-hop's most popular and innovative to pushing its mainstream into full existence, *Rolling Stone* would eloquently note of the B-Boys that "unlike nearly all white rap acts, the Beasties aren't white boys in blackface. They're the embodiment of the modern lower-Manhattan street kid. If hip-hop is as much a New York thing as it is a black thing, if keeping it real means faithfully representing your social aesthetic, if it's another way of saying perfect pitch, then the Beasties keep it as real for their peoples as Jay-Z and Snoop do for theirs. For modern lower Manhattan, *Kids* is *The Godfather* and the Beasties are Sinatra." Putting the group's influence in a legacy context, it could be argued that when music's most respected historians are gathered around hip-hop's water cooler years from now discussing and debating the coolest and arguably most innovative—where samples alone were concerned—rap album in the genre's greatest hits bin, *Paul's Boutique* will almost certainly be sitting on the tips of their tongues and top of their favorite piles of vinyl. Consider the assessment *Rolling Stone* has already made that, with the album, "the Beasties pioneered psychedelic hip-hop, which was mind-expanding in text and texture. It would take seven years until the world would catch up with the expansive grooves and mind-set of *Paul's Boutique.*"

Released in July 1989, though *Paul's Boutique* would eventually be ranked #156 on *Rolling Stone's* list of the 500 Greatest Albums of All Time and hailed at the time by the BBC as "a genuine masterpiece," commercially the LP fell on deaf ears. Critically, however, it would give the Beastie Boys an artistic credibility that had eluded them entirely on their wildly successful debut LP, evinced by *Billboard's* conclusion that "few pop records offer this much to savor, and if *Paul's Boutique* only made a modest impact upon its initial release, over time its influence could be heard through pop and rap, yet no matter how its influence was felt, it stands alone as a record of stunning vision, maturity, and accomplishment." Most importantly, it could be argued that while it would take the industry years to catch up and on, *Paul's Boutique's* greatest success, for the band, came with the fact that it "allowed the Beasties to operate at their own speed," as the aforementioned BBC—already an avid fan—would later reason.

While rap went mainstream at the turn of the decade in ways both good (Dr. Dre, De La Soul) and bad (Vanilla Ice/MC Hammer), the Beasties went underground. In what would prove a radical departure from the sampling dynasty that *Paul's Boutique* had established, the Beasties would make a move longtime coproducer Mario C confirmed was motivated at the time by the group's feeling that "after *Paul's Boutique*, they felt like, 'We went extreme on the sampling,' spent a grip of money on the studio, and so heading into the next record, the group thinking was one of: 'You know what, we spent $100,000 on the last record, we can just buy a tape machine and a board and rent a place and start our own studio.' They had signed a two-record minimum deal with Capitol, so they had to make another record, so about a year after *Paul's Boutique* had been out, they said 'Let's go work on the next one. We got the money, we got the budget, let's do it.'"

Deciding to invest their next recording advance more conservatively in the context of their creative environment, the group charged Mario C with overseeing the construction of the group's first customized studio, G-Son. Promoted to the position of lead producer, Caldato recalled that "we found a building in Atwater Village in L.A., near the Los Feliz area and Hollywood, it had been a community center or ballroom previously, had a wood parquet floor, and a half-curved, cylinder-type ceiling. So the guy who had been there before we took it over had a studio space and used part of it for rehearsal, but the problem was, the downstairs was a drugstore and so you couldn't make any noise till after six o'clock. So we'd start our day at six and go home at two in the morning."

Dusting off his blueprint for the studio's gear layout, Caldato shared his memory that

> when we set up shop, it was a big room, and already had a wall built but there was no door, so Money Mark—who was a carpenter by trade—said "Let's put a door here so we can make a control room with a window so we can see out into the big room," which would be the recording room. So we set up shop with a 24-track Tascam, a two-inch tape machine, and a Neo-tech Elan mixing console, which was a 32-channel with 24 buss, three band EQ, and then I had all the outboard gear and all the mics. The outboard gear included reverbs—the Yamaha Rev 7, the SBX, and three Ibanez delays: the HD 1000, HD2000, and HD 1500 with the harmonizer. Then I had a Yamaha compressor, and had bought a pair of blackface 1176s, which was the first time I had some real nice compressors. Then I had some DBX 160s with the VU.

Once the studio was up and running, the Beasties made the wise decision—in the context of time—to take themselves off any kind of outside clock, moving only at the pace of the music they had quietly begun making together *as a band*. This marked a shift in tempo that Mario C revealed the band had reached in reaction to, "at the time, being totally burnt out on the sampling. So once the studio was set up, they had started horsing around and jamming together, and previous to that, Mike was playing drums in a local band called Big Fat Love, Yauch had a band called Brooklyn where he played fuzz bass, and Ad Rock played everything. So we'd set up the live room with instruments, added Money Mark in on keyboards, and this band was born."

Most fans of the band would argue a new sound had been born as well, one that the band took literally years to let develop, such that, as Caldato recalled, "that album took three years to make. We started at the end of '89, six months after *Paul's Boutique*, and recorded up through 1992. For the first couple years, we only focused on instrumental stuff, so there was no there was no vocals, just jamming." Providing the band with a rare opportunity—unheard of in the modern world of major label recording—to hone their chops as a live band—a necessary step in the context of being taken seriously down the road by fans—Caldato felt that, indeed,

> with the jamming thing that went on for a year and a half before the rapping started, it brought up the musical level of the band because the guys were playing together every day. Mark was helping them construct instrumentals, and showing them changes and new chords, and it was all building up. It was a special thing, to take three years, which nobody does nowadays, to be on the clock, and slowly make a record that we had no idea at the time how it would turn out as a finished product, it was an amazing experience to come together and be part of it.

With their move toward live instrumentation, *Billboard* would later argue the band had successfully "repositioned themselves as a lo-fi, alt-rock groove band," and over the course of the Beasties' musical reinvention, Caldato—who had witnessed the evolution firsthand sitting behind the console documenting every one of its notes to tape—recalled capturing what he considered among his—and the album's— most enjoyable musical moments. Operating from the premise that every jam contained a germ—and at times gem—of a musical idea that could play into the album's broader composition, the producer treated every jam as a recording session, recording "all their ideas, which is something I *always* recommend to any engineer or producer, even if it's in the rehearsal room, because you never know what the band will come up with."

Painting a picture from the technical side of the gear in play during the record's instrumental recording phase, Caldato—beginning with Mike D's drum sound—volunteered that

> it was pretty basic. Mainly Sennheiser 421s on the kick and toms, a 57 on the top of the snare, overheads were 451s, and the hi-hat was a 460. There were eight mics on the drums, which stayed stationary, and then there were times I'd throw a 414 room mic in the middle of the room. MCA's stand-up bass—for that thing, I used a 414 condenser mic, which was my best acoustic mic. For keys, Money Mark had a Wurlitzer we used quite a bit. We did have a Rhodes, but he mainly used the Wurly, and we ended up using a Korg through the Leslie on some stuff, which sounded very close to the Hammond. He rocked that quite a bit, and then there was also an acoustic upright there.

As the band amassed a vault of instrumental jams that Caldato estimated to be "up into the hundreds because we recorded everything over that three year period," when it came time to begin mining the vault for potential keepers in context of the broader album, the producer detailed a process of

> listening back and clearing out and picking out the keepers, like "This one's got potential," so there was a lot of reviewing and analyzing, and we had time to do it. It didn't put any pressure on anybody, so nobody was afraid to try a wacky song or something nutty, then we'd live with it for a while and see how long you were into it. Then the stuff that stuck made it to the record, so everything you hear on the final *Check Your Head* LP, everybody in the group was really pleased with, and happy as a whole on the record. It was like it passed the test of time after three years of making and listening to it, it still sounded good when we finished.

The record's next creative evolution came when the group finally decided they were ready to return to rhyming. Ironically, the song that wound up launching *Check Your Head* also launched the vocal phase of the album's broader recording when, "one random day after a year and a half, two years of just jamming," Caldato recalled,

> Yauch came in and said, "I have this idea, I want to record it and surprise the guys," and he didn't want to do it at the studio so he came to my house in South L.A. and we demoed it there. That song was "Jimmy James," and he'd found the Hendrix loop, the Turtle beat, and we looped it up at my house, arranged it, and did a demo with Yauch doing the vocals himself. Then we brought it back to the guys and they loved it, "Aw shit, I want to rhyme on that!" And all of a sudden, they were all hyped and all wanted to start rhyming, so that set it off.

Taking their creative cues as much from one another as from their own internal inspirational processes as the album's rhyme-schemes were hatched, Caldato confirmed that as the lyrical phase of the record's creation got underway,

> it was definitely a group effort, and everybody contributed. When they recorded vocals on any given song, we would try it out and actually have all three of them recording at the same time, and they would break verses up between them. As far as the arrangement of mics, it was odd, because I'd set up three mics, and one guy would be in the big studio room, one guy would be in the control room, and in between the big room and control room was a little cubbyhole—literally a foot and a half wide—to where you could just fit in it because it was a double-door. So I rigged up a mic in there so the three of them could all see each other and be close, but the voices would be separated.

As the group wove their way through crafting the album's lyrical tapestry, they were—in the process—pushing "their rhymes to Byzantine new heights" in a sonic context, *Entertainment Weekly* would later argue. This innovation was achieved thanks to the band's success with starring—in some cases wildly—experimental vocal effects on lead vocal performances; and not just on album cuts, but hit singles as well in the case of smashes like "So Whatchya Want." An ideal time for such a traditionally risky commercial experiment given the inherently *experimental* nature of the broader alternative-rock genre itself, the group was taking the true gamble with their hip-hop fans, whose ears hadn't been accustomed to much outside of the basic reverb or delay leading up to that point.

Painting a picture of how the group successfully utilized the latter technology as an instrument creatively in the studio, Mario C recounted the creation of the aforementioned hit, "So What'cha Want," beginning with his recollection that

> when we got into "What'cha Want," we had this B-studio, which was for when one of the Beasties had another idea and wanted to go work on it. So in that smaller room, we had a 4-track set up with the instrumental music, and a little cheap Sony Karaoke mic that featured a built-in distortion, and had an octave thing where you could make your voice sound like a Martian, and a computer scrambler effect—just some weird effects all built into the mic. So at first, they would use that to demo stuff on, and that little mic sounded cool because it kind of overloaded when you cupped it, and it sounded pretty awesome, so we kind of got used to that—the demos with this sound.

Reflecting minds as musically open as both the territory and possibilities they were pioneering via production decisions/directions like the latter, producer Mario C recalled that the sound was catchy enough that

> it grew on the guys to the point where they started saying, "I want to use this mic to do the real version on the record," because when they would do it on the 58, it sounded too clean and didn't have that intensity. So "So What'cha Want"—a smash hit—was recorded on the $29 Sony Karaoke mic! That microphone was the effect, there's no other effects of any kind, that was the sound. They wound up using that on the record, any time you would hear a distorted voice. From that technique, I would try out some other hand-mics, like a hand-radio mic and cheap mics I would plug in and distort with the pres, but that Sony Karaoke mic was the main go-to, with no extra distortion or nothing. So from there, we used that on everything, it was the primary effect on songs like "Jimmy James," "So Whatchya Want," all the songs that have distorted

vocals on them. The rest of the records' vocals were recorded with 58s, and on *Check Your Head*, we did everything on hand-held mic, so they never used mic stands during vocal tracking.

Speaking beyond mics and more broadly to the exciting array of effects at inspirational play during vocal tracking, Caldato recalled that

when they were tracking, they all loved effects on their voices, the more effects the better, so they'd always be like, "Yo turn that shit up, give me more echo," in terms of what they had going in their headphones while they recorded. What we kept of that we played by ear, sometimes we would record it when the shit was just banging, like if it was tape delay, then we'd record that, Yauch on one song was really into that, and wanted to record it exactly like that and commit to it. For the vocals, we mainly used short delay and long delay, and I would just adjust them according to the song. So like a short delay to get it tight and kind of fatten it up, and then a long delay for the echoes and that kind of part. Then we'd do panning sometimes on the echoes, and as far as reverbs, I had the Yamaha Rev 7 digital reverb, which I used as a basic reverb, and then would use the SPX 90 more for special effects, like when I wanted a gated reverb or reverse, or flanging or phasing, or auto-panning—any kind of weird stuff. That was basically it.

As the sound of the broader record began to morph sonically and stylistically and the group shifted creative gears toward a focus on crafting its accents and more idiosyncratic textures, the Beasties would stumble upon yet another musical innovation for hip-hop. Where sampling had previously defined much of the instrumental character of rap productions—even its most cutting edge circa *Paul's Boutique*—on their new LP, the B-Boys wouldn't re-embrace sampling as a production technique, but rather re-invent it entirely. Treating the presence of samples throughout the album as a tool to color the personality of songs rather than define or dictate their overall direction, the group had broken free of the derivative chains that many would later argue had held hip-hop back until that point from claiming an authentic original identity as a musical genre. As the group made their own sampling selections this time around, Caldato again painted the process as a team effort, wherein "there were three heads with the Beasties, and then Marc and myself, so five heads just listening and adding ideas, 'Hey, check this out,' etc."

Taking readers inside the science behind this signature aspect of the group's broader sound, the producer explained that "we'd basically fill it up and leave three tracks for vocals, and one for Simpti. So that left us like twenty tracks for music, so typically we'd add a bunch of loops, beats, kicks and snares, scratching. On *Check Your Head*, Ad Rock did all the scratching, except for Yauch did all the terminating, like the stuff at the beginning of 'Jimmy Jam'— pretty much the rest of the album was Ad Rock." Aided greatly in their looping process by the cutting-edge samplers that had emerged at the dawn of the 1990s, Caldato recalled that

> on that record, we were using the Akai MPC 60, that was the main one. At the time, that was the new shit, and allowed you to do like thirty seconds of sampling, you had multiple pads, at the time it was just the popular sampling drum machine out there so all four of us had one, except Marc. That way we could work, and if somebody got an idea at home, they could bring it into the studio, so it was interchangeable, you could bring the discs and it was easy to use. We also used the EMU SB1200, which is what Ad Rock used, he mainly worked on that one. Then we had an 808 that was linked up as well.

Elaborating on the actual tracking process, the producer added that "as far as the timing and the synching up, back then, you didn't break down every single hit or beat, you just kind of took a loop and massaged it into the rough BPM, and it wasn't quite perfect, but you got it as close as you could to where it felt right, which made the stuff really funky." Breaking new musical ground beyond their own subgenre for broader hip-hop with their success—according to *Alternative Press*—in "reinventing sampling and hip-hop's parameters," Caldato volunteered "Professor Booty" as an ideal sonic/stylistic summary of the latter in play, recalling that "the samples on that one came from all kinds of sources, I think the movie *Wild Style* was sampled, Ad Rock brought in some elements. Those guys had a lot of B-Boy background, and they tried to utilize that as much as possible—a lot of old school stuff. That's got a bunch of different loops on there."

As production wrapped on the "aural joyride"—as *Spin* would later muse—that was *Check Your Head*, and attention turned to the daunting task of mixing, coproducer Mario C recalled that the first challenge in this process came with settling on "the album's final 20 songs, where there were probably about 50 total ideas for the record. There were a lot of little things that turned into other things, and on the bonus CD they put out, *Skills to Pay the Bills*, a lot of that stuff surfaced later. But at the time, it was difficult, because every one of those fifty cuts the band considered their babies." *Check Your Head was* reflective of a competitively broad array of musical styles the Beasties had made part of a musical odyssey that, according to the BBC, featured "tracks fluttering from low-slung funk to caustic rock 'n' roll via bona-fide mega-hits and jazz-tinged instrumentals . . . in lounge-jazz territory."

With *Check Your Head*, the Beastie Boys didn't just rebound, they reinvented; recreating themselves, in the esteemed opinion of *Rolling Stone*, "as a total cultural experience." Ranked #5 in the *Village Voice*'s list of the 40 Best Albums of 1992, *Entertainment*

Weekly would later argue that the Beasties' comeback LP had successfully "left a much bigger bootprint on pop than *Licensed to Ill,*"*large enough that Billboard* would declare the record "an alt-rock touchstone of the '90s."Twenty years later, the BBC would conclude that the record "remains to this day the quintessential Beastie Boys collection," an assessment that—on a personal level—producer Mario C concurs with, sharing that "*Check Your Head* is still a very special record for me, being the first step into that world, and having three years to work on it, and the friendship and everything just building and being created naturally was really wonderful."

Discovering they'd been missed on the road as well as the charts, Caldato—who also acted as the group's live concert sound engineer—shared that "after we released the album, the band went on tour immediately, which was needed because they'd been off the road for three years. We toured for the whole year, maybe a year and a half, and as we were on tour, in between sound checks, they'd get ideas and I'd record them as they popped up. Well, out of that process, some ideas started forming for the next record." With their creative fires no doubt inspired and roaring on high from the radically improved response *Check Your Head* had received vs. its predecessor, rather than re-invent the wheel musically on their next studio LP, Caldato recalled the band was eager to keep it spinning in the same stylistic direction, such that

> after the tour finished, we were focused on getting back in the studio to do another record—we were ready. We'd just traveled all over the country and world and had bought records all over the place, and were really excited from being on tour. And while we'd been on the road, we had the drum machine on tour, and were already actually sampling some stuff, and kind of getting some homework already done. I think all we had was the drum machine and a 4-track DAT, and so whenever they would get an idea at sound check, I would run a stereo mix while they were jamming, just keeping the ideas flowing.

Diving headlong into recording, the band initially set up shop in their native New York, mirroring the jam-writing sessions that had defined *Check Your Head*, albeit with a much shorter time frame in mind, such that

> we wound up going to New York for one month, and so for the first four weeks of recording we were in Manhattan, recording all the jamming material that became all the basic instrumental material for the record—like "Ricky's Theme," "Sabotage," "Bobo on the Corner," "Sabrosa," "Futtermen's Rule," "Shambala," "Transition," and "Eugene's Lament"—those were all done in New York, the basic tracking. By this part, Bobo, the percussionist, was now part of the band, along with Money

Mark on keyboards, and of course, Ad Rock on guitar, Yauch on bass, and Mike on drums. So that first month was great, a change of scenery, and it turned out to be a great idea. We were tracking on an old custom console, a tube board, that had a lot of tube-Pres.

As the band jammed their way through a by-then signature side of their sound that *Rolling Stone* would later observe successfully continued "the formula established on *Check* — home-grown jams powered by live instruments . . . buried under the warm hiss of vintage analog studio equipment," and noted "an artistic maturity" in the Beastie Boys' sound. From a production vantage point, Mario C explained that he'd selected the size of the New York studio for how it helped to shape the character of the group's sound, reasoning that the room made sense

for those New York sessions because everyone basically played together in these very tight quarters, which give a tight sensibility to the sound. By contrast, the G-Son studio in L.A. had a big stage, it was a big room, and felt much more spacious, where this space was opposite, again, a little tighter—so the band could see each other and play off each other, plus the musicianship had improved after touring for so long and just playing a lot. I remember Yauch always being very motivated and creative in the studio, always working on his bass sound. He was playing on a fuzz bass and a stand-up bass. So the confidence in the room was high.

When the B-Boy camp wrapped live instrumental tracking in New York and headed home to G-Son Studios in L.A., Mario recalled that where Yauch had taken much of the compositional lead with the group's original material, Ad Rock would prove the driving force for the album's more traditional, loops-driven hip-hop tracks. Beginning with the album's opening track, "Sure Shot," Caldato recalled that, instrumentally, "Adam came up with that flute loop from *Howlin' for Judy* by Jeremy Steig, added a slamming beat, and the track was done. I don't even think it was a whole bar—the beat. He found the kick and snare, and he sampled it, I don't even think it was separated, it was together, it was a noisy beat, a noise kick-snare. We added some 808 on top of it, and there was two elements of the beat and loop and that thing was done. We added a couple other sneaky elements on the chorus, and that was it." In the band's CD booklet for the *Sounds of Science* anthology, Ad Rock would later share of the song's creation that "I like this cut a lot. Just straight up hip-hop. Like a lot of our songs, it's arranged like a hardcore (punk) song. Mathematical. Intro - verse - chorus - verse - chorus - break - chorus - verse - chorus - end. Nice. The flute line is from the elusive Jeremy Steig. Off the SP1200 it sounds nice."

Often rumored to be the true Beatle of the group—creatively speaking—in the studio, Mario C spoke of what he felt were Horovitz's greatest assets as a producer: "Ad Rock had a great instinct and talent for putting beats with loops," adding that the emcee as producer possessed a talent for "take a chance, and through that, discovering different avenues musically for the albums by putting different styles together—he really enjoyed doing that." Offering a look at those skills at play in the course of creating two of *Ill Communication's* most popular cuts, Caldato pointed to the making of the hit single "Root Down," recalling that

> that song came off a live Jimmy Smith album. I remember I was with Ad Rock on tour when he bought the record, and we listened to it in the car, heard that bass line, and he was like "Oh My God, I gotta loop that shit up," so he called it. It was so fat, that they just used the hook, "I kick it root down," there you go, it's done. So that loop was basically the record, I just re-edited it. We took four or five different loops, and put them in different orders with the guitar and all that shit, and I don't think there were any instruments added to it—that's Jimmy Smith, straight up, reedited in a different order with some scratching. "Do It" was another slamming Ad-Rock track. It's super-funky, I think that one was Bob Dylan song. And as that loop comes in and you hear all that scratching, that's Ad Rock scratching as well.

Along with "Do It" and "Root Down," Caldato recalled "all the rap joints we did when we came back to G-Son in L.A, including 'Sure Shot', 'B Boys,' 'Get it Together,' 'Update,' 'Alright Hear This,' 'Fruit Loop,' and 'The Scoop.'" Tapping the creation of "Alright Hear This" as a sample of that process in action, the producer recalled that

> that track originated from a sample I heard on an '80s hip-hop TV show in New York, and there was some guy on demonstrating scratching, and he said, "Don't try this at home on your dad's stereo, only under hip-hop supervision," and the guys were all about using that kind of influence as much as possible to keep the B-Boy element strong. That was Yauch playing acoustic bass, he made that up on the spot, and that song was a great example of how Yauch had grown pretty hot on his bass chops, and really stepped it up in the studio on *Ill Communication*, he had some really great musical moments and ideas.

Speaking on his technique for micing MCA's acoustic bass, a driving presence on cuts like the aforementioned, the producer explained that Yauch's sound came from an acoustic stand-up bass with the big body and he generally used that for recording. At the time we were making that record, I'd just started buying tube mics, and would have had a Neumann

U-47 on Yauch's stand-up bass, and sometimes I would use an 87 or a M-49. But on tour, we wound up buying a Z bass, which is an upright bass without the body, and has a small, hollow kind of body that has a little bit of acoustic sound to it also, but was just easier to transport. So sometimes we'd use that in the studio as well, mic it up or line in and EQ, but generally always miced and at times processed a little extra.

Proceeding much as they had on *Check Your Head* when the tracking of lead vocals got underway, Caldato shared that the trio was aided greatly by the practice they'd had rhyming together onstage night after night on tour, such that "things went very smoothly overall. Occasionally we'd do an edit, if we didn't get it right, so we'd go on and record the next part, then punch back in and make an edit, but we generally got it together on the first or second take."

For all of the album's easygoing moments, Caldato revealed that it was out of the group's most challenging production that they would find their greatest commercial success. Recounting the genesis of what would wind up the Beasties' biggest hit of the 1990s, a song that was born during the band's New York jam sessions and evolved into an experiment with the unremarkable code-name of "Chris Rock," Caldato said of the song's musical roots that

> at the time, we were into funky, jazzy sounds, and we had an acoustic bass happening where Yauch was really rocking it, going for the exotic sound. So one day we were in the studio fucking around, and Yauch was really jamming—really into his fuzz bass thing—just rocking away on that thing, he came up with "Chris Rock" while he was ripping on that bass. So that lead riff on that song, that's bass, and when he started playing that shit, I remember being in the control room knowing he'd stumbled onto something great, what producers call a gem vs. a germ, and I immediately yelled to our percussionist, 'Go in there Bobo!' So Bobo went in there, but didn't know what do to, and started going 'Na-Na, Na-Na,' just like you hear that little part in the final song. Then as this is developing, Mike D walks in, and I was like 'Mike, go in there and follow Bobo,' so Mike hopped on the drums, and the two of them brought that start-stop rhythm part to life that the song starts and ends with. So they just jammed it out and created the basic rhythm track that you hear on the record, and is it would turn out, on radio.

Confirming his instinct that the group was onto something catchy, Caldato added that

> the funny shit was, after we did it, the studio owner Chris came walking in, and day after day leading up to that one, he would routinely say, 'Man, you guys need a hit . . .' Well, when he walked in that day and heard us playing that track, he said, 'Now *that's*

what I'm talking about! That's a fuckin' hit right there!' He called it, he knew, and that's why we initially wound up calling the song "Chris Rock"—because he'd bugged out on it so much. In fact, it stayed an instrumental almost up until we were ready to turn in the record, because it was just too challenging, nobody wanted to sing on a rock song, because to them it was going back to "Fight for Your Right to Party" on the first album—they didn't really want to do that. I remember they actually tried doing some vocals on the song, there might have been one attempt in New York, then when we got back to L.A., a few months later I think Ad Rock tried something, but it wasn't fitting right.

The stars would finally line up for the song in a nick of time that came close to costing the group what would become their biggest radio hit since "Fight for Your Right to Party," with Caldato recalling that

two weeks before we're planning to turn the record in, after the whole album is done, we still hadn't come up with any personality for the song lyrically, so at that point, "Chris Rock" was going to be on the record as an instrumental because it sounded tight. Then Ad Rock calls me up one day, and says, "Dude, I want to try the vocal one more time," and I go, "Well, okay, the song's already mixed. You want to just do the idea at my house?" So he came to my place, where I had a studio set up, and I just loaded up a 2-track premix of the instrumental, gave him a vocal mic, and he nailed it in a couple takes! He had the attitude, and the lyrics, and just went off, screamed into it, and when he was done, I remember immediately saying "Oh shit, that's dope! That's fly dude," so we had him add some scratching, and the song was done. I bounced it onto my Adat, added the two vocal tracks he laid down, the two tracks of scratching, used the premix of the instrumental to mix it, and it was done. It ended up sounding banging, and when Mike and Yauch heard it, they were understandably excited because it had finally come together. The song had to go through all that process for it to be the right moment and the right energy and attitude and Adam nailed it hard! We knew there was something exciting and different about it, but even then, at first the Beasties had some reservations about putting it out as the album's first single because, again, it was a rock song, but they eventually embraced it as part of the record.

When attention turned to mixing *Ill Communication*, Caldato headed into the process with an "if it ain't broke" approach, explaining that he had that luxury because

we were working on the same board, outboard and everything for mixing *Ill Communication* as we'd used for *Check Your Head,* except now we were all a little bit more on our chops, so mixing was always a snap. The whole record we'd completed record-ing in six months: the first month we spent recording in New York, then the next five months building and mixing as we'd go, so we recorded song by song and I would mix as we finished recording each song. So we'd work on a song for weeks sometimes, keep working till we get it right and can't do anymore, then go on to the next one, and then go back and revisit or remix. The board, the way it was set up, you couldn't just fly around, so we did it one song at a time.

Raising the Beastie Boys' profile as one of rap's most clever crossover successes upon release as school was letting out in late May 2004, "Chris Rock," aka "Sabotage" would be-come the summer's top party anthem and MTV's most requested/rotated video of the sea-son. Debuting at #1 on the *Billboard* Top 200 Album chart, *Ill Communication* would inspire mainstream critics like *Entertainment Weekly* to celebrate its content as "the most tantalizing ear candy in years," while *Billboard* would conclude that "with this record, the Beasties confirm that there is indeed a signature Beastie Boys aesthetic, with the group sticking to a blend of old school rap, pop culture, lo-fi funk, soulful jazz instrumentals, Latin rhythms, and punk, often seamlessly integrated into a rolling, pan-cultural, multi-cultural groove." Having earned their way back into arenas, it would be another four years before the Beast-ies returned to the top of the charts, leaving their fans for the moment with plenty of musi-cal mojo to tide them over.

Hello Nasty (1998) would remind critics and fans alike that the release of a new Beastie Boys LP served not only to celebrate hip-hop's past, but also show where it was head-ing. *Billboard* would reinforce the power of the Beasties' creative instinct in this respect with their assertion that throughout the group's career, they had consistently released re-cords "that both set trends and predicted them." As a consequence, the *L.A. Times* would add that "none of the Beasties' peers enjoy the contemporary relevance that Ad-Rock (Adam Horowitz) and his bandmates Mike D (Mike Diamond) and MCA (Adam Yauch) carry." Reminding fans that it was not just cool but also inspiring to take chances where those new directions were concerned, for many Beasties' fans and critics alike, *Hello Nasty* marked their bravest effort yet, so powerfully that *Entertainment Weekly* boldly declared the LP as "unguarded as the Beasties have ever been," adding that, as a result, "the mélange makes for a looser, more free-spirited record than their earlier albums; the music invites you in, rather than threatening to shut you out."

Crediting Ad Rock once again as one of the dominant creative forces driving the re-cord's direction musically, producer Mario C recalled that, by that point,

Adam was really on top of his game, and was responsible for 85 to 90 percent of the music on that record. He was really on fire, and had a backlog of a lot of tracks and ideas, and he was just ready to go. He had a little studio in his house, in the back room, and he came in with this box full of discs, and they're all little songs and ideas, and he'd just pull them out, like "Let's review this. Let's review this. That's a good one, so is that. Hey, maybe we can put those two together?" Adam's taste in music was very eclectic, and he wasn't shy to try nutty things. He'd show up just thrilled because he had four new songs he'd done on the SB12 the night prior when he'd gotten home from the studio, and he'd show up with all these ideas. And the guys would be like, "Oh shit, that's dope! That one's even better," and that was really his strength—his ideas, and for him to be able to do that so easily and focused.

As a natural byproduct of the passion Horovitz was pouring into the project, Mario recalled that once principal recording was underway, "Ad Rock was usually the first one to the studio, and we would be working and spent most of the time together because he had the tracks, and we'd lay them down and then Mike and Yauch would show up." Adding that Ad Rock's lead role was fully endorsed "by the guys, who were very proud of him. When I recorded him in the studio, Adam was always *very* quick and he would get his parts in a couple takes—that was it. That's the thing, his attention and his time was short, so he'd go in and nail parts and it would be done. That means we would just move onto something else at the studio once he had that track done.

From a conceptual perspective, the producer recalled that heading into recording, for the Beasties,

the main focus of *Hello Nasty* was to be a rap album. They wanted to come back hard, we did the two records previous where there was jamming and playing and screwing around, and I think they realized that they maximized that kind of as far as they could with their abilities at the time—musically and with their talents. So the attitude was one of: "We had fun doing this, and have done everything we wanted to do: our Sly Stone, our Meters," and all these influences we were listening to. All these different elements were done, and now it was like, rap was at a stage where it kind of needed a revitalization, and they were amped to do this."

Seeking a change of vibe and scenery for their latest studio endeavor, the Beasties returned to their—and hip-hop's—birthplace of New York City, with Mario reasoning that the move made sense because "the focus on that record was mainly making rap tracks, we were going back to New York, and wanted to make a hip-hop record, so that was the vibe. The New York City backdrop was hugely important in crafting that vibe too, because it was like a home coming, almost ten years after *License to Ill*."

Having danced on technology's cutting edge without missing a beat for years in the course of their record-making master craft, with the advent of digital technology, the Beast-ies were provided that much more of an opportunity to excel at just that, with Caldato con-firming that because "the Beasties were always into the new stuff, especially for the kind of music we were doing, which was always innovative, we embraced digital right off because it just allowed us more tools. Working for the first time in the digital recording realm was definitely exciting and opened up more possibilities by having everything in one computer, and being able to manipulate it, like tuning was much easier, truncating, trimming, just working with it was a lot easier than working with the drum machine. So from my process, it made things easier."

Delving more specifically into the areas where he had upgraded his recording rig to be current with both the technology and times, Caldato explained that

> basically I was using the computer as the recording unit. I had sixteen tracks of Pro Tools, analog outputs, and then I had an 8-track called a Sample Cell Card, which was basically a sampler with eight outputs, and the sampling time was endless. So instead of on the drum machines, I was now sampling in the computer. Ad Rock was still using the SB1200, and so he'd work on that, and then I'd transfer what he did into the computer, and then we'd reprogram it on Studio Vision. So I was using Studio Vision, the sequencer program, at the time, and I was using Pro Tools hardware to record the album.

Aided greatly by the creative mobility of Pro Tools, Caldato said of its benefits for the group's individual members that "by then, because we were basically recording everything to digital, going directly to the computer, the writing process for the record was much easier and more streamlined technically than on previous albums because we all had D-88, the digital 8-tracks at home, that way somebody could take the music home on a stereo track, and that way, they'd have six tracks they could add vocals on at home. That was a medium we used for vocals, so the vocals you hear on the final album got recorded on those D-88s a lot of times."

Still, for all its conveniences, trouble for Mario entered his creative paradise in that, as the Beasties brought their home-made into the studio,

> that benefit for them created more work because for me because there were also more possibilities now, so the guys would be like "Well let's try this version," or "Let's try this version!" So I'd be copying the song over, and trying different edits, and differ-ent versions instantly, which was something we could never do when we were working on tape. You'd have to mix it, and then would have to edit it, so it opened up a lot of channels, and was a great too, everybody was into it and excited, so Yauch could

say "Hey, let's repeat that again," and it was like "Cool, done," and literally took ten seconds as opposed to: "Hold on, let me get a half-inch machine, and copy it, and tape it, and edit it."

Feeding off each other's creative energies, the producer recalled that, individually,

usually Ad Rock would have one or two ideas ahead of time, and then from there to- tally go off his head and feel from the moment and just come up with a rhyme. Yauch, by contrast, would definitely have his thing thought out more and written—you knew what he liked to say, and he'd already have that in mind and figure out how to finalize it. Mike was also 50/50, he'd have some ideas and then come off the cuff sometimes too with some crazy rhymes, because he'd hear Ad Rock say something silly, and then he'd come back with something ridiculous. He liked to be as silly as possible with his rhymes, and it worked—it was just very normal.

As an aid to inspiration, Caldato volunteered that, as with past albums, "they definitely all liked a lot of effects, and that was the first thing they'd ask for in the booth, like 'Yo, give me some verb,' and they didn't even have to ask, I already had the reverbs and delays ready, so once I checked the level, it was just turning on the delays—that was a given." By contrast, in a technical departure from previous records, he shared that "for vocal mics on this album, we used Sennheiser 421s, which had a tighter sound. With *Check Your Head*, they used hand-held and were mainly 58s and the Karaoke mic, and the other radio hand mics and all that stuff, and on *Ill Communication,* it was a similar setup. So by the time we got to *Hello Nasty*, we went to the 421s to change it up, and sometimes it would be hand-held, but a lot of times it would sit on the mic stand—so it went back to a more precise kind of performance."

Caldato also found his digital recording medium helpful in the process of producing as precise a performance as desired by the group on any of the record's sophisticated sound- scapes, such that

whether it was with editing vocals or loops, being able to cut up more stuff, because our sources is what was mattered—the source of the old record; the source of the old sample, or the dirty beat, or the nasty sounds. That's really where the heart of it is; the editing and the sequencing was just a tool that aided and improved immensely the production part of it, and allowed us to do so many tracks and so many songs, and everybody was a fan of it. Especially now, I could comp vocals as opposed to just having one vocal take, and punching in. We could do a few takes, and take the best ones, and put it together much more easily.

In the course of crafting what would be celebrated as the Beastie Boys' most eclectically rounded fusion of styles yet—a blend that *Rolling Stone* would conclude was "a sonic mix that's about sixty-five to seventy percent the frenetic, sample-crazy hip-hop eclecticism of *Paul's Boutique* and about twenty-five to thirty percent the funk-punk fun of *III Communication,*" and one whose "sonic adventures" Billboard would praise—Caldato utilized a treasure chest of effects that he recalled included "the Yamaha, the Rev7, and the SBX90, and the Ibanez DM2000—those were my standards—that's all I needed was two reverbs and two delays and I can get that sound. Then I had a couple compressors for the vocals, and that's all we really needed to get things done. Because the rest of the stuff was samples, stuff that was already treated, except occasionally where we'd do something special."

Turning his recollections to some of *Hello Nasty's* most poignant cuts, beginning with the smash hit "Intergalactic Planetary," Caldato revealed the inside story of the creation of the song's infectious, effects-driven chorus hook that starred Ad Rock:

> I had just bought a vocoder the day before, and I was horsing around with it, testing it out, and we tested it out on that mic, so that's his voice you hear on the chorus: "Intergalactic Planetary," and as he's singing in the mic, I'm controlling the vocoder that's hooked up to a keyboard. So as you trigger the notes, it sends the pitch up and down and that's determined by the key but also by the oscillator on the unit, and I was manually rocking it while he was saying the chorus vocals. So we created the sound together, and we looked at each other as I was recording it, like *"Oh shit!"* So afterward, we cut it up, and were like "That's the one!" We knew it was banging, it was just ridiculous. For the other effects in play on the lead verses, I used the Lexicon 280 reverb, and the 2290 PC delay—there's no phasing or chorusing.

Starting a creative domino-effect of sorts that worked to stoke the band's creative fires, the producer shared his memory that

> when that one came together, it just sparked more interest and more anxiety for those guys to hurry up and get this shit together. It provided fuel for the fire, and led to "Body Movin." I remember when we decided to do "Body Movin" that day, we were like "Okay, this is the joint with the steel drum band playing," and Mike was joking, "That will make this like some exercise-type shit, Body Movin' . . . " So when he went in the booth, I turned on the harmonizer, and that's the effect you hear on his voice for the chorus, and when I threw it on there, all the guys went "Oh shit, that's perfect!" So it's mainly Mike, but all three of them wound up on that chorus, with a double harmony with a high and a low one from the SBX90 stereo harmonizer. It was just perfect.

Moving from Sean Lennon's basement office, where the band had tracked "90 percent of the record" to the more traditionally decked out RPM studios to mix *Hello Nasty*, the producer recalled that "mixing was pretty focused on sonically getting things to sound right, and I had a technique and formula I kept with, which meant having the beats tight; making sure the samples sounded a certain way; and then treating the vocals a certain way. There were a lot of little nuances, and a lot of time and focus and energy into making sure the record sounded perfect." To ensure he had ample room to address each and every sonic detail of the album's twenty-two tracks, Caldato employed an elaborate technical setup that consisted of "an old Neve that was either thirty-two or thirty-six channels that was hooked up to the computer using sixteen of Pro Tools tracks and eight on the sampler, so that's twenty-four, and then the rest were outboard. We utilized everything on that console."

Though he took the lead, Caldato recalled that throughout the mixing of the record,

we all pitched in. I definitely spent and dedicated an entire year of my life in New York working with the Beasties, and realizing this dream that was this record. It was a serious commitment and I'm very proud of it. There was a bit of pressure on *Hello Nasty* to get finished after four years since the last record, and there was a lot of anticipation, but we were very confident. I remember when we finished the record, we all felt it was the hottest thing we could come up with, I don't think anything else could have touched it. We were actually nominated by the Grammies for Album of the Year in 1999 for that LP. We didn't win it but being nominated alone was just an incredible honor, for me, just as one of the producers on it.

CHAPTER 3

Butch Vig—The Architect Of Grunge

Back in 1990, when the blueprint for popular grunge was still sitting in Butch Vig's head, he was thankfully imprisoned in a recording studio alongside Billy Corgan plotting rock's escape from the chains of hair metal with a little engine of change called *Gish*—a revolution on record that would be a new generation's first breath of pure air and ultimately their revolution against the musical mediocrity that had come to represent and speak for teenage angst as the decade closed. Although *Nevermind* would be Vig's ultimately fatal blow as a producer to hair metal, *Gish* put the genre in ICU to begin with. Billy Corgan was a musical revolutionary without question, as he introduced the world to a sound we'd never heard even hints of before, and his technical innovations as a player and producer—beginning with *Gish*—will be studied for years to come. Along with *Gish*, the release of another Butch Vig production—Nirvana's legendary *Nevermind*—would fully thaw out rock listeners from hair metal's numbing, but *Gish* would be the first flame that led them to the light. The sound Vig and Corgan founded with *Gish* would make those ears sharp again, would motivate rock 'n' roll—and its fans—to stand up for something, both in demanding change, and celebrating its arrival at the same time.

One of Butch Vig's greatest gifts as a producer—first showcased within the music layers of *Gish*—was his ability to hone guitars to their times, both socially and in the context of the broader moods of rock 'n' roll, to be aggressive yet celebratory, derivative yet ground-breaking, tight yet experimental, where the chords needed to bend like a new turn in the road he and Corgan were taking us down as listeners. The journey Vig would take us on as a producer would be epic—an adventure for the ages, and thankfully a commercial block-buster that forced a healthy musical conformity that saved rock from itself as the 1990s began. *Rolling Stone* hailed the band's music as "distinguished from most other grunge rock in its incorporation of the high production values, ornate arrangements, and melodicism of such '70s bands as Boston and ELO." According to the producer, at the outset of his col-laboration with the Smashing Pumpkins' mastermind, Billy Corgan "had a pretty specific idea of what he wanted sonically." Vig's role then, as he viewed it—in overarching terms—was to act as something of a technical translator—in a recording context—for Corgan's methodically perfectionist method toward achieving the latter. Patience was Vig's first ally in that process, as the producer explained that "in contrast to producing Nirvana, where Kurt went through a solo once, and he wouldn't want to do it again, Billy would do it 200 times before he got it exactly as he heard it in his head." Still, Corgan's meticulous recording process wasn't laborious for Vig, as it was also his natively in terms of a preferred approach to record making, with the producer recalling that

> when I started working with him, I loved it, because I'd been in bands where we're trying to craft songs, and as much as I loved punk rock, I loved great songwriting, and I wanted records to sound good. And I wanted the performances to be really tight. There's nothing wrong with being really tight, to mastering your instrument. And so it was the first chance, when we made *Gish*, to spend some time really, really pushing ourselves. I really pushed Billy, and he really pushed me back. We'd go in the studio for 14, 15 hours a day, and just go to battle. And it wasn't like we were yelling at each other, but we were constantly trying to up the ante: "Well, you can probably do that better," or he'd say "I don't think that sounds right, you can get a better sound on this." So we were just constantly pushing each other. I loved that, I respected that, and I think it's one of the reasons we had such a close working relationship for a long period of time.

Texturally, the studio construction of *Gish* was rooted heavily in Corgan's signature, multilayered guitar tracks, of which *All Music Guide* in its review of the album observed, "there's no denying his gift for arrangements. Like Brian May and Jimmy Page, he knows how to layer guitars for maximum effect, whether it's on the pounding, sub-Sabbath rush of 'I Am One' or the shimmering, psychedelic dream pop surfaces of 'Rhinoceros.'" For

Vig, the process of tracking Corgan's compositions, from the aforementioned guitar tracks up, "was tricky because Billy's songs always evolved from start to end." Of great aid to the producer in navigating each song's compositional fluidity was the foundational synergy of the band, specifically between Corgan and drummer Jimmy Chamberlin, whose musical chemistry Vig described as one where

> in terms of playing, a lot of that sort of feel in his guitar playing came from his playing with Jimmy Chamberlin. They had a real sort of unconscious feel for how they grooved together, it was sort of a push-pull thing. One of the best things about Jimmy was he was usually able to dynamically play those parts, but then we would spend a lot of time going back in the overdubs changing the sound, and trying to match the dynamic that the song called for. When we tracked in the studio, we were primarily going for drums and a rhythm guitar part, which Billy would play along with him. We were primarily looking to get a drum track, because Billy would always go back and redo the guitar if he didn't like the sound or if it was out of tune. But I was always amazed how they had this sixth sense for locking into a groove together.

Once the album's basic instrumental tracks had been laid, as Vig began to develop a sonic sense of how Corgan's songs would play in context of the band's larger sound, he recalled a production process wherein

> one of the things I loved about that band as a whole was they could roar and rage and then get very vulnerable and delicate, where Billy's singing was almost feminine at times. It just had this wonderful lyrical quality, and a very delicate balance between the vocal and guitars and drums. So there was a lot of time spent overdubbing, using different microphones and guitars, depending on how we would dial it up and dial it down. I remember times when he would be playing and I would be running the volume on his guitar, where the chord would swell up to full volume when he played, and then I would cut it back. So we actually would find spots in songs where it sounded good, which is not easy to do when someone's standing over you playing guitar, and you're trying not to get in their way, but still work the volume on the amp. Again, that's one of the things I loved about the band was that they weren't gonna just hit the distortion petals and rock out for three or four minutes. They had a great sense of dynamics, and theatrics in some places, where their playing could just be over the top. Billy and Jimmy were both fantastic musicians, and trying to capture those dynamics in the drums too was very tricky. That was all recorded on tape, so at times in a song where it would get really quiet then go full blast, to capture the range of that without mangling the sound up was really tricky.

Vocally, Vig's technique for tracking Corgan was identical in process both on *Gish* and subsequently during the recording of *Siamese Dream*, wherein, as the producer recalled,

for Billy's vocals, I had kind of a standard setup I used with him where we would do takes, and I would adjust levels for the verse where he might be singing quieter, and then louder for the chorus or whatever. So I'd have to watch how hard he was singing, but for *Gish*, and most of *Siamese Dream*, we used one of the older, first mics I'd gotten at my studio—a Shure SF7—because I'd read somewhere that Michael Jackson had used it to sing on *Thriller*. So I found a used one for $200, and I would use either an Eve or API Preamp, and I loved these Summit TLA100 Mono-Compressors. I've used those on vocals on pretty much everything I've done for the past 16 years, and so there was a certain chain that he was used to and I was used to. The thing for Billy with vocals was that it was really important for me to get the right blend in his headphone mix, which sort of goes back to Kurt in that what a singer's hearing when they sing dictates how loud or soft they sing. So it's a very crucial balance, in terms of getting the track so it sounded good at just the right volume, and his voice at the right level in proportion to how he wanted to sing. Because sometimes if I would take the volume level down just a couple of DBs, he would sing louder and it wouldn't sound right in the verse. Or sometimes it would be the opposite where he was singing too quiet in the chorus. I sort of came up with a system once I knew how Billy wanted his mixes to be, because the console mixing board aux fader can be very flaky, so I would put tone on a reel, that I would set to calibrate to come back to the aux fader so I could set up to get the headphone mixes right. So when I knew how Billy wanted the mix during a vocal take, I would put up his calibration reel, and run tracks 15 and 16 in stereo guitar, plus I could look at the tones and know "Okay, he liked them when they were +2.5." So then when I would put the song up, it would come up exactly where Billy wanted it to be, which really helped a lot in terms of his singing. These days with Pro Tools it is a lot easier to do, but back then we were using analog. With Billy, sometimes we recorded with effects going, but a lot of times, I'd have them running on another track. If it sounds amazing, and that's part of the vibe, then I'll record it. Particularly with Garbage, if it's the guitar, or the drums or the bass, and it sounds cool, then we just go for it. But back then, a lot of times you're not sure—this sounds great at the moment—but are we going to use this? But if it sounded good enough, and was hard enough to maybe get the sound back, you may as well record it. With Billy, a lot of times, as soon as we had a vocal take, I would go back and print the effect on another track.

Once production on *Gish* had wrapped and the album was released in the very early a.m. of grunge's coming dawn, critics were early birds with their recognition of the importance the album held for the coming decade in the context of shaping its trends. *All Music Guide's* review acknowledged that "arriving several months before Nirvana's *Nevermind*, the Smashing Pumpkins' debut album, *Gish*, which was also produced by Vig, was the first shot of the alternative revolution that transformed the rock 'n' roll landscape of the '90s." Still, before Vig could have his *Siamese Dream*, he would have to achieve Nirvana, heading into the studio with that band following a production wrap on *Gish* in the late spring of 1991. Over the course of May and June 1991, while toxic wastes of airspace like Ugly Kid Joe and Trixter polluted the rock radio and video waves, a new generation of rock 'n' roll reckoning was beginning to boil toward overflow—and boil over it would by the fall of that same year upon *Nevermind's* release. For Vig, in context of plotting the album's production path, he recalled an air of unpredictability about the project that no one knew was akin yet to the times. In the same breath, Vig admits to knowing something was brewing ahead of his heading into the studio with the band, motivating the producer to subtly lobby for the gig, explaining that "usually, before you take on a project, you want to know what the album's songs are like and where they're going. In the case of Nirvana, I had done six or seven tracks at Smart that were going to be a Sub-Pop Record, and those demos ended up getting them into a major-label bidding war, and by the time they had signed to Geffen, I wasn't sure I was going to get the job, but had said to them, 'Sure, I'd love to do it.' "

In hindsight, it would have been any producer's dream gig, but for Vig, in actuality heading into preproduction, he expressed some nervousness over the album's material based on the fact that "Kurt sent me a boom box tape of them recording in the basement, and it was so distorted and shitty sounding that it was almost impossible to hear the songs. And I could kind of hear the 'Hello, Hello' on 'Smells Like Teen Spirit,' and I heard 'Come as You Are' and some of the other songs." Still, everything felt in the moment for the producer where the vibe of the project was concerned, even down to the fact that "I got a call a little more than a week before they wanted to go into the studio." During the album's brief preproduction period, Vig explained that "I had established a good relationship with them through working on those demos," a foundation that gave him an opportunity to poppify Kurt Cobain's demos in terms of an accessibility that would be key to the final album's commercial breakthrough.

As Vig explained his methodology at work in the latter process,

> because I got the gig last minute, I didn't really get a chance to digest Kurt's demos until we got to L.A. and were in the rehearsal studio. And the one thing I had realized was: I was a fan of "Bleach," but my favorite song was 'About a Girl' because it had such a great melodic sensibility. It sounded like a Lennon/McCartney song to me. And the one thing that was apparent between then and now was that Kurt had become

much more vicious in terms of his songwriting, just melodically and chord structures, so it still had the energy of punk, but had much more of a pop sensibility.

Rolling Stone would hone in on the latter aspect of Cobain's songwriting in their commentary on "Smells Like Teen Spirit"—the group and genre's breakout single—upon its release, noting that "the killer hook is a stuttering chord progression similar to the stuttering chord progression in Boston's 'More Than a Feeling,' a hit fifteen years earlier, utterly transformed through Nirvana's trademark loud/soft dynamic and dark, surreal mood. Following Ezra Pound's call to arms, Cobain made it new." For Vig, capturing that musical lightning in a bottle began with his preproduction process

> when we started rehearsing, just tightening those songs up, it was basically cutting sections down, because on the demos, they had just been jamming in their basement. So, in some cases, we'd shorten verses, or maybe drop the bridge out. Like in "Smells Like Teen Spirit," there's that little jag at the end of the chorus, that was originally at the end of the song, and they just repeated it over and over till it basically just collapsed into disarray, and that was the way they were approaching the song. So I suggested "That would be a cool little transition to get from the chorus back into the verse.

In terms of Cobain's receptiveness to Vig's suggestions, the producer recalled that during preproduction, "Kurt was totally open and easy to deal with when it came to that process. He knew the songs were good. I think, for him, he had a little bit of a struggle understanding that these songs were really poppy, which is what he wrote, but I think he was afraid and still wanted to keep the punk theme. But he was totally open to trying to move choruses around or whatever would make it a better song. I didn't have to force them to drastically rewrite anything."

Still, while the producer remembers Cobain as being open to suggestions where writing his songs was concerned during preproduction, once proper recording had gotten underway, Vig encountered the opposite in terms of their recording, explaining that

> within the recording process, I think the most difficult thing was trying to deal with Kurt's very fragile psyche. Because he could be very sharp and funny and totally engaged, and then without knowing why or when, he would shut off, and go sit in a corner, and not say a word. He was very bipolar, manic-depressive, so it was very hard for me to gauge, early on, when to push his buttons and when to leave him alone. So I knew sometimes I only had a small window to really motivate him, and a lot of times he didn't want to do things more than once.

With a pop theme in mind, and perhaps recognizing Cobain's genius on the level with that of his idols—as the world at wide later would—Vig employed a strategy in tracking Cobain's vocals in which "I would have to use Psychology 101 to get better performances, so for instance, when I wanted to double-track his guitar or vocal, he'd say 'Oh, I don't want to do that, that's fake.' And I'd go 'Well, John Lennon did it on just about everything he ever recorded . . . ' and he'd go 'Okay.' So if I could find a reference that he respected in terms of why I wanted to do it, then he would agree to it."

In spite of Cobain's moodiness toward the recording process, Vig found that once they were on the same page in terms of performance, "Kurt's greatest strength in the studio then was: He always totally went for it—whether it was playing guitar or singing, he didn't hold back. Even if it was something quiet like 'Something in the Way,' just the sort of emotion that came out of his voice, it's not a song that's confrontational by screaming, but it kind of is by the way he whispered. And when he was on, and you would actually hit record, he was amazing." Describing the atmosphere he set for Cobain during vocal tracking, Vig explained that "I tried to vibe it up, I try to do that for everybody. Keep the lights low so there are no distractions, try to keep people from wandering around the control room or in your line of sight." In terms of the technical specifics of tracking as Vig tailored them to Cobain's vocals, he recalled that "Kurt didn't want to wear headphones at first, so I tried setting up a couple speakers out of faze in a triangle from the microphone, and it worked on a couple of the things where he sang really loud, but when he was doing quieter songs, it would end up feeding back. So I had to work really hard to get a headphone mix that he liked, because he didn't really like hearing the music that way. Basically, I would have to crank it super loud and turn the guitars up super loud."

Reading into Cobain's fragile approach toward committing the revolutionary songs he had written to tape, Vig found the core of what he felt made the singer's songs so important in a commercial sense, reasoning that

> at the time, I didn't know *Nevermind* was going to become this huge critical and commercial success, but I did know he was special, and you could tell he was a very damaged soul. I think one of the reasons he became such an icon was because when he sang, somehow, the pain inside him came out through his vocal chords. I think more than anything that's what people responded to. If you took *Nevermind*, and put a different singer on that record, it would still be a good record, but wouldn't be the same thing. The sound of his voice was like exposing a raw nerve, and I think in some ways, that it's really the intense emotional quality from listening to him sing, is one of the reasons he touched so many people.

Perhaps realizing the responsibility he carried as producer in terms of balancing artistic integrity with commercial salability, Vig explained that ultimately

> in making that record, I walked the line of really crafting the songs and pulling the hooks out so they were really in your face, but still keep the energy of punk rock, and sort of the passion of it. Kurt had an innate genius for melodies over chords. A lot of times, he'd be sitting in the corner, playing acoustic guitar and humming something, and my ear would catch it, and I'd go "What's that? We should record that." And he'd go "Oh, naw, that's just some punk bullshit that sounds like blah, blah, I don't really want to do that." But he was constantly doing that, just noodling and singing these little things that were gorgeous. I knew that Kurt was special, that he was extremely talented.

Assessing Nirvana's historical importance to forever reshaping the landscape of commercial rock is best left to mainstream critics like *Rolling Stone*, who would conclude upon the release of *Nevermind* that Kurt Cobain had joined "only a handful of musicians . . . (who) have been able to catch their zeitgeist and watch their music resonate far beyond their fan base into the culture at large." Nirvana's debut LP would prove the archetype, both in concept and commerciality, for a genre and generation that followed, and for Vig in setting up his next project, Smashing Pumpkins' follow-up to *Gish*. The timing couldn't have been more opportune or ideal for what Billy Corgan heard and had in mind with *Siamese Dream*. Perhaps seeing opportunity, Corgan seized ambition by the neck of his guitar and dove headlong into his second collaboration with the producer. For Vig, the pressure he felt heading into production on *Siamese Dream* was as layered as Billy Corgan's guitar tracks, and in terms of the latter, perhaps—in terms of what he faced heading into the studio—Corgan's ambitious plans for the album's guitar sound offered the producer the most intensity in terms of focus on planning.

As Vig recalled his preproduction process with Corgan,

> Billy was a mad scientist with the guitars, so a lot of times I would have to draw out a map, literally, of the song for his guitars, with all these arrows, going "Okay, this one goes to track 14 for the clean guitar through the second verse." For instance, on "Soma," that was one of the biggest guitar maps I ever had. I remember that was an epic, and literally so in recording it, so much so that I remember having to flip over the back of the track sheet and continue the map. And when it came time to mix that, I remember showing the map to Alan Molder and he freaked out and goes, "What the fuck is that?" I explained that it would help him get through mixing the song.

Describing Corgan's equipment setup, Vig remembered that "Billy brought in his amps, and I can't remember exactly, but I think they were mostly Marshalls, and he had some different preamps he had hot rodded, so they had more gain, so it had a certain kind of fuzzy crunch coming from the preamp before it went into the amp." Once amps were hot, guitars were plugged in, and tracking was underway, Vig recalled a coproducing routine with Corgan that rivaled any he had ever experienced prior thereto, explaining that

> *Siamese Dream* at the time, that was by far the most ambitious undertaking I had done. We spent five months, fourteen to sixteen hours a day, six and seven days a week recording. Then we mixed it for thirty-six days straight. It was brutal, and we almost killed each other in the process, but at the end, I felt really proud of that record. We tried to do a lot of things dynamically and sonically that were above and beyond any of the other records I had produced up to that time. And again, I really have to give Billy credit because he pushed me hard and I pushed him hard, and we wanted to make it sound cooler and weirder and more fucked up than anything else out there, and to have these spots where it just ripped your head off, and then blow through the stratosphere.

Key to the album's overall musical synergy, as always, was that of Corgan and drummer Jimmy Chamberlin, who Vig recalled, in setting the pace for the record's overarching groove, "became this sort of hypnotic pulse. Billy's guitar playing and Jimmy's drumming together really I think is how the band developed their style." *Rolling Stone* would even note the pair's kindred spirits as players, highlighting "the virtuosic interplay of Corgan and Jimmy Chamberlin" in their coverage of the band. Elaborating on Chamberlin's drumming style as it related to driving the album's overall in terms of groove, Vig explained that "Jimmy was never really good at using click tracks, which is great, but if you analyze the tracks, they are not like rock steady/click track steady. Sometimes within the same bar, he'd push at the start of the bar, then pull back, and push and pull very subtly, but in a way that made the music hypnotic." Using his technical approach to tracking Jimmy Chamberlin's drums to offer broader commentary on his approach thereafter on a host of multiplatinum rock albums, Vig explains that

> for starters, hopefully the drummer is really good, as Jimmy definitely was, because you can have a kit that sounds good in a room, and have two different drummers go in and play and it's going to sound very different. So the first thing you usually try to do is sit in the room and listen, without putting a mic on anything, and find the best place where the room sounds good. Then just understand how the drummer plays, is

he really heavy on the cymbals, does he play medium on the snare, or are the dynamics really exaggerated, or is he pretty consistent? And sometimes that would help you pick the mics you were gonna use, and where you were gonna put them.

While Corgan and Chamberlin remained in sync, as they would for more than a decade to come, Vig recalled that Corgan's relationships with the band's other members, namely guitarist James Iha and bassist D'Arcy, were considerably strained due to Corgan's recording method of tracking every instrument but drums himself. As Vig recalled, "it was hard work, particularly because the band was dysfunctional at that point, so aside from all the technical end of it and trying to get the best performances, there was also dealing with the fragile psyche of each individual band member. They were not getting along all the time, and there were moments when Billy was like 'Fuck you guys, I'm gonna fire you all, I want you to go home.' Then we'd get together, have a band meeting, and then smooth things out for a while."

Critically, *Siamese Dream,* upon release, rose volumes above even its hype in the context of praise and promise for the return of the guitar gods to popularity as part of alternative rock's mainstream. In the latter pursuit, Corgan led the charge with an album that *Rolling Stone* hailed for making "the waters safe again for six-string assault . . . With Butch Vig coproducing, *Siamese Dream* is guitars and more guitars—streamlined or sludgy and often aping such dinosaurs as Boston and Queen, stacked in sonic layers . . . This 13-song collection asserts main man Billy Corgan's fondness for the thick tone and hot chops beloved of post-metal '70s-crazed players." *Siamese Dream* was nominated for Best Alternative Music Album at the Grammy Awards of 1994.

As a renaissance producer who has experienced just that in the course of his remarkable twenty-five-year career, Butch Vig, in spite of all the accolades and platinum plaques that line his studio walls, still feels, as he did from day one, that

for me, the best thing about making records is the process. By the time I'm finished with a record, have gone through the mixing, and listened to the mastering, I don't necessarily want to go home and listen to it, which is common. So it's the process of actually creating that's the fantastic part. It's not so much the part where you get the finished product, put it in the CD player. It's the process that's fascinating, because every day is different. When you go in to cut basic tracks, for instance, you have no idea what's going to happen. There's always a million little decisions you have to make on the fly that you're not even aware of—the feel of the performance, does it sound right? Is this the right kind of approach we're going for? But it's not like you have to sit there and ask yourself those questions, they just happen all the time. There's always little technical things to be aware of and make sure are all going in your favor. So you can sort of plan out your day when you go in the studio, but there's always some massive curve balls that get thrown toward you, which is part of why I love it so much.

From a legacy vantage point, rock 'n' roll as it was defined throughout the 1990s cannot be played without hearing Vig's influence in shaping its broader soundscape. Consider *Rolling Stone*'s summation of the producers' career, wherein the mother ship of all rock critics concluded that Vig "rewrote the pop book on distortion with Nirvana's epochal *Nevermind*. Quickly he became current rock's best shaper, a quietly logical guy who could navigate the complicated corners of, say, Sonic Youth and still remember the big beat, chewy tunes and adolescent aggression that make pop fly." In offering a closing assessment on how the aforementioned collaborations rank not on the commercial charts but personally on his own in terms of greatest and favorite hits, Vig describes how each informed his overall record producing process:

Looking at working with Kurt Cobain, I realized so much of the sound of them was capturing that raw, primal emotion, and trying to get to the point where it sounded really focused, but was real and honest. Same thing with the Pumpkins, but different because Billy would want to work the part over and over again, and in some ways, when I finished *Siamese Dream*, it's one of the records I'm most proud of because it was sonically much more vicious then *Nevermind*—the layering and what we were trying to do. Not that the songs were better, I think there's great songs on both records, but just the different approach to recording because at the time, I had never really done a record of that sonic scope. I just remember it almost killed me, but was an immense achievement for me personally. I can't really rank one over the other. Both of those records are in my top five records I have ever made.

CHAPTER 4

Linda Perry—The Gift

Legendary pop songstress Laura Nyro once said of her craft that "songs come in cycles; next year I may write one song. That kind of song writing is cyclical, seasonal; it's the culmination of a deeper experience. It's like nature; it takes time to seed and then it blooms." For the twentieth century, Nyro was arguably pop music's most gifted and prolific female songwriter, penning #1 hit singles for a variety of pop acts—including the Fifth Dimension's renditions of "Wedding Bell Blues," "Stoned Soul Picnic," "Blowin' Away," and "Sweet Blindness"; "Eli's Comin'" by Three Dog Night; "Stoney End" by Barbra Streisand; and "And When I Die" by Blood Sweat & Tears among countless others—that defined pop radio in the late 1960s and early 1970s. Thirty years later, in the twenty-first century, one-time 4 Non Blondes leader Linda Perry has kept the next season of generation-defining pop abloom and fertile, writing hits for the biggest names of the day, from Christina Aguilera to Pink, Gwen Stefani to Courtney Love. In spite of being tapped as Nyro's heir apparent in terms of both her sheer number of hit songs and their thematic focus on the female experience, Perry is the first to admit it's the last thing she expected to be doing with her gift, explaining that "it definitely was not a plan for me to start writing and producing for other artists." For as unplanned for Perry as her second career as a songwriter/producer is, so too is her process for pairing songs with recording artists. She explains: "I don't match up songs—write a song and go 'Oh, I'm going to give this song to that person.'" Once Perry has accepted the challenge of adding substance to an artist's sound where style has been the prevalent factor driving the artist's commercial popularity without compromising album sales—as was the case initially with both Pink and Christina Aguilera—and which has become her signature as a collaborator, she explains that "it's a challenge to do that, to get people to see beyond the bad stuff, like when you hear Christina hearing 'Come on Over,' it's like 'Okay, please give me a break.' Then you have to win all those people that thought she was a blonde, little Gonna-Be-Like-All-the-Other-Girls, and then to get real people, like musicians, that are standing and going 'Oh my God, that Christina song you did was amazing,' that's it. To me, that moment right there is what it's all about for me."S

Perry's journey to reaching that creative crest was an intricate one that began with a process of letting go personally: "I go through an internal struggle of letting go of every song I write that someone else sings." Offering one of her collaborations with Christina Aguilera as an example, Perry explains that:

> Christina just did it to me again. There's this song she has, her single "Hurt," that song I wrote about my dad. I had lost my father a year ago, and it hadn't even been a year when I did the song. And she came to me, and had these two chords that her and this guy wrote, and she was like "I really like these chords, can you turn this into a song? I want the song to be about losing someone." And inside of me, I'm going "You little fucking bitch, you totally know I lost my dad, and now you're gonna milk me for my emotions." And I wasn't gonna go there, I was going to be stubborn, and just give her a mediocre make-up-what-I-think-loss-is, and pretend there was no emotion behind it whatsoever, and it ended up being this beautiful song about losing my dad, and the pain that I'm going through, and the guilt, and regret for not being more present for him. So it's really hard, and this is where the producer part of me comes in, because I have to go "Linda Perry would have never done 'Beautiful' that way, Linda Perry would have never done 'Hurt' that way." I would have done a completely different type of production, and had a completely different way of singing it. But you know what? It's Christina Aguilera, so I have to figure out how to get her where she needs to be but still maintain the integrity and emotion, and have it sound like Christina Aguilera, and not Christina singing a Linda Perry song. So it's a lot of struggle. I go through struggle all the time with songs.

It is Perry's inimitable ability to first mirror her collaborator that allows the broader musical metamorphosis to blossom, as she explains:

I have this chameleon thing I can do: I can totally adapt someone's character, and I'm very empathetic. I can just sit and take one someone, and feel their pain. I can feel them. I'm very, very extremely sensitive to people's energy, and all of a sudden, I can be in a place where, if they're describing something to me, I can be there with them. So then, when they leave, it's not that they're asking me to write a song for them, I'm going to write a song with them, but sometimes what happens is after they leave, I have time to absorb their energy. I'm left with them still, and I'll start walking out the door half the time, like "Okay, I'm gonna go home." But then something pulls me back into the studio, and I go sit down, and turn on the recorder, and sit at the piano for a bit, and all of a sudden, an idea will start showing up. And then all of a sudden, here I am feeling this person and where their pain was, or their happiness, whatever, their state of mind. So then when they walk in the next day, I go, "You know what, I didn't mean to do this, but after you left, I didn't mean to do this, but I came up with this idea." And they're like "Whoa, how did you do that?" And I'm like "I listened. I listened to what you had to say, and just wanted to give you what you wanted." So I don't know how it happens, but that's the process.

In other cases, Perry writes a hit before it's even paired with an artist, as was the case with what is arguably her—and Christina Aguilera's—biggest hit to date, "Beautiful" from 2003's *Stripped* LP. In addition to staying atop the *Billboard* Top 200 Singles Chart for weeks and driving the album to multiplatinum status, the single also won the 2004 Grammy Award for Best Female Pop Vocal, ironic considering that, as Perry recalls,

that vocal—her scratch vocal from the first time she ever sang it—is the vocal that's out there on the finished single, that's on the record, that was on the radio, that was her very first time singing it. I fought for seven months for that vocal, because she kept trying to perfect it, and I was like "No Christina, this is the vocal. This is the vocal that sold me, and it's gonna sell everybody else." And she said, "It's not perfect." And I said, "That's *why* it's perfect, because it's not perfect, it's believable to me, you gotta trust me on this." So finally she agreed, and let me have my scratch vocal."

In instances like "Beautiful" where Perry has completed composing a song before she gives it to an artist, her process of getting to know the artist ahead of their collaboration in recording the song is equally important to the writer/producer in both mapping out the song's production in the studio and many times determining which song she'll give the artist to record.

Elaborating on the genesis of "Beautiful" becoming Christina Aguilera's, Perry recalled:

How "Beautiful" came to be was that when Christina and I first met, and she came to my house, and she was feeling a little shy, and was talking about how much she loved my voice, and asked me, "Well, would you play me a song just to break the ice and make me feel a little comfortable." And I had just written "Beautiful," and it was basically my favorite song at that point because I just knew it was great, and so I played it to her, not to give to her, just played her the song because she had asked me to play something. So I was like "Okay, I'll play her 'Beautiful.'" So I sat down at the piano and played the song, and she got closer and closer to the piano, and by the end of it, she looked at me and asked, "Do you have a demo?" And I said, "No, I just wrote this." And she asked, "Can you demo this for me, and write out the lyrics." And I looked at her and asked, "Why?" And she said, "Because I want it." And I was looking at her in shock like "Huh?" It didn't even click. Then I called up my manager and said, "Christina wants this song of mine, 'Beautiful,' and I actually played my manager the song over the phone, and she's like "Well, she's coming over again tonight, have her sing it and see how you feel about it." And I thought that was a good idea. So that night when Christina came over, I wrote out the lyrics for her, put her in front of the microphones, listened to me sing it a few times, got the melody together, I put down a piano demo of it, and she sang it. And while she was singing it, it hit me like "Okay, she can have that, because that was my vocal."

In revealing the inner workings of her truly inspired songwriting process, Perry explained it is never deliberate:

I never try to write, I only write when there's a song to be written. When it's time to write a song, I sit at the piano, and the melody is there, the chord structure is there, and then the lyrics I ad-lib. I just start singing whatever the hell comes out of my heart, and then words start forming, and I record everything, so I don't write things down. You should always record everything, even if it's just a little rinky-dink recorder, anything. When you are going to sit at an instrument, push *Record* on whatever is around you, because words that you say, like adlibbing I think everyone should learn to be confident enough to just open up their mouth, and say whatever stupid thing comes out. Because that's where you get the real emotion, that's where the song is, the song cannot be written with lyrics first for me. I'm sure they do it all the time, but I have never written a lyric before writing the music to a song. I've never had a concept, I've sat down at the piano or guitar and just played, and the melody shows up, and then the lyrics come. I felt stupid the very first time, for instance, "I am beautiful" came out. I was like "What the fuck? I am beautiful, no matter what you say? What the fuck is this shit?" But I kept going with it, because I felt that what a weird statement to make for me, because I am so not that, I don't think that whatsoever, but then I started hearing what my lyrics were turning into, and was like "Oh, I'm trying to convince myself that I am. That's what this song is about." Someone is so insecure, they're starting to learn themselves that "Hey, you know what, I am beautiful in here somewhere. And hey you, you are too." It's a cheesy concept once it ended up, but I was just like "What a beautiful one at that too." So for me, that's the only way I've written, I've never tried to write.

The latter compositional routine alters itself somewhat when a collaborative writing situation occurs, as was the case with Gwen Stefani. In that scenario, as Perry recalled,

with Gwen, it was an interesting manner, with her it was completely different from my past collaborations. She would come and kind of tell me what she wanted to do. Gwen, her biggest strength to me is how down to earth she is. She is really open-minded, also very clear about what it is she wants to do, she's very clear. She knows what she wants, and is really open-minded about how to get it. We only wrote really in the same room one song together, called "Fine by You." It was right then and there we came up with it. So we did this first song, and she was really hesitant about being in the studio, really kind of dragging her feet a little bit. And I could tell she wasn't 100 percent comfortable with me yet, and also she was really nervous about doing the solo album. She had a lot on her mind, and I got the impression she'd rather be in bed, eating pizza, watching TV with Gavin, because it was all too overwhelming. So she had left that night, and then I had stayed up all night, because as soon as she walked in the door, my first thought was "I wonder what she's waiting for?" And so I just went in, and started putting this beat together, then the guitars started showing up, the bass line, and all of a sudden I had this chorus, "What ya, What ya, What ya waiting for?" And put the chorus down, melody ideas in the verses, the bridge, just kind of making up words. But I did the track overnight, and was there till probably four in the morning. Then came back to the studio the next day, and said, "Hey, what's going on?" Just being all mellow. And I said, "I have an idea," and she's like "Okay," and I just played it, and she was like "Dude, what the fuck was that?" Everything changed, and from then on out, she came to life. That was the first song, that was her first single. But she was really open to everything, she's very talented, I love Gwen. She's funny, goofy, and kind of a dork, very dorky. She can just go and go for vocal takes, but we didn't have to do that many. She pretty much nailed it. She corrects herself very quickly, and by the next take, she'll go "Oh, I know exactly what I did wrong." Then—Whamo!—she'll be nailing it from there on.

One aim Perry habitually has in mind with any demo is for the song to stand up on its own as a finished product—naked of any production touch-ups. Offering "Beautiful" as an example, she explained that a song like "Beautiful" is a great song all on its own. That's what I strive for, is the songs that are just good all on their own, that you're not thinking of production. With "Beautiful," to me it was a '70s Beatles type of song, so in my mind I could hear it, but I was so focused on the song itself. Sometimes when a song is that good, to me if it can sound that good just on piano it's kind of hard to imagine where it can't be, because I don't need to imagine that. Sometimes if I don't write as good a song, the production and what is going to make it better starts popping into my head. I'll think, "You know what, this is fucking great but I know that I can't just play it on the piano right now, so what I want to happen here is this on the bass, with a B3 with strings, and that will allow me to open up the melody better. But right now I'm just not getting the point across, so I gotta get the production happening somewhere around there in order to really get the song where it needs to be."

An important part of achieving the latter, according to Perry, involves

as a producer, you having to really understand the atmosphere that you're putting around your artist, you have to understand the artist and really listen to them. You have to let go of ego. When an artist walks into my studio, my ego is out the door, it's no longer about me, it's about them, and that's what makes me a great producer—none of my stuff sounds the same. It all sounds completely different, because I become the artist, the artist does not become me. And experiment, experiment with sounds, there's no how-to, follow your instinct. If you want to put some weird-ass $50 microphone in front of the bass amp, just do it, and if it sounds good to your ear, then that's all that matters.

Turning next to another bedrock rule where her master craft of hit writing is concerned, Perry explains via her multiplatinum collaboration with Pink that, with any of her collaborations, no matter how big the star:

The thing is, you can't predict these hits. There are songs I thought should have been hits, that never were hits. I thought that Pink song "Dear Diary" I thought if they would have released that song, it would have set up her career better. It frustrates me only to a point, but then I realize it's a label and they're stupid. So you have to understand and appreciate the fact that that's what's gonna happen. But the thing is—and this is the big misconception—it's the artist, not the label. If the artist was strong enough, and fought hard enough, they could have anything that they wanted. But the truth is, the artist gets scared, because the label starts threatening them, so then they back down, and cower, and then they end up making a record they don't wanna make. If I hear "That wasn't me. I didn't make that type of record. My label made me do it. I hate it." If I fucking hear it again, I'm gonna kill myself. Because it's like: who are you fucking kidding? The label couldn't have done anything without you sitting in front of that fucking microphone and recording it. So you allowed it to happen, not the label.

One instance in which Perry always defers her opinion on a final production upon initial delivery of a song are those collaborations in which she is not producing a song she has written for an artist, explaining that "I've had to part with a couple songs I wrote that I didn't produce. One was 'Fine by You' and another is going to be on Gwen Stefani's new album that I wrote, but Nelly Hooper produced those records. I wrote a song for the Dixie Chicks called 'Voices in My Head,' and they already had Rick Rubin, but really wanted to work with me as a songwriter, so he did that production. I am definitely not a stickler for that." Still, there are instances where the producer seems clearly to feel her production would have benefited the end result, citing her collaboration with Lisa Marie Presley as an instance in which "I didn't get to produce the stuff I did with her, which I really wish I'd had the opportunity to do that. Personally, the demos of those songs—the vocals were way better. They were more relaxed, more raw, they were fatter sounding, and I think she was in a comfort zone, and loved the energy of my place, even though where she recorded her record was her house. But I can totally hear the difference of the vocals I have from the demos to the vocals that are on the record. So it really depends on the artist."

Because of the latter, Perry—judging by the trends of her production resume—almost always seems to prefer producing those artists for or with whom she writes, viewing the two steps as one process. Toward that end, while postproduction compromise is something she has come to expect through years of experience, during the creative phase of record making, Perry maintains an environment completely free of any constraints, beginning with who is allowed in the studio during tracking. Perry explained that the latter typically

depends on the artist and on the song as to whether it's just them and me in the studio. I had one artist that where they were just so stiff when they were doing the vocal that I made people actually go into the room and start taking pictures of them to loosen them up, and really kind of distract them from their head. I've brought strippers in. Christina really likes to be alone; it's just me and the protocols guy and her. And sometimes when she starts loosening up, people can start coming in. But other than that, it's a closed session, because she's a perfectionist, and she doesn't want anybody to hear her hit a wrong note, which she never does. Rarely does Christina hit a wrong note. So everybody's different, and if it's an energetic song, I've had people who I get them drunk, because I need that slur, I need that swagger, and they're being again too stiff, and not enough energy. So I'll make a party out of it. I had to do a

Christmas song the other day and I put a Christmas tree in the live room. My studio itself is amazing, it's beautiful, has tons of vibe, so even just being in my studio automatically gives you tons of vibe. I don't go into other studios.

Critically and commercially, Perry has become inextricably linked to the artists she produces, with *Rolling Stone*, for one example, in a review of Pink's *Mizunderstood* LP, noting that Perry's "songwriting and production dominate the album," while in a review of Lisa Marie Presley's *Now What* LP, the magazine concluded that Perry's "tracks do possess the best melodies." In the case of Kelly Osbourne's LP *Sleeping in the Nothing*, the magazine similarly observed that "with crucial help from songwriter Linda Perry, she translates family stuff and rehab stories into pop confessionals." Aside from Osbourne and Presley, the majority of Perry's collaborations have been repetitive—both in the results they achieve for maturing artistry and record sales—over the course of multiyear relationships she has built with artists like Pink, Courtney Love, Gwen Stefani, and countless others. Still, in spite of her successes, Perry emphasizes to up-and-coming songwriters and producers the importance of checking formula at the door every time:

As a songwriter, I think it's really important that you let the song be what it wants to be. You can't control the song. So in order to do that, you have to trust your instinct, and just get out the guitar, and just let it flow, let it all come out and open up your mouth, and just start singing whatever comes out of your head. It's when we get into the mind, too thought out and now it's becoming scripted, but if you just open up your mouth and let your heart kind of come out, there's going to be really magical things that are gonna come out that you would've never written if you were thinking about it. And a song will be written when it's time to be written, but when you try to write a song, and it's three hours now and you don't even have anything, walk away, give up and move on. It's not gonna happen. The only thing that is going to happen is some contrived piece of crap that's not gonna mean anything. So that's my best advice to songwriters is just let the song come, you can't find the song, the song has to find you.

CHAPTER 5

Mike Fraser—Rock Steady . . .

Whether it was Aerosmith off taking a *Permanent Vacation*, the Cult building their *Sonic Temple*, Joe Satriani exploring a *Crystal Planet* or pushing toward sounds *Super Colossal*, or AC/DC perfecting their *Stiff Upper Lip* or sliding along *Razor's Edge* or across the *Black Ice* as agelessly and authentically as they had twenty years earlier on generation-defining classics like "Highway to Hell" and "Back in Black," throughout his thirty-year career, producer Mike Fraser has earned the kind of studio loyalty from some of rock 'n' roll's biggest living legends that is afforded only the most trusted keepers of its platinum grail. Fraser is one of those trustees, after three decades of making the kind of "favorite playlists" that only show up in the league of legends like the aforementioned artists.

Sitting in his Vancouver studio in 2011, Fraser reflected in the same kind of amazement anyone would, confessing proudly that "with a lot of the bands I've worked with—Aerosmith, AC/DC, Metallica, Van Halen—I pinch myself every day, because I can't believe I've been lucky enough to be in this business, and for as long as I have, and still pull a paycheck from it. I get paid to listen to music, and work with some great musicians and great bands. I'm living a dream." That dream—one that tens of thousands of sound engineers hold up as high as the even millions more guitar players who dream of stadium stardom the way engineers do of shaping its signatures in the studio—is one that came true for Fraser almost by accident. Recalling that he began his music career like so many of the latter dreamers when he was in high school, the producer shared that "I played guitar in a little sort of garage band, played a few school dances, and when I got out of school, my dad and I had our own logging operation for a while. So I drove logging trucks and gravel trucks and bulldozers, and after a while, I got tired of being laid off in the winter. So I finally asked myself, 'Well, what do I really want to do?' And I loved music, but wasn't a good enough guitar player to pursue and make money at that, but still knew I wanted to work in the business."

Pivoting from that ambition, Fraser next recounted that his big break came when "I found a studio, Little Mountain, that needed a janitor, got hired, and thought it would be the perfect way to get my foot in the door." Reflective of a down-to-earth bedside manner that would serve him well in the years to come, Fraser found his blue-collar work ethic would soon pay off. "After a couple of months, I started assisting on some jingle sessions, and at that time Bob Rock was starting out as an engineer, and was working at night with all the Vancouver punk bands. I would basically sleep at the place, staying all night after working days to help him do that, and we became a team, and there you go."

With Bob Rock needing no introduction to rock fans who grew up on Mötley Crüe and Metallica records, Fraser recalled of the fundamental production underpinnings he took away from his years working alongside Rock that

> coming up under Bob's wing, one of the main things he really taught me was, as an engineer, how to listen and how to hear, not only sonically, but also how to listen to a song for its qualities (i.e., is it strong melodically, is it got a good riff and tempo, etc.). He was *really* good at that, but *most* important was how to hear things, and how there's two ways to listen to a song: one is sonically, and as you listen through a song, even on the radio, you zero in specifically on the kick drum or snare or guitar sound. And you can listen to a song just as a song, which is how most people do it as fans.

That instinct would be honed over several multiplatinum collaborations Fraser would record with Rock, including the Cult's classic breakout LP, *Sonic Temple*, which the *New York Times* would hail as "an exceptional hard-rock album," and a record so pop-palatable it would grab the attention of mainstream critics like *People* magazine, who warned rock fans to ready their ears for "rude, aggressive guitar attacks that will slam you up against the wall like a Utah state trooper after martial law has been declared," adding that "with all the wimp rock floating around today, *Sonic Temple* is a bracing tonic."

Detailing the sonic fundamentals behind the album, whose sound the *Times* would add "washes blunt, powerful sound over the broadness of most of the band's strokes," Fraser recalled that the LP "was recorded at Little Mountain in Studio A, which is a fairly big room, then off to the side we'd have a doorway that led into a loading bay, so we'd record the loading bay separately. On *Sonic Temple,* we were definitely going for a big, roomy sound." With much of the band's power rooted in the stellar beat-keeping by then drummer Matt Sorum, Fraser—who personally miced the set that captured Sorum's thunder on tape—said of its technical blueprint that

> on Matt Sorum's drums for that album, on the snare drum, I miced the top and bottom with a Shure 57, and on the kick would be a Sennheiser 421, and on the toms, I again used a Shure 57 on the top skin, and on the bottom, miced it up with a Sennheiser 421 as well. I like the Sennheiser because it's got a really good sort of attacky quality to it, and I use 57s and 421s on guitars as well because I find the combination of both those mics are great because a 57's got good top end and tone, and then the 421's got that great midrange thing. So when they meld together, you rarely have to EQ because you're getting all the qualities you're looking for.

Singing his praise of Shure mics, which would become a key tool of his micing technique in the years that followed, Fraser explained that his preference for Shure as a go-to drum mic was rooted in the fact that "they can take a lot of abuse and you can even sort of hit them with a drum stick and they'll keep on working. The only difference in the mic I use for maybe a real heavy hitter is maybe not mic the drums as close, to get a little more distance on it. Because when you hit a drum really hard, the sound jumps up so fast that it sounds like a smack, so you've got to catch that sound wave a little further away from the instrument, because that's where the tone comes back in." As he and Rock worked side-by-side creating the album's drum sound once principal tracking was underway, which Fraser recalled was recorded at "Studio A of Little Mountain on an SSL 4000 console," the engineer-producer added that in years since, his preferences have expanded to include a love of "recording on Neve or API boards, for drums and guitars especially, they just have this warm, punchy characteristic that's great, and for mixing, it's always an SSL for me. I think the combination of something being recorded on a Neve, and mixed on an SSL is the perfect combo."

Describing tracking lead axe-man Billy Duffy, whose guitars blended with Sorum's thundering drums so succinctly that *The New York Times* would add in its review that "the guitars and drums come in like a wave, finding a riff and . . . suddenly there (is) . . . intoxicating . . . sound exploding everywhere," Fraser shared his memory that "I used a 57 and a 421 on kind of opposing cones. Every guitar part, every song we used a different setup, so sometimes we'd put room mic on there to catch a little bit more of the room sound of the guitar, every part was through a different head. I know we used a lot of Marshall heads, but also know there would be a lot of hi-watt stuff in there." Using the album's biggest hit single, the anthemic 'Fire Woman,' to reveal his and Rock's bag of tricks for creating the song's blazing guitars, Fraser said:

> We manipulated the guitar sound on that song on the setup. Bob was always into cap-turing the guitar sound and not leaving something to later, 'Oh, let's add that effect in the mix.' So it would be through a combination of pedals, I remember we used a lot of multiple-heads per sound, so we'd have a hi-watt setup, as well as a Marshall setup, mic both amps, and then find the blend we were working for. With Billy's style, and the way Bob liked to do it, they liked to record the effects at the time. Say a delay or a chorus through an amp sounds a little different—when you fire it through the amp—as opposed to adding it to the recorded sound later. So it has that sort of speaker quality to it, that's what we're looking for.

Fraser's producer Bruce Fairbairn, who would sadly see his star burn out far too soon following a tragic passing to cancer in 2001, was a mentor who *Billboard* would call "one of the most successful producers of the 1980s, helming massive hits" for bands including Bon Jovi (*Slippery When Wet, New Jersey*), Aerosmith (*Permanent Vacation, Pump, Get a Grip*), AC/DC (*Razor's Edge*), Van Halen (*Balance*), Kiss, Yes, and Ozzy Osbourne among others. Fairbairn and Fraser's success in reinventing/relaunching Aerosmith for a new generation of fans that would follow over the course of hits like "Dude (Looks Like a Lady)," "Ragdoll," "What It Takes," "Angel," "Love in an Elevator," the Grammy-winning "Janie's Got a Gun," 'Living on the Edge," "Crazy," "Crying," "The Other Side," and "Amazing" led to another generation-defining collaboration with *Razor's Edge*, the twelfth studio LP by fellow hard-rock legends AC/DC.

Entertainment Weekly would praise Fairbairn's production and Fraser's engineering ac-complishment as responsible for producing an album that served as a wildly successful mu-sical reminder that while "hard rock and heavy metal are young people's music . . . often it's the older bands that prove most dependable." That album, AC/DC's *Razor's Edge* LP, which Fraser would record alongside Fairbairn, heading into the last decade of the millennium, was one that the engineer-producer recalled came to Little Mountain in an odd fashion:

> AC/DC had started *Razor's Edge* with George Young in the U.K., and there had been a family illness, so they basically had everything but vocals and lead guitar overdubs recorded. So when they got to Little Mountain, initially we thought it would be a breeze because all we again had to track was Brian's leads and the other overdubs I men-

tioned. Well, when Brian started singing, we quickly discovered that the keys of the songs were in the wrong key for Brian, so we started rerecording the guitars on them to change the key and bring it down a whole step. Well, the band liked the sound and process of that better than what they already had tracked, so we wound up doing everything again, down to even cutting two or three more drum tracks with Chris. We kept a lot of the basic bed drum tracks.

In spite of a signature sound that plays to the ear so easily its existence is taken for granted by most critics and fans, ironically, Fraser would share that, in reality once the tape was rolling, "they're a tough band to produce, because they already know what they want and how to get it, but they just need that third member of the band, so to speak, to help guide them to those ends. In the dynamic between Bruce and the band, they liked his approach in general. Bruce is a take-charge kind of guy, and so he was the perfect guy for them." Setting the band up in Studio B at Little Mountain, Fraser recalled that in spite of the thundering drums throughout the album, "Studio B is a fairly small room, and it didn't have a doorway into the loading bay, so you had more of the small room sound. With AC/ DC, they like the tighter, closer sounding drums." Elaborating on the technical side of the drums' tracking, which he supervised, Fraser next recalled that—for again as loud as the album's final mix projected itself rhythmically:

> It's funny because Chris is actually quite a light drummer, he doesn't hit very hard. When you watch him on videos, it looks like he's really laying into them, but in the studio, when he hits the cymbals they barely move. That's sort of the clue, and some of those drummers who hit with a little bit more finesse, it's actually an easier sound to record, because the drum skins react a little better. They don't shut down with the force going on. So especially on overheads, I'd mic him a little closer because he doesn't put all his weight into it; he's more of a finesse guy. The overheads I used on Chris were probably AKG 452s, which have a really nice silky top-end, they don't get too thin—it's still warm, but has a nice silky top-end, that's why I like those.

Over top of those drums, Fraser recalled, the process of recording what MTV hailed as "AC/DC's mammoth power chord roar . . . [one that] became one of the most influential hard rock sounds of the '70s . . . [and] spawned countless imitators over the next two decades as 'amazing.' On *Razor's Edge* it was a little different from later records I made with them, because the songs were already recorded, so we were just doing overdubs. So on that one they didn't play at the same time." Delving into the specific setup for brothers Angus and Malcolm Young as they recorded their respective guitar parts simultaneously, Fraser explained that "we set up the amp heads in the control room, and Angus would sit there with a cigarette hanging out of his mouth and play. I miced him up with 57s on his Marshalls, not much of a room sound on them, because both he and Malcolm like a little bit tighter, close-miced type of sound."

Detailing from a soundman's ear how the Young brothers' synched style of guitar interplay worked to flesh out the heart of the band's sound, Fraser explained that, on tape, "Angus and Malcolm's interplay together as guitar players is really uncanny and that's why they're such a great band, because they're brothers it's so instinctive. Malcolm is there holding down the groove and the rhythm, and that leaves the room for Angus to kind of put all the flourishes and whatnot in, and their two sounds really mash together nicely." Offering a unique look inside how the brothers' respective guitar parts wound up so perfectly placed in the broader mix of the band's finished songs, Fraser described a recording routine where:

> with all the records I've done, Malcolm's on the left side, and Angus is always on the right. There's always only the two guitar parts. Sometimes if the song needs it, Angus will play a single power chord track, and that will be panned right in the middle, but way back in the mix so it doesn't clutter. The only other overdubs are Angus's little leads or flourishes, but it's basically Malcolm on one side, Angus on the other, no double-tracking or anything. It's quite funny, because when he's solo, Malcolm's is a very, very clean sound, and other bands come in the studio, say "Oh, we want this AC/DC sound," and they've got this really overdriven thing, which is not the case at all in reality. Malcolm has a really clean, almost shiny sound, and then Angus has a crunchy sound that isn't overly distorted, and somehow when those two are meshed together, it creates the illusion that it's bigger than what it really is. I think that's the secret of their sound; less is more. We just end up getting such a bigger sound when we don't have to layer all these guitar parts.

Waxing poetic on rhythm stronghold Malcolm's side of that guitar mix, the *L.A. Times* would later say that "to use a fancy word, Young is a minimalist. He may have played a dazzling array of notes in his solos Saturday, but each move of his fingers on the fretboard related tightly to the next. In his style, Young mixes the blues with rough-edged garage rock, breaking down the combination into a few sharp and aggressive phrases that he then repeats until they're bloody from overuse. The effect is primal." For his part, Fraser fleshed out the latter analysis with his own very qualified opinion that "Malcolm is one of the best rhythm guitar players I think I've ever worked with. His sense of rhythm and groove is amazing, and if you watch AC/DC live, most of the guys in the band will watch Malcolm for all the cues and tempos and all that stuff."

Turning specifically to brother Angus, legendary lead guitarist—who *Guitar World* concluded "wrenches solos from the neck of a battered Gibson SG with all the grace of a drunken dentist . . . [yet] Angus Young's hands have fashioned some of the most memorable guitar riffs in rock history"—Fraser quickly formed the impression while working with Angus during the album's principal tracking that the lead guitarist "has just this great, singular knack for coming up with stuff in the spur of the moment. Again, when we were doing *Razor's Edge*, we were doing his solos, and I remember he'd done a pass on one song, and I said, 'Hey, that's great, let's just do another one just to have an alternate,' and he played a completely different solo. Then we did a third one and it was an *entirely different* solo, and they were all three competitively great. So now it was like 'Great, how do we choose between these?'"

Offering the band's smash single 'Thunderstruck,' as an example of Angus's mastery in action, Fraser recalled what he counted as an amazing recording experience:

> recording "Thunderstruck," that was so cool, because Angus said "Well, we have this little intro thing," and whipped out that little opening part, and it was only going to be on the intro. So as we start recording, Angus goes through the intro, and then as the first verse came up, he was still playing, and Bruce went "Okay, let him roll, and see where it goes," and he wound up continuing to play it throughout the *whole* song in *one take*! By the end, he had this big long ash of a cigarette hanging out of his mouth that he'd smoked throughout that one take. If you listen to the finished song, you can notice in the mix we faded it in and out, so it sort of disappears a little bit in the verses and choruses, and comes in and out, but it's played top to bottom, all the way through, one pass—it was awesome.

Turning to the tracking of the single's famous chorus backing vocals, Fraser recalled that

> we had Brian all sung and the main vocal comp done, and for the big gang "Thunder" vocal, that was Angus, Malcolm and Cliff. We never get Brian in there for backing vocals because his voice is so distinct that if you add him to the backgrounds, it will kind of take over. With any harmony type parts, it's usually Cliff who does all those. We use an 87 or 414 for the backgrounds, because you don't want to load up all similar sounds on the vocals, you want a little bit of variety. So for instance, because the 58 mic has its own characteristics, if you did all your backgrounds with that, it would start clouding in the way of the lead vocal.

Turning to another of the album's big-selling singles, "Money Talks," the engineer-producer felt it was an equally poignant example of the band's knack for pulling out hard-rock classics that seem almost to write themselves, such that "I remember it all coming together really fast, they're a really fast band in the studio, even if they're not rehearsed, they're such a great band at what they do after playing together all these years. So they come in, and there will be a quick bass, drums, two-guitar setup, and away we would go, and after a couple hours, there's the song." Fraser also remembered the session as a fantastic example of those times when he—as engineer and/or producer—has had occasion to recognize a hit from the moment it's birthed out of the band in the studio—well before A&R, fans, or the radio have gotten their hands on it, citing "Money Talks" as a musical moment:

> When you hear a song for the first time that you know is going to be a hit, you can usually know that right from the get-go. That said, I treat all songs the same, because you want them to be the best. In saying that, in the early '80s, when we were mixing, I remember we'd mix a song for the album, and then if it had been picked as a single, we'd do an additional little side-mix for the radio—only because at that time still a lot of radio stations were mono. And so you had to mono-ize your mix, because if you take a stereo mix and fold it down to mono, the balance changes, so what we in essence were doing was mixing a song to be played on mono radio, so that all the levels are still important. So that would be only different kind of change on my end, because I've always wanted each song to sound as good as it can be, whether for record or the radio.

The album would prove a hugely revitalizing hit for AC/DC, moving five million copies at retail and inspiring *Billboard* to hail it as "arguably the Australian headbanger's strongest album in over half a decade." *Entertainment Weekly*, for its part, would add to the chorus of praise, declaring the LP 1990's "one really great hard rock record." Over the course of his work with the band on *Razor's Edge*, in 1994, the band rang Fraser up to invite him to helm the console for their next studio LP, 1995s *Ball Breaker*, which this time out would feature already-a-legend-in-the-making Rick Rubin as lead producer. In adapting from one mega-producer to another, Fraser recounted the process as a seamless one for him, quite simply because

> right from the get-go, from when we'd done *Razor's Edge*, the band had really liked the guitar sounds I helped get, and because I've been an AC/DC fan right from the very beginning, I also sort of *got* their sound, and, as a fan, appreciated it and could help them get it and retain it. Because I understand that sound, unlike other engineers who go in and start putting reverb on the drums and making Angus play through a delay pedal or something, and that's not who they are. So because I get their sound, and understand completely what they're like, they like that comfort level, and so no matter who's producing them, they know I'm watching their back as well, and won't let it get out of hand.

Though the band would again reunite with Fraser to engineer/coproduce 1995's *Ballbreaker* and 2000's multiplatinum *Stiff Upper Lip,* it was 2008's *Black Ice* that would take the band to their greatest commercial heights since the release of the *Razor's Edge* album twenty years earlier. The band's first studio LP in eight years and Fraser's fourth studio collaboration with the band in twenty would inspire *Rolling Stone* to declare of the rock 'n' roll institution's latest offering that "no one this side of Chuck Berry has written so many great rock 'n' roll songs about rock 'n' roll, and no band short of the Ramones has so militantly refused to reach beyond the basics of the form. AC/DC offer a vision of the Stones if Keith had won every argument: no concept albums, no keyboards, no disco, no ballads, no gospel choirs. And *Black Ice* is their best argument in years—maybe decades."

As much as to the outside listening world it was no surprise the band kept to routine when recording their new LP, to the band's insiders, it came as equally small a shock that the group opted to put Fraser in the control room driver's seat, navigating the console dials and faders as the band created a sound where the *Sydney Morning Herald* could conclude, "thankfully, for all concerned, in just about every track we get the signature solid thumping rhythm guitar and four-square drums in lock-step to remind us that AC/DC are really the ultimate marching band." While producers have come and gone, the band's loyalty to producer Fraser—a staple of many of his long-term artist collaborations over the years—is a testament to the producer's talent for and mastery of knowing at a gut-sonic level precisely how to maintain the band's signature sound in the traditions their fans demand album after album.

Recalling the invitation he received in early 2007 from the band to return to the studio after eight-plus years off from the recording studio, the call itself was evidence of their innate comfort with Fraser as the right engineer to trust with tracking the new LP. Though the band had aged a bit, according to Fraser, their classic/signature sound as a rock band had not, such that, the first day they set up in the studio and plugged in to begin principal tracking, "though nine years had passed between albums, it was like no time had lapsed at all." Critics would later agree with the end result Fraser and the band produced, with the BBC reasoning that *Black Ice* was yet another musical extension of the "big, dumb, formulaic fare that's studied the same blueprint since the 1970s—but if it ain't broke, why not channel several thousand volts through the thing and make it dance even harder?" In more straight-ahead praise, the BBC would conclude in the title of its review of the album that "time had not withered" the band in the slightest.

Fraser was joined this time out by producer Brendan O'Brien, who at the time was on a particularly hot streak following multiplatinum productions with iconic rock vets including Bruce Springsteen (2002's *The Rising* and 2007's *Magic*) along with a long-term collaboration with Pearl Jam (from 1993's *Vs.* and 1994's *Vitalogy* through millennium-era hit 2009's comeback LP *Backspacer*) and Stone Temple Pilots (1993's *Core* and 1995's *Purple* thru 1999's *No. 4* and 2001's *Shangri-La Dee Da*) that mirrored Fraser's own with bands like AC/DC. Describing what could have understandably been an awkward introduction for O'Brien and Fraser with the band having taken the rare step of coming into the collaboration with their engineer in-tow vs. allowing O'Brien as producer to pick his own, Fraser candidly acknowledged that, heading into production,

> especially in Brendan's case, it must have been a funny thing to walk into because I've worked with the band for so many years, and he's walking in brand new, first time he's met the band. And they've got me there, and Brendan's an engineer himself, so for the band to insist on having me there was probably a bit of overcoming for him to walk in on. But again, he's a professional and he walked in and we all got along great. There's a little bit of feeling-out time, and Brendan was a big AC/DC fan as well, and so the first couple days of working with them I imagine was probably a little bit intimidating. But he's a great producer, and was really good at pulling the best out of those guys in the studio.

Rather than any ego clashes, Fraser—knowing his way around the band's sound as well as he did—flexed his talent for blending into their natural creative fabric: "My being as intimately familiar as an engineer with the band helped to free Brendan up as well to focus more on production. An engineer's role is to be a liaison between the band and producer, and especially on *Black Ice* that was even more so the case because I'd worked so much with the band, and understood their sound." Taking advantage of his sonic expertise in all things AC/DC, Fraser painted an atmosphere of teamwork:

> I remember when he first came in we talked about the approach of the record and whatnot, and he said, "I know you've worked with them in the past, so I'm just gonna let you do your thing. But I'm an engineer too, so just so you know there might be times I'm gonna jump on the board and change a few things, are you cool with that?" And I said, "Of course, we're here to do a record together, there's no ego," and it actually ended up that he didn't do that too much. We quickly earned each other's respect, and had a great time working together collaborating. I think he quite enjoyed being able to just be the producer, and not have to worry about other things. He knew I had his back on the soft side.

Discussing the album's pre-pro process in more detail, Fraser recalled that:

with the songs in such a new stage, Brendan would help a little bit with some of the arrangements, and suggest "Well, let's do that six times here instead of the four times," and he had quite a soft touch with them, because AC/DC doesn't really need to be produced. They just want sort of a collaborative effort to get the best down on tape, and Brendan handled that great. Him being a guitar player as well really helped meld him in with the band, and earn their respect. He would listen to one of their writing demos on the laptop, and he and the band would sit together and he'd say "Yeah, that's really good, but I would get to the chorus faster," or "Let's do a double-chorus here," and the band would quickly on acoustic guitars try his idea out, and if they liked it, they'd go with it. He'd also help them work out a tempo, or say "We need a mid-tempo song, so let's try this one out," and that kind of thing, just helping to guide the process as opposed to trying to take it over.

Discussing what the team decided on as an overarching sonic strategy for the album's production, the engineer-producer revealed that the band was desiring a departure from their most recent studio effort. "Consciously, I think we all talked about the fact that *Stiff Upper Lip* was a record that they wanted to make a little dryer and more bluesier—which was a departure from their usual direction—but on *Black Ice*, they wanted to get back on track with their classic sound." Recounting the specifics of the band's preproduction writing process, Fraser revealed that once the band and soundmen got together to flesh out the album's songs:

they hadn't done any rehearsing or preproduction at all, they all flew in from different parts of the world and said, "Hey, let's do a record." Angus and Malcolm write, and bounce ideas off each other. They have a little studio in England, so they go in and record quick writing demos, and bring those ideas on their computers. So just before we'd do a take, they'd play it to the rest of the band, explain "Here's the riff, here's the chord progression, etc." I remember before we started tracking the first song, I was sitting there thinking to myself, "This should be interesting, nine years, they haven't played together, maybe it will be a little rough at first." And right from the first get-go, it was on. It was like "Holy shit! These guys are so good, they can take nine years off, barely warm up, and away they go." They were just amazing that way!

Along with the band's otherworldly creative talents, Fraser attributed the ease with which production got under way to the fact that "they're one of the most sweetheart bands I've ever worked with—they're just so down to earth, and there's no egos or anything like that about them. They're just absolutely lovely people to work with." Sticking to the same classic musical basics that had worked for the band over the thirty-plus years prior, Fraser and O'Brien took a similar approach as they began tracking the album's bed tracks. Beginning with drummer Phil Rudd—whose work the *Village Voice* would later praise as "a marvel of simplicity"—Fraser recalled from a technical angle that "I separated the drum tracks a little more than, say, I would have done back in the 24-track tape days, because you were more limited. I always keep the kick separate, and I like the two snare mics separate. A lot of times, say if there's three or four tom mics, I will bounce down to a stereo pair, just to save a few tracks. With all the overheads and close-stuff, I'll usually put them down to a stereo pair, then usually throw up a couple of room mics. I use basically the same mics on AC/DC's drums as I always have."

As focus shifted from drums to arguably the star attractions of the band's sound (i.e., the sibling duel of Malcolm and Angus Young's guitar performances), the brothers would both garner heaps of individual praise, beginning with the BBC's observation that "each song starts with a stuttering riff from Malcolm Young; for years the world's most unsung guitar hero," while *Spin* magazine drew critical attention to brother Angus, concluding that "Angus shoots lightning bolts from his Gibson SG," adding that as a sum of their respective parts, the Young brothers "still sound strong and hungry thirty-five years on, as if they could pulverize riffs in perpetuity." Offering a look inside his formula for recording that legendary sound, Fraser said of his science that with

> each guitar part I like to keep to one track, but sometimes I'll do a separate track with a room sound I'm not sure I want to use quite yet. But when I record tracks, I like to get them down on tape the way I want the balances to be, I don't want to record all these mics on separate tracks, then have somebody else come along and redo the balance if they're going to be mixing it later. I want to kind of lock in an idea that "This is what we're going for, this is what we want," and so I kind of lock it into that. At the same time, keeping my options open too, so I wouldn't record a big giant room sound on the guitar track, and then later on go "Oh, I want it to be dry now," well you can't undo that. So I would put a room track on a separate channel to protect that option.

Keeping the critical chorus of praise going where lead singer Brian Johnson's vocal performances on the album were concerned, *Entertainment Weekly* celebrated the singer's "terrific, growling performance" on the album's smash hit "Rock N' Roll Train." Still, in spite of the latter critical approval, engineer Fraser revealed that back in the studio, he and producer Brendan O'Brien were presented with certain recording challenges attributable simply to the fact that:

Brian had aged as a vocalist, and with his style as a vocalist, for really any age, you just have to be really careful not to overwork him or over-sing him, so I only record him for maybe an hour to hour and a half a day, not wanting to burn his throat out. When he's getting tired in his throat, you have to rest him, because if you push him, it will take him two or three days to recover from that, because when he sings, there's so much power coming out of him. So that's really the only thing I have to watch with him. Having said that, when we were doing *Black Ice*, there had been about nine years in-between records, and when he isn't singing, Brian owns a racing team, and races almost at the Formula One level, and the guy has six-pack abs, and is in just *great* shape for a sixty-three-year-old guy. So when he was tracking vocals this time around, being in such good shape, he actually had more power and more stamina in his singing than he's ever had.

As principal tracking wrapped and the production team's attention turned to mixing, having been a principal party to the mixing of the band's past three studio albums, Fraser found himself again in relatively familiar sonic territory, volunteering that while

with each record, you mix a little bit differently, with AC/DC, they do have their sound, and haven't really changed that fundamentally, but if you listen to their catalog of records in chronological order, the sound does change a bit in the mix. But again, one of the very cool things about AC/DC, and part of why they have so many fans, is that they don't stray away from what they are, they don't go with the trends. So the changes in their sound come more with the fact that they might be recording in different rooms from album to album, but their fundamental sound is the same.

Focusing on another of the album's hit singles, the stadium-ready 'Anything Goes,' to touch on some of the specific fundamentals he has long kept close in the course of mixing the band's patented brand of radio-ready rock, Fraser offers that

at the end of the day mixing AC/DC, the bottom line is emphasizing those instruments that are driving the song—drums obviously, but sometimes the guitar parts are a little more riffy, so the bass can be back in the mix, or sometimes, as in "Anything Goes," it needs the bass out there to help drive the song, so that's the direction we went in. With "Anything Goes," on that song, the bass line really helps carry that song, so that's probably why it ended up more apparent in the mix. But generally, in mixes, the band likes the bass sort of as a background role.

Black Ice was released in the fall of 2008, and Fraser and O'Brien's accomplishments in terms of production would inspire *MelodicRock.com* to conclude that "there is something comforting about getting a new album and just knowing how it is going to sound before you even put it on." The world felt an equally instant affinity for the group's first new album in almost a decade, debuting at #1 in twenty-nine countries, including atop the U.S. *Billboard* Top 200 Album Chart, moving over 800,000 copies in its first week of release. Reflecting on what he felt continued to attract such generational legions of fans album after album, in spite of what would be career-killing lapses in time for most any other rock band, Fraser feels the secret to the band's continued success rests in the fact that "with AC/DC, I think it's because there's such an honest approach: this is what we are, this is what we like, and this is what how we like to do it. Over the years, they haven't really changed their style much. And some people will say 'Yeah, but they only play three chords,' but that is their formula of rock. That sound has crossed over a lot of age groups and genres, and because they aren't trying to be trendy at all, they just play honestly what they want, and it's just good old, foot-stompin' fun music."

Turning to another of Fraser's long-term collaborations, established over a multialbum collaboration with guitar legend Joe Satriani—who the *San Francisco Chronicle* in 2010 rightly hailed as "rock's leading instrumentalist and hero of a thousand guitar magazine covers"—Fraser contrasted how he approached working with a solo artist vs. a group like AC/DC, said:

> Working with an artist like Joe who doesn't have a singer, your role as a producer changes a little bit in terms of what you pay attention to because there's a lot more guitar layering. So there will be some rhythm parts put on there, then the melody/lead guitar sort of becomes the vocal, so you have to make sure with each sound of the guitars that they're not going to keep building up the sound on top of each other. To do that, you have to make sure they leave room and space for the other guitar parts to work, and for that melody guitar to come up in the middle, front end of the mix and still really sing.

Reflecting on what he feels has made him and Satch gel so well over the course of a two-decade creative collaboration that has included 1998's *Crystal Planet*, 2000's *Engines of Creation*, 2004's *Is There Love in Space?*, 2006's *Super Colossal*, 2010's *Black Swans and Wormhole Wizards*, the all-star 2011 *Chickenfoot III* LP, as well as the live *G3* concert recordings, Fraser said, "I think Joe and I work great together because I'm a fan of music, and even though I'm not a trained musician, I feel it, and I know when it's sounding right. So I think he likes the play-off between the two of us." Explaining that the greatest lesson he gleaned from his experience crafting records alongside the Beethoven of modern instrumental guitar, the engineer-producer said, "The biggest thing I learned from working with Joe is I'm never picking up a guitar again, because he's so amazing, and watching him, he makes it look and sound so easy. But in all seriousness, the biggest thing I learned from Joe is how to sound-scape all the different parts of a song, because he layers a fair amount, but in the end result it all sounds like it works together. It's pretty cool to listen to all the little qualities that you can hear in there, but without sounding cluttered."

Blue-jeans-and-leather-style rock is as enduring as the fashion that has outfitted the fans themselves over the past thirty years. With bands like AC/DC, Aerosmith, Metallica, Mötley Crüe, Van Halen, and Joe Satriani, Mike Fraser has sonically outfitted more rock 'n' roll over that time than any other engineer in terms of songs permanently in rotation on jukeboxes and classic-rock radio in bars, pool halls, and cars across the U.S. Reflecting back on that star-studded mega-list of rock 'n' roll fan favorites, Fraser says,

> I love my whole catalog. The '80s was a fun era, there was a lot of partying, and a lot of fun went on—the budgets were huge, so it was sort of the heyday. Everyone was getting paid really well, and it was a lot of fun to do. I think if you listen back to the music from that era now, there were actually some really good songs, but by the end of that era, where it was very big hair/big makeup, it's hard to believe I was a part of that. But I just do this because I love making music, so I can't say I have favorites. It would be akin to asking me if I had a favorite kid, because I love them all!

Emphasizing love of music and the art of making it as core motivations any new pro-ducer should possess heading into the business today, Fraser adds, "I always advise people who ask me, 'Hey, if you're into it and love it, hell yeah, do it, but don't think you're getting into this lucrative business you're going to make millions of dollars at, because it's highly unlikely.'"

Keeping the latter in mind, as Fraser reflects in closing on the platinum album plaques that line his walls, his awareness of the role luck has played in that legacy is not lost on him, coupled not surprisingly with a feet-on-the-ground vs. head-in-the-clouds perspective that has served him well

> over the years, as it has occurred to me that I've been lucky enough to work with almost every one of my heroes, from when I was back in school. I've done stuff with Alice Cooper, Van Halen, but in any of those settings, I just go in and do my thing and don't really think about it. But after the day is done, it is fun to look back over my dis-cography. The most important thing for me is that I just absolutely *love* what I'm doing. It's not a job, I'm not going to work every day; it's a lifestyle and I love it.

CHAPTER 6

Scott Humphrey and Tommy Lee—Methods Of Mayhem

Back in the early millennium, Scott Humphrey's recording studio sat high up in the Hollywood Hills in a nondescript mansion, a gated fortress that acts as something of a cross between a space station and a flophouse for rock stars. Humphrey explains that his unique choice of setting for a studio was rooted in his desire to

> work in an environment where everything was always ready to go. All the guitar amps were always set up, always miced, always plugged in, always assigned, so that if you wanted to play guitar parts, you could go over and literally enable a channel and start playing. Same with the drums. I put the drums on input, and they're ready to go. In a commercial studio you have to go in and set everything up, and "Okay, I got an idea for a drum part," and you have to stop for three hours to get drum sounds. The same with bass, vocal mics, acoustic guitars, amps, Leslie cabinets, percussion. Pretty much anything you can think of, any keyboards, effects, everything I always plugged in and ready to go. Getting to the creative side as soon as possible was always my goal. I always felt really cramped in traditional control rooms. I wanted a huge control room, because that's where you spend most of your time.

Desiring a space to accommodate the spirit of the new frontier he was exploring stylistically and sonically at the outset of the millennium, Humphrey explained the space design:

> My idea was to have a big space that was wide open, where I felt like I had space to breathe and it was also comfortable for the artist. The reaction from the artists that I've worked with has been very positive. It seems to make people comfortable, and I think that makes a big difference when you're trying to inspire someone to give their best possible performance. Some classic records have been recorded in nontraditional studios. For example, *Led Zeppelin IV* was recorded in an old mansion in England, Deep Purple's *Machine Head* was recorded in an empty hotel in Montreal, the Red Hot Chili Peppers' *Blood Sugar Sex Magic* was recorded in a mansion in Laurel Canyon about a half mile from my studio. There is enough evidence to exemplify this theory. One of the things I like about working here is, if I want to stay overnight, I can. If I'm going through a phase where I'm not sleeping well, I'll stay at the studio, and if I can't sleep, I'll get up in the middle of the night and work on parts or edit or mix. Also, artists have stayed here before whom I work with more in a one-on-one capacity.

Appropriately named "The Chop Shop," the studio has always been Humphrey's lab, and as a producer, he is something of a mad scientist, constantly struggling with the genius of his own formula as it remixes and reinvents itself with every record. Many of Humphrey's closest collaborators he also counts among his closest friends, including both Tommy Lee and Rob Zombie. Over the last twenty years, Humphrey has established himself as one of rock's most innovative and commercially reliable producers, in that most of the records he produces are copiloted with the artists, evolving out of a creative nucleus that merges man and machine into a sound cyborg comparable only to a James Cameron movie in terms of its futuristic presence in the most modern model of the record industry. His sound can be routinely heard in science fiction and fantasy movies like *The Matrix*, *Blade*, *Daredevil*, and *End of Days*, and it would not be a far leap into the future to say that Humphrey's creative mind works in much the same way as a science fiction writer's. Blending elements of rock 'n' roll past into his futuristic rocktronic soundscapes, Humphrey works each of his songs with its own personality, creating through his catalog a sonic reality unto itself, impossible to recreate, equally as difficult to generically prototype, and impossible to ignore from a commercial perspective.

The genre he founded and helped make a multiplatinum monster via his hit collaborations with Rob Zombie and Tommy Lee, among others, rocktronica began as a millennium-minded fusion of electronic programming and drum loops layered beneath screaming rock guitar riffs and derivative rock/metal vocals, which also experienced their own revamping through futuristic-sounding reverbs and delays courtesy of Pro Tools, the principal digital recording medium in which Humphrey worked. Offering one of his favorite illustrations of the genre he helped pioneer in play, he recalled:

> When I was working with Zombie on *Hellbilly Deluxe*, we were specifically trying to do something different that no one had done before. We were trying to merge together the technology at the time, and mix that with heavy guitars. There were maybe certain things I discovered making that record that bled over to the next couple records I did afterwards—a combination of the ways the guitars were recorded. A lot of the bottom end was scooped out on those records, so they were really aggressive and really bitey sounding. And I remember distinctly doing that and wanting to make things sound different than everyone else's records.

A key element of Humphrey's seemingly complex formula for making records from the jump of his career has been to simply have an open mind. People were beginning to do the same in 1995 and 1996 as Pro Tools became more and more the mainstream for studio recording, but as the digital age dawned, it was complex in that it mixed with society's traditional ways of communicating, and even more so for record buyers. Where the breakthrough in introducing the Internet to consumers came with the mass advent of e-mail, so, too, did that of digital recording in terms of its effects on rock's overall sound with the introduction of Humphrey's own style of record production. His soundscapes were sophisticated but accessible because of their roots in rock 'n' roll guitars and related instrumental influences. Fans responded approvingly by taking the same chances Humphrey was taking in the studio at retail, spending their hard-earned dollars on his productions and proving to major record labels that his sound was both accessible and viable. Once that machinery got behind Humphrey's blueprint, there was no stopping its inevitable takeover of mainstream rock music. The result was a whole new breed of bands spawned out of Humphrey's rocktronica subgenre, including Rob Zombie, BT, Spineshank, Powerman 5000, Crystal Method, and a host of others. Humphrey broke additional new ground by reinventing several rock stars who had begun fading around the time his started to shine, including Tommy Lee (as a solo artist and with Methods of Mayhem) and Rob Zombie.

Humphrey's style of production is unique compared to many others within the rocktronica medium because it is inherently collaborative; because of his expertise with programming, his natural ability as a musician, and his pop sensibility, he invents sounds rather than sampling them. He uses the technology to help him define his sound, but he doesn't ever allow the sound to define his writing or substitute in the creative process at any point, for that matter. Humphrey explained the process via his collaborations with both Lee and Zombie:

On the *Methods of Mayhem* record, I kind of took Tommy's demos and expanded from that point. We got his demos and played over top them and kind of took the best of—a combination of taking drum loops, electronic stuff, and then picking out a bunch of things I liked—and then he played a bunch of live passes, and then we sat down and looked at what sounded best, what was working the best. From section to section it might vary. One section might be totally programmed, and he might come in with a live fill leading into the next section with all live drums. I think I've done it both ways, where I've recorded the band live, and then later on put loops or samples over top of it. Or, in the case of Rob Zombie, we would write all the songs using machines and computers, and then have people drum over top of it, and then see what would work best from section to section.

For as "futuristic" a sonic direction as Humphrey's productions began to take rock's millennium sound at the dawn of its first decade, the underpinnings of his recording method were as old school as those of his mentors, who included Pink Floyd producer Bob Ezrin and Mötley Crüe and Metallica producer Bob Rock. Arguing that engineering a record while also understanding the production aspect is an art largely lost on today's students of record production, who have a computer to provide samples of a guitar sound that Humphrey had to capture manually, he said,

As a producer you need to know how to do everything, even if you don't do everything on a day-to-day basis. They're the tools of your trade. You need to know what you're doing, especially when the people you're working with don't . . . When you're a producer, you need to know everyone's job—the singer, the drummer, the guitar player, every piece of equipment, every amp, every pick up, every drum head . . . Nowadays, there is a tendency on the part of producers to want to know the computer but to forget about the rest of it.

Humphrey's comparison to the older school of analog producers is appropriate in illustrating the importance of the underpinnings of reel-to-reel recording as they naturally exist within and apply themselves to digital recording in the millennium. By doing so, he also exposes the potential downside to digital recording in terms of the shortcut it offers around artistic performance and laziness on the part of the producer/engineer in working hard to naturally capture that performance as it was once naturally required with analog,

A lot of bands are very aware of Pro Tools and what you can do with it, and that has developed a serious lack of musicianship. Records get piecemealed together, one track at a time, and the reason for that is musicianship. A lot of guys can't play and need Pro Tools to chop subpar performances into some kind of magic, and it doesn't always work. That's not to say I haven't completely piecemealed a Zombie song together, but that was our intent, not the result of a bad performance. I view digital editing as a way to comp performances or to be creative rather than a substitute for a good performance. My early exposure to digital editing was to edit great performances together and adjust things as you went along, and now it's gotten to the point where a musician gets in the studio, plays the part down a few times, and tells you to make something out of it. In that sense, I think it's lowered the bar.

Longtime collaborator Tommy Lee agrees, echoing Humphrey's sentiment from an artistic point of view that is unique in that Lee has existed in both worlds as a recording artist: "That's so bizarre that there're producers who don't know or do any of it. How could you possibly do a job that you don't know all the sub floors of? You know what I'm saying? I mean, for another artist, I would recommend they seek out a producer who fucking knows what they're doing, which equates itself to being as versed as Scott is, knowing how to do all of it." The lesson in this reality, as least for Humphrey as a pioneer in the use and innovation of digital recording, is to attempt a consistent balance in which both the producer and the artist attempt to remember where they came from in the rush to get creatively where they want to go, reasoning to that end that

there's a natural speed factor with using a computer and not having to wait for the tape machine to rewind or not having to switch reels or having to switch reels plus put up a rough mix. When you load up a Pro Tools session, it's there the way it was when you did it last time. So it's better in that sense . . . Some of the other innovations or benefits of Pro Tools are, for example, editing, the ability to edit and comp performances. If you look back twenty-five years, when you were maybe on a 16-track machine, they got to a point in the recording process where they didn't have any more tracks. So say you were working on a guitar part, you didn't have the ability to do, say ten takes. You might only have one track, so you'd have to keep recording on that same track and get to the point where you'd just drove over what was the great performance. You kept saying to the player, "You can do it better," and realize three or four takes later that you taped over the good take. People take that for granted, that you have unlimited amounts of tracks to do it as many times as you want.

Contrasting the process of recording between his solo work in the last few years with the heyday of *Mötley Crüe,* and in the process, placing emphasis on the creative energy that is freed up by the convenience and ease of digital recording, where it might have been eaten up in the time consuming process of analog recording, Humphrey said:

Technology is fucking awesome, dude! I think back and I go like, "How did people ever make fucking records back then?" I mean, I made them back then, when it was like "Okay, we got the fucking drum track, bring in the guitar player." It was like the mythology of the same old bullshit—"Okay, guitar overdubs, bass overdubs. Got the bass and drums? Okay, guitars." For fucking two weeks, Werman, Bob Rock, fucking tape machines is like the old-school way of doing things, but everybody did it that way. It's like now, you can do things backward, forward, start in the middle, wherever the fuck you want. It's definitely an enhancement, technology. It fucking rules.

Humphrey agrees in theory but rounds out Tommy's argument by pointing out that the innovation Lee speaks of has to begin with the artist or, for that matter, the producer, knowing what they want and what they are doing musically and technically within the digital medium so that they remain in control of the creative process rather than allowing it to think or invent artistically for them.

With Tommy, even if it's just like a simple guitar part you're working on, he's so good with rhythm. He'll take a simple guitar part and go, "No, let's make it like this and make it more syncopated," or with a vocal line that's stagnant, he'll have some syncopated vocal idea that will totally turn it around, where you'll be listening to it and go, "This is amazing. It has all this energy." Rhythmically he has a way of injecting his rhythm, natural rhythmic syncopation that he can take something that's really flat sounding and turn it around and make it sound like a hook.

Though Lee's point is valid in the context of the present, Humphrey still calls up from within the bedrock basics of his producer's manual lessons he learned from observing the master craft of both Ezrin and Rock:

Bob Ezrin was known for really pushing singers, really pushing them hard, and that resonated with me. A singer may come in and sing it one way, and that's not necessarily the best way, although it might be the best way. You don't really know till you explore and push to sing it a bunch of different ways, working a vocal syllable by syllable if you had to, and comping it by syllable. I don't think up till then I'd ever seen anyone work that crazy on a vocal, and that's one thing I definitely took away from working with Bob Ezrin. In my own productions, I really like to do vocals really early on. I like to get my bed tracks done and then get to vocals right away so you have a lot of time to live with them, so you know they're right. It's amazing how many times the first take is one. That's why it's so important to have your signal flow, level, and headphones together on the first take.

Revealing another of the principal lessons he learned from his work under the tutelage of mega rock producer Bob Rock in capturing a great drum take, Humphrey highlighted the importance of

having a good drum sound to begin with. Every drum has to sound good on its own before you can put a mic on it. If it doesn't sound good in the room, it's not going to sound any better when it's recorded. In fact, it's going to sound worse when you record it. For example, if you have a weird ring in a tom and you put a mic and compressor on it, that ringing's going to be even more apparent. It really comes down to having the sound right at the source, and that's the shell, the edges of the drum itself, and the head. My preference has always been Remo heads, either single or double ply Ambassador or Emperor heads, depending on the drummer. A guy like Tommy Lee could never play Ambassadors because he would just rip right through them. You might get through one take, but the heads are either going to be dented or broken by the time he gets through it. For a heavy hitter, the Remo Emperor heads would be my first choice. Even with a head like that, with a guy like Tommy drumming, you may have to replace the heads on the snare, every two or three takes because he hits them so hard, cause it'll start to dent or start to get weird overtones in it. But it's really about the sound at the source. If it sounds good in the room, then all you have to do is put the mics on it. Dynamic mics on the snare and tom, as far as overheads go, some guys like 67s on the overheads, as far as room mics go, I have a pair of vintage German RFT mics I like for the room, they have a really interesting midrange that really cuts through the drums that I use quite a bit, that really helps to define the drum sound.

Tommy Lee, speaking to Humphrey's greatest strengths as a production cohort in crime, says that he has stuck with the producer over the past fifteen years primarily because Humphrey has excelled, as any great producer should, at

always pushing me to the fucking limit. He's always like, "This is not good enough." He doesn't settle. It's awesome. He's always pushing you to your maximum fucking potential, and he doesn't really settle for, "Mmmm, that's good." It's like good isn't ever good enough. So just by watching what he did and knowing how things worked, and then literally understanding the possibilities by watching, like, "Oh really, you can do that!" And then all of a sudden, your mind starts expanding with possibilities and everything. So he sort of taught me the possibilities of a lot of things. I didn't know you could do that, and then I'm like, "Well, if you can do that, then I can take this part and put this part over here and do this," and by watching, I learned so much. And then I started realizing what was capable, what the possibilities were, and was like, "Oh! Oh my God, we *can* do that!" The possibilities are endless working with Scott. Sometimes we start with just a beat, and as you're auditioning beats, you try a different beat, as the song's playing, try a different guitar part. That's the cool thing about Scott. He's always open to trying everything. He's never like, "Nope." He's always like, "Yeah, let's try it." And by trying all these other ideas, you eventually find the one, and are like, "That's it!" You know? And that's how he works. He's always open to trying fucking everything, which is awesome. Some guys aren't like that at all as producers. They're like, "Nope, that's it. This is the way we're doing it," and you go, "Wait! It's *my* record!"

The relationship between Humphrey and Lee is unique, especially considering that much of their synergy relies on an equal fascination with the technical side of creating and recording. In the eyes of an artist like Lee—who, being a drummer, naturally gravitated toward the rhythmic emphasis in Humphrey's sound—the producer's expertise with digital recording also played a large role in his initial and continued attraction to working with the producer, in addition to their creative chemistry on a musical/songwriting front. As Lee explains:

No disrespect to guys like Tom Werman and Roy Thomas Baker, but in this day and age, as a producer, if you don't kind of know about all this new technology, then you open a bed-and-breakfast in fucking Nantucket somewhere. There're guys who are just plowing right over you who know what the fuck is going on. I don't think the old way of doing it really works anymore. That's why these guys aren't making records anymore. And in like '85, '86 on the *Girls* record, we were fucking with drum samples and electronics, and John Purdell to me then was like Scott. He was this guy who was into doing new shit. So I would watch every day, and we would together try to do something new. And we were doing samples, and back then the technology was fucking wack. I remember like the drum samples were all late, shit wasn't right then—just wasn't up to speed. And we spent a lot of time where we knew what we wanted to do, but we spent a lot of time fixing shit. Where now, it's better. Technology's fucking amazing. The possibilities are endless. You can fucking go nuts. And with like working with Tom Werman, I gravitated toward John Purdell, because John was working doing some new shit, while Tom was like sitting there, drinking his wine, typical producer guy, not doing anything, smoking his cigarette. And would just kind of walk around the room and this cat, Purdell, was over here fucking doing some new shit, and I was like, "*That*'s the guy I want to be hanging with." Werman's one of those typical fucking producer guys, or like Roy Thomas Baker, who wouldn't even show up. He'd fucking show up two days later, and go, "Hello, Darlings . . . Okay. Sounds great," and leave. I was like, "Where's he going?" I didn't get it. I didn't get any of that. So I always gravitated toward the engineer or the guy who was making it happen—not the guy who came in and checked on it, but the guy who was making it happen. A producer who knows his shit technically behind the board and gets the whole deal is night and day to the guy who comes in and is just an extra set of ears and eyes.

Another important element to the creative chemistry between Humphrey and Lee, according to Lee, is his own understanding of the artist putting in the time to learn the digital platform so he can avoid becoming a repeat of the hands-off producers Lee so resented from his years in Mötley Crüe. "From years and years of working with Scott, everything I know now, from driving the computer to recording and editing, I learned from him, by sitting next to him while he was working with Bob Rock. And Bob Rock would say to Scott, 'Okay, go sew it all together,' and Scott would be in there for hours, and I would just sit there and watch him, like every fucking day. For-fucking-ever I watched him. And by watching is how you learn. You learn by watching and doing. You know what I'm saying?" Humphrey clearly appreciates Lee's continual enthusiasm for the digital recording medium, specifically his willingness to put in the time to learn the advances of the medium as they happen, making the overall coproducing process that much more creatively cohesive: "Sometimes, too, when you're working with an artist who knows what you're doing, you communicate much easier. When he can see what I'm doing, then the conversation doesn't even have to happen."

As Lee elaborates on the benefits of the latter creative coherence:

It's cool as an artist to sit there. If I'm watching Scott edit, whether we're recording or writing, or whatever we're doing, it's cool to be able to sit there and look at the screen and know what he's doing and not sit there and go, "Oh my God." Because I *know* what he's doing, I *see* what he's doing, so your comfort level and creativity are just going, because I'm like, "Oh, okay, I know what he's doing. He's moving that over to here, and we're going to try that edit there." I know what he's doing next. Dude, how many millions of times have we sat there and not even said a word, and I know exactly what he's doing, and am like, "Dude, that rules," and he knew it before he was doing it, and I knew it before he was doing it, because I was watching him, and we were in tune?

Scott Humphrey has achieved the best of both worlds in his craft and would be quick to point out to anyone focused on the digital side of his medium that he began at the other end of the pool and learned everything he knows about the basics of record producing from legends like Bob Ezrin and Bob Rock, who created their catalogs entirely in analog. As time goes on and Pro Tools advances in its own generations of sound and innovation, Humphrey continues to transcend all potential contemporaries via his own competitive relationship with the world of digital recording as it continually evolves. He has reached a point of accomplishment with the fundamentals of Pro Tools that, aside from keeping up with its newest software offerings, he has begun to shift his focus from the technical back to the musical:

> Nowadays, I'm more focused on musicianship and performance and just trying to get the magic rather than just trying to be involved in the technical end. I mean, I do jump in when I'm mixing, and I do get technical, but I come originally from a musical background, which is why I feel like I've come full circle. I started off playing music, then got crazy technical with the computers and editing, and now I find myself spending more time at the keyboard or guitar working on arrangements or playing with the bands. You just kind of go with it, and all of a sudden, twenty years have passed, and you're looking back, going, "Wow! I've done this and this and learned that," and you just pick up little bits as you go, and also from just staying up late at night reading manuals and experimenting. It's a ton of hard work.

Humphrey has always played down the notion that he has a signature sound, as he aspires to constantly reinvent that sound, though he has made peace with his own importance in rock's annals as a producer in terms of helping to discover and introduce the connection between rock and electronica as a viable and vital commercial medium. According to Humphrey:

> Maybe there is a connection, but I'm always trying to change it. When I was working with Zombie on *Hellbilly Deluxe*, we were specifically trying to do something different that no one had really done before. We were trying to merge together technology at the time and mix that with heavy guitars. I think that's what Tommy and I were trying to do with the *Barb Wire* soundtrack, with "Planet Boom," a few years earlier. Early on we started doing that, going, "Well, let's put drum loops, electronic sequencers, and heavy guitars together." That single on the *Barb Wire* soundtrack was really the first time I tried to force all those elements together and try to make sense out of it. I think we refined it on *Hellbilly*.

Still, Humphrey, perhaps out of a fear of being pigeonholed, and thereby limited, within the aforementioned framing, constantly seeks to reinvent and innovate his own discovery, and in doing so remains very much in touch with the inspiration that first propelled him to bridge the sounds: "I feel like, right now, I feel the same way I did on *Hellbilly*. I'm trying to do something different, something that hasn't been done. I feel like that whenever I start a new record."

CHAPTER 7

Hugh Padgham–Synchronicity

Legendary British producer Hugh Padgham's style of new wave crashed down upon the U.S. as the 1980s began with a force that would almost single-handedly reinvent the British invasion in a modern context. His sound wasn't just a matter of cutting edges, but rather reshaping them into new pop boundaries that he could further explore and expand upon with each epic he helmed. Consider, for one example, *Rolling Stone*'s review of the landmark *Synchronicity* LP, in which it singled out the fact that "the Police and coproducer Padgham have transformed the ethereal sounds of Jamaican dub into shivering, self-contained atmospheres. Even more than on the hauntingly ambient *Ghost in the Machine*, each cut on *Synchronicity* is not simply a song but a miniature, discrete soundtrack." As new wave became a progressively more mainstream genre throughout the early and mid-1980s, each hit Padgham helped to craft was another step forward in defining mainstream art rock throughout the 1980s, such that, in 1985, Padgham won Grammy Awards for Producer of the Year and Record of the Year.

Consider landmark anthems like "In the Air Tonight" and "Take Me Home" by Phil Collins, or classics like "Every Breath You Take," "Every Little Thing She Does Is Magic,"

"King of Pain" and "Wrapped Around Your Finger" by the Police; "Senses Working Over-time" by XTC; "Blue Jean" by David Bowie; "Hampstead Girl" and "Indian Summer" by the Dream Academy; or "Invisible Touch," "Land of Confusion," and "Tonight, Tonight, Tonight" by Genesis. In the later 1980s and throughout the 1990s, many of the artists Padgham had shepherded through their transitional periods from the alternative into the mainstream continued to work with the producer, crafting some of their most memorable classics and biggest smashes. Consider Padgham's work with Sting on solo hits like "All this Time" and "Fields of Gold," or Phil Collins with the LP *But Seriously*, which won the Grammy Award for Record of the Year in 1990 and produced hits like "Another Day In Paradise" and "I Wish It Would Rain Down"; or on Melissa Etheridge's *Your Little Secret*, which produced the mega-hit "I Want to Come Over" and won Padgham Producer of the Year and Album of the Year Grammy Awards in 1995; and *Yes I Am,* which produced the smashes "Come to My Window" and "I'm the Only One."

Beginning in the late 1970s, Padgham made his first mark on the new pop soundscape that would become New Wave with the groundbreaking drum sound he invented with Phil Collins—the gated reverb drum sound effect that was introduced to Top 40 radio via "In the Air Tonight," one that would reverberate as a signature in the experimental drum sounds that would define some of the most innovative and popular art rock/New Wave records of the 1980s to come. As the coauthor of its creation, Padgham recalled that the origins of the

whole experimental drum sound Phil Collins became widely known for first came to-gether in the first place from my working with Peter Gabriel on his solo album, because I used to do quite a bit of engineering with Steve Lillywhite before I started producing Phil, who prior to our collaboration was playing drums on Peter's solo record. So the roots of that sound were developed through experimenting on Peter Gabriel's third solo LP in 1979—partly through the fact that we had a brand-new SSL console—and it had this reverse talk-back mic on it. All consoles had this button where you could talk to musicians through the headphones, but no console I'd ever seen up to that time had a button you could press that opened a microphone that was specifically hung in the studio, that was then rooted to the control room via a very, very heavy limiter, because obviously with a talk-back mic, you always wanted a big compressor on it so you could hear anybody and everybody talking in the studio. Well, it just so hap-pened one day that I had that talk-back mic open when Phil was playing the drums in the studio, and we had a very live room that was a relatively unusual new concept in those days. Up till then, most of the studios in England had been very deadened up very much with soundproofing, and the drum sounds were dry, so we were reacting against that. So when everybody heard that drum sound coming from the talk-back mic, we all said "Wow, that sounds good," and got the maintenance engineer to re-root a feed off the compressor to a jack, which we then rooted into a channel and therefore onto tape. The song in question was called "Intruder," and also not what we did above, but the SSL was also the first console to have a compressor built into every channel, and a noise gauge, so when Phil was playing this pattern, I started fooling around with a noise gauge on it. So when Phil stopped playing, with this great room sound, suddenly it sucked itself into nothing through the noise gauge. And the opening and closing of the noise gauge happened to work naturally within the tempo of the pattern he was playing.

Padgham's work with Collins would be truly kindred, as both engineer and drummer morphed into producer and solo star in the course of their first collaboration, transforming a genre at the same time via a revolutionary drum sound that alt-pop contemporaries like famed producer Don Was later remarked was "pretty amazing. I don't know anyone who's ever bought a record for the snare drum sound, unless if it's for something like 'In the Air Tonight.'" Collins's debut solo LP, *Face Value,* would be Padgham's as a lead producer, and evolved out of

working with Phil on that Peter Gabriel tune, so that six months later when it came time for Phil to start work on his solo album, he remembered the drum sound from the Gabriel session and called me. I think part of his interest was piqued out of the simple fact that Phil—like many drummers I imagine thought in those days—was just a drummer, to where you just hit those things, and that was that. Whereas, with the whole way I was working and experimenting, it was amazing to hear it that way, because before that, a drummer was just a drummer. So that work with Peter Gabriel, by extension, showed up on "In the Air Tonight." Phil was always very experimental with drum sounds, especially in his solo career, going back to his first album with "In the Air Tonight," the drum machines available back then were very early Rolands, and it just had very basic samples. I remember for instance it had *Rock* and *Bossa Nova*. For that song specifically, Phil came into the studio with the beat programmed into his Roland, and when we attempted to start the song, we could never get it to feel as good as it did on the original tape, so we actually just copied it off the original demo tape. Also, the main synthesizer that starts out the song, we said, "Oh hell, we're gonna copy the drum pattern, why don't we copy that as well?" Because we reasoned after playing around for a bit with the synthesizer in the studio that we weren't going to get that sound again, so we actually built that song up off the demo, and did some other songs on the first album that way.

Using "In the Air Tonight" as a template, another element of the song's hauntingly ambient, sci-fi sonics—and by extension the album's—that made it so innovative was the harmonizer effect that layered Collins's voice, whose technical genesis Padgham explained:

> In the studio was about experimentation with the vocals and things, because Phil came in with most of his material already written. Recording Phil vocally, he was absolutely mad keen on harmonizing then, so really the effect on all those tracks was basically just a harmonizer, but also nearly always, some sort of dynamic microphone through very heavy compression. Where we used this compressor that was called a mini-limiter, which is how you get Phil's very sort of guttural vocal sound, it would come from this very heavy limiting that had a slow attack and a fast release. We'd always record his rehearsal takes, and then usually three or four more. The rehearsal take we always used to call the Bridesmaid, and then three or four more, but very rarely more than that, because often the singing would really take it out of him physically, and his voice wouldn't be in such good shape after three or four vocal takes. And of course, in those days there was no such thing as vocal tuning, or any electronic, digital device whatsoever. It was all proper old stuff.

Padgham's success in bringing Phil Collins out from the shadow of Genesis into his own light as a solo star with a singular sound was best summarized in *Rolling Stone*'s review of 1981's *Face Value*: "With the notable exception of the three Peter Gabriel [solo LPs], every solo album from a Genesis member or ex-member has proudly displayed the lessons learned in that band—and been the worse for it. But Phil Collins's *Face Value* . . . [is] aggressively likeable." By the time of the Police's 1981 *Ghost in the Machine* release, Padgham was in the captain's chair piloting the console, and the band, according to *All Music Guide*, by that point, had "certainly demonstrated that the punk spirit could have a future in pop music." The producer's goals, sonically, for the Police certainly appeared headed in the latter direction, with Padgham explaining that

> with the Police, the dynamic creatively between Sting and I, another artist who I have had a long-term creative relationship with, in the beginning it was funny because we never really talked about it. We really just all rolled in there and made a record. Having said that, from a production standpoint, I was very keen on developing Sting's songs properly on tape, because—although I loved the Police before then—the first three albums sounded very raw to me. What I wanted to do with the Police—from the first minute I heard the songs we'd be working on—was to develop the music as 3D, almost like a movie, with respect to some of the textures we can put into the music, which is the way I've always looked at making records.

Producing smash radio hits like "Every Little Thing She Does Is Magic," "Spirits in the Material World," and "Invisible Sun," Padgham's first collaboration with the Police was hailed by *Rolling Stone* for its success in maintaining "*Zenyatta*'s approach via well-modulated singles . . . [like 'Every Little Thing She Does Is Magic,' which stands] out like [a] glowing gem." The album was a stepping-stone to the seminal *Synchronicity*, which would lift the band to its commercial peak. Heading into preproduction for what would be the band's final collaboration, Padgham admitted he "really remembered having a massive pressure on with 'Every Breath You Take,' because that song was definitely a hit from the first time you heard it in the demo studio. And also Miles Copeland would pull me aside and say 'That's a God damn hit, I hope you're doing your job boy!' So I remember being quite nervous about that." Elaborating on the song's development process from demo to #1 smash, the producer recalled that

> it wasn't a bad demo at all, it had pretty well the riff on it. I remember the one difficult thing with that song was it never really had a proper middle bridge, so we agonized over that part for a long time. That kind of one-note piano thing was actually kind of my idea in the end, because we were almost into the mixing stage doing overdubs, and Sting was sitting down at the piano trying still to come up with something for that part. And I was always into the simple things, and he kept hitting this one note, and it was just like "Yes!" and we had it.

In capturing that sound to tape, Padgham explained a surprisingly simple technical setup wherein

> the Police really didn't have that much gear, all the Police stuff was played through Roland JC120 Chorus Amps, and it was miced up on both speakers; one speaker was the fade, and the other was the chorus, and we'd double-track it, put one left-right, and then reverse left-right on the double track. On the heavy stuff, that was usually done through a Marshall, and all the guitar-synthesizer stuff was all done through Marshall as well. In that way, we just played with what we had, and it just came out in the way it came out. We were very much helped by analog as well. The backing tracks for the Police were always done as a live thing.

The most trying part of the recording process for Padgham seemed to be tracking Sting's lead vocals, due in large part to what the producer described as an

> impatience with the process where he wanted to cut tracks quickly all the time. What was good about that was some people have this sort of perfectionist element about

them, and I think people when they become too perfectionist about something, all the serendipity gets sucked out of it. So in the studio, Sting's strength was speed, and when he was working, he was very impatient. So for a bass track, or whatever he was doing, he would say, "That's fine, that's good." And sometimes even I would have to stop him to redo something, but in general, it was a good approach from a vibe standpoint creatively.

The album's biggest hit, "Every Breath You Take," would hypnotize radio for the summer of 1984, just as Padgham and Genesis had begun work on what would become their most commercially successful album ever. With *Invisible Touch*—which seems in hindsight as much an ode to Padgham's production savvy as anything else, the producer would take advantage of the times, in terms of both technology and trends, to craft a postmodern art-rock masterpiece rivaled only by Peter Gabriel's *So*, released the same year. The album's drum sound was an archetype of that which Padgham had refined with Collins over the first half of the 1980s. Still, *Invisible Touch* further expanded upon those innovations via a blending of progressive-rock instrumentation with pop-driven, melodic hooks over the course of smash singles like "Invisible Touch," "Tonight, Tonight, Tonight" "Land of Confusion," "Throwing It All Away," "Anything She Does," and "In Too Deep." Revealing a bit about the band's preproduction and songwriting process, Padgham mentioned

an interesting element of Phil Collins's solo career, which was the fact that before then, in Genesis, I don't think anyone—including himself—thought of Phil as a writer. Phil started to write as a result of the problems he was having with his marriage, and also the solo stuff was a release for Phil because it was a source of frustration for him in Genesis that Mike and Tony and Peter were the writers. One of the first songs Phil ever wrote was called "Misunderstanding," off of the *Duke* Genesis album, and it was one of the band's first hits in America. So by the time he thought of 'Invisible Touch,' he had their respect as a writer.

Padgham continued:

I'd worked with Genesis for two or three records before that, so by then it was fairly routine, in that we didn't have any specific conceptual goals, I think in a way that record was just sort of a process of accumulation—whereby the way they used to write, they hadn't seen each other in ages, because Phil by that time had a very successful solo career. So they would just sort of meet up in the studio and jam for two or three weeks with a tape recorder, putting everything onto cassette. So there might be one bit from one day that someone in the band would go "Okay, let's go with that bit from that cassette on that day," and so one bit might be the chorus of a song, and another bit might work as the verse, and the songs would just sort of come together like that. And then they would more or less draw straws for who was going to write the lyrics for that song. With their song development, as a producer, I think my role was to help evolve the sound, and I've been lucky to work with a lot of great people like Phil and Mike and Tony, who are all very talented in their own right. I don't write myself, I'm not the type of producer to sit in the studio and say, "If you change that chord, and put a different sort of note on the bottom of it, it will sound better leading into the chorus, or something like that." A band like Genesis is fairly self-contained that way, and I think I'm not threatening in a creative way—from a writing point of view—to them, so if I made comments, it was more from an arrangement or musical suggestions. I think where my forte is is just really understanding what they're trying to do musically, and trying to make it sound on tape how they want it to sound. I just think that album was a peak in their creative period together.

In addressing *Invisible Touch*'s dazzling rhythmic foundations, which Collins and Padgham accomplished by coupling programmed and live drum tracks, the producer explained this was inspired by

a time drum-wise where there were a lot of electronic drum elements and influences around at the time. So on *Invisible Touch*, we got that sound by juxtaposing real drums and electronic drums, and programming as well. When Genesis recorded, there was always the three of them playing together in some semblance or another, but invariably, Phil would always go back and play the drums. The great thing working with Phil as an artist was that he was such a great drummer. Very often as the song would progress, he'd go "Oh, I think I'll play that again a bit differently," and very often the last thing that would go on the track would become the live drum track for the whole song.

Explaining the intricate mic setup he utilized to capture Collins's live drum sound, Padgham explained that

when I'm micing drums, the main thing was I used to take an incredible amount of care in micing the drums, from choosing the mics to their placement, and so on. The drum kit is quite a hard instrument to mic, and in the '60s, you might have two or maybe three mics on a drum kit. By the '70s and '80s, the whole thing was much more closely miced with more mics, and when you introduce more mics in proximity of each other, you're gonna get problems with respect to faze relationship and coordination between the mics. So having a technical background, I understand exactly what that means, and so I would spend a lot of time with microphone placement; rather than just fiddling straight away with the EQ controls at the console in the control room, I would go and change the position of the mics—it's just a change of attention. I've always felt that the backbone of any record—whether it be a jazz record or a pop record or an experimental record—is that if the drums sound good, the likelihood of everything else sounding good, technically as well as emotionally, is much better. As far as recording drums, I hate digital recording, because it doesn't sound as good as analog. I still try to do my basic recording on analog.

Following the massive mainstream success of the *Invisible Touch* LP, which had cemented Padgham as among the premier art-pop producers working behind the boards, he next reunited with Sting—now a multiplatinum album and several hits deep into a solo career amid the departure from the Police in 1986—for *The Soul Cages*, in 1991, where the duo were in perfect creative synch. As the producer explained it, the album conceptually stood opposite to his last LP in that "*Soul Cages* I think, atmospherically, as a finished product is reflective of the desire to strip down some from the *Nothing Like the Sun* album." Written out of the sorrow of the passing of both of Sting's parents, and amid a severe writer's block that followed the tragedy, the sessions for *The Soul Cages* sounded something like an Irish wake of sorts, with Padgham explaining its creative vibe as one in which

the atmosphere on the record was somewhat dissimilar to that of his last album be-cause we lived a very decadent lifestyle during those sessions in a hotel just off the shores of France, stuck in this room all day tracking. Then at night we'd rehearse, and watch and laugh at all the transvestites lined along the roads, then go back to this very expensive, Caribbean hotel and usually hang out in the bar till one or 2 o'clock in the morning. Then on weekends, Sting would go off on his own to a house that he'd rented off the coast, and lock himself away writing the lyrics. It was quite weird really, because even though both of his parents had died, that's not the mood of the record-ing in any way. Then we packed up everything, rented a mobile unit down to Italy, and that's where we did all the overdubs and vocals. And we had a rather grand chateau where he set up to do vocals, which was bizarre from where I was stationed with the mobile recording unit. Another bizarre circumstance of the recording of that album was that the World Cup Soccer Tournament was on the whole time, so at times we found ourselves distracted from the recording by that. So even though that album had a somber feel in terms of the songwriting, there was quite a bit of jolly music with very personal, heartfelt lyrics overtop.

As sonic therapy, the results Sting and Padgham achieved were hailed by critics and fans alike, who welcomed the artist back with golden reviews like *Rolling Stone*'s declaration that the LP was "highly serious and sonically gorgeous . . . Sting's most ambitious record yet—

and maybe his best." Producing the hit single "All this Time," the success of 1991's *The Soul Cages* led an artistically and commercially revitalized Sting to 1993's *Ten Summoner's Tales,* which he again recorded with Padgham helming production. A much more commercially pronounced outing than their last collaboration, the producer's fifth studio collaboration with Sting was much more upbeat in a pop context.

Specifically addressing his approach to tracking Sting's much-hailed vocals on *Ten Summoner's Tales*, Padgham explained that

> recording Sting vocally on that album—as with always—the rule was: as long as it was as quick as possible, then that was fine. In those days, if there was a flat note, we'd have to go back and do it again, which he didn't like doing at all. Having worked with him before, I knew if it was a chorus, or other vocal part that would be tracked up with double tracks or three or four harmonies, where there would be eight voices there at the end of the day, you didn't have to be as particular as you had to with the lead. I just had to work out in my mind the best way to fix mistakes, so as far as technical problems, as far as I was concerned as a producer, I would sort them out in my off time. When we were doing vocals you've got a vocal on its own; it needs to be a lot more perfect than the five harmony tracks behind it. So in the Police, if we went through each of those harmony tracks and made them each perfect, collectively it wouldn't have the same thickness of sound it had when you're less than sort of perfect. There's a certain magic about it. For instance, as a bass player, Sting was a very accomplished musician, but he wasn't a perfectionist, so in the studio, we would go for vibe over perfection *any* time because he had great feel.

As the 1990s progressed, Padgham, now among the upper echelon of pop producers, with multiple platinum albums and Grammy wins, changed direction from alt/art-pop to a more mainstream collaboration with Melissa Etheridge on the 1993 smash LP *Yes I Am,* which produced acoustic-rock hits like "I'm the Only One" and "Come to My Window." Looking back retrospectively over his highly accomplished chart of timelessly classic, legacy-defining #1 hit singles and albums, Padgham reflects most fondly on

> the *Synchronicity* album, because it was so difficult to make because the band members were fighting like cats and dogs. To have finished it and have had it become such a success was rewarding. The other was *In the Air Tonight*. I felt it was quite revolutionary at the time, and I was very proud of making that first album we did together. I think the Phil Collins bombastic drum sound is something I'll be remembered for, which has been widely copied—whether it be samples or on drum machines or whatever—that's something that is attributed to me in terms of helping to evolve.

In offering closing advice to the millennium generation of engineers and producers, all of whom have invariably been influenced by Padgham's sonic blueprints across the universe of subgenres that have bloomed out of his pioneering work mainstreaming art/alt-pop rock, he feels that

> it's very difficult for kids to come up the way I came up. I got a job in the studio and worked my up. Today, half the studios are closing down, and that position no longer exists, so the art of engineering has gradually disappeared. I think it's just evolved into something different, but a lot of the fundamentals are the same conceptually. I'm lucky. When I started working at a studio, I figured I could do this for four or five years and then go to college and learn architecture. And here I am 30-something years later, so I feel very blessed.

CHAPTER 8

Bones Howe—The Heart of Saturday Night

As great American songwriters go, it is impossible and irresponsible not to recognize Tom Waits's singular genius in speaking for the underdog. A poet and musical advocate for the "real people" of the world, Waits's words twisted along the boulevards and back roads, through the fringes and frays of life's most authentic moments, in terms of both errant adventure and consequence after the "thrill" is gone. Tom Waits was an advocate for the urban dwellers who were arguably the white counterpart demographically to the black working class that artists like Sly Stone and Stevie Wonder spoke for musically and socially in the early 1970s. Waits's songs were like modernized passages from S. E. Hinton novels like *Rumble Fish* and *The Outsiders*, which gave an identity and sympathetic light to the underdog for perhaps the first time to viewers and listeners. Often, he seemed to write from the vantage point of what they had left. At the same time, he sang of the beauty of redemption like no other because there was nothing shallow about the backstory of his characters' triumphs in terms of their adversities. Waits's musical novella was a reality television show for every human emotion, offering characters so vividly described and embodied that you felt you knew them, or were perhaps like them in some significant vice, mannerism, or experience.

The legendary songwriting society ASCAP commented in their bio on the performer that "[between 1974 and 1980, Waits released] *The Heart of Saturday Night* (1974), *Nighthawks at the Diner* (1975), *Small Change* (1976), *Foreign Affairs* (1977), *Blue Valentine* (1978), and *Heartattack and Vine* (1980). It was an incredibly prolific period for Waits and one that solidified his reputation as one of America's new leading songwriters. As a singer, his trademark gravelly voice became one of the most unique voices ever heard in pop music."

The counterpart to Waits's lyrical carnival of vagabond city dwellers and their downtown adventures was a jazz-based musical foundation underneath as improvisational as the characters' fluid lives that Waits sang about overtop. Throughout the latter 1950s and the first half of the 1960s, Bones Howe's studio credits piled up as high as the stacks of hit jazz LPs and singles he was recording for artists including Ornette Coleman, Bud Shank, Bobby Troup, Bill Holman, Bing Crosby, and the Big Band All Stars. Transitioning into the world of pop in the mid-1960s, Howe logged time as an engineer alongside Phil Spector for the Righteous Brothers' "Ebb Tide" hit, as well as with the Mamas and the Papas and the Crickets, before stepping out into his own as a pop producer in 1966 with the Turtles, creating a greatest hits collection's worth of jukebox smashes, including "You Baby," "She'd Rather Be with Me," "Happy Together," and "Making My Mind Up" among others. The Turtles gave Howe his first taste of commercial success as a Top 40 pop producer, but it was his next collaborations with 1960s folk-psychedelia groups the Association—via hits like "Windy" and "Never My Love"—and the 5th Dimension—via hits like "Up, Up and Away," the seminal "Stoned Soul Picnic," and "Let the Sunshine In (The Flesh Failures)"—that would make his reputation, the last song earning the group Grammy Awards for Record of the Year and Best Pop Vocal Performance by a Group. By the end of the 1960s, Howe had arrived at the peak of pop production, and based on his reputation as one of the lead specialists in capturing live bands in a studio context, the producer was drafted for one of the biggest gigs in the business—Elvis Presley's comeback television special in 1968, recalling that "By the time I got around to producing Elvis's television special in 1968, I had won Grammys for my work with groups like the 5th Dimension and the Turtles."

As the 1960s came to a close, and the rock-rock heavy Top 40 era of the 1970s began, Bones Howe was in the market for a new sound:

> A very close friend of mine, David Geffen—who I had known since he was a junior agent at William Morris—I had put together with the Association, because David wanted to handle the Association as a live act. And David and I remained friends through the years as we moved up the ladder of success, and eventually, he started Asylum Records. And I'd produced Warren Zevon's first record, and had him signed for a time to my company as a writer, and David signed Warren for his second record, on

the recommendation of Jackson Browne. So not long after that, David called me up, possibly returning the favor, and said, "I have an artist I think you should hear, I think it's different than what you have done, but I think you and he will really hit it off." David always had a great gut about putting people together, and he was a big fan. He always promoted me. He'd wanted me to do Crosby, Stills, Nash & Young, and we had a couple meetings and I told David "We'll kill each other." I loved Buffalo Springfield, but by the time they had started a band together, they were all doing drugs, and I told David "I don't do drugs, and we're all going to end up hacking each other to death, cause they're going to get high in the studio . . ." I always believed the studio is business, and so for them, I guess all of that lifestyle was part of the business. So working with a group during that period was really, really difficult, but with individual artists, I always had really great working relationships. So it just wasn't meant to be, and I didn't take things—no matter how successful I thought it would be—that I felt I couldn't be a part of.

Regardless of the initial mismatches, the next Asylum artist Geffen would pair Howe with would be truly kindred, and the work Howe and Tom Waits produced together over the next decade would found a new subgenre of rock out of their process. As the producer recalled,

David next called me about working with Tom Waits, and I said, "Send me a tape." And he said, "No, no, I want you to come to my office." So I went to his office, and he played me a few tracks off of *Closing Time*, Tom's first album, which Jerry Yester had produced, and who I knew because his brother had been in the Association. Anyway, I asked David if Tom was a folk artist, and he replied, "Well, I'm not really sure what he is. He's not really folk, but he's different. I saw him at the Troubadour, and he's great live, so I signed him and made this record. But it's not exactly what I think he is." So after listening to a few tracks from *Closing Time*, I decided he was somewhere between Tom Waits and Bob Dylan, but there was kind of a jazz-tinged quality to it that I thought was really quite interesting. So I asked if they were going to do another record like this. And David told me he was working on some demos, and that when Tom was done with those, he would send them to me, and if I liked them, then Geffen would set up a meeting. That's the way David always worked, one step at a time.

Recalling his first impressions of Waits's vaudevillian, jazz-folk style of Beat poet blues-piano rock, Howe explained that

They sent the tape over to me the following week, and I thought "God, this guy's like Jack Kerouac." I had done a record with Norman Grant that Jack had done in a hotel room in Miami, where he'd read his works and poetry into a microphone and tape recorder, and they in turn sent them to Norman, who bought them, and sent them over to me and said, "Make an album out of this. I can't make heads or tails out of it, you want to take a shot at it?" So I said "Sure,"' and I sat with those tapes for two or three days, sorted through them and made an album out of them. In those days, if you were lucky, you could get an hour of spoken word if you used both sides of an LP. So he seemed like Kerouac to me, Waits did, he had that kind of Beat Generation sound in his writing, but there was a folk quality because he was playing an acoustic guitar along with a lot of the material. But there was also beauty, in some of the songs where he played piano and accompanied himself, like "San Diego Serenade" and "Blue Skies," which was almost like a Ray Charles song to me. So I thought, "God, this guy's got all kinds of things." So I called David, and said, "I love what he does, I'd like to meet him, and if we like each other, we can make a record together." So he set up a meeting, and I sat down with Waits, and we ended up talking about Jack Kerouac, and Steve Allen, and I told him I'd made a record with Kerouac. So he next asks me, "Did you know Steve Allen made a record with Jack Kerouac?" And when I said no, he said, "I'll send you a tape of it if you'll send me a tape of yours." So we started off exchanging Jack Kerouac tapes, and then he talked about a lot of stuff from the Beat Generation, and I talked about the jazz musicians I had worked with, and we just immediately liked each other.

Once the pair had clicked on a personal level, Howe recalled that immediately thereafter "we began talking about his demos, and how we'd record the songs, and Waits said, 'Well, I don't want to do a record like I did before. I want to make a record with some musicians in the studio.' So I got a rhythm section together, and the pianist, Mike Melvoin—a jazz pianist, had also been an arranger, so we had a jazz rhythm section, with a couple of horns, and went in the studio and made *Heart of Saturday Night*. It's a lovely album, and just kind of the beginning of where we were starting." Crafting a subgenre at the same time with their first album together, Howe explains that *Heart of Saturday Night* would serve as a blueprint to the duo's approach to record making for the next six albums. Describing Waits's approach to writing songs and their subsequent development in the studio, Howe recalls that

it was always the same with Tom and I when we were shaping the production of the songs. First of all, he wrote all the songs, and in some cases, the kind of quality of the song was in the way it was written and that he presented it to me, so if it was a folk song he played on the piano, then it was a ballad by definition. For instance, "San Diego Serenade" was a ballad, and the joke about that song always was it could go on for a year, because there were a lot more verses than ended up on the record. He would come up with a verse talking about it—there were dozens. So the first thing we had to do was choose the verses he was going to do, and figure out from there how long the song was going to be. And this was the beginning of our working relationship, so we were kind of feeling around a little bit. And there were some songs that were just gonna be kind of down and funky like "Depot, Depot," those kind of things were gonna be what they were, and there was no way you could change them. But "San Diego Serenade" was a song that could almost have a pop flavor to it, so we let it go that way a little. Waits could always get his arms around these things, it was never meant to be a big production, it was meant to be a Tom Waits record.

Revealing a bit about what thematic direction he felt the album was moving in as tracking continued, Howe reasoned that

a lot of the record thematically was about being on the road. He was fascinated with bus stations, and people on the road, and truck drivers and that sort of transient part of society that's out of the mainstream, and almost has its own world and language. He was fascinated by a lot of the language that goes along with that. On "Shiver Me Timbers," like "Semi Suite (Truck Drivin' Man)," again that song arose out of Tom's fascination with people who worked on the hourly wage, the working class. Any of those kind of people he was fascinated with, and these ideas just bubbled out of him. He'd come into the studio with lyrics scribbled on a piece of paper. He was a great poet. The couplings and ideas that go together. There are people who I speak to who are songwriters who say, "All the really great lyrics have been used." And I say, "Un-uh, just go back and listen to some Tom Waits records and you'll find lyrics you haven't heard before, and haven't heard since." He wrote this album on Skid Row. I'd ask him, "Tom, what did you do today?" And he'd say, "I went down to Skid Row, there's some interesting people down there. I bought a pint of rye, went down to skid row, I talked to those guys. Every one of them—a woman put him there. I drank that pint of rye, went home, threw up, and wrote "Tom Traubert's Blues.""

Given Waits's improvisational approach to both living life and reemulating the aforementioned in his songs and sound, Howe explained that in the studio

Tom to me musically was like a jazz artist, so as his producer my job was *not* to force him into a mold like I did with pop artists. He was not going to get played on the radio, so my job with Waits was to deliver the baby. He was the talent, and I was the one who was there to help him find the direction, cement it down, and then go on to the next thing. So there's a lot of arrows pointing in different musical directions on that first record we made together, and he could have gone in a lot of different directions if he'd wanted to. After we were done tracking, we would just get together, usually in the evening, sit down, open a beer, talk about the sequence of the album, because all the pressure's off at that point. You're just gonna decide how to put the record together, and quite often out of that process, Tom woul d say to me, "You know, I think if I go to the studio and sing this by myself it will be better." So you'll find on those albums tracks where it's all him, by himself, just sitting at the piano playing.

Describing his technical approach to capturing Waits on tape, Howe recalled that "I'd go hang a microphone, usually a 77, and two mics on the piano, a U47 on the low strings, and something with a real wide pattern on the high strings, because I had no separation or leakage problems, it was just Tom at the piano singing live with a mic hanging in front of him, just like he would be if he was sitting onstage singing."

Following the success of *Heart of Saturday Night,* Waits and Howe took a different approach to their first follow-up, in the form of a live album, common to the 1970s but unique in how the duo chose to track the record, with the producer recalling that "out of our conversations posttracking for *Heart of Saturday Night*, out of that recording, came the band that played on *Nighthawks at the Diner.*" Now two albums into their collaboration, the producer and artist had established some norms to their recording process, with Howe explaining that

on average, we made a record a year. And the way we would work was, he would write the songs, then he would go into a demo studio, and just put down a demo on tape of all the songs he wanted to do, in whatever shape they were in. Some they were incomplete, sometimes it was just an intro and a verse, sometimes just a chorus with his voice saying, "Okay, there's a verse here, and then it goes dadada." And then he would send me the tape, he'd never play those demos for me live. He'd always lay them down on tape. And then I'd get a copy of the tape, and I'd go through it, and then we'd have one of our "production meetings" at Duke's or one of those coffee shops on the Sunset Strip. And we'd sit there for three hours and talk about it—I'd talk about the flavor, [what] the feeling of the album was. Then we'd talk about what the album was gonna be like, and then the atmosphere of it. That all developed out of these conversations. By nature, I was very disciplined about coming into the studio to do your work, and unbeknownst to me, it was an approach that Tom really liked because he had absolutely no discipline in his life at the time. Tom was developing as an artist still at that time. He was living in that motel, and was eating at a diner, and performing at dives, and was just a hangout guy. He had all these friends who were down and out, a lot like the characters in his songs. So in terms of the structure of the recording sessions, he called me after we finished the live album and said, "The next record we make together, I want you to spread the sessions out, because it's over too quickly. We go to the studio, go home, then go to the studio, and it's done." And I think there was something of a father figure component to our relationship, and he's the only artist who I worked with through all those years that I miss talking to.

Having set a pace by the time of their third collaboration in 1975, *Small Change* would mark an evolution for Waits in terms of his and Howe's approach to studio recording, with the producer recalling that

from the time of the *Nighthawks* album on, it began to change, because Tom and I would see each other quite often in between albums, and would have long talks at Duke's over coffee about what the next record would be like, the atmosphere, and what was going to happen. So one of these "production meetings" usually began with Tom saying, "Well, tell me about those records you made in the '50s with those jazz musicians." And I would explain that it was live to 2-track and mono, and so he said to me, "You know, I want to do a record that's live to 2-track and mono, because I like performing that way, being out there." We had done some multitrack recording obviously for safety's sake on the live album, and we'd done some on *Heart of Saturday Night*, and Tom then said, "I think there's an immediate feel to doing recording that way." So we began recording that way for the *Small Change* sessions, and even the reading of "Small Change (Got Rained on with His Own Thirty-Eight)" is the live reading over a live orchestra to 2-track. We did make multitrack safeties, but we never used them, and all those recordings are first-generation 2-track CD. I mean, when you hear those albums on compact disc, they were transferred right from the original 2-track tape, so you're hearing it the way I did come through the monitors when I first recorded it. It's amazing, and looking back on the original recordings for *Small Change*, they were something that was a lot of fun to do.

Discussing his approach to mixing the *Small Change* album, and by extension, Waits's albums in general, Howe explained that

for me, engineering personally was always part of the whole process. I generally mixed without the artist in the control room, and gave them finished mixes to listen to. It's one thing to be in the studio and singing, doing something you're really comfortable doing in the studio. But when it comes to mixing, it's not something that you do, and you were also mixing—particularly in the 1960s and '70s—because you knew it was going to come out of a radio first. And you also had to think about how your audience is going to hear it, so it's not as pure. With Waits, it was purer because we never expected to get played on the radio, and then always did. Tom and I mixed the first two records together, and after that, there was no mixing. Tom would listen to a take of a song back after tracking in the studio, and approve or not. Occasionally, he would say something like "I want to hear the saxophone louder on the call and response parts." So we'd do it and make another take, but basically we never had those kinds of discussion.

With their third studio collaboration, Waits and Howe produced what *All Music Guide* said "proves to be the archetypal album of his '70s work . . . a jazz trio comprising tenor sax player Lew Tabackin, bassist Jim Hughart, and drummer Shelly Manne, plus an occasional string section." Utilizing jazz foundationally for both the album's technical and musical approaches to writing, performing, and tracking, Howe elaborates on the specifics of the title track's development in the studio, explaining that

for "Small Change," that song was done with the whole rhythm section and Jack Sheldon playing trumpet in the spaces between the verses, kind of an improvised little jazzy thing that we did. Often, what would happen with Waits and I is we would do something with the saxophone and bass, or trumpet and trombone, whatever the ensemble would be. We would do it all live to 2-track, so there was no mixing, as Waits would say, "There's no kitchen drudgery." On the reading of "Small Change," he's talking about gangsters and gambling. He kind of made this circle through this underbelly, and it was always an adventure. On "Small Change," when he said he wanted to do this reading, I said, "Well, we should score it like a movie." And he said, "Oh God, what a great idea." So I got Bob to write some underscoring. What Tom did was just lay the reading down on tape, then we gave it to Bob, and Waits played some things in between to show Bob how he wanted it to go, and in turn Bob turned it into a film score. That was kind of the beginning of what we did on *One from the Heart*. So I said, "Here's what we're gonna do, we're gonna just put the orchestra in the studio, and they're gonna play, and Bob's gonna conduct, and you're gonna recite it. Bob's gonna listen to you through earphones in the same room, and conduct this orchestra at the same time, and underscore it like it's a movie." And that's what we did. It wasn't like million-dollar recording budgets. Our records never cost more than $50,000, so we recouped with the first shipment. We always knew what we were gonna do, we went in, did it live, there was no overdubbing, and then we went in and put the album together. And even though sometimes there was a lot of production on those albums, we always went in and did them very quickly.

Touching on some of his personal highlights from the album's recording, Howe explained, "The Piano Has Been Drinking (Not Me)," of which the producer explains "the reason he wrote that song was because he would do it live at the clubs, we never did it on a record. There was a club owner that he really hated, and the guy used to get on Tom because he ran up a bar bill, so Tom wrote an ode to him. We recorded that just as if he was playing it live."

Elaborating on the band's setup in terms of sonic dynamics and instrumental arrangement, Howe explained that

> I organized Waits's rhythm section like I was scoring for a movie—I did my share of movie scoring, so it was set up like a scoring orchestra, which means not every instrument has its own microphone. Sections have their own microphone, and you mic the sections because you mic them from farther away. You don't mic each instrument right down in the middle of the horn for instance, so sections have their microphones. Or in some cases, you may have two, like with the woodwind section, you may have flutes and clarinets, and you can't mic them on the same mic because they're different animals. So you mic the flutes separately and the clarinets separately, but for the most part, they're treated as sections and not as individual instruments. With a scoring orchestra, everything is in the background, and not just in terms of volume, but also in terms of distance. Distance is what makes it possible for the music to be really loud and you can still understand the dialogue. Being the traditionalist I am, I recorded Waits on the microphone up close like he was reciting or singing, and the orchestra in the background, which meant the orchestra could be up pretty good. It didn't have to be way down, because you had the depth of the room, and the feeling that the orchestra is in the background. The trick is there is no trick, you just make sure to keep them from being as close to the mic as he is. And then you get a little room sound, which changes the wave form, and it kind of runs the music all together, and ease up close next to the mic and it's very clear, so you can hear Waits's voice and still have the music pretty loud. My one big regret with Tom was that, he wrote such great melodies, but you didn't often get the melody because of the gruffness of his voice. Every one of the songs that went on *Small Change* is a gem, and they were fun to record. On *Small Change*, a lot of the songs were recorded with almost an orchestra, those were recorded live with Tom singing live while the band was playing. Some of the songs on that record were recorded in one take, others were three or four times through, and then we'd maybe put it off to the next day. Everything I did in terms of engineering when making those Waits records was based on things other than engineering.

By the time of 1978's *Blue Valentine*, Waits and Howe's fifth studio collaboration of the decade, the producer fondly recalled that

> By that time, Tom said he and I were like "an old married couple." I would argue with him about sequence, and say, "Don't you think the rhythm section ought to be such and such or so and so?" But we always came to an agreement that we were both excited about. It was never somebody giving up something for the other person, except when it came to the sequences. Sometimes I would be so sure that we needed to open the album with a particular cut, and he would disagree, and we would have this long, drawn-out argument about it. I would keep prodding at him and prodding at him, and he would finally say, "Un-uh, that's the way it's gonna be." That's the way it was with us. I would make a suggestion, and he would say, "Well, okay let's try it." But if he was set on something, then we would do it. For *Blue Valentine*, Waits wanted to do a blues album, and Tom's blues album is entirely different than, say, a John Lee Hooker album. A Waits blues album is a *Waits* blues album, and it defies definition. He found some guys that he wanted to play on it, and he had gotten fascinated with second-line rhythm sections, like those in New Orleans. So we had put together some players for the record, and for this rhythm section, he said he had heard this sound in his head when he was creating these songs. So once the band was in the studio, and starting to do them, they began to shape themselves into that mold. So you hear some things which are more traditional Waits from the records before, and then some things that are completely different in terms of the ways they moved on. Every record had its own kind of musical personality, and that was the personality of *Blue Valentine*. In a way, *Small Change* and *Foreign Affairs* are in a period, there's a lot of stuff that's the same about them, but then Tom started getting caught up in this idea of second line and blues."

Upon *Blue Valentine*'s release, the new direction Waits had sought to endeavor on with his sound was readily embraced by fans and critics alike, with his most constant admirer, *Rolling Stone*, commenting that "*Blue Valentine* is as solid a record as Waits has made . . . The LP's best cuts—'Christmas Card from a Hooker in Minneapolis,' the title track, and 'Twenty-Nine Dollars'—rank high among the sentimental sagas that contain Tom Waits's strongest writing . . . He's a great storyteller."

On Waits and Howe's sixth and final collaboration, the magazine would accurately observe that "the patron saint of America's hobo hipsters returns to the sentimental ballad style he abandoned for jazzier, less song-oriented turf after *The Heart of Saturday Night*." Perhaps coming full circle in the development of a sound that had begun almost ten years earlier, Howe still felt that because of its electric guitar-dominated theme,

"*Heartattack and Vine* was an entirely different kind of feel from any album we'd done before." In describing how Waits stumbled upon the sound that would define the album overall, Howe recalled that

> what he did was, Waits and I were sitting in a rehearsal room in the back of his manager's office, and there was a set of drums in there, and Waits brought in an electric guitar, and started playing, and I hopped behind the drums. So he hit the few open chords to the song, and I started thumping on the drums, and he said, "That's the sound of the record." That's how we came about the sound for that record. The production was done the same way we'd done all his albums previously in terms of tracking live to a two-inch reel. We did everything live, because there's an immediacy about tracking live that always worked well for him. The only exception to that approach was on "Jersey Girl," because he wanted to do a rip-off of the Boss by putting the bells on the end of the song. It's like a celeste, a keyboard instrument, but when it's played it sounds like orchestra bells, and we did that as an overdub. In terms of the guitar sound on the album, that's just the way Waits's amp sounds when he plays it. It's got a broken speaker and how it sounded naturally on tape. Putting these things back in context, you have to think about what was happening then. I bought Tom a copy of an Asia album, because I wanted Tom to hear how strong the jazz influences had come into that area of pop music. And he wanted to get away from this kind of pretty piano sound, to something more funky, that was part of his purpose. He didn't want to do blues, he wanted to do it funky.

Recalling some of Waits's defining conceptual moments as a songwriter on the album, the producer begins with the album's title track, explaining that

> Tom would write the songs, then we would pick them, and then talk about what they were going to be, and there was always a link backwards to what he had done before, and always something new. With *Heartattack and Vine*, the way the title came to him, there used to be a bar on the Sunset Strip just east of Western Recorders, called the Ski Room. It was a bar downstairs with a sleazy hotel upstairs, and Tom used to go drink with the characters at the bar, and he would get a lot of ideas from what he'd hear at the bar. So one day he came to me and said, "I was in the Ski Room, and there was this guy sitting at the bar, and he had obviously had too much to drink. And he kept asking the bartender for another drink, and the bartender kept refusing, and the guy finally said, 'You have to give me another drink, I'm having a heart attack.'" So Tom walked out of the bar, which wasn't at Hollywood and Vine—it was about six blocks from there—but he said, "Heartattack and Vine," and that was the title of the

song and album. It was the ultimate down-and-out-in-Hollywood song, without really talking about Hollywood so much.

Heartattack and Vine marked a significant departure for Waits, comparable to Bob Dylan's decision to go electric on *Blonde on Blonde*. With the 1980s dawning, Waits wasn't just making changes in his sound, but also to the personnel involved in creating it in the studio. Howe recalled that "'Jersey Girl' was about his future wife Kathleen, and he was entering his electric period. His life was changing rapidly at that point, he and Kathleen were deeply in love, and he'd moved out of the hotel, and had informed me he wanted to produce his next record himself. We had a very amicable parting. I told him, 'You know the kind of record I'll make with you, so if you ever want to make a record like that again, call me and I'll be waiting.' That was the last time that we ever talked about working together personally." Examining the impact of his production sound and style in the broader context of a legacy fifty-plus years in the making, Howe offers the following wisdom:

> To me, producing is just like projecting a movie on a screen, those aren't real people up there, those are light images. But what happens is you suspend disbelief, you watch them, and you get emotionally involved with them. The same thing happens when you make a really good record, that has good sound, you get caught up in the feel of the music, and the emotion of that event. It's an illusion you're creating, it's not the real thing, it's not a real singer there. There [are] two 12- or 15-inch cones of paper, it's not a real band. So how do you make that sound good enough, enough like a real band, that a person listening to that will capture the emotion they get from hearing that music live? That's the best way I can explain record production—you make up devices to help people to suspend disbelief so they can have the full enjoyment of the music. I think the biggest mistake people make in the entertainment business is they plan their voyage before they get on the boat. It's never what you think it's going to be—it can't be—this business changes too quickly. It was changing when I got into it, and it's constantly changed since. My tendency is toward positive thinking, and I always say, "Get a job in the business. There's two states of business—you're either in it or you're not in it." Get in it doing anything, because one thing they'll find—if they can stay in the business, continue working in the business for ten years, they'll be making a really good living at it. Chances are they won't be doing what they started out to do, but most of the people I know who started out trying to plan it all, ended up as lawyers and accountants, and the people who wanted to be producers ended up as managers. It's the kind of business that if you get in it, you can stay in it, and work in it day in and out, and you'll gravitate to the thing that you do best.

CHAPTER 9

Bob Rock–Dr. Feelgood

In 1991, grunge washed over the world of hard rock like the 500-year flood, leaving virtually all its various species of hard rock and pop, hair and heavy metal extinct. One *Rock* survived the musical tsunami, and became the foundation on which the next two decades of hard rock and heavy metal would survive and flourish commercially. It sounds almost satirical to say they named that rock *Bob*, but there was nothing to joke at in the soundscape he created with bands like Metallica, Mötley Crüe, Bon Jovi, the Cult, and others that single-handedly allowed hard rock and heavy metal to survive throughout its dark years over the course of the 1990s. The musical bedrock of Bob Rock's sound has been credited for Mötley Crüe's seminal 1989 release, *Dr. Feelgood*, which went seven times platinum and launched Rock into orbit as rock and metal's hottest producer. The album that would give him credibility and unleash heavy metal's greatest sleeping monster upon the musical mainstream in 1991 was Metallica's *The Black Album*. Heavy metal's *Appetite for Destruction*, Metallica's first collaboration with Rock in a relationship that has lasted almost two decades, reshaped the landscape for heavy metal from an underground genre throughout the 1980s into a commercially viable one in the 1990s. Becoming almost grunge's only counterpart in terms of competitive sales, Metallica were already legends by the time they approached Rock to collaborate on *The Black Album*, and *Rolling Stone*, at the time of its release, credited the band based on the musical merits of its fifth album as "no longer (being) the cutting edge of metal, as it was in the beginning, but . . . expanding its musical and expressive range on its own terms. This can only be a positive step for a group that is effectively bridging the gap between commercial metal and the much harder thrash of Slayer, Anthrax and Megadeth."

Ironically, Mötley Crüe—a band with whom Metallica had had a musical rivalry among fans dating back a decade in terms of genre, image, and musical substance— brought the latter group together with Rock to begin with based on the work the producer had done two years earlier on *Dr. Feelgood*. As the producer recalls, "Metallica told me that they sought me out to produce *The Black Album* based on the drum sound I'd gotten for Tommy on *Dr. Feelgood*." The aforementioned pair of rock and metal masterpieces, considered by most historians of both genres to be the seminal releases for both bands, are also his personally as a producer. He explained: "I guess it's as simple as wanting to be remembered for helping the bands I work with make the best albums they could, but the intro to *Dr. Feelgood* and *The Black Album*, I'll take those. *Dr. Feelgood* and *The Black Album* will be just fine, if they go 'Yeah, this is the guy who did that.' I could live with that, that's enough for me."

Regardless of genre, any classic album will be a timeless one. When a rock 'n' roll listener puts on a magic record, its effect is much like a time machine, taking him or her back to childhood, to a time when that album's hits represented the theme songs of the formative years. For Metallica fans, perhaps the band's music offered a means through which to understand and navigate teenage angst and frustration. For Mötley Crüe fans, perhaps the band's music offered a way to celebrate the survival of that angst. For millions of music fans, *Dr. Feelgood* and *The Black Album* represented the popularly termed "soundtrack of our lives," and the reason why both Mötley Crüe and Metallica are still playing to sold-out arenas almost two decades after the release of both of the aforementioned records. Rock's sound aims for legacy because he only settles for the type of *best* that defines the times, even if he sees himself as only working in the moment of that sound when working on a given album.

Using *Dr. Feelgood* as an example of that model in action, Rock focused on working with Mötley Crüe to make their fifth album the vehicle by which the band could overcome what they had felt were major limitations in translating their monstrous live sound in the studio on past projects. According to Rock,

with Dr. Feelgood, I was just trying to make everything as big and powerful as I possibly could. My production at that point was more to do with sonics, being in the '80s, production for the most part, a lot of times was about sonics, about the sound. And coming from an engineering/mixing background, I went into Mötley Crüe with that in mind. Just to make it big and powerful, and there was no preconception as to what I was doing, it was more like, "Okay, let's just get in there." I had heard a couple of their songs for the new album, and I thought for these guys, it sounded like the demos had been made while they were sober. So in talking to them, and then listening to their songs, it sounded like this could be really good. So we just went in the studio, and I tried to make each instrument and Vince's voice kind of big and as real as possible.

Prior to entering the studio to record *Dr. Feelgood*, Rock took Mötley Crüe through the same preproduction boot camp he indiscriminately puts any of his bands through regardless of their popularity, wherein "preproduction, with me, for every band is the same, and that is every time I've short-changed preproduction, it's never really worked for me. So I try to get into a rehearsal hall with a really basic tape recorder, and work on all the songs—the structure, the riffs, and find out what's missing. Work on the drum beats, guitar parts, and vocal parts, and figure out what needs to be worked on. It just always works, and any song worth recording should stand on its own with just one mic in the room. So that's what I try to do."

A key focus for Rock, foundationally, in the course of building *Dr. Feelgood's* wall of sound was capturing Tommy Lee's thunderous drumming on tape in a way that properly reflected his full power, such that,

going back then, it was always a combination of really I think Tommy and Nikki, mainly Tommy in terms of the drums, his whole thing was basically, back then, it was the whole beginnings of hip-hop, and I think bottom was becoming bigger and bigger. A lot of Tommy's drumming, back then, I think the big shocker there was I had to open up the mics because he was such a loud hitter that he would actually compress the drums. He just hit so hard that the drum would almost compress itself, so I would have to back off the mics, and I remember doing that. It was really just a question of trying to tame that energy, and getting the right distance on the cymbal mics because of the size of the cymbals. I think the big thing with the sound of the drums on the album came in the mixing, and in the mixing, it was pretty much Tommy pushing me, and me kind of figuring out a way to make it happen. By using samples in conjunction with the drum kit to get the weight of the drums, and the size of the drums. For instance, we'd want to get a nice big bottom, and he'd tap me on the shoulder and say "Rockhead, could I have a little more bottom." And then, of course, we'd add bottom to the kick, and then the kick would be thumping, and there wouldn't be bass. Then we'd increase the bass, and then the definition would be gone. If you listen to the beginning of *Dr. Feelgood*, what I did was, with an AMF, I triggered a bass tone just like one hit on the bass that's hammered. And that's with the kick drum. So in mixing the drums on that record, it was just a question of detuning, and finding the right balance between all of those drums and the guitars.

In terms of exploring his general approach to micing drums, Rock explains that

the mic techniques that I had at that point were all ones I'd picked up from working with the different people I had worked with, and then in time adopted my own sound. Everything is derivative, so for instance, when Claremont was in the studio working with Bryan Adams, I'd go in at night after session, and look at all the mics, and combine that with other people I had worked with through the years. But it really was a question of learning good micing techniques, but really the difference was it's pretty much stayed the drum sound without being mixed, is pretty much what I get these days. Back then, I used a 421 in the kick, an RA 20, and usually a 57 or 86 on the snare, for overheads, I used 87s or 460s, and room mics were condensers, and for tom mics I've always double-miced my toms, top and bottom. And that's stayed the same pretty much to today.

By contrast to his approach to recording Tommy Lee, Rock's method for capturing Lars Ulrich's madness on *The Black Album* and beyond was a matter of adding

maybe another 40 percent of top end on everything, so I think everything became a little tighter, and there was a lot more dampening. The best thing I can do to describe that and then what I did on *The Black Album* in comparison to Tommy's drums on the *Feelgood* record was weight. I tried to give as much weight to the drums as possible. Metallica records are slightly different from Motley records in terms of the drumming. To me, Tommy as a drummer is kind of like an open nerve end, whereas Lars, to me, is probably closer to Keith Moon than anything. Tommy is a classic back-beat drummer, he is the basis, he's a rhythm kind of guy. And he does have syncopation and all the other kind of stuff, but he's a rhythm machine, whereas what makes Lars Ulrich's drumming so wonderful and so unique is that he's reactive to the music. *The Black Album* was him consciously trying to be more of a backbeat, keep-the-time kind of guy. Whereas most of his fills and unique drumming all come out of the fact that he plays to the riff of the music, much like with the Who. The Who and Metallica are very similar because Keith Moon played to Pete Townshend's solid rhythm playing, and Lars Ulrich has always played to James Hetfield's solid rhythms. I believe Lars doesn't think in the terms that most drummers do, I think he thinks in a musical world that is kind of unique. I don't really know how to describe it, other than he plays to the riff rather than trying to control the riff.

Shifting focus to Rock's approach to capturing the monster guitar sound he achieved for both Mötley Crüe and Metallica, the producer explains that his key has been

to always try to get the guitar player involved, and get what he wants. I think that comes from my engineering background, and being a guitar player myself. Just knowing that, I had some early experiences in the late 1970s and early 1980s when I started, literally the producer and the engineer used to, in some cases, would supply the drum kits and amplifiers, and say "Here's the drums you're using, here's the amps you're using. I don't do this . . ." There were so many rules, and growing up in the industry, I was thinking, "You guys got it all wrong. You're supposed to try and capture what these guys are doing, rather than trying to force them into sounding like this or that." So I think right from the beginning, I learned to get in synch with the guitar player and his sound. Like with Mars, he kind of said all the sounds he'd gotten previously—and I'm certainly not criticizing Tom Werman or anyone else—but they'd all been mini and small, and he said, "This is my sound." And he played it for me, and I went, "Whoa! That's not what I've been hearing on the record." Mick's sound is about size and sheer volume, not unlike James Hetfield or John Sykes, or other players who have a big, monster sound. That has a lot to do with Black Sabbath—Tony Iommi, that style of playing with single-note riffs that sound like a monstrous power chord. It's the size. That has to do with the playing, and Mars has this style that is very much his. Very light strings and a very soft touch, but very loud. So I just tried to get on tape what I heard. We went through all the cabinets, and I got him involved in the control room, and we just did it till we got it right, and that was it. The big thing is Mars, like James Hetfield, has different amps, and you get four different Marshalls, you get four different sounds. Back in *Dr. Feelgood*, I think Mick was pretty rattled from his experiences prior to me, so we took a lot of time to get his confidence back, and just take the time and get the feel back. Instead of being ahead of the beat, kind of get that feel, to where it felt comfortable and natural for him.

In addition to getting both Mars and Hetfield involved in translating their live playing style and sound on tape, the biggest asset Rock feels he brought to both players as a producer was

using multiple amps and using the differences in fazing and cabs and heads all combined to get one sound. Different volumes on different amps for different frequencies and clarities, and that's basically what I've always done to record guitars. Multiple amps and multiple mics, and just finding that sound. It's basically just a process of building the sound in the studio, because some people, like Eddie Van Halen, throw one mic in front of an amp and make it work. Whereas I think realistically, sometimes you have to build that sound. I use 57s, 421s, 87s when I'm micing amps. I think the big thing with amps for Mars's sound was that he used Jose-modified Marshalls, which John Sykes was using, and I used that same amp on *The Black Album*, and really every album I've made since. That became a mainstay. Really I think that's the big thing that I brought to both Mick and James Hetfield.

In terms of identifying what he feels the greatest strengths of both guitar gods, in the case of Mick Mars, Rock feels that,

as far as Mick Mars's playing, I think it comes down to him being solid as a rock. I think he's highly underrated, and to me, this goes back to some of the better players that have had these great signature sounds in bands—it's Tony Iommi, James Hetfield, and Mick Mars. These guys are the backbone of the band, there's always the drummers that are responsible for the rhythm and everything. But I think one of the reasons why Tommy works is because the guitar playing is so solid. Tommy can't do what he wants, all the syncopation, and all the other stuff he likes to do without a solid player behind him. Mars is like Pete Townshend, he's really rock solid. Like now, listening to the DVD, he's just right on the money.

Regarding James Hetfield, Rock is quick to point out that, "when I group Mick Mars and James Hetfield together, I do so for what they bring to their bands. As players, make no mistake, I would say James Hetfield is absolutely the best rhythm signature sound guy I've ever recorded. It's just phenomenal, I can pick up the same guitar with the same amp a minute after he's played, and it will sound like crap compared to him. He's just got that. Mick Mars is much the same way too, I can't pick up Mick Mars's guitar after he's played and can't make it sound like he does."

In comparing the two players, Rock points out, "I would say the sound of Metallica is built more around James, where I would say Mars is the collective in Motley. They have the same function as guitar players because they're so rock-solid. Mick just brings it all together, the wildness that Nikki and Tommy have respectively, Mars makes it solid. Even in his solos and the little things he does in terms of accentuation, nothing is wild. It sounds wild, but it's really well played and executed."

In exploring Rock's approach to capturing vocals, a key for the producer again seemed to be rooted in understanding where the singers he worked with were at in terms of who they were as singers, as well as where they wanted to go creatively with the material they were singing.

Elaborating on the latter, Rock compares his work with Mötley Crüe and Metallica:

James Hetfield, during *The Black Album*, became a singer. It was something that he wanted to work on, where with Vince, I think he likes to do his thing and that's it. I don't think there's any conscious effort on his part to say like "I want to be somebody else, I want to work on this and improve." Vince is a realistic guy who knows what he is and what he does and that's fine with him. To me, I think back in *Dr. Feelgood* days, it was just a question of getting Vince in tune and in time, and just trying to get the best performance out of him. I used multiple takes and comp, and it was very laborious. I do a shorter version of that now with him, because while everyone else has been doing solo projects, Vince has had to make a living by being on the road, so he's been singing non-stop. When I record Vince, I think the big thing is he just wants to get it done. I think he's been singing long enough that he just does it straight. The last time I worked with him, he was real pro, he does what he does very well now. I think the only trouble he has as a vocalist is pronunciation, but that's everyone. I think the greatest thing about Vince is he's exactly at the level of what people want Mötley Crüe to be. Right from the image to the name, he is the singer for that band. Any kind of difference, if he had more of a range or level, it wouldn't work, it doesn't work. It is L.A. rock 'n' roll, it's kind of like Morrison in a way that Morrison had his sound that was L.A., and Vince has his sound that is very much Motley. His voice is a signature voice, and has its limitations like every singer has. But I think it works really well for what he does, and it is what it is. I think one of the reasons why they became popular was the combination of the four of them, what each one brings to it. People want Motley to be trashy and kind of just punky and sleazy and simple, but I think it's the elements of Nikki's wildness, and Mars's rootsy thing, and Tommy pushing the envelope on all that other stuff, that's what musically made it great. And I think Vince is the blonde, surfer bling-bling kind of singer that has a very unique kind of voice. It's Vince's sound that makes him unique. He's got his thing. To me, if you look at Jagger, and you look at David Johansen, or Johnny Rotten from the Sex Pistols, they've got their limitations, and they've got their sound, and Vince sits within that. His voice has a very definitive, L.A. surfer, '80s rock sound.

In broader terms of the Grand Canyon–like ground that Bob Rock broke through his first musical collaboration with Mötley Crüe, and more elaborately with Metallica, *Rolling Stone* proclaimed that *The Black Album's* "sonic textures and audio depth of field are a revelation." For Rock's part, he recalled that his achievement musically with Metallica came in great part from getting to know the individual members of the band as well as he did, as well as how those personalities related to their collective dichotomy musically, such that, with Metallica, the personalities and opinions of both Lars Ulrich and James Hetfield were as life-size as their sound. Elaborating on the latter, Rock explained that in the makeup of Metallica, "Lars and James are kind of equally the lifeblood of Metallica—that is a marriage when it comes to Metallica, those two are not at all short-changing Kurt. Kurt has always been the guy who's sort of the mediator between the two, but James and Lars are kind of like—when they're both strong, they're the sound of Metallica. Whereas, when one or the other dominates in any situation, it changes drastically. In contrast, realistically, Nikki is so much the lifeblood of Motley, and the other guys really add all those other elements that make the band work."

Elaborating on the inner workings of Motley's musical personality, the producer explained that,

> to me, the life blood and driving force of Mötley Crüe is Nikki Sixx. I think Tommy, Vince and Mick make that work into a functioning kind of band, and bring all those other elements to make it work. But the lifeblood is definitely Nikki, and as of late, Nikki has done his best to rein everybody in to get them to work. Nikki's definitely the leader of the band, but I would also say the guy he works with if he wants to work on something solid is to work with Mars. When he wants to work on the energy of the music, it's Tommy. Nikki brings the kind of wildness to Motley, he's the wild guy in terms of ideas. All his ideas are always just all over the place. So if he writes a lyric, it's the most extreme lyric. If he writes a riff, he goes, "I want it loud, I want it punky." He's the extreme guy in terms of ideas. And I think the balance in terms of Nikki and Mick Mars is Mick's a little older, he's a little more blues-based, he's a little more entrenched in '70's rock, instead of punk, where Nikki's a little more rooted in punk. A little younger. I think what Tommy always brought to Motley was pushing the muso-quality of the band. He was always trying to push, like with the different beats. For instance, with *Dr. Feelgood*, things got a little funkier. I think, in terms of the rhythms and stuff before, it had always been pretty straight-ahead. So all of a sudden with *Feelgood*, Tommy sort of broke away from what had been their traditional drumming sound. Like Mars, he's the backbone musically, he's the one who strings it all together. And Tommy's so solid as a drummer, that he adds all those accents and stuff. Nikki's the idea guy in that band, it's fair to say he's the pulse of Mötley Crüe. To me, Nikki knows where Motley should be, he knows what it should be all about.

One of the keys to Bob Rock's long-term relationships in helping to shape, refine, and continually modernize the directions of both Mötley Crüe and Metallica's sounds respectively lies in the trust he has with each of his bands' members' musical personalities. By being so well versed with their respective strengths and weaknesses as musicians, Rock is able to keep a collective eye on where each band is at with one another and the times they play in.

My philosophy is, with any band, an individual's mind will ruin anything good. Basically, logic in bands and individual personalities destroy bands. In music, there's a certain amount of logic, but I think it's underrated from rock music and heavy rock music. Both are as artistic as classical or jazz, and there's a dynamic into it that's very delicate and mysterious, much like some of the greatest bands and artists of our time. It's a delicate balance, within all those personalities, the time, the music—there's so many things that come into it. I think working with both Motley and Metallica through the years, as well as any other band that I've had a long relationship with, it's just realistically individual personalities, and those people and their thoughts and their logic, and some of the things they come up with just ruins the music and the bands. For bands like Motley and Metallica that have stayed together so long—even with members going in and coming out—I think Nikki's version of what it should be is best translated by Tommy, Mick and Vince. Bringing their qualities into his mix makes Motley what it is. The collective of the four guys, just look at it as something unique, and that unique thing, that trademark of Mötley Crüe, is something they've worked very hard for almost twenty-five years to create. And there's a reason why it works, through that collective force. You can do all those other records all you want, and have a really great time, but both coexist, and eventually you will always come back around full-circle to Mötley Crüe. It's just my job as their producer to understand what that core *band* sound is.

With the latter in mind, Mötley Crüe has worked with Rock almost continually over the past seventeen years, to both the liking of the band and fans' ears. For the producer's own, he has tried to keep them tuned to what works best for rock's current climate given that Motley's musical core and foundation is largely intact. A prime example of the producer's success with the latter came with the recording of four new songs in late 2004 for what became a wildly successful Mötley Crüe reunion tour in 2005. The majority of the new songs appeared on the platinum *Red, White and Crue* compilation album, including the hit radio single "If I Die Tomorrow." Perhaps Rock's biggest admitted challenge was bringing drummer Tommy Lee back into the Crüe's inner fold, which was largely achieved by producing a sound that would satisfy Lee's seeming insistence that the band not sound dated, such that,

in recording the new material, realistically, all I tried to do with the songs Nikki wrote, specifically the one with the Simple Plan guys, was create a modernized, radio song which they needed. The other songs were kind of all there to represent the band now. It was really a case of trying to get them to work again together. I mean, Tommy couldn't be . . . it was tough to get Tommy to come to the table. I helped Nikki try to get it together, and it was really tough to get Tommy to play on the stuff. Now that they've been out on the road together, it's gelled, but it was tough.

While Rock acknowledges his long-term relationships with both Mötley Crüe and bands like Metallica have worked to produce something of a foundational sound and approach to making records that works well for each band, surprisingly, he still hopes there

isn't such a thing as a signature Bob Rock sound, because I've worked this many years so that doesn't happen. I like making records, and I like making records that interest me, and there's not supposed to be any formula in that. To be quite honest, I'm just not into being a career record producer, it's not about my career. There was a time in my life where it was, but realistically since the *The Black Album*, more and more I've just tried to be a better producer, and work with bands I find interesting at any given moment, and challenging, and help them realize what they want to do. It's not a Bob Rock record, it's never been about me. On a personal level, it's always been about trying to make the band happy, because I know, through personal experience, what it's like to make a record and not be happy with it. I lived with that earlier on in my career, and it's just the worst thing. So I've always been an artist-driven producer.

In closing his discussion on a career with a legacy of years already behind it and many more platinum records to come, Rock keeps his ear close to the street because his feet are firmly planted on it, his head out of the clouds, preferring to leave the stardom to the bands he produces and the dreams to the fans who buy the music he creates. For his own part, while Bob Rock has created a production sound and style over the past twenty years that virtually every subgenre of hard rock and heavy metal is modeled after, he remains impressively modest about his own security within the business. Even with the safety net of his legacy to fall back on, Rock does not see his future in the industry in terms of the hits he is almost sure to produce; rather, he is hopeful for the opportunity just to continue making those hits at all. The majority of his confidence is rooted in raw experience and a love for music that he points to as

the biggest thing in my life, second only to my family. And that's what I live for, and I think it's a huge commitment in terms of the love of music, and the time and work that you have to do. It's not something you can learn, to me, in four or three or two years. All that phase of it gives you is the basis of going out there to get the experience, that to me is what it's about. It's kind of interesting because I think youth brings energy, and I think that's a fantastic thing, but with age and experience comes another aspect that I more and more cherish. And that's with anything, whether it's people who play or produce music that are older, or people who make movies. There's this experience thing that you just can't underestimate. So I'd say to anyone who is young: just work your butt off, absorb as much as you possibly can, and use whatever tool you have in front of you to do the best job you can. So the bottom line is you just gotta hang in there if you're young, and do as many records as possible, and just work really hard. With every job I do, I just work at that record so I get to do another one. I'd say it's always been like that—with Motley, with Metallica. I don't take any of this for granted, because I work at the pleasure of the band. It's always like "God, I got to do the best I can cause I hope somebody likes it. If somebody hears it, maybe I'll get another gig." And I mean that with anybody. I want to do the best I can so I can get another job again, that's what it's about, that's what it's always been about. The day after *The Black Album* went number one, I was worried about where I was getting my next job. I still do. It's part of the business. I still hear all the things that are wrong with *Dr. Feelgood*, and *The Black Album*, and all the records I've made since and before—things I would change. Like I said, I feel like I know what I'm doing, but I still feel like I learn every single day.

CHAPTER 10

Flemming Rasmussen—Master of Puppets

For the past thirty years, the world of metal has been one largely according to Metallica, beginning almost three decades ago with the release of 1984's *Ride the Lightning*, from whose sheer raw power iTunes would years later point out "listener(s) can detect the beginnings of the cataclysmic shift occurring in metal." Producer Flemming Rasmussen would helm production on the band's trifecta of 1984's *Ride the Lightning*, 1987's *Master of Puppets*, and 1989's *...And Justice for All*, a trio of metal masterpieces that would come to define the blueprint for the broader heavy metal genre, one where *Rolling Stone* would later declare that Metallica took "the raw material of heavy metal and refined all the shit—the swaggering cock-rock braggadocio and the medieval dungeons and dragons imagery—right out of it."

Recounting his very early impressions of the band, Rasmussen considered it so foreign to anything he'd heard previous that it reminded him of *jazz*, in that

> as soon as I started in the studio, my partner and most of the people he worked with come from a jazz background, and all these people kept banging me on the head, saying "When you grow up, you'll learn to appreciate real music and jazz," and all that. So when Metallica came around in 83 and I started recording, I got blown away by the

energy, and couldn't get my hands down, because I thought, "This is fucking brilliant," and we were starting to develop a good collaboration and the sounds were getting there, but everyone who heard it would say, "But they can't play!" I would always reply, "Who gives a shit, listen to the energy!" And they didn't understand that, but I really loved their combined energy.

It was Rasmussen's collaboration with Rainbow on the band's 1981 *Difficult to Cure* LP that would first catch the ear of a then-unknown American metal band. Metallica crossed the Atlantic ocean from sunny California to freezing Denmark in November 1983 to seek out Rasmussen. The band was eager to enlist the producer's assistance in realizing their ambitions for a sound that *Billboard* would later celebrate as "stunning, exhibiting staggering musical growth (from their debut LP, *Kill 'Em All*) and boldly charting new directions that would affect heavy metal for years to come." Ahead of changing the course of metal history, the producer shared that, heading into the studio,

> they'd done one album and I hadn't heard that, so I had no reference whatsoever. I'd never heard about them and didn't know who they were. They brought the first LP, *Kill 'Em All*, to listen to, because James loved the guitar sound on that, and the amp he'd used on that first record had recently gotten stolen, so he wanted it to sound something like that on what would become *Ride the Lightning*. They came mainly because they'd heard the Rainbow albums I'd done, and thought they'd sounded great, and were basically looking for a good studio with a good in-house engineer to create the sounds they wanted, and they came up with me.

Heading into recording on the album, unlike other collaborations that had preceded his work with the band, Rasmussen recalled that "on *Ride the Lightning*, there wasn't any preproduction, because in those days, Metallica didn't demo elaborately. They made really good demos that almost were finished productions basically." Because the band's tidal wave was just starting to rise by this point, unlike his work with Rainbow or Cat Stevens, the producer found quick luxury in the fact that "I didn't have to take any commercial considerations into account whatsoever, so that freedom we had in the studio was important to helping their sound evolve." Still, though the band had all the creative freedom they desired heading into production, Rasmussen quickly discovered that, internally, "creatively, things revolved around James and Lars mostly, and Cliff—they were all participating. We had some days off where I locked them into the studio and they rehearsed, and it was everybody's fight against everybody, it was great."

Drawing inspiration from the band's indifference to musical conventions of any sort where their genre was concerned, Rasmussen proudly recalled that "back then, their whole attitude was that they didn't give a shit. They were in this for the music and the rest didn't really matter. That was their whole attitude, that we'd show the world what real music was about, and that was it." Backing that attitude up with a power of performance rooted-in the combination of rhythm guitarist/lead singer James Hetfield and drummer Lars Ulrich, whose style the *New York Times* would rightly describe as "thunderous," the band's producer said of the tracking process for Ulrich that

> we had three rooms in the studio, and that big warehouse in the back, and that's where Lars's drums were set up. It took a while to get started, because this was in November, so it was freezing cold, so we had like gas burners out there to make sure the temperature was so Lars could survive at night. We'd start at seven at night, and spend the first half an hour to hour to tune drums and make sure everything was cool, checking sounds, and we spent a lot of time changing heads, because Lars would go through skins on the snare in a couple of hours.

Flemming elaborated on the specifics of micing Ulrich's kit:

> We actually had Rick Allen from Def Leppard, his snare drum, flown over for that album. He'd just been in that famous car accident where he lost his arm, so he was laid up, and because the two bands shared the same management, Lars had called Rick up, and said, "That snare from Pyromania, can I borrow that?" That was a Ludwig. Lars was playing a double-bass drum, which I would mic with two D-12s, one on each, and with Metallica, there was no front-skin, or at least a hole in the front-skin on each bass drum. For toms, I used 57s all the way around—those were my go-to mics, and probably on the floor toms, I used Electro-Voice RE20s, which I liked because it was a bit more live than the 57, and was a bit rounder I thought for the floor toms. I used KM-84s, three or four of them, for overheads.

Adding Hetfield into the blend of the band's root rhythm sound, Rasmussen next said of the sound's construction that "first we'd do James's rhythm guitar part—which was tracked with Lars while he drummed—and then we'd double James's part. For micing James's amplifiers, I started using a combo of 87s and 57s, one on each speaker, and then we had some AKG gold tubes—which was like a remake of the C-12, which I set five feet from the corner of the cabinet in a 45 degree angle, which captured the umph from the cabinet. So it was always a combo of that, then I had a room mic or two, so it was pretty elaborate."

Hetfield would receive consistent praise from the band's earliest days, both critically and internally via Rasmussen recalling that he formed an almost-instant impression upon hearing Hetfield live in the studio that "James was probably in my opinion, the best rhythm guitar player in the world—he's the tightest, meanest, rhythm guitar player I've ever heard." But the broader outward sentiment toward drummer Ulrich on a purely skill level was markedly different. In defense of the drummer, the producer said that "Lars—I know a lot of people said he couldn't play drums in those days—I would argue it depends on your definition of playing drums, because if you ask me, Lars's main focus on drumming was doing fills, and at that point, he was probably the best drummer to play fills in the world, because that's where his focus point was."

Once the mics were hot and the band blazing through bed tracking, the producer next recalled that "we recorded everything analog, and the band tracked live off the floor," adding that from the control room, he was recording the band

> on the first console we ever got, which was a Trident A-range, and had that all the way up till 1992. The owner of the studio, Freddie, had come from the A-Range at Rosenberg Studio, and he'd worked a lot with Roy Thomas Baker—who'd helped develop it. We liked the punchiness and the really special sound the console itself had that kind of added to the sound of the record, just going through one of the input modules (as opposed to doing nothing). I just really like it, and to me it's the ultimate rock 'n' roll desk because it sounds loud and crunchy, and you can really put a lot of volume output through it without it cracking up. We were working solely on [Lyrnix two-inch machines], twenty-four tracks, and we had all our tape machines adjusted so we could go +14 on tape.

Of those twenty-four tracks, Rasmussen revealed that—due to Ulrich's elaborate kit—"we had a lot of assigned to Lars, it was two bass drums, one snare, a hi-hat—that's four, I probably bounced the toms down to stereo, that's two tracks for a total of six, and then overheads were seven and eight, and then four room mics for a total of twelve."

Discussing harnessing the power of bassist Cliff Burton, who *Bass* magazine would later hail as "the king of metal bass" in part because of his playing prowess on *Ride the Lightning*, Rasmussen recalled feeling right from the jump that "Cliff was a fabulous bass player, especially when he started doing all his solo stuff, and fiddling around with his Moby wah-wah pedals, and he had some parts that were difficult, as most of the guys had." Turning to the technical aspect of bringing the legendary bassist's sound roaring fully to life on tape, Rasmussen shared a special trick he developed exclusively for recording Burton: "One of the reasons why I always recorded the low-end of Cliff's bass amp is so you have that low-end crunchiness, because distortion on a DI sounds pretty crappy. Cliff had a huge stack of amps, and I'd mic both of them, and then run a DI line as well. If you listen throughout all their records, even the distortion parts, the DI is always ahead of all the pedals, so I'd have a clean signal at all times, and that mixed in with the amps is what does the trick with the low end and definition." Tracking his bass parts following the completion of Ulrich and Hetfield's drum and rhythm parts, the producer added that "Cliff usually needed half an hour or so to warm up, because some of their numbers he had to play really, really fast, so he'd come in, I'd have him play through the songs four or five times, and he'd be warmed up, then we'd record bit by bit or sometimes in huge chunks."

When lead guitarist Kirk Hammett—who in 2012 became the first inductee into the *Guitar World* Hall of Fame—plugged in to begin tracking his lead solo overdubs, Rasmussen said, it was a process by which "Kirk would come in after we'd done the rhythm guitars and drums, and dub on his solo parts. He'd more or less worked them out at home, so once we were tracking vocals and bass and rhythm guitars, he would like to assign solos. Lars was there a lot during Kirk's tracking." Explaining the purpose of Ulrich's presence during the creation of Kirk's solos, the producer explained the drummer's role as something of a compositional filter wherein because "Lars is good at composing songs, once Kirk was doing his solos, if he'd laid something down and I'd said 'Yeah, that's nice,' Lars might chime in and ask 'Well, can we put something there,' and I'd maybe help translate that to Kirk, for instance, 'In this part, you should probably go down low because you've been in the high register for a while,' so shaping the final solos was a collaboration between me, Lars, and Kirk."

Sharing that the band favored Marshalls during *Ride the Lightning's* recording, Rasmussen recalled that:

> The first album was more or less all played in Marshall amps because James had had his amps stolen just prior to going into the studio, we had every single Marshall that was in every single band in Denmark in the studio, so he could check out which ones he liked. I think Kirk played through that, and had a Marshall preamp where he could store different settings, which he also had on Master. Kirk's guitar micing was the same setup as James, just with more room mics. All of Kirk's guitar sounds would have the three mics: a 57, a U 87, and then a tube mic that was away from the amp, and then the room mics—and it would all be a combination of how they were mixed and phased.

When the time arrived for singer James Hetfield to lay his lead vocals, Rasmussen said, at that point in his career Hetfield

> wasn't much into singing, so it was more about capturing the shouting thing, double-part, more "I'm an angry young man and need to get my expressions out." He was good, don't get me wrong, but the playing was a more important element to the band's sound at the time for him than the singing. When we tracked, typically, it

was just me and James. We did it bit by bit, because it took a lot of breath, so we did a couple of lines at a time and would just progress like that. On the first couple of albums, I doubled him on almost everything, and they would be centered, both of his lead vocal tracks—one three to four dbs lower than the other. I would use either an SM-7 or a U-87, but we used the SM-7 a lot on his vocals. I would make little notes as we recorded regarding delays, and stuff, and we'd actually record some of those while we tracked too.

As principal tracking wrapped on a record that *Kerrang!* would later hail for including "melody, maturity and musical intelligence" and Rasmussen's attention turned to mixing, he explained that that process started for the producer well before recording had finished, with his main mix-focus during tracking on guitar arrangement:

They both had a rhythm guitar part, Kirk and James. After James's rhythm part tracked with drums, then we'd do Kirk's rhythm guitar part and double it, and all the melody bits would then be put on the tracks. Because in those days, there was not a lot of automation, I'd have a track that would say "Kirk's guitar left side," "Kirk's guitar right side," and then some of them would be assigned to center, depending on which parts. So you'd sometimes wind up with three tracks, because there had to be a centered track. Some of them, I layered with different sounds, and placed the same way as appropriate.

Depicting the band's mixing process as much a group effort as principal production had been on the album, Rasmussen described a team effort wherein "they were the ones who came up with ideas, but I executed all of that from the production side. It was a *big* collaboration. I think my willingness to offer a certain element of latitude as an engineer was one of the reasons they kept working with me as time went on.

Keeping the reins throughout the entirety of production, Rasmussen shared that "I mixed *Ride the Lightning* as well as produced it," saying of his inner blueprint for that process that

while I was recording that album, I made a timeline on the 24-track sheet: Intro, verse, B, blah blah. With Metallica, I had to have it in a separate group for each song, because when you have a song that's seven and a half minutes long, you needed to map it out. All of *Ride the Lightning* is on a maximum of forty-eight tracks, so that's forty-six minus the two code-tracks, and twelve of those was drums, one was bass, and recording each mic separately when you have multiple mics on a guitar amp, I'd always mix then as we record.

As he laid out some of the specifics of what would become the staples of Metallica's signature sound to follow, Rasmussen recalled concerning the guitar tracks that most of the mix assignments were "done as we made it, because rhythm guitar one was always assigned to the right side, and if it was Kirk's part, it would go on one side, if it was James's part, it would go then on the other."

More broadly, Hetfield explained that planning was his secret weapon where Metallica's intricate mix arrangements were concerned, such that "I always had it laid out because in those days, I couldn't automate-pan. For instance, on the beginning of 'Sanitarium,' when it starts out I have some AMS stereo delay with some pitch-change on it, and that all starts out in mono, and then as we recorded, after the first part of the intro, I flicked the switch and everything is stereo—and I recorded it that way." Speaking of some of the legendary album cuts that fans quickly made live concert favorites, for Rasmussen, a personal favorite to date remains "For Whom the Bell Tolls," which he recalled "was written in the studio by the band over a weekend, and then they played it for me on a Monday, and I thought right off, 'That is fucking cool.' That's probably the first song that we played to a click track because it kept speeding, which was something they'd never tried before."

With the release of *Ride the Lightning* in 1984, it was quickly clear that Metallica had their finger on the pulse of where metal was heading, largely because they were steering it, reshaping the genre in their image, such that iTunes would years later argue that the LP "proved Metallica were more than the American metal movement's brightest stars— they were now its leaders." Concurring on a personal note of satisfaction, Rasmussen recalled, "When *Ride the Lightning* was done, I thought it was really great, I was really proud of it, and still am—it was a really good album, and sort of set the tone for that whole metal scene that followed." With an album that *Rolling Stone* would hail as "a titanic step forward" under their belt—though *Ride the Lightning* by its natural predatory power in shaping the broader genre of heavy metal had made Metallica an overnight force to be reckoned with—the band and Rasmussen took it all in stride. Heading into their second studio collaboration, *Master of Puppets*—the producer recalled that "it was pretty much a repeat of the first album, just that we were getting better at what we were doing—we were refining everything, all the work processes as we went along. We actually spent two weeks in the States trying to find a studio that we could use, but the band ultimately decided to do it in Copenhagen at my studio."

Sensing the spirit of ambition and adventure in the air, Rasmussen remembered feeling the band was in a perfect place to seize the moment that *Billboard* would later hail as "the band's greatest achievement" because everyone in the band had improved as players by that album, so we tried more elaborate things on *Master of Puppets* because they were able to do it. Everybody was getting better at what they did musically, and the roles within the band were more defined, so the arguments were less. I would say looking back that *Master of Puppets* was a really pleasant record to make. *Puppets* was more or less laid out from scratch. They'd been in a rehearsal studio in Lars's garage, and had more or less worked out the songs the way they were going to be recorded. The arrangements were all done, which made my life easier.

Tracking the album's bed tracks live off the floor, the producer added his memory that "we recorded solidly from noon till around two a.m., and as a band, when we tracked, we'd usually go through two or three takes of each song—with some we did more, and with others we did less. Three takes was the average."

Proceeding as they had on *Ride the Lightning* with Lars Ulrich's drums going down to tape first along with James Hetfield's rhythm guitars—since "we always recorded Lars and James together first before everyone else"—Rasmussen recalled that in addition to Ulrich's overall performance improvement, the team was further aided by the fact that "Lars had a new drum set, and he'd found a new snare drum in a shop in Copenhagen, one that had been sitting there for sale for like ten years, so we got it at a really good price. So the whole kit was better sounding, and everything had been upgraded a bit." Along with the drummer, Rasmussen added that the studio had upgraded on the equipment side, adding "some new mics, and two new 24-track by then, and effects was probably the biggest area where we'd added new gear, as more and more things were coming all the time: more and more AMS reverbs, Eventide stuff, and probably a couple of LA-2 Teletronics by then.

Turning to his memories of the physical process of bringing to life a drum sound that *Billboard* would later celebrate as "thick and muscular" and varied "enough in texture and tempo to hold interest through all its twists and turns," the producer candidly revealed that "recording the drums was a hard work, a lot of hard work, but I was loving it. There was a lot of tuning drums, and doing takes again and again." In one departure from *Lightning* Rasmussen felt was necessary given the complexity of epics like "Battery," "Welcome Home (Sanitarium)," "Damage, Inc.," and the album's title track, "we used click tracks for parts of these songs." Doing much of his mixing work while he tracked the album's drums, the producer explained that where placement assignments were for the different pieces of Ulrich's kit, "I'm always deciding on the spot. I had this ideal picture in my head and tried to get it to sound like that. I wanted the bass drum to be able to cut through, so that's why it's got a pretty defined click to it. I used a graphic EQ on the recording of the bass drums, to more or less shape the sound the way I wanted it."

To achieve that end technically, Rasmussen added that as he tracked,

> I used a DN-22 Claptechniques 11 Band graphic EQ unit. This particular EQ had 11 different frequencies that start in the low end and go through the whole spectrum all the way to the top. This one is on faders, but if it's a knob, when you turn—it's neutral in the middle—and you can add or subtract. So what I do most of the time is add as much as I can in one frequency to hear what that sounds like, and if I didn't like the sound, then I'd take it a bit below zero and keep going. And in that time, you can shape the sound exactly the way you want.

When harnessing the power of Metallica's signature kick drum on tape, the producer preferred to keep the sound relatively raw, so that "it felt natural, and the dynamics of the playing did that most times, although it's pretty massive all the time, there's still dynamics in there. The compression that's on there is more or less tape compression, I'm pretty sure I didn't use any compressors on the drums for any of those albums—definitely not in recording."

In prepping Ulrich's drum sound for the compliment of Hetfield's rhythm guitars, which—in what had by then become a norm to Metallica's recording routine—were tracked in real time with Lars's drums, Rasmussen began with broader sonic considerations, sharing that "I would have taken out some of the midrange in the bass drums in order to make room for the bass and the low end of the guitars. And then I would have added some high-end around where the click is to make the bass drum more defined. And also in the low, low end, I would add that to make it go 'boom.'" Turning to his micing blueprint for the latter guitar sound, the producer recalled that "mics-wise, everything was pretty much the same setup as *Ride the Lightning*, except that I think we'd gotten some Cable DPA *4007 Omni* Directional Condenser *Microphones*, which are like test mics—they're these linear mics. I used those for room mics on the album's guitars because they can handle excessive amounts of pressure, so that really brought it. We had like six rhythm guitars solidly through the album on the heavy parts. That added the fatness, of course, and all of those guitars were played by James because he's so unbelievably tight."

Pulling back the curtain on exactly how Hetfield's legendary crunch was created in the studio, Rasmussen shared that the wall of sound was one that went through some reconstruction after its initial tracks were laid: "I remember for most of the songs on *Master of Puppets*, once we'd done the rhythm guitars, we thought it was a bit too fat and not crunchy enough, so we actually did another two tracks of rhythm guitars that were thinner and crunchier so that we actually had two more guitars we could blend in and out to make sure we had the right amount of crunch in certain passages of the songs."

Delving further into the heart of the signature sound's creation, the producer added that

> that crunch came mainly from the amps, which at this point were Boogie amps. We got new guitar amps because the band had gotten an endorsement deal through Boogie guitars. I wasn't too happy about that, because I thought they sounded pretty crappy. I started tweaking them as much as I could, fiddling about, so I would set the amps up in the main room, they'd play, and they had a graphic EQ on them which I'd fuck around with trying to get a tone out of it. So what we'd do on some songs, I'd tweak it around to get a sound I liked in the room, obviously I'd mic it and fuck around with the mics till I thought it sounded good. Then we'd do a rough take of one, then quickly double it to see what that sounded like.

Feeling as though he really was catching lightning in a bottle when he worked tracking Hetfield's equally speedy rhythm playing to tape, the band's producer seemed happy to testify as a witness to the Metallica front man's "best-of mantle" as a true title indeed because "he's extremely fast and he's extremely precise. When we were recording, he'd work pretty intensely with his playing craft, so we'd do a section and he could feel when he didn't have it. So we'd normally agree on that, go back and punch in on it, and he'd play it all in a punch. This was in the analog days, so there was no undo buttons."

When it came time for Cliff Burton to weave his own masterwork on the bass into the band's blazing mix, Rasmussen recalled,

> I never record the bass till I've done the guitars when I do metal, so I recorded Cliff after the guitars were done. I think it's really important because metal is so guitar-riff oriented, I want the guitar player to lay the riffs where he wants them feeling-wise. I don't want him to have to change their feeling because there's a bass there that maybe has a slightly different feeling. The bass player's part in Metallica is supposed to be the low part of the rhythm guitar, except for like Cliff, who was just the way he was—all over the place sonically, which is brilliant.

From the technical side, the producer added his memory that part of Burton's sound came thanks to his "pedalwork, where he was doing wah-wah and stuff, it was brilliant, and added a flavor to the tracks. Cliff did all that himself, deciding where to use his pedals, and it wouldn't be consistent, just when he felt it fit."

Reflective of the sophisticated nature of the band's musical arrangements, which the BBC would later hail as "complicated, aggressive and hugely technically ambitious," Rasmussen recalled that ahead of tracking, "Cliff needed to warm up, because some of the songs were really, really fast. When we were recording, he would do four or five takes to get a whole song, more or less, and we'd pick as we went along. We didn't have five tracks to do bass, we had like two or three, so for the bass we'd decide right away. I hate leaving decisions for later, and at this point, the band was by nature the same way." When attention turned to lead guitarist Kirk Hammett's inspired lead playing, the producer shared his memory that during recording, "Kirk had this Marshall half-unit where he could store sounds, so this was one of the first Marshalls where you could actually store your settings. I had these B&B Audio Equalizers inserted on the amps for the frequencies, I still had that going."

The BBC would give equally powerful praise to lead singer James Hetfield's lead vocal performances during this era of the band, dubbing the vocalist "a master of establishing; maintaining and manipulating musical tension and mood, creating songs that really suck you in." Recalling that in its recording basics, he and Hetfield employed the "same basic approach as *Ride the Lightning*," Rasmussen added that as tracking for the album's lead vocals commenced, "James wrote some lyrics as we went along tracking vocals, he had plenty of time to do that, because we were in the studio for four months." When the tape was rolling, the producer revealed that the notoriously-shy-off-stage Hetfield preferred to "track vocals alone, and then Lars—who was at the studio but not in the control room during recording—would come in and they'd discuss it. Most of the time, they'd leave it where it was, but James would always consider Lars's opinion. There weren't a big of arguments in those days. James also did all the backing vocals on that album."

Metallica's—and arguably metal's—first masterpiece, *Master of Puppets,* would prove a sonic vacuum that sucked the entire metal universe through its filter and succeeded at doing so, the BBC argued, because the album featured "hard, fast rock with substance that doesn't require the listener to wear eye-liner or big fire-hazard hair to enjoy." *Rolling Stone* would double down on the BBC's point that the album worked because it had "a sonic theme: really loud guitars, played fast, with no regard for the hair metal on the airwaves," while *Billboard* added in grander summary that "some critics have called *Master of Puppets* the best heavy metal album ever recorded . . . [and] if it isn't, it certainly comes close." Agreeing with the critics like *Rolling Stone*—who would also add that "produced . . . with Flemming Rasmussen, *Master of Puppets* is the real thing,"—Rasmussen would offer his own conclusions regarding *Puppets'* greatest achievements that "with that album, I wanted it to sound better and louder than *Ride the Lightning*, and I think we achieved that. So going in that direction with that kind of sound, I think we nailed it on *Master of Puppets*, because it's 10 percent better than *Lightning* sound-wise, if you ask me. I wouldn't change a bit on that—I think it's perfect."

As the band began 1988 plotting what *Billboard* would later argue became their "most complex, ambitious work," the album's spare, dense production and dark musical tone throughout the writing reflected their musical mood at the time, following the death of beloved bassist Cliff Burton. They were defined fundamentally by the absence they felt without their brother in arms, and the BBC underscored that fact by noting that throughout the album, "there's little in the way of bass—the lack of bass. That decision was the band's sole responsibility, meaning James and Lars." That decision Rasmussen matter-of-factly confirmed with his recollection that, indeed, "there was no bass on the album basically. Jason didn't have any real parts like Cliff, who just took his parts. With Jason, he was told what to do and he did it on that first record."

While he wound up behind the console for *...And Justice for All*, initially, the reteaming almost didn't happen, because, Rasmussen recalled, unlike the first two LPs,

> they wanted to record it in the States, which meant a new studio, and they decided on One on One Studios in L.A. They wanted to start January 1, and I couldn't do it, so they basically got someone else in there who was supposed to do the whole album, and I got a call from Lars like three weeks into January and he went, "It's not working, help! When can you be here?" So I postponed my sessions and went over there on February 14 to begin recording the album. They'd already been at it for a month, but hadn't done much of anything, and so we didn't keep anything recorded before I got there.

Once the band and their producer were back on track, in spite of their loss with the death of bassist Burton, Rasmussen recalled that, as recording began, "to me, we were just starting back up from where we'd left off with the last album. I would have liked to have done the album in the first place, I just didn't have the time for it when they had been scheduled to start recording. I was really busy in Denmark at that time, but I was happy they called me to come in and do it anyway, it made me feel like maybe I'd done something right with them on those first two records."

Heading in the opposite direction of AC/DC, who'd used *Back in Black*—their first LP following the death of their lead vocalist to craft an upbeat tribute to late singer Bon Scott, Metallica channeled their aggressions into a sound that *Billboard* would call a "bone-dry production." Filling in the absence of Burton with an expansion of the experimental, the BBC would later say, had the result that, "as the sound has become thinner and tauter the songs have grown grander and more epic," adding that "these are musicians becoming more ambitious craftsmen and experimenting." As Ulrich and Hetfield began laying out the album's concept to producer Rasmussen, who recalled that the pair "had a pretty clear view in their mind of what they wanted, and I think that was aided by the fact that over the years they had developed an internal intuitive understanding of each other, and they can look at each other and know what they mean. Along with having a pretty clear view of what they want, they definitely have a pretty clear view of what they don't want—which is sometimes equally important."

Along with a recognizable *lack* of bass, the producer recalled that, in overall sonic terms, "with that record, the band was looking for a sound that was dryer and louder, because on *Master of Puppets*, it's so loud and ambient and huge sounding." Beginning foundationally with the record's ambitious rhythmic soundscape, Rasmussen recalled that this time out, the production team allowed as ambitious an amount of room in the way of tracks as required to accomplish Ulrich's vision for the record's drum sound, such that

> on that album, we had twenty-two tracks on the drums, so on . . . *And Justice for All*, we were using one whole tape reel for the drums. So we would start off the session with them playing, defining some tempos for the different parts in the songs, mostly around James. And Lars would play to a click track, fitted to the tempos and changes, with James doing a guide guitar for Lars to play to, and we recorded drums for the album a couple of days per song—because of how elaborate they were. When you're on the edge of your own technical ability in terms of playing, you're ready to use tricks like that. We wanted the drums on *Justice* to be so tight and so fat and so loud that it topped all of the previous albums.

Aided greatly in his goal by the fact that "over those three albums, Lars had gotten better and better technically as a drummer, and much, much tighter as an all-around drummer by that point," Rasmussen highlighted the epic "One" as a moment where all the drummer's ambitions exploded into a synergetic symphony of precision rhythm that would later inspire *Rolling Stone* to conclude featured "stunning drum work by Lars Ulrich . . . works up to a ferocious rhythmic whirlwind, executed with the precision of a close-order drill." Rasmussen would use "One" as an opportunity to underscore why he felt Ulrich's "greatest strength can be heard in his fills, his drum fills are some of the best in the world—take for instance the machine-gun part in 'One.' He just keeps coming up with new drum fills, which is brilliant."

Revealing the technical blueprint for how Lars's epic kit was brought to life on tape, Rasmussen recalled that

> there was only one mic on each kick, an RE-20, sitting right in the center of the bass drum, and they didn't have any front skin on them whatsoever. And I recorded those through a UA-21 graphic EQ, and the bass drum was always dead-center in the mix. Because of the way the rest of the band plays, if the bass drum's not there there's no

energy left—so we push the music forward via the bass drum and the guitars. So the bass drum mics were two RE-20s, and we had some AKGs on the cymbals, and Lars had recently acquired some Touch mics that were sitting underneath each cymbal, so we had that mixed into a stereo feed that was recording. The toms were 57s again, as was the snare. The big change from *Master of Puppets* was, again, that the bass drums were RE-20s, and that the graphic EQ on the bass drums was a UA-21 band instead of Chloric Techniques 11 band—that gave us a lot more high-end on the bass drums than was heard on the previous album.

The results Rasmussen and Ulrich achieved, in the estimation of *Decibel* magazine, "combined with the album's savagely precise riffery and bottomless power grooves, the overall effect is like a battery of machine guns spitting serrated razor blades through the listener's face."

Bringing his game to a Jordan-level status as a player in the course of . . . *And Justice for All*'s nuclear attack of rhythm guitar tracks, Rasmussen confirmed that, by that point, James had arrived, such that "for the first couple of albums, we were kind of inventing the sound at that point, but later on, there would be discussions between me and James for the rhythm guitars, and we'd set up something to see what it sounded like, and if we didn't like it, we'd tweak it." Working within an if-it-ain't-broke formula that broke the mold entirely in the course of their first two collaborations with Rasmussen, on *Justice*, the producer recalled that "James would play to Lars's drums, which was the foundation for everything in Metallica." As Hetfield and Ulrich worked away creating the equivalent of a musical force on *Justice*, so powerful that *Rolling Stone* magazine argued that "*Thrash* is . . . channeled aggression," Rasmussen revealed that the band's go-to amplifier throughout this process was "the Boogie Amp, which I tweaked by inserting an Effects EQ effect looper on the amps while they recorded, so I would be able to sit with an EQ in the control room and could control the sound of the amp in the studio."

As the band built their perfect beast track by track, section by section, they were in the process constructing metal's most powerful monster, one that overshadowed even Black Sabbath's legendary "Iron Man" in making eardrums rumble with a sound that *Billboard* argued "revealed (Metallica's) determination to pull out all the compositional stops, throwing in extra sections, odd-numbered time signatures, and dense webs of guitar arpeggios and harmonized leads." That compositional tapestry of sound was rounded out with what *Rolling Stone* hailed as "breakneck tempos and staggering chops [that] would impress even the most elitist jazz-fusion aficionado." Decorating that sky with his own shine over the course of solos that would all take their starring role in song after song, Rasmussen would single out the aforementioned "One" as an instance where "the end solo on 'One'—the really long one—is probably one of the best solos ever in rock 'n' roll history." For the album's epic acoustic guitar adventures, the producer shared that he captured the record's pristine sound via "the U-87 / KM-84 combination I used a lot. I would sometimes do a double, but in some parts, it's just one guitar just stereo with two mics on each side."

In a change for the producer, working for the first time with the band outside of his home base in Denmark, Rasmussen said of the studio shake-up that

> they had an SSL desk at One on One, so luckily they had an old Neve sitting as mod- ules in the wall, so I used that and basically just used the SSL desk as a monitor. I thought the SSL sounded flat and dull, it had a high-end in the EQs, and a lot of things I didn't like about that. On the bass drums, we were using RE20s because we were in the States, and there was just no EQ, so you'd take a mic up, listen to it, and it sounded boring, and if you did the same thing through the Neve, it sounded interest- ing—the Neve sounded fuller, fatter and bigger.

When the discussion turned to James Hetfield's lead vocals, Rasmussen recalled that as a benefit to the singer's vocal ambitions for the album—which included proper singing for the first time in the band's recorded history—"he was a much better singer by then, and it was his ambition to sing more on *Justice* than past albums. Recording him was more punching, where we'd do a long bit, then redo small bits, like that." As production wrapped on an album that *Decibel* would later hail as "Metallica's finest hour," Rasmussen recalled feeling that his proudest accomplishment from the production—not surprisingly—was "One," saying the "machine-gun drum part on that song is my favorite, and the whole thing from where it starts getting heavy and all the way out with that long solo, that's totally up there as one of my faves."

Upon release in August 1988, Rasmussen's final production collaboration with the band launched them into worldwide rule over the metal genre, beginning with . . . *And Justice for All*'s Top 10 debut on the *Billboard* Top 200 Album Chart, and the rocket that was "One" that didn't stop until it had smashed the ceiling for metal's commerciality. Rasmussen had felt the band's potential for the latter stardom that would follow in the studio by way of "the energy, the power that's in the music and the energy you get from listening to it. You can feel that these lads mean business, and that was even down to the way we acted. They were really devoted to this project and they put everything they had into it." Those results would famously garner a Grammy nomination—the academy's first year—for Best Hard Rock/Heavy Metal Performance, lost through industry politics to Jethro Tull. What the band had earned from the popular reaction to . . . *And Justice for All* was—arguably for the first time in the history of the heavy metal genre—a body of music that could creatively, critically, and commercially compete with anything else out there, such that iTunes would conclude years later that *"And Justice for All is so precisely rendered, so expertly conceived, and so flawlessly executed that listening to it is the musical equivalent of watching an Olympic team perform in an event for which it spent years training. . . . And Justice for All* to stand as the insurmountable pinnacle of . . . metal."

CHAPTER 11

Don Was—The Sonic Translator

Don Was, as a producer, is perhaps pop-rock's greatest artistic translator. Fluent in multiple musical languages, Was possessed a unique talent for communicating almost any artist's vision into a universally palatable musical result. As he said:

> The essence of my job—once the songs are there, for instance with someone like Bob Dylan—is then to help them communicate whatever it is the song's about—whatever the emotional message of the song is. You learn this in Art 101: that you have to communicate something that has to be received. Good art is art that people understand, and it's the same with making records as with say painting—you capture what's almost like a moment of emotional videotape. You feel something, and you freeze that moment by transforming it from emotion into a song, into another medium. You're taking something emotional, and giving it some other facet so that you can communicate something where conversational language fails you. So you're freezing this feeling, that's half an artist's job, is to freeze it and give it some form. The second part is to communicate it to someone else, the process isn't complete unless someone receives the message, and feels what you felt, or feels something as strongly—their own version of it. That the song awakens something emotional in them, and then you've

gotten to them. So that's the whole process in a nutshell, and the producer's job is to do everything possible to ensure that's expressed as strongly and clearly as possible.

While his countless Grammy Awards and multiplatinum albums only work to illustrate his success at the latter, he himself has always philosophically handled success as a double-edged sword, doing his best not to internalize his own hype for fear of it drowning out his ear's ability to hear a fresh idea that might run counter to commerciality. He explained that

> the biggest danger, the biggest pit I ever fell into was—after winning all those Grammys for Bonnie Raitt's record—I went from not being employable to having everyone want to hire me—so that for a year and a half, the people in line were Iggy Pop to Elton John to Bob Seger to Bob Dylan to Neil Diamond. It was a wild array of people, and they were the biggest people around, and they want to believe you're gonna help them out; that you have some mojo going for you so that whatever you did to win those Grammys, they want that juice. And I think because people want to believe in themselves, you start believing it, that it's because of you, and you're fucked. Everything goes out the window, and it takes at least five years to realize: "I get it." Something else is moving that groove, and I was part of it, but I don't know how it happened. I think you get over that when you throw everything out the window and go back to trying to treat it like it was your first time again—being open to anything regardless of how it might look at first like it will translate commercially.

While *Rolling Stone* has called Was "a master of makeovers," that is the very type of stylistic branding he has sought to avoid via collaborations with the universe of stars who have sought out his creative counsel over the years, reasoning that "the idea I think is not to force someone into a direction that's not their choice, but to help them achieve what they want with the best possible result. I try to avoid a signature sound, I think being invisible is a really good thing." The latter serves both Was's and his artist's purpose in erasing the pressure of expectations from the creative constitution of a recording session, allowing an artist to see performance in terms of art and not commerce, and in the same time freeing Was from those same chains by extension. From the producer's perspective,

> I see myself as a producer kind of as Ben Franklin, I hold my kite up and let the lightning strike the key. Someone's gotta hold the tether to the ground, and that's the producer's job, to let them go out and stretch and try to create a situation where they can be the best they can be—where they're fearless, not self-conscious, pumped-up and enjoying themselves, and want to do more . . . I just put myself in their place. I've been produced as an artist, and I know what it's like to give a performance that you know has got truth to it, and comes from a real place deep inside of you, and to fin-

ish the take, have ten seconds go by, and then have some guy push a button and go, "Can you do one more." And you know that they didn't hear it, and missed it, and it's disgusting. You lose respect for those people . . . Why do people become musicians, let's start there—because they don't wanna have a job. Already you're dealing with independent spirits who don't want to be told what to do. Any musician worth his salt does *not* want to be told what to do by anybody. So some punk comes in the studio and starts telling them what to do, most times they won't listen. So, as a producer, you have to put yourself in the place of the artist to have any success in the studio.

On the subject of whether that aforementioned status has ever proven intimidating and thus a distraction for Was, independent of label pressure, he pointed to his collaboration with Bob Dylan.

The very first day I worked with Bob Dylan, in 1989, someone thought they were being nice, and had kept a DAT recorder running all day, which you never do to Bob Dylan. And at one point, Bob Dylan was standing at the piano, telling me what he wanted to do, and I was telling him why it wouldn't work, before I'd heard it even. Then I thought, "What the fuck!" Bob Dylan's my hero, I'd waited all my life to work with this guy, and then I wasn't letting him be Bob Dylan. It was an outrageous thing, I just wanted to hide in a dark room for a couple years, but for the most part, artists will tell you what they want to do, if you come without an agenda and just open up to them. All they are focused on is the music, and that is all you should be as well—not who they are in terms of fame and expectations as a result of that on any level.

Was's collaboration with Dylan also taught him another valuable lesson early on in his producing career:

the value and importance of a feel of a performance. When I worked with Bob on "Under the Red Sky," I didn't know what the fuck I was doing. I could have done a better job. There were things he clearly stated that he was trying to achieve, that I wouldn't say I dismissed him, but I didn't try hard enough to go after. I remember when we were mixing "Under the Red Sky", one of the things he said when he came in to hear the mix was "it's fucked up, I can hear everything." He didn't mean it literally, but he meant something by that, what he meant was that it was too clean. He wanted it to sound more like the Chess Records, which today after being cleaned up with remastering, actually sound pretty clean. But what he was really saying was "I want it to sound like we imagined the whole Chess Records era to sound." And he achieved that on *Time out of Mind,* which Daniel Lanois produced. The minute I heard the finished record I realized "Oh man, that's what he was talking about ten years ago." I would say the thing that stands out about Bob's voice is he had a great sense of feel, feel was very important. He really did know. My engineer on that record and I just coined a phrase, "Bob knows," because he knew when the thing was grooving and when it wasn't.

In offering a contrasting scenario in which his paying almost exclusive attention to performance helped develop a hit song, Was cites his collaboration with the B-52s on their 1989 smash "Love Shack", which he recalled

wasn't even a song when we started making that record. They had five songs, maybe six, and we just finished a day early, and things were going so well that they said, "Well, we have this other thing we need to finish." And it was about twelve minutes long, and the way they write, they do stream of consciousness, sing anything and record it, play it back, and maybe they'll just play on a groove, they call it jamming. So they'd jam on a groove for a half hour, then listen back, and maybe someone came up with one good line that they liked, so whoever sang it usually writes it down on a piece of yellow legal paper, and they tape it up on the wall, and whenever the paper gets to the floor, they have a song. And "Love Shack" was about fifteen minutes long, and nothing ever repeated, the "Love Shack" part was in there, the "Tin Roof" part was in there, and so we sat on the porch of the studio in Woodstock, and I went, "Okay, this love shack thing seems to be the common link here, let's make that the chorus." And then, we just edited the song down in about a half hour. And it was only because we had an extra day at the studio, so we went right in—we were on the steps in the morning, the last day—and we went into record, and the first take was amazing. The first take felt good because no one had ever played it before, and no one had any preconceptions about what the thing was supposed to be, and we were in a good mood, and it was fun and there was no pressure because it wasn't even supposed to be recorded. And I think what makes the song feel good when you hear it is that everyone had fun playing it, I do think people can hear in the grooves, and they can tell when you're struggling. They can tell when the people making the record are having fun, and they want to hear that.

Given the fluid nature of Was's recording process, he holds a rather unconventional view of preproduction:

It's good to have a plan, as far as preproduction goes, but you have to be prepared to abandon it in a second. You have to stay on your toes, and don't try to plan it, because it's gonna change—either because you're wrong or because things change. For instance, when I did *Voodoo Lounge* with the Rolling Stones, I know that they write in the studio, I know that they always have. So in my first few meetings, I went over to Dublin when they were at Ronnie Wood's house working on some songs, and I suggested simply, naively, "Wouldn't it be great if the songs were actually written before we started, and we can really focus on doing tracks that are appropriate to the song, that are emotionally in synch." So they go "Yeah sure, we can do that, no problem." So I go back to L.A. and a week later I get a fax from Keith saying "be in Dublin on Tuesday, we're gonna start recording some songs." And I said, "Wait a minute, what songs? There's nothing written yet? I thought we agreed . . ." And so then I got another fax back from Keith that said, "Just remember when you get to Dublin: improvise, adapt, and overcome, and P-fucking-S, don't paint yourself into a fucking corner." So I'd only met Keith twice at this point, and my knees started to give out, and I thought "Oh fuck, I've lost him already." So after that, I made a T-Shirt from the fax, and showed up the first day and gave it to him. What I learned was: had I made a plan, had we prepared for it, we would have had to throw the plan out the window, because the album's gonna go the way it's gonna go with them. You can make all the plans you want, but they're gonna hit the studio, and are just gonna take off from wherever they land. And if you have a plan, you have to waste time unlearning the plan, and then catching up to wherever they already are. You gotta be able to roll with it, and you may not come out with what you thought, but you're always gonna come out with something good.

To attain that end, Was employs a gorilla recording technique mentality and approach:

When I'm recording, I don't care how it happens to get that great take, by any means necessary. I use the Malcolm X method. Sometimes you get in a jam and the first time you solve the problem you do it on intuition and creativity—"I don't know how I'm going to get out of this," but you try this and try that, and eventually land on something. But the next time, if you go back and say "Well, this is what I did with Iggy Pop and it worked," where's the creativity in that? It's a recreation, and a different neurological response. Creativity is what makes music, not re-creativity, so that's the danger of falling back on experience.

Commenting next on his work with Iggy Pop on the *Brick by Brick* LP, Was's boundlessly open-minded recording style was put to the ultimate test by the singer simply because

he's a pretty uncategorizable cat. Every line's got a different personality, all of which are part of his outlook on life. He's a really interesting guy. With any artist, you try to get a point of view, you try to figure out what someone's point of view is, and then try to make that as clear as possible musically. Really, he reveals himself quite eloquently in the lyrics to the songs, and you can see the components that make up his psyche. That "I Wanna Be Your Dog," that's part of him, but he's also highly intellectual, and then the third part of him is he's a really sweet guy. He played with such enthusiasm, and such an exhilarated spirit that you can hear it on the tape. It went from lackluster to staggeringly powerful—Iggy's performance—in about fifteen seconds, and it was by the sheer constant energy of Kenny's personality as a player—totally altered the mood of the room 180 degrees musically, by fusing the thing with such positive energy. And all we had to do was go back and punch the first twenty seconds.

While Was is happy operating in the moment—whether in real time it translates to a handful of days or in the case of Bonnie Raitt, the span of a couple of years—he remains equally committed to traveling whatever distances are required to complete an artistic vision, explaining that in Raitt's case

for *Nick of Time,* I'd say we spent a year and a half doing demos at my house, with just her either playing piano or guitar and singing, with the idea that if a song didn't work with her alone—no matter what we did production-wise, or how many people we added, orchestras or whatever—it still wasn't going to work. So a song had to work with her alone, and then you could expand on that. I firmly believe that, and unfortunately you don't always have the opportunity to do that, so you gotta be able to roll with anything and be open to everything. There's an experience I had with Bonnie Raitt making *Nick of Time*, and repeated with her two subsequent albums we made together where hunting through songs was the largest part of making the record.

Once the right songs are in hand, producers across the board recommend next turning a focus to their vocal performance. In the course of collaborating with many of the most distinctively legendary vocalists in pop music, Was offered the following in terms of what he has learned about the craft, saying that the process

is very simple but yet it's very complex, getting a great vocal take. Does it touch you; do you feel anything from it? I don't care if a note's sharp or flat, or if a guy's yelling, but does it make you feel anything, and make you feel the right thing too? Does it sound like they mean it? It's all about emotion, and the story telling—that's what pop songs are, they're stories. Take Bob Dylan again, for one instance. He's an emotional singer; he's got the feel. It's irrelevant technically, because I don't think it makes a difference if it doesn't make you feel anything, and Bob Dylan has obviously aroused very strong feelings in people, and tapped a nerve. In working with Willie Nelson, I learned with him when we went back into the room after doing a take, I only really paid attention to his vocal, because when he got a great vocal, it meant the band was playing the right thing. It left him space in the right place, so if there were mistakes in the band track, they could always be fixed, but we'd choose the take based on the vocal, not whether we had the arrangement together. When he sang the shit out of it, that was the take, and then it was incumbent on me to correct whatever might have been wrong in the music track.

For the work he has done, Was has been acknowledged with the highest award the business has to offer to a record producer: the coveted Producer of the Year Award in 1994. Still, he seems reluctant to take credit for the results his collaborations produce, preferring to stick to his tried and true outlook that

the reward for producing records is in the moment, when you have one of these magical takes where everything works and just all falls into place—whether you've been struggling or a fresh take—when it really works and it's so good that you're moved by it, and get goose bumps and your hair stands up, that's the reward. That's what you make the records for. It's immediate, and you got to be part of that moment. It's right up there with raising kids and sex. That may be the most important thing we touch on all day, is that if you're doing it for some later reward, it doesn't make you whole. With winning a Producer's Grammy, here's what I've learned to do: you really have to define what success means. I think what you learn over the course of a lifetime is that your idea of success under the influence of testosterone pushes you in your twenties, and is quite different from what the truth of the matter is. Grammys were good for business, and turned me from a pariah into having a year and a half of top-notch artists lined up overnight to work with me because of that. And I'm grateful for that, I don't want to sound ungrateful, but what I'll tell you is when I won Grammy Award for Producer of the Year, in 1995 or 1996, it was the beginning of a really bad period in my life personally, which I think reflects professionally, because I didn't wake up and look in the mirror in the morning and go "I gotta win a Grammy," but in the back of your mind you know this is like the highest accolade you can get awarded. Well, it didn't mean anything to me, I was glad I didn't lose. That's what I remember, but there was no joy there I could grasp onto, there's nothing to grab onto because in the end, it's a golden trophy that people give you for something you did years before. So the real lesson there was: a little trophy, even if it's on national TV, doesn't make you whole. It's the shit that has almost nothing to do with music that can kill you, and if you allow your self-esteem to be determined by sales or trophies, you're fucked. When I look at my life overall, every dream I've ever had came true, I'm living well, and I'm not worried. I'm worried about the world, but I hope the world will as last as long as my bread does. It's been really great, and I'm doing only things I want to do now.

CHAPTER 12

Stephen Hague—The Prince Of Synth Pop

Dance pop owes its modern-day mainstream popularity to a wave of British synth-pop that swept Europe and then America in the mid-1980s, via superstar innovators like New Order, the Pet Shop Boys, Orchestral Manoeuvres in the Dark (OMD), and Erasure alongside the production genius of Stephen Hague, who recalled the roots of his own fascination with sound recording having come "from the time I was a teenager, a friend of mine had an old Roberts tape machine, and we used to push it backwards and that kind of stuff you do." Knowing he'd found his calling at the right time, but in the wrong place, Hague recalled that because "I'm from Maine originally, which is not exactly the land of opportunity, I bailed out of there pretty young and went to Los Angeles, and kind of fell in with some players. I was originally a guitar player, then switched over to bass and ended up with keyboards, and when I switched to keys, it was right when synths were starting to happen. Mini-Moog had been kicking around for a while, but Oberheim started making stuff, and the Yamaha CS80."

Hague's training in multi-instrumental performance would give him a rounded experience as a player that would later inform his process as a producer, whose own roots began to take hold, such that

> it clicked for me in L.A. and I started playing with some bands, went on the road with some people, and was doing quite a lot of studio work with a couple bands that were signed, and through that process, I found I loved to be in the studio, although starting out I didn't know anything about it. At the time, I was making a living as a player playing on demo sessions for songwriters or whatever work I could get, and as I assembled more and more bits of gear—one of the first things I got was one of those Tascam 3340 tape machines. When I started to make a little money—beyond paying the rent and car and stuff—I started to assemble little bits of recording equipment, I found a little place in Los Angeles, a couple of garages that I knocked together, set up and started to get a few mics together.

Taking a bigger and bigger interest in the art of record production, Hague found he was able to "start steering demo work to my studio. I did quite a few things for other people, just on, not things that were released necessarily, but where I would just take it to myself to play all of the instruments just because I could."

In looking back on how that he felt his role of musician aided him in that of producer, Hague shared that

> one thing that I brought forward into that part of the process from being a player is that I knew what it was like to be on the other side of the glass as they say, and you know, like how a player feels when he's sort of on the spot or if he's not playing too well or if he's having trouble getting something and now it's so freewheeling because so much, so much you can do after the fact, you can change the sounds, you can change the structure. You can make someone sound a lot more together than they actually played it if that's the choice you want to make. But back then when you recorded to analog tape, you know, you really, and this is something else that I suppose that's been, not lost, but has been changed by the technology today, is the performance, the on-the-day performance was of the utmost importance. And also you had to decide on the sound of the guitar, for instance, when you were doing the guitar. And if the guy was having trouble, and the other guys in the band were freaking out, that was all part of the deal. You couldn't just say, well, let's do five takes and I'll go home and sort it out, you know. It wasn't like that back then.

Reflecting a broad palette of influences that ranged from the psychedelic pop of the late '60s to the art rock sound of the early '70s, in turning to the ambient/synth side of that universe of influences Hague would bring into the studio with him as time went on and his signature production style firmed, he said that

> one influence that was really major for me that was going on for a couple years was instrumental music coming out of Germany via groups like Cluster, they did a collaboration with Brian Eno, and Brian Eno himself—his solo albums, and the instrumental solo album he did with Robert Fripp—who came out of that prog sensibility. There are a few other groups like that from around that time, as well as some synth people like Morton Subotnik, I was into quite a lot of instrumental music that, although I have a little bit of a taste for classical, really served as my classical music at the time. Just things where they didn't even want vocals—sometimes you hear instrumentals where it sounds like they just stopped writing the song at some point. But these things really just existed as little slabs of ambient entertainment, and you can listen to some of my work from later on like some of the stuff I did early on with both Pet Shop Boys and New Order.

As he began to craft his some of his production sound's fundamental sonic and stylistic tenets, Hague recalled being guided by his aforementioned heroes: "I was trying to emulate the sound and the vibe you get from records you really like, that's what I was doing at the time, even if it was subconscious. It all goes in on the stuff you like, you make your taste calls, and kind of choose sides about what types of music you find most engaging, and then you find yourself not necessarily wanting to make that sound, but certainly the sensibility from your tastes in records has a lot to do with the choices you make." Honing in on another key fundamental to his broader production style that solidified during this period, the producer added that "the biggest general thing that I think I took out of my love from a lot of those records—the three- and four-minute singles—was structure. What follows what, the A-B-C elements of pop records, and I always get this certain feeling when the payoff doesn't come at the right time, or the second verse is too long or too short. That's something I'm sure was ingrained from the stuff that I loved to listen to, and that's something that still serves me well today, even when I hear things on the radio."

One of Hauge's first big—and most groundbreaking and genre-shaping—breaks as a producer came via his work with OMD on their 1985 breakout *Crush*, which *Billboard* would report had succeeded via "the lightweight synthesizer pop of *Crush* in (representing) . . . a nearly complete reinvention of the band's original ideals, trading in the influence of Ultravox and Kraftwerk for the more contemporary fare offered up by The The, Howard Jones, et al." From a commercial standpoint, the move paid off, breaking the band into the U.S. Top 40 on the strength of singles like "So in Love" and "Secret." Ahead of that success, in the studio, the band was making a style of music the *New York*

Times would later hail as being "at its most adventurous . . . (sounding) both hearty and arty, two qualities that don't ordinarily go together." For Hague, that exper imental synthesizer-and-beat-based production and performance direction for the band was in part an extension of

> everyone was trying to figure out how to do something like that at that time. We were all listening to Kraftwerk, them being the forefathers of that genre, and one thing that a lot of people don't realize about a lot of records made at that time is that there was a lot of hand-played stuff going on, because it was almost impossible to get stuff to synch up together. It wasn't anything like today. There were free-standing sequencers that wouldn't really lock properly to anything else, drum machines weren't spitting out Midi-clock—this was *before* Midi for one thing.

Delving into some of the earliest synthesizers he utilized in creating what would become the synth-pop subgenre that followed, Hague recalled that

> on the record I did with OMD and on other stuff I did around that time—like the Pet Shop Boys' first album—I was using a bit of the Fairlight, and it was always very challenging because you'd have to print this oscillator tone on the multitrack, and then kind of tune it back into the Fairlight using an oscillator thing where you had to actually get the waves to line up on the grid. It was very hit and miss and things would drift like crazy. When Midi came along, that was exciting, but a lot of us were using it to link keyboards together and still hand-playing them. So when people did start to get their hands on drum machines in the early and mid-1980s, we were looking toward stuff to make people dance, and I think people were emulating some of that, like very, very simple things. Not that type of feel-type drummer playing, where there's a tasty fill going in here and a cymbal-crash there, it was all quite mechanical and we found it attractive and thought we were doing something you didn't hear every day. But it being a pop song, we thought it was all going to work out, because it wasn't like you were asking the listener to swallow some experimental piece of music on top of a slightly experimental approach to the production—they were pop songs.

Those foundational elements of Hague's production shined through the release of OMD's *Crush*, which CMJ would later rank ten in their "Top 20 Most-Played Albums of 1985." From a commercial standpoint, the move paid off, breaking the band into the U.S. Top 40 on the strength of singles like "So in Love" and "Secret." The producer—singled out by the latter publication for his decision to keep "the arrangements clean and simple"—

would years later count the album as among his personal high points, revealing that "the *Crush* album, that's one of my favorite albums that I worked on from that period, and there are definitely three or four things on there that speak directly to that influence. If you listen to the album *Crush*, it's one of those albums that is I think overlooked—not just because of my work on it, of course, although I like to think that had something to do with it—that record had some things on it that were a real signpost for the things that were going to happen over the next four or five years."

Riding the wave of newfound success he'd attained with OMD, Hague's next studio collaboration with the then-unknown Pet Shop Boys, a duo who the BBC reported "took their inspiration from the early '80s dance music emanating from New York, combining a very English sensibility with hi-NRG dimensions," creating in the process "a very brilliant pop thing" that made them "one of the finest pop acts of all time." Heading into the studio with the Pet Shop Boys, in spite of the latter critical conclusions, Hague said that, at the time, "We were all quite green. On that record, everyone chipped in, and if one of us could play something better than the others, we did it. If there was something that a member of the band felt comfortable playing or wanted to play, even if it took a bit longer, that was part of the process as well."

Breaking down what he felt the band member's principals—Chris Lowe and Neil Tennant—each brought to that process in the way of creative strengths, Hague said that Lowe "would kind of mess around a bit on synths, and was like an ideas guy, and Neil was the real melodic element, as far as top lines and stuff like that." While many of the band's songs were written in the studio during production, Hague recalled that on the future smash single "It's a Sin," "they had done some work on that with someone else, so I inherited a bit of stuff." Still, on the larger margins, Hague and the band were taking the British Pop movement in an entirely original direction, both in terms of the brand of new wave dance-pop they were creating and with the emerging wave of synthesizers, samplers, and drum machines they utilized in crafting that sound.

Delving into some of the specific gear utilized in the course of recording the band's debut LP, *Please*—instrumental soundscapes, according to *Alternative Press*, where "synths and drum machines form the perfect carpet for Neil Tennant's funny and intelligent lyrics to walk over"—Hague revealed that

> on "West End Girls" and a couple of other songs on that album, the entire backing track was created using just the Oberheim DX drum machine and Emulator II keyboard—in a lot of cases, just playing the factory samples. If we wanted to incorporate an outside sample, you could go through a very involved process burning stuff in, and at the time I

was doing bits of field recording and trying to put together some sounds I thought were interesting that weren't available on these fledgling sample libraries. We did some work on that album with the Fairlight [digital sampling synthesizer] as well.

By the time Hague and the Pet Shop Boys wrapped work on their debut, they had broken enough ground to inspire the BBC to conclude the album was "a textbook example of how brilliant a pop debut could be," while MTV— throwing a nod the producer's way—honed in on the LP's "evocative . . . production." Selling upwards of three million copies, the Pet Shop Boys' debut LP would break the band, and arguably the burgeoning synth-pop genre itself, in both Europe and the United States via radio smashes like "West End Girls" and "Opportunities (Let's Make Lots of Money)." Heading into his sophomore collaboration with the band on their follow-up, *Actually*, the next year in 1987, Hague and the group kept the hits coming with smashes like "It's a Sin" and "What Have I Done to Deserve This?"

For Hague, while many of the team's internal production fundamentals remained intact, by virtue of the still-experimental nature of the musical equipment they were utilizing to craft the band's songs, the process itself remained fluid, with the producer recalling that "on the Pet Shop Boys albums, everything is hand played except for the drum machines just running patterns—I never did any live drums. Once again, this was pre-Midi, so nothing was linked up." Through that ironically organic process of creating with musical machines like the aforementioned, Hague felt the group broke the greatest ground for the genre via "our use of that whole pad thing, me and the Pet Shop Boys I think made up that thing of like a drum machine with string pads." With 'Actually,' another multiplatinum worldwide smash, *Billboard* would conclude that the band had successfully "perfected their melodic, detached dance-pop. Where most of 'Please' was dominated by the beats, the rhythms on 'Actually' are part of a series of intricate arrangements that create a glamorous . . . backdrop for Neil Tennant's tales of isolation, boredom, money, and loneliness."

Turning the discussion to another key instrumental element the producer utilized heavily in the course of constructing synth-pop/new wave dance hits with groups like the Pet Shop Boys and New Order during this late '80s period, Hague recalled of his keyboard collection that

as far as the stuff I had at the time, I did a lot with the original BMI DX7, and I also liked some of the early Oberheim gear when Oberheim first went polyphonic. I had one of those early polyphonic synths, the Yamaha CS-80, which I still have actually, and I remember that thing was as big as a tank. I never owned a mini moog, but with

New Order, we always had one around and we would use that. I also used some of the early sample-playing keyboards, so as I mentioned, the Emulator II, that was a *big* favorite of mine for a while. I also had a Selena string machine, the Profit 5, and the Roland Jupiter 8.

Putting all of these pioneering pieces of equipment to work crafting the new material that rounded out New Order's first "Best Of" collection, the producer recalled that a certain magic momentum was at work creatively, such that "we were really lucky, because those first songs we did were both written, recorded, and mixed in ten days, so that was a very productive little stretch."

That productive stretch would continue with successes for Hague outside of the electronic music realm via his multiplatinum 1989 collaboration with groundbreaking post-punk new wave innovators Public Image Ltd., helmed by the already iconic former Sex Pistols front man John Lydon. An ideal teaming from the point of view that, as the *Los Angeles Times* attested, the group had "experimented with dance and electronic textures throughout its career," the production would give Hague the opportunity to go deeper into the realm of live band recording. Discussing the making of a record that *Billboard* would later argue was brilliantly "split between a modern rock record and a dance producer-derived one," Hague recalled that "PIL, a real proper band, with Bruce Smith on drums, who was a very, very good drummer, along with their guitar player, John McGeoch, who was excellent, a really top-notch guitar player, which made my life a lot easier."

In spite of his famously defiant public image, in the studio, the producer found that "Johnny was very much a professional," a disposition the producer reasoned was aided by the fact that "he seemed to trust me. So he really did kind of put himself in my hands, because he knew that they, the consensus in the band was that they really wanted to try to make a commercial record, you know. They'd had some success up to that point, but they wanted to have something like a hit, so he went on the assumption that I knew more about that than him. With PIL, we were also dealing with people who really play well together, and fill out a really good rhythm section." Hague was equally as excited about making the most musically of another of the band's unique instrumental talents—that of singer John Lydon's eclectically colorful vocal range—recalling that in the studio, "John was very cooperative, and it was really about him singing, just doing what he does. That part was quite easy, I remember, we just piled through some of the vocals where it was so much about attitude. In the case of 'Disappointed,' when he heard it finished, he loved it, then we took it back to London, and we put the girls on."

Throughout the last thirty years, Hague's catalog, along with the aforementioned superstars, would go on to include high-profile collaborations with a who's who of alternative rock icons, including Blur, Matthew Sweet, Siouxsie and the Banshees, Soft Cell, Robbie Robertson, k. d. lang, the Pogues, Erasure, Manic Street Preachers, James, the Pretenders, A-Ha, and the Jesus and Mary Chain among others. Offering sage words of closing advice where the heart of producing records is concerned, Hague shares that the process,

> for me, not as much of a thought process as it is a feel thing that you get—for instance, when you can tell you've settled into the right tempo for a track, or when you've finally found the right key for a singer to deliver a certain song in. To me, it's the same thing where I find myself not thinking about it, but instead just going "Okay, this is what should happen here." You don't really know why you think that, but then when you do it there, at least you try it out and immediately know whether it does or doesn't work. The bottom line for me is: I don't want to bore anybody.

CHAPTER 13

The sonic possibilities of psychedelia as a music genre were flirted with in the late 1960s, but it didn't truly come into full fruition as its own rock 'n' roll subgenre till the early 1970s via an aptly named band, Pink Floyd, via the groundbreaking *Dark Side of the Moon*. The album would stay on *Billboard*'s Top 200 Album Chart for seven years (or 566 weeks), selling over twenty-three million copies, and lay the musical rationale for what would become the most influential, brilliant, and musical odyssey the genre would ever experience. The band would achieve even greater heights with *The Wall*, their 1980 double-LP opus that was destined from its conceptual beginnings to define a new level of success for art rock commercially, selling fifty-five million albums around the world and inspiring a multigenerational psychedelic consciousness among music fans that spanned art rockers to fraternities. *The Wall* had something musically communal to offer everyone, finally making acid trips sensible through its brilliant musical imagination. *The Wall* was at its most basic a blueprint against which all past and future psychedelic rock would be measured as the '70s came to an end and the '80s dawned.

By the time Bob Ezrin came to produce *The Wall*, he already had a well-established track record producing multiplatinum rock smashes for many of the biggest rock icons of the 1970s, including theatrics-rock pioneer Alice Cooper (*Killer, School's Out,* and *Billion Dollar Babies*), Kiss (*Destroye*r), Peter Gabriel's self-titled debut, and Lou Reed (*Berlin*), and scores of others. In his collaboration with Reed, Ezrin perfected a mastery of skill as a psychologist that would serve him well in his later collaboration with Roger Waters during the making of *The Wall*. As for his prep work with Reed, Ezrin recalls frankly that, "I wouldn't call that lots of fun. That was more like being in a psychiatric ward. That was creatively inspiring, very, very challenging, such a stark project, that I can't say we had a lot of fun doing it. It certainly was soul filling." Ezrin's collaboration with Pink Floyd was one of which he recalled, "First of all, I went into boldly, as I went into everything at that stage of my life. I was too stupid to be nervous. I just sort of figured, I'd heard the material at the beginning of the album, I knew what they were capable of, and I figured that together we were going to do something really special. In fact, I already had a sense of how special it was going to be."

Ezrin's first job as producer on the project was to organize the maddening but brilliant world of Roger Waters's art-rock opera into a series of acts that would make sense outwardly to both the rest of the band and to fans. He definitely had the respect of both Roger Waters and Dave Gilmour going into the project, and as both knew this would be the band's, and in many ways history's, seminal political rock statement. Each musician had a well-placed appreciation—given their own notorious history of artistic feuding—for what they viewed as Ezrin's unique talent for uniting and transforming a band's internal artistic vision into a commercially palatable aural presentation. Above and beyond making studio sense of the band's musical, lyrical, and conceptual ideas, Ezrin also contributed his own artistry to the product as a musician, perhaps most profoundly in his decision to pair a theatrical, orchestral score alongside the band's experimental, art-rock style. Ezrin is largely credited with advancing Pink Floyd's *The Wall* as a concept from an album to a movie—though he had nothing to do with the production of the film—and made the transition conceivable by charting Waters's story line in a way that had a literally visual fabric.

This revelation, according to the producer, was the true catalyst for bringing the band members on board as a team to complete the record, as he explained:

In getting started working on *The Wall*, there was so much going on, including setting myself up with a place to stay in London, getting a car, finding a studio, figuring out all of my sort of personal needs in order to be able to be there to do this record, that I was distracted enough to not really need to worry. I just showed up, and the challenge began almost immediately. The call was for ten in the morning, and I was driving myself in London for almost the first time, and I had to find the studio, which because of its location wasn't easy if you knew where you were going, so I just got turned around, lost, and finally found parking, and was already in a pretty bad mood when I arrived at the studio on the first day. And I was jet lagged. So I got to the studio. As I'm going up the stairs toward the control room, I meet the rock engineering equivalent of Igor on the steps, coming down with his back bowed and his eyes glazed over, and he looks at me and says "Are you Ezrin?" And he says in an English accent, "They did this to me." And moved on. And so I walk into the control room, and you could already cut the atmosphere with a knife. It's already not feeling like a grand bunch of guys. it's definitely feeling like somebody's not happy about being there, or not happy about the way in which they're there. We were actually building the record as we were going. Roger had written a lot of material for this project, and he had a sense of direction, but the original writing was not what—a lot of it's on the record, but not all of it's on the record. And a lot of what's on the record was not yet written when we began the project. We actually had to find and grow that material during the project's preproduction.

Continuing with his recollection of the album's compositional evolution, Ezrin revealed:

The experimentation from pre-pro actually inspired some of the music, too. We would get together every day from ten till six in the studio, and at first, my plan was to get my hands around the material that already existed, and I started off with no real form in my head for the album. I simply knew this was going to be a double album. There was no way we were going to get all this stuff onto two sides of an LP, so I kinda knew that was not gonna happen. And I knew there was a thread, a story-like thread to the thing, but I wasn't comfortable with it yet. So I decided to get started by focusing on some of the technical stuff, some of the arrangement-oriented stuff, gaining their confidence as a band, creating relationships, while I was getting my head around the totality of the project. It didn't take too long before I had an epiphany one night, and I just sat down and saw the film in a sense. This is tough because I know there is a movie called *The Wall*, and I had nothing to do with that. In fact, I didn't agree that it should be done; I know so many people love it, but I think that in a certain way, it diminished the album, on a certain level, by removing the element of imagination. What I saw was the concept for an eyelid movie.

In elaborating on his process for charting out *The Wall* scene for scene, act for act, from start to finish, Ezrin continued:

I drew a movie out of this wonderful aural experience. I got a story line, and it just all made sense to me, and I wrote it down, like a script, like, literally, like a film script. Opening shot, cut to, the dialogue was whatever lyric we happened to have at the time for the songs, and the description of the action—instead of saying "Roger moves around the house, close up of him," it was, "start with spare, dry drums, and rolling bass line, pick up the bass"—it was a description of arrangement. That was my description of the action. And by reading it, you could have a pretty full understanding of what the album was going to be, except it had a lot of holes in it. There'd be a lot of places where I'd get to a certain spot in the story line, and we didn't have something that said what I thought needed to be said there, so it would be "to be written." So I wrote this whole script out, and it changed the sequence of things we already had, and eliminated the autobiographical element of it, because initially, it was about Roger Waters, and although there's still a lot of that in there, I wanted to take out the obvious, because I didn't think anybody really cared about—the kids at that time weren't going to care about an aging rock star. But they may care about every rock star, so if we worked to create an everyman, and the idea was—I'd heard that in a song before, "Which One's Pink," and I thought well, that's our guy, he's pink. He'll be our everyman, he'll be our gestalt rock star. And we'll build a story around him. It won't be specific to anyone; it'll be an amalgam of the rock stars we can think of. So anyway, I wrote the script and brought it in the next day, and I was just on fire when the idea came up, it so captured and ignited me, that I just started writing and writing and writing, and I didn't stop until it I'd typed the words *The End*, and I got it copied and bound, and put it into complete script form. And when the guys arrived, we had a table read, which is a real trip if you think about it. You're making a rock record, and the first thing you do is sit down and do a table read, but we did. We sat down and read through the script together, and I just asked for everybody's indulgence. "Just roll with me on this one for a minute, and if you all think I'm completely out of my mind, you can fire me." So we talked through the album and all the material, and at certain points, played songs in the order that they were coming up—rough, rough versions that we had—guitars, vocals, something we had already recorded in our first couple weeks messing about. And you could see it, you could feel it and see it, and you knew basically what the form of this thing was going to be. Everybody agreed, and we, the next day, launched into the process of crafting that thing we had all read. It made it so much easier to do; I think, in fact, it made it possible.

In the figurative context of a film set, Ezrin was acting as a director of sorts, with Waters and Gilmour playing the main characters, in a dynamic where the producer was able to continuously utilize the strengths of Waters's conceptual gift for lyrical genius in descriptive, character-tangible storytelling and song structure alongside Gilmour's gift for adding color and detail to those characters, and complex, melodically emotional atmosphere to the basic story line Waters had constructed. It was Gilmour and Waters's creative tug-of-war that gave *The Wall* its exponential number of innovations, most of which evolved out of compromises Ezrin brokered, which the guitarist confirmed in an interview with *Guitar* magazine. Gilmour explained, "Bob Ezrin was in there partly as a man in the middle to help smooth the flow between Roger and I, whose arguments were numerous and heated." Ezrin also fit in well with the band's musical culture because of his technical expertise, which was naturally required by the experimental nature of their studio recording process. With a firm hold on the creative and technical reins, Ezrin continued evolving the epic double-disc masterpiece by explaining some of the cutting-edge technologies and equipment required to even attempt what the album's musical challenges necessitated.

> I had to voice the control room, and get the speakers sounding better, and again, they just sort of flew with me, because I kind of sounded like I knew what I was doing. Their technical staff loved me, their technicians and guitar techs loved me, because I apparently understood their language. I brought in the concept of doing this on multiple machines, which is something Pink Floyd had never used before. In fact, not many were doing multimachine recording. And not only that, I wanted them to use a specific kind of tape machine. I wanted them to use a Transformulus Tape Machine and do my basic tracks on 16 tracks, so that I would get more tape coverage, more density of iron oxide, and consequently, better bottom end and more density to the sound. So we cut all the basic tracks to the sixteen tracks.

Recalling a production so intricate that, "we actually even scripted some of the many sound effects," the producer added:

> Then the plan was to experiment with different ways of making bombs fall. Some of the sound effects we made were after the fact, were not in the script, but were thought up once we—when constructing the scene—found an opportunity, or something not musical to advance the story line. But like the album's connective tissue, that baby bomb falling, breaking down the door, that sort of stuff was written into the script. Then all we had to do was figure out how to do it. That process worked through visualization. We never saw this album as anything other than a dramatic work, and that's important because I never said "heard." It had a story line, it had foreground action, it had background action, it had subscore—meaning, music underneath the action that was happening. That's how we saw this, which made it possible to pull off something like this. We didn't just write a bunch of songs, and figure out later how to get them all together. Doing it that way, doing it, kind of, extemporaneously, can be really magical, but can also be really awful, because you can end up with a bunch of stuff that just doesn't fit together. And you never sort of know. The thing about *Dark Side of the Moon* that made it such a magical work was that they were all in such a place, that was the sound—that album reflected the sound of them at that time—in

the world at that time. It captured London in the early '70s, the sound of an art band, and that pervaded the entire record. So everything about it had a similar character or quality; that's what made it come together so brilliantly. With *The Wall*, I think it was a little more deliberate, because by that time, they all were in a very different head space. Dave was not where Roger was, and vice versa, and London didn't have a sound. In fact, we didn't cut any of the final record in London, the rough versions, but then we went to France to make the record, and came out to L.A. to finish it off. So we didn't have those cultural or personality threads that would naturally knit the thing together. Because there were no boundaries, basically, we could do anything—anything we thought of, we found a way to do it. And we were very resourceful, and some of the things we did were really goofy. If you'd seen us, you'd be laughing. Some of the sounds, like "their fat, psychopathic wives beat them within an inch of their lives," and then you hear them getting smashed. That sound is so pointed and colorful, that was a cooking tin. In a live room, it just kind of made the noise we were looking for. As far as music effects, we already knew what we wanted to do, and I'd come up with a suggestion, when I had one, for something that they ought to do. But very often, when we were working on the music, Dave was already there sonically. He was already where his guitar needed to be, and it was just a matter of him playing with his toys to figure out what sounded like what he was hearing in his head. So, rarely did I have to go to Dave and make suggestions because he'd already be there.

While Roger Waters enjoys taking historical credit for *The Wall's* majesty, namely because of his central songwriting role, lead guitarist Dave Gilmour's role in translating and launching Waters's conceptual vision into the instrumentally experimental universe that Pink Floyd had long been known and celebrated for traveling cannot be understated during the album's recording. Bob Ezrin, for one, walked into the project with an established reverence for Gilmour's mastery of not only the guitar itself, but perhaps equally importantly in terms of the band's sound, the technical adornments designed to expand the possibilities of the instrument's ambient reaches. In elaborating on Gilmour's strengths as a musician, and in terms of his technical knowledge relative to the instrument's metallic amplitude, Ezrin boldly states that

Dave Gilmour is one of the best musicians I've ever worked with, and I've worked with some amazing people. Just great instinct, unbelievable musicality and sense of melody and sound; an amazing musician. In the course of recording *The Wall*, Gilmore was always experimenting, experimenting with new gear, different-sounding pedals, and a strange range of amplifiers, and different kinds of delays, and he has—he's very instinctive, and instinctively facile with new technical gear. As soon as you bring him a new piece of gear, he twiddles a few knobs, and he's got it. And he starts to make music making the sound he's created.

In terms of his relationship with the band's mad scientist, Roger Waters, Ezrin expressed a mix of admiration and what seems to be a sense of quiet liberation. Summing up the duo's artistically volatile yet brilliant partnership as one in which every battle was hard fought, and respect was well earned by the product their compromises produced, Ezrin explained that working with "Roger Waters was difficult and challenging, but he was the most exciting and inspiring collaborator I ever had." Validating the latter, Ezrin recalled a scene on the first day of recording for *The Wall*:

> I walk in the room at 10:45 or 11:00 a.m., or whatever it was, and the call had been for ten, Roger Waters stands there tapping his watch, and I flipped out. It had already been such a difficult morning; I'd had so many dramas just trying to get there and set up that that was the last straw of the morning. There's this guy standing there tapping his watch and looking at me like I'm some kind of recalcitrant child. So I pulled him outside into the hallway, and said, "Look, I already got a father, and he doesn't talk to me like that in public, so do me a favor—treat me with respect, or I'm out of here, now." He had dressed me down in the control room, too. And he settled down; it was sort of like testing me. But he settled down, and gave me a laugh and a smile, and we started working together right then and there, making decisions and changes, and bringing in new ideas.

To date, Ezrin considers Waters to be his true coproducer on the project, a dynamic that was often

> difficult, because he's so brilliant. So quick on his feet, so incredibly imaginative and creative. Never a minute where we sat around bored. Always blasting off ideas, firing off concepts. Dave played a key role musically in the making of the record, and James Guthrie played a key role in the sound of the record, and the other guys played key roles in the playing of the record, but really the concept behind the whole thing, the concept behind the show, which we created at exactly the same time as we created the record, by the way, was Roger's and mine. We worked really closely on that, visited the architects together, and looked at the illustrations and animations, worked on the bricks together, constructing the bricks out of the appropriate material so they would collapse down to a small space, and could be shipped, and that sort of stuff. And finally, when we had completed the first stage of album recording, before we went into final overdubs, and mixing in L.A., while we were still in the south of France, we

put up a table—Roger and I—and we did, with little men and little cutouts of the stage and the wall and all that other stuff, did a kind of dress rehearsal version of the show. That was really cool. We played the music and moved the little men around, and you could really see the show; it was just great. And that was such a thrilling thing, to be working with someone who thought in those terms.

As an artist, Ezrin holds an equal respect for Roger Waters, citing his particular brilliance for spontaneity by describing a particularly legendary skit from the album in which Waters yells,

"If you don't eat your meat, you can't have any pudding, how can you have any pudding if you can't eat your meat?!" That's completely Roger, yelling. I didn't write that in, because that's not something I ever would have thought of. Roger has a tremendous affinity for dialogue punctuation behind musical points. He's the guy who comes up with strange voices saying strange things in the background that refer to whatever's happening in the foreground, and he did a lot of that. He loves dialect, he loves to act. He's a good actor, and so that stuff came from him.

Of all the musical accomplishments of *The Wall*, Ezrin's personally finest moment, and arguably the album's, was the musically innovative and conceptually boundless achievement of "Comfortably Numb." It perfectly bottled the lightning that struck amid Gilmour and Waters's storm of electric, creative chemistry; the controversy produced an anthem that gave a new kind of light to the world of rock 'n' roll. Ezrin recalled highlights from the recording the song:

"Comfortably Numb" is my favorite song from *The Wall* for a variety of reasons. One of them being, Dave brought that music in with different lyrics. It's funny; I was looking for a song in D to fill that spot where we were telling the story of the breakdown, and Dave had written and brought "Comfortably Numb" in. When I got there, it had mostly been Roger songs, and I thought it was really important to have some input from the other guys because they were so important to the sound of the band in the past. Dave was the one who really stepped up with stuff. One of the things he presented was this great song—I can't even remember what it was originally called—with this fantastic chorus with a high-strung guitar, and just soaring melody, but no verse, and no real story line, and I said to Roger that I wanted him to take it and finish it, and he was really not happy. His whole thing was that it was his album; he was going to write it all; he didn't like the idea of including this other material. But to his credit, he came around, and I asked Roger if he'd write the lyrics, and at first, he was really snappy and not happy about this at all. But he took the challenge, went home, and maybe the next day came in with that unbelievable verse, and what I think may be the most interesting, literate lyric in rock history—"There is no pain, you are receding, a distant ship smoke on the horizon."

Outside the scope of the album in which his legacy will always be cast, *The Wall*, Ezrin has had a colorful and wildly successful, multiplatinum career producing many of the greatest rock anthems and musical moments the 1970s had to offer. In commenting on his experience working with some of the bands with whom he produced these moments, he offers a unique insight into the lighter side of his studio personality, in terms of bands like Kiss and Alice Cooper, whose music didn't require or reflect the conceptualism or experimentalism of Pink Floyd, Peter Gabriel, or Lou Reed. Ezrin had perhaps his most fun with Kiss in the course of making *Destroyer*. "It was like being at summer camp. In fact, I had a whistle, and I used to call them campers. We just had the greatest time. Funny, and hard working, maybe not the most accomplished musicians in the entire world, but what they didn't have in technical ability they certainly made up for in heart and dedication and hard work."

Summarizing Ezrin's legacy is like attempting to comment ultimately on a setting sun. It can't be conclusive because you know it's sure to rise again, and shine even brighter. Some of the jewels in Ezrin's production crown have arguably outshined the sun itself in terms of their influence over the varying subgenres of rock they helped to shape, or came to define outright, as well as over rock 'n' roll in a larger sense where they are, still today, among the brightest stars in rock 'n' roll's universe. With Ezrin's productions, he's traveled even further in terms of experimentalism, where he's charted and crossed an entire sonic solar system. Along with Brian Eno, he is arguably most responsible for inventing and sculpting the subgenre of art rock. Moreover, by helming production on the empire that *The Wall* became, Ezrin will always remain as timeless and legendary as the album itself. Perhaps the greatest beauty of *The Wall* is the fact that it draws no competitors, only admirers and proud imitators; much like a priceless portrait in a world-famous museum that millions travel the world over year after year, generation after generation, to see with their own eyes because of its ageless allure. Bob Ezrin's *Mona Lisa* is *The Wall*, and as listeners, we are her eternal votaries. Just as one could sit for hours staring in the latter metaphor, as rock fans, we sit for hours, generations listening to Ezrin's musical magnum opus, as we will for ages to come.

CHAPTER 14

Don Gehman—The FM Veteran

As the centerpiece to the rock radio-listening and record-buying demographic, the working-class rebel theme has always been prevalent in rock 'n' roll lyrical and visual imagery. Whether life was imitating art (i.e., the foreign styles of the rock artist becoming locally those of the artist's fans, i.e., Kiss makeup in the 1970s or alternative rock fans wearing black clothes and eye liner to imitate Robert Smith of the Cure in the 1980s) or art was imitating life (i.e., the singer capturing the day-to-day life of the small-town character he was depicting in song, as with Bruce Springsteen), the formula sold millions of records. During the 1980s, the working-class rebel theme—commonly embodied in a character named Johnny—was further exploited via movies like *All the Right Moves* starring Tom Cruise, *Young Blood* starring Rob Lowe and Patrick Swayze, *Footloose* starring Kevin Bacon, and *Reckless* starring Aidan Quinn and Daryl Hannah. The theme of small-town listlessness was depicted through the eyes of teens dreaming of something greater.

The soundtracks to these types of movies often featured thematically generic songs that suited specific scenes within the movie where that rebellion was acted out, but never songs that the "real" small-town teens those movies represented would be caught dead listening to in their own cars or clubs. The artists they identified with most were those like

Bruce Springsteen and John Mellencamp, who had walked in their shoes, and sung narratives that were like documentaries that mirrored their own lives and feelings rather than the fictional movies where everything worked out in the end. By the mid-1980s, Springsteen's *Born in the USA* had become the most authentic mainstream soundtrack to these listeners' lives that any popular rock artist had ever created. Springsteen was the Boss, and his only true competitor was Mellencamp, who spoke for the Midwestern heartland faction of Springsteen's larger working-class demographic. While Springsteen was already well-established by the time John Mellencamp finally broke out in 1982 with the release of *American Fool*, Mellencamp quickly became competitive with his smash hit "Jack and Diane," the first song to speak eloquently and accurately about small-town teenage life since Springsteen had ten years earlier with *Born to Run*.

Producer Don Gehman's collaboration with Mellencamp began in the late 1970s, with the future producer still an engineer, working alongside brothers Howard and Ron Albert on the singer's 1979 self-titled *John Cougar* LP, which produced his first radio hit, "I Need a Lover." Mellencamp was still in his infancy as a radio hit-maker, and while the breakout success of that single would put him on the FM map, 1980's "Night Dancing" and 1981's *Nothing Matters and What If It Did* performed underwhelmingly for the singer's label, so that by the time he reunited with Gehman to coproduce 1982's landmark *American Fool* LP, as far as the producer was concerned, "the record company had basically dropped us." The lack of label support ironically worked to the benefit of Mellencamp in terms of the rock sound he was trying to capture on *American Fool*, which Gehman recalled conceptually as a nightmare because

at that time, I was fooling around a lot with multimachine recording so I could save everything. It was a pretty scary idea, and was something the Bee Gees were playing around with a lot. We'd just finished doing two records with Barbra Streisand and then one with the Bee Gees where we'd had multiple 24-track recorders locked together, thousands of tracks. And I was trying to bring that technology into the Mellencamp thing, and was kind of coming up against a brick wall, because John really wanted to make a very simple record, modeled after a Credence Clearwater kind of thing. And I had just come to a place where we had absolute and total perfection in storing everything, and fixing everything, and timing everything—kind of what Pro Tools has become. But we were doing this in 1981, with pitch benders, so it didn't really work, and the whole album was kind of crippled by that as well because I was saving a lot of pieces, because I didn't know what we had. And it became kind of a chain around our necks. Eventually, we simplified the whole thing; once we had all the pieces, we put it all back onto one machine. But the *American Fool* record was immense. We made records later on, with *Uh Huh* on, that were extremely organized, and we knew what we were doing, did things quickly. But our method was developed during the *Ameri-*

can Fool album, and developed very much out of the fact that nothing was working. On that record, I think we made twenty-six songs, during that summer of 1981. The concept was: we were trying to do things all at once and finish it, and it didn't work because we didn't like anything we did, and the record company hated everything that we were doing, and wanted to fire me after turning in those songs.

After submitting an initial batch of tracks for consideration that Mercury Records rejected summarily, the duo perhaps felt they had nothing to lose, or maybe threw out every method they had been employing out of desperation. In either case, the recording sessions that followed in the fall of 1981 were a breakthrough both for the album's completion in the short term and for Mellencamp commercially in the broader scheme of his career. One key to that breakthrough came with the recording of "Hurts So Good," which Mellencamp seemed to write in response to the pressure from the label, along with "Jack and Diane," both of which became the album's hit singles. As Gehman recalled, "we came back about six months later, recorded 'Hurts So Good' in Los Angeles, with an engineer named George Tutco, who had worked with Rod Stewart, and also taught us a great bit about rock 'n' roll recording." Elaborating on the differences from previous sessions, as well as the effect those changes had in allowing the record and blueprint for future recording to conceptually gel, Gehman recalled that

> "Hurts So Good" was recorded in Los Angeles at Cherokee, and it was one of the first things Kenny Aronoff played on. In terms of the song's micing, in those days I used Shure microphones on the Snare, the 57 mic, and a lot of times we used the RE20 on the kick, we used 421s and 451s a lot for overheads on the toms. We'd gotten into this thing where we'd started to copy a lot of Shelly Atkinson's technique of double-micing things. He always put two microphones together to make the diaphragm size bigger. For instance, he would put a 451 and a 57, a dynamic and a condenser mic, put them right next to each other, both on the snare. The kick would be two microphones too, maybe a 47 on the outside of the head and the other inside, and then we'd move them around until we got the sound we wanted on the kick drum. We used 421s on the toms. For the guitar sound on that song, we used an SG for most of the song, and we ended up giving it away because it was too much of a pain in the ass to keep in tune. So then we moved to a Tele after that, pretty much universally.

In the groundbreaking case—both for the album commercially and in establishing the experimental and urban rhythmic foundation that would develop within the instrumental fabric of Mellencamp's larger sound in the years to come—the recording of "Jack and Diane" was one Gehman recalled as peculiar case, because we used both a drum machine called the LN2—it was one of the first models Lynn had built—and a live set of drums. I was trying to make one transition to the other for dynamics, and we had a great deal of difficulty coming up with a live drum sound. The room we were working in had just been built and was a brand new room, and was highly trapped, meaning it had no reverberation in it whatsoever. And I couldn't figure out why I couldn't get a good drum sound. It took me three months, and then finally David Bowie's guitar player—who was a friend of John's—came in one day, spent that one day with us, and turned us on our heads by showing us how to get a drum sound using some gated echoes. I'd never heard of that, and so we took the feed from the snare drum on the mic, gated it down to a little snap, turned it into a plate, gated the returns from that, and all of a sudden we got this huge slap. Up until then, we were trying microphones and mic positions, and compressing, and were getting nowhere with this horrible, thin sound.

Continuing, Gehman explained that

once we had the dynamic sound, we were able to make a huge entrance with the drums. So we'd had the first three minutes of the song pretty much figured out in a day, and then it took the rest of the summer to get the drum sound. John had heard this song called "In the Air Tonight," and had the idea to make the beginning of the song be real hypnotic, then have drums come with a huge entrance, and then rock out from there. So that's the thing we were trying to do, and we came up with the little drum machine pattern pretty quickly, printed it, and all the hooks were there and the verses, and a lot of colors. But then when I got to the bridge, we could never figure that out. It was a sonic problem in that we could never make it mean anything as far as the sound, and the other thing was we could never make it mean anything as far as the sound. The other thing is, we weren't quite sure what the part was. So it was just over and over trying it.

Describing the method by which he captured an acoustic guitar sound that would become the norm for Mellencamp records to come in how they were recorded and sonically presented to the listener—Gehman explained that

in the '70s, I'd been doing a lot of live mixing, and Stephen Stills was one of my clients. I was mixing live monitors for him at the time. And in 1974, he invited me to his Caribou Ranch to make a record, and I was there because I understood how everything worked—I had a good understanding of what a compressor did and what an equalizer was, but I had no idea what the medium of tape was all about, nor what making a record was all about, but I knew how to operate the gear, which was a foot in the door. In terms of what I learned from Stephen, he's the first guy who showed me there are ways of doing things that work, like for instance, how to get a great acoustic guitar sound. Basically, the idea that an acoustic guitar works really well when you put an 87 on it, then run it through a Pultec, then shave the bottom off of it with a big wide shelf that a Poltec has, then add a little bit of airy top with the 12 k, and you use the bandwidth to dial in how much of the pic you want, then run it through an 11-76 to touch it up, and make it sit in the track. You put that at 4-1 or 8-1, they're like settings, which Stephen gave to me and had learned from Bill Halverson, his previous record producer. At the studio where we were working at the time, he would show me how to patch it all together, what order things needed to happen, and then how it all needed to fit together to make a mix. He really did lay it all out in a very methodical way.

Incorporating the latter into Mellencamp's signature acoustic-electric blend in the course of "Jack and Diane," Gehman explained that

that spot in the song where that little "didididit" part that follows the electric guitar part, on acoustic where nothing else is played instrumentally with about eighteen zillion compressors on it, is what makes that sound the way it does. On that song and with all of my records, the acoustic guitar is not a picky little rhythm instrument that you kind of hear in the background. it's as close as you can get to an electric guitar as possible. We would mic things and compress them, and roll out bottoms, and push up middles, and pull out pick noise, until we could get the most sustain out of these things as you possibly could so that they could rock. And that they would be able to be heard against a full-on electric guitar. Most people don't do that;, most people want an acoustic to be a little bit of a feather. John and my guitars didn't do that; they had to be able to make time and hold up against it, and that had to do with the layers of compression, and pushing a lot of 500 cycles out of it, to really make the boxiness come through where the sustain is—with wood equality. Probably with every record I've ever done has been to try and make the most of those guitars. When you do that and add an electric guitar to it, this bristling thing starts to happen in the record—and with future Mellencamp records.

Once the duo had retuned the album's guitar sound, Gehman, describing some of the specific gear and playing styles, recalled that

we got into these Ampeg V7s that eventually became what we used for electric guitars. Mike Wanchic always had these 12 x 12 boogie amps that he used with his Strat, and that was his sound for a lot of the decade we worked together. Mike would play power chords, and that was about it, where Larry Crane was really the guy who would layer in most of the record. We had a technique that involved mix-ing acoustics and electrics together. The mixture of guitars is probably the sound that became what it is more than anything, and it was pretty evolved. Every song would have, usually, a set of stereo acoustics that came in in the chorus, and then played the whole way through the song. Then there was an electric that doubled op-posite, and those two things together became the core Mellencamp guitar sound. We were using 87s a lot for the low-end off the bottom for acoustics, and I really still employed the Stephen Stills technique in those days for recording acoustic guitars of using an 87 with a Poltec and an 1176. We did record to our mix very much, so we didn't pin it down flat; we processed a lot to get them toward a spot we wanted it to punch.

Addressing the album's ever-prominent drum sound, Gehman described a by-design approach that sonically suited

the relationship between John and everyone, which was always very confrontational—with everybody all the time. The Mellencamps are very much about in-your-face, which worked well for John professionally. Personally, Kenny and John had more of an employ-er-employee type of relationship—Kenny being more of the outsider than Mike and Larry were, not from the area, he was from the East Coast. So they were always very much in a competitive stance—certainly having fun a lot of the time—and as a studio drummer, Kenny Aronoff had this unending positive energy. He has incredible drive, and an obses-sive energy toward getting things the best they could possibly be.

Mellencamp and Aronoff's perfectionist approach to record making was thematically contagious throughout the sessions for *American Fool*, such that Gehman recalled:

I'd say that's what we all had in common was an extreme amount of almost obses-sive energy to be the absolute best, so consequently our record-making process was always about: "Can we get it better? Can we do ten more takes and get it better?" And everybody would be willing to do that, and then we would put that up against the idea that—in focus—we would want to have our record done in a day or two tops. So we'd come up with an arrangement, we'd track it for almost a whole day, get it really perfect with the drums and bass and maybe one guitar part. Then spend another day just layering lots of overdubs in, and at the end of that, we'd have pretty much what you heard.

Describing his approach to tracking Mellencamp's band, Gehman explained that "when we were tracking, lots of times it was just drums, bass and two guitars, that's the way we would track, and even sometimes we would cut it down to a trio, then do a guide vocal. Eventually, we did some experimenting to where we would use a click for maybe the first half of a song, and then let it go so it would have some excitement toward the end."

Concerning his approach to recording Mellencamp's lead vocals, Gehman explained that

from the very beginning, we found out the 67 was his mic, and we stuck with that for all the records I did. As I recall, we also used a combination of limiters, usually two, and we liked the Neve front end, though sometimes we'd use the Triton front end, and the LA2A along with the 1176. Generally speaking, we never did a lot of late-night stuff, because John would get up earlier in the morning, and had a more normal work ethic in the studio than some that I've worked with. I liked working in that 11–noon start time also because as soon as his throat opened up to record, we'd go till nine or ten at night. John did *not* like to have other people around while he was recording vocals. I'm sure he was insecure about being a studio singer, probably more so than he was pushing everyone else, and I would say he also realized that this was the name of the game: performance, which comes from confidence. In capturing vocals, my style has always been to let people perform, and I try to pick and choose what I like. On "Hurts So Good," we did a lot of comping, which involved six vocal tracks that I comped together, almost syllable by syllable. We had issues with tone and pitch, and I'm sure a lot of it had to do with the ability to work with headphones, which was always a problem. Also, the whole thing of trying to perform and push, and then keep your pitch center. And what we discovered was, for John, it was about confidence too, because by the time we got to "Pink Houses," it was one take from one end of the song to the other. So he became a great singer in the studio, and later on, our routine became he would do a couple takes, we'd talk about it, I'd put the best of it together, or we'd punch one in. If he hadn't done well, it was "Let's try that again," but generally speaking, "That's good enough" became our mantra because he had become that good. That became our approach to tracking John's vocals on all the subsequent albums we made together.

Upon completion, to the surprise of everyone involved, *American Fool* became one of the best-selling rock albums of 1982 and established John Mellencamp as both a radio and video star via the massive, generation-defining success of "Hurts So Good" and "Jack and Diane." Critically, *American Fool* was also the first solid nod Mellencamp had gotten from mainstream critics like *Rolling Stone*, who hailed Mellencamp's band as "an engine . . . (that) is a tight, unpretentious Indiana band, and Cougar, who produced *American Fool* with Gehman, seldom lets it idle. Guitarists Larry Crane and Mike Wanchic know how to raise a ruckus, and drummer Ken Aronoff is good at interrupting it with an authoritative thump." Based on this sonic blueprint for the massive series of successful collaborations that would follow, Gehman would proceed with the singer sitting at his side as copilot the entire way, in an arrangement as

coproducer, which was the only way John would do it. The thing that made all of John's records stand out from many others was the fact that John never wanted anything to happen in a record unless it was needed and unless you really felt it happen whenever it came in. So during mixes, he was always standing over our heads kicking us—literally—if, for instance, the guitars didn't come in loud enough at the top of "Hurts So Good." He'd be there saying "Come on, make them come in." And the way that all those pieces fit together is because we're moving faders around on the console like crazy, and that is not the norm for most mixes. Most mix engineers tend to try and make things carve together so that they sit with faders sitting still. We didn't do that—we made everything have a big fat sound, and then you'd turn it up into the bus compressors to make something happen on the guitars, then you'd turn up the drums, and then you bring in the vocal, then put in a guitar solo. And because we only had one guitar, one set of drums, and one vocal, you can do that, because it's about whatever's featured in that moment. And that is the Mellencamp formula, it became more sophisticated as we went on—but generally, everything is written, arranged, and produced so that one thing that matters happens now, and we move everything else out of the way. John was difficult to get along with—always has been. He pushes people to their limit, and sometimes didn't back off. So consequently the band was a group of really talented people with a leader that was just maniacal. He would be focused to the point where he'd have something of "this is what we're trying to beat." It was crazy-making, because you really can't compare records that much. Having said that, John is a very good taste master and an excellent entertainer as well, but he just has this gift of design where he understands how things fit together artistically.

Elaborating on what he felt are Mellencamp's strengths as a sonic visionary, Gehman explained that

he was an excellent arranger, and Steve Cropper produced the record before *American Fool*, and John credits him with being the guy who taught him how to arrange songs. Personality-wise, he always looked to me to be the responsible one. I was the guy who kept him from going off the rails. I'm a good planner, and he knew with me that the studio would work and that I would get things done—I'm reliable. Not that John isn't; he's very professional, but in the studio, he might come up with a wild idea, and I might try it for a second, then go, 'This is not working. I don't know what you're thinking, but we're going to have to try something else,' and he would listen. John didn't have a lot of patience; he's one of those people who will listen to something one or two times, and if it's not working, he'll go, "Next." I might by contrast say, "This is working, but we have to get it right. Go do something, come back and I'll have it done." So there was that kind of trust in our record-making process. What we wanted was to bring in something we didn't know how to do; he trusted me to go find that person. We have a very good personality blend: I'm very patient, and methodical, and focused, and John's passionate and impatient, and so the combination of the two are a good result.

Heading back into the studio the following year to record *Uh Huh*—whose sessions progressed much more swiftly (sixteen days) and with far greater organization than its predecessor—Gehman attributed the latter to

a routine we had developed from album to album that allowed us to repeat what we did where we all took a lot of notes, and were all very scientific about what we evaluated, in addition to using our gut. So Kenny became a professional drummer during that process. When we found him, he was a fusion-jazz drummer and couldn't play a rock beat if he tried. Over the first period he worked with John, John's technique was always to give people about fifty songs to learn that were kind of his palette for the album we were making. So the band would learn all those, and then we'd draw parts for "Under the Boardwalk" or "Five O'clock World" and would use that as a technique to pull our production out. I've never been a big fan of preproduction; I always found it was a good time to learn everyone's name, and also a good time to get a sense of who people were, and maybe figure out what they might be capable of doing musically. So consequently, all of my productions, I never did more of a day or two. Hootie was two days; we ran through all the songs, and I got a feel for what I could expect. John maybe did a little bit more for his records because he had his own studio that I built him, and everyone was on salary. So we could all get in together and hammer away at things.

One important technical difference from the first album to the second in terms of Mellencamp's signature acoustic guitar sound was Gehman's discovery of a new microphone: "From *Uh Huh* on, I had a specific mic I liked to use for acoustic guitars called a Frank Church mic, which was something specific for acoustic guitars, basically a 47 mic with its own electronics added—and built in 1955. There were about 500 of them made, and it's an incredible kind of condenser version of a Shure 57, not a very broad sound. Much more of a certain midrangey quality, and a tremendous amount of attack tone, which was good for the acoustic guitars. We used that from *Pink Houses* on."

Another adjustment in the duo's recording process on their second collaboration that would become permanent concerned Kenny Aronoff's drum sound, specifically the snare sound, with Gehman recalling that after "Hurts So Good," we got into the Rolling Stones type of snare-drum tuning. I had an old Ludwig student drum that I had found somewhere, it was aluminum and had an unusual kind of ring, "boink" thing to it whenever you'd hit it. So I brought it out to the studio, and we liked that ring, it was really obnoxious, and that became our snare sound. That is what the John Mellencamp-Kenny Aronoff sound is—the sound of a highly cranked-up, almost Jamaican-style snare drum that is tuned to ring too loud, and when you put that in a rock 'n' roll track, it just sounds unbelievable. That, combined with multiple echoes, where we would put three or four digital echoes on it, gate them all together, and make a real dense, kind of impact wooden sound after it.

Offering some insight into Mellencamp's growth as a songwriter between albums, Gehman explained that

after *American Fool,* John would come in with an acoustic guitar song, sometimes in the wrong key because he wrote it late at night, and play it for the band. And usually, even without me, he would start doing preproduction arrangement. And a lot of that was working with Larry Crane and finding a guitar riff, or a certain kind of motif for the song John was working for. A lot of that was worked out before we got in the studio, and invariably it changed a great deal once we got in, but John would have a pretty good familiarity with how he was going to make it into a record before we even got started. Then once we were in the studio, it would take off and take on a life of its own. John would come in with a pile of songs, and we knew which ones were our singles pretty much always going in, and would make attention toward that. He was always focused enough in his songwriting to know which stuff had everything it needed and which required special attention toward radio. Then other things he would feel functioned more to speak to what he was all about or what he believed, and he was always more concerned about what he was saying than anything else. The writing process I pretty much left alone to him and George Greene, and generally speaking, I always felt like what he was saying was amazing. That was never an issue; if I had anything that I was questioning, it was whether or not it was really a hit, or whether we went too far on something, or didn't do a good enough job yet.

Commenting on the band's overall improvement in efficiency and creative direction, Gehman felt in hindsight that "the first year making *American Fool,* we were lucky we made it though, but by the time we got to *Pink Houses*, we had figured it out. We'd also figured out how to manipulate it, and move it every record. *Un Huh* was the last record that we did the 'Hurts So Good' format, and when we changed the production style up, people didn't realize we were still using the two guitars, bass, and drums format." Mellencamp and Gehman's third collaboration, *Scarecrow*, would mark a departure from their past two electro-acoustic-dominant collaborations in that, as the producer explained,

> we'd electrified so much, that everything went to ten, and all of the sounds became much denser. It was probably the most rocked-out album we ever made." Another change in sonic direction, according to Gehman, was the albums being "more highly produced than the first two John and I had made together. That seemed the next logical place to go, because we'd figured out how to capture our sound, and I was always into more highly produced product. The more simple thing was always John's idea, and the engineer we were working with had worked on a lot of stuff with Shelly Yakus and was accustomed to more pieces as well.

Mellencamp had by now commissioned Gehman to build the singer his own signature studio near home in Belmont, Indiana. In describing its design, the producer explained that

> during that era, we were working with an engineer, Greg Edwards, who had worked a lot with Shelly Yakus and Jimmy Iovine, as well as David Thoener, an engineer who had built a studio in L.A. called Rumbo, which had a room in it I really liked: it was a simple design, and the control room made a lot of sense to me, had the same kind of console. So we got together with an architect who was building a house for John around the same time and drew up plans for a simple add-on to a little place out in the woods John had bought, on five acres of land, near his home in Indiana. I basically designed my own recording space, because in line with the "Mellencamp sound," I knew we were looking for a really garagey drum sound. Literally, the two-car garage size is a great drum size; it's 25 x 25 by some ceiling height that in this case was pretty high, a 12 or 14 foot average. But we did it all with dry-wall, a very simple design, and then broke it up with some diffusion—we had different shapes going around so that I think I had five sides to the room. It wasn't a square room when we were done, I tacked booths onto the corners. I wanted a lot of ISO booths so I could put the guitars one place, the vocal in another, the drums in another, the bass in another, so I built all those containment places with air-locked windows that allowed all the band members to see each other. We built the whole thing for under $100,000 which is less than we spent on an album at another studio.

The creative freedom the studio's price included paid for itself a million times over in Gehman's estimation, first and foremost by the fact that Mellencamp's band could spend as much time as they had rehearsing and refining their sound for the album without worrying about the cost of studio time. As the producer explained,

I built the studio for him in 1984, and by that time we had a small group which was two guitar players, the bass and drums, and maybe the engineer—and those guys were always around. They may have been outside playing basketball or watching TV, but were in and out of the control room. Our process of making records was always inclusive of everyone, and when we were done, we were all very proud of the results. We were totally aware by then of what actually made the sound for everything, so we bought all the pieces we needed to do a good snare chain, a good guitar chain, a good bass chain, a good vocal chain—and wired them all together through a relatively inexpensive Triton board.

Addressing the setup for Kenny Aronoff's drum sound on *Scarecrow* and future albums, Gehman recalled that

for the mic setup in the studio where drums were concerned, we had a D-12 mic for the kick drum that we were using by then, and we had a 47 set out in front of the kick drum. Then sometimes we'd build a tunnel out in front of the kick drum with another shelf that allows it to isolate the kick energy to the microphone. Then 421s on toms, 451 AKGs on the hi-hat and snare as well, and AKG 412s on overheads, although the overheads changed a lot. We also had some M-49s that we used for room mics that were kind of at waist level. They are very warm, which is what you're looking for in room energy, you want to get a lot of fusion and impact out of the room tone. They're not too trashy, and we kept them low so we got more drums and less cymbals. They weren't more than probably twelve feet away from the snare drums. I think we used nine tracks to record Kenny's drums—kick, snare, hi-hat, toms—and we had overheads and rooms separate. That was the same setup for both *Scarecrow* and *The Lonesome Jubilee*.

In discussing the album's electric-guitar-dominant sound, Gehman explained that

Scarecrow was the full-on Telecaster, electric-acoustic thing, and we'd converted to this D7 Ampeg amp with a 112 in it. The whole thing with electric guitars in making records is if you have a lot of parts, the distortion part of the guitar tone kind of multiplies; it gets fuzzier the more tracks that you put together. So if you've got a really trashed-out, heavy power chord, and you try to put another one on top of it, invariably the power chord obliterates everything. So the whole trick is getting these guitars to have a sound that has some sustain and some character, but if it gets distorted, you can't put a lot of parts together—countermelodies, chords, picking, et cetera—they just all kind of mumble up. Well, the thing that was cool about the Ampeg amp was the way it focused this particular Tele sound in a way that we could stack up six or eight guitar tracks, and they would all maintain some integrity where you could tell what was going on in the song. Usually, we had about eight guitar tracks—that was typical. We might have had a stereo pair of acoustics, either that played throughout or in sections. We did a lot of things that were sectional, where we'd have a set of tracks that maybe played in verses and the bridge, perhaps the solo, then another set of tracks that were just in the chorus. Then you might have some arpeggios or power-chord stuff that would come in on the chorus, just in addition. So we did a lot of stuff where we would have scene changes between choruses and verses, or B-verses to chorus, and we did that by literally turning the guitars off in those sections. Or he would only play those parts, so that you'd have things disappear and you'd go to a totally new guitar sound in the chorus, and that tone would come in and make a big difference. It also made it easier to mix because you could just turn those up in the chorus and they would come slamming in, so you didn't have to worry about making them move. We usually used a 57 and 67 mic on that amp, right next to each other, and we'd move them around till we got what we were looking for. On acoustics, for that album, we used the Frank Church mic and mainly Takamine guitars. John didn't play guitar on anything at all. He's not a great guitar player; he knew enough chords to write a song and that was it. Even playing the song for somebody, it was rudimentary at best. He's become a much better guitar player over the years, but back then, Larry Crane really was the unsung hero of all those records. He's just an amazing rhythm guitar player, probably one of the finest I've ever worked with. Larry and John were like brothers; they had grown up together in Indiana, and Larry was like the Keith Richards of that band. Not the writer perhaps that Keith Richards was in that team, but nevertheless, the sound that we know John Mellencamp for is about guitars, and that came from Larry Crane.

Upon completion of principal tracking, Gehman recalled that the album's smooth recording sails lost their wind momentarily when it came to

settling on a final track listing, because as always, it was a process of weeding out. Usually, we over-recorded quite a bit, and the process of figuring out which songs stayed and which went was normally one of going back and forth over stuff that I liked that he didn't want to keep. John had a pop side to him that I liked that he didn't, and I'd say "R.O.C.K. in the U.S.A." was a good example of one that we almost threw away that I thought was amazing and everyone in the band hated. Eventually, we all agreed to put it on in the very end, but there were others like that that were pop songs he didn't really want on his records. That's what gave him his credibility—the fact that he didn't do too much of that.

With a final track listing that would include smash-hit singles like "Smalltown," "Lonely Ole Night," "Rain on the Scarecrow," and "R.O.C.K. in the U.S.A.," Gehman and Mellencamp headed into mixing, which he explained was

the first album done at the completed Belmont Mall studio in Indiana, and it took us a long time to get our bearings, so consequently what we wound up with when we mixed was three engineers that were all probably capable of doing the job on their own, all mixing together. So it was a pain in the ass, but it was a very good result obviously, but I probably mixed that record four times. The whole trick with mixing a record is to try and make something fit together with musical frequencies and compression that gets you the illusion that things have a lot of space and power. We labored the most over the orchestration of the people working together—because we kept on ripping it down and starting over again. Add to that the fact that John was there the entire time. We had a lot of trouble—some of it was understanding what the room actually sounded like, because mixing is always a perception of what you're hearing. And it might be what you want to hear, but also involves a discipline of understanding what you're actually getting—aside from what you're hearing. It requires a lot of comparative listening, and people who aren't skilled at mixing listen on face value and can only comment on that, and that's what would happen in our dynamic all the time. John would listen and say "I don't like the way that sounds." And then I would say "Well, if you listen where I am in this spot in the room, and then imagine how loud the guitar is in relation to the snare drum, it's actually very loud. You want it to be louder, and that would be ridiculous." So you'd have to then get into this educational process of size and relative position within the field, and it's extremely complicated. But he trusted me enough to know that when I would dig my heels in, he needed to get himself out of the room until I got what I wanted. And invariably, when I was happy, he would be happy as well. We were both pretty stubborn and strong personalities, and we'd had enough success by then that he trusted me to where we were never at each other's throats.

Scarecrow, released in 1985, would become Mellencamp's most demographically defining collection in terms of its lyrical focus on the everyday lives and struggles of the American farmer, and by the time Mellencamp and Gehman began preproduction for *The Lonesome Jubilee* near the end of 1986, Gehman recalled that Mellencamp was gearing up for another stylistic evolution: "John was looking for a new sound—as always, and every record was a new place he was trying to shift to." Aiding Mellencamp's ambition, the producer recalled that "we had a different engineer that was involved in the mixing, which was a big style difference. Invariably, all these records were coengineered amongst a group of people, and I would be the common thread, but every record we made we would reinvent. Some of that would be accomplished by bringing in new blood." Ahead of production beginning, Mellencamp had also added new instrumentation to the band in the form of a violinist and saxophonist, which naturally worked to alter the band's sound. According to Gehman, out of these additions, Mellencamp had discovered what would become a thematic musical presence in the instrumental textures of *The Lonesome Jubilee,* such that "by playing around with having a fiddle on the record, he had added Lisa Germano on violin and someone else in the band was playing sax, and somewhere along the line the squeeze box idea came out. I think what happened was, at one point, John had asked Lisa to come up with a melody for 'Check It Out,' and asked John Cascella to double on an accordion. And when he heard those two things together, he thought he had found something unique."

In spite of the instrumental additions and alterations to the band's sound, Gehman relied on some of his most tried-and-true tricks in the course of capturing that sound on tape, beginning with

> that Frank Church mic, which I used on the violin, and on a lot of things on *The Lone-some Jubilee,* for percussion, backgrounds, acoustic guitars. It was kind of a utility chain we had set up with a Neve front end and an LA2A compressor, and it was kind of the thing that sat out in the room we recorded a lot of things with. The process by which we tracked that record was once again, as a trio, and then we layered it up. The arrangements of those songs had been evolved quite a bit further than some, where they were played as a band before we started recording. Then in the studio, we refined them, but generally speaking, people knew when they came in. We had a living room at the studio where everyone kind of hung out, and got called in to put the part on, as we worked our way layering up. Then we would make changes as needed, but essentially it was all done piece by piece.

Another addition to the record that Gehman felt helped it evolve musically was Mellencamp's own maturity as a songwriter: "John wrote this group of songs that were more adult than any he had ever done before. More emotionally aware, more socially aware, and that's why that album thematically has that sound." Still, in spite of the serious tone of the songs Mellencamp had written for the album, his approach to recording them vocally was as laid-back as ever. According to Gehman, "Vocally he had become an accomplished singer, so by the time of *The Lonesome Jubilee* we never worked on vocals. For that album, he would spend all of a half hour on his vocals, where he'd go into the booth, sing it once or twice, I would put it together, and that would be it. If he didn't like it, he'd go out and work on it again, but most times, he'd lay down a first take designed to be a guide vocal for the band, and it would turn into a master half the time."

Where Mellencamp did focus his time and attention vocally on *The Lonesome Jubilee* was with background vocal arrangements. As Gehman recalled,

> A lot of times it was because we would lock so many things to it, like background arrangements, which became more and more the norm—piles of background vocals, and events where Pat would sing on this line, and Crystal would sing on that one. We had always used background vocals, and as we got more accomplished, we used them more for color more, obviously, and as events, and less as just background vocals. By "event" I mean if you listen to any of the songs on the album, the background vocals don't always just double what the lead's doing; they have an event happening all on their own. It might be an "Oh yeah," or whatever, but they reflect more what the lead vocal is talking about. We would talk ahead of time about what we wanted to go there in the way of a background part, and John would write something, and tell them to go out there and "pretend you're the Stones."

The Lonesome Jubilee reflected leaps in maturity both musically terms of the sophisticated arrangements and topically in terms of the lyrical subject matter, which now had evolved to represent the entire country's downtrodden. Critics clearly felt Mellencamp had come full circle in his sound and message, refining the two down to a science in terms of commerciality on *The Lonesome Jubilee,* with *Rolling Stone* hailing the singer's "complex, moving new album."

Commenting on the financial considerations of making a living as an engineer/producer in the millennium age of recording, Gehman advises striking a balance between art and commerce. In closing, he says,

> I've always tried to focus on recording what the artist is, or what I think the best vision of that artist would be, and because I never had much luck doing things that I wanted to do, I always had to kind of do what came my way, it was all over the map. And I think that's part of the reason I'm still here. I'm working on country records now, which is never where I thought I'd be. So if you focus only on one genre, you might get stuck into that one corner, and never be able to get yourself out if the commercial tides turn against you. It's always good to try and work with people who you enjoy being with, but be open to anything.

CHAPTER 15

Tom Werman–Girls, Girls, Girls

For any hard-rock fan growing up in the late 1970s or throughout the 1980s, the sound architect who produced many of the biggest hard-rock and metal acts of the era, including Ted Nugent, Mötley Crüe, Molly Hatchet, Twisted Sister, Poison, and Cheap Trick, is Mr. Tom Werman. In a dual role shaping the era's rock sound, Werman, as vice president of A&R, was responsible for discovering and/or signing many of the biggest selling hard-rock acts on Sony's roster in the 1970s, including Boston, Ted Nugent, Cheap Trick, and REO Speedwagon. Back in Werman's heyday, A&R, as he wistfully recalls, was based more on a gut instinct than anything else: "There is very little in common when you compare A&R in the '70s to A&R in 2002 . . . When I was doing it, it really was more based on instinct—you could actually afford to sign a band that you liked, as long as you had a vision for that band."

Werman's foot in the door as a producer came via his discovery as an A&R man of Ted Nugent, where Werman was given the reins over the production of his new signing's debut album. This was virtually unheard of in the 1970s, with the producer recalling that

the actual transition from A&R man to producer came because I had started doing all the edits for singles for Epic Records. They always talked about what cut they liked, and they'd give it to me, everything from the O'Jays, to the Hollies, to Argent, to Harold Melvin, I did all the associated labels. And by doing edits, and by taking seven- or eight-minute songs and making them like 2:50, I learned about the internal structure of songs, and producing in ways, because I had to listen to see where I could go in and out. Sometimes I would think an edit was going to work that I'd find I was cutting in a place where going into it, the guy was on the hi-hat, and going out of it, the guy was on the ride cymbal. So I said, "Wow, he's playing a different cymbal." I began to understand arranging. So from that I determined that I could probably produce records as well as some of these people. And that's pretty arrogant, but it was true in time.

From his success with Nugent, Werman recalled growing naturally into the role of producer:

I kind of just backed into it, with Ted Nugent. He was the first artist I produced. I kind of just muscled my way into the control room. And sat down, and was present for the making of the record. And then, when I was busy for the mix somehow, someone else mixed the record, and I didn't like it at all. So I went down to Atlanta, and went back there, and remixed the album with the engineer. And I had asked Steve at Epic Records for like $7,000 more to mix the album, and he had agreed. And what we came up with was the Ted Nugent album with "Stranglehold" on it. And all of a sudden I was a big hero, immediately. I went from goat to hero, from $18,000 a year to $260,000 a year; they decided to give me a nickel a record. And we sold so many records, that I made a lot of money, so I was very happy about that.

Werman's lucky streak would continue with his next signing, Cheap Trick, which also extended his pattern—a first for the industry at the time—of an A&R man also acting as producer for his band's records. Werman's time in the studio with Cheap Trick he views in hindsight as a truly inspired one, and perhaps his most satisfying as a producer.

I never had as much fun when I worked in the studio as I did with Cheap Trick; it was like a vacation. It was fantastic. Because we would get so much done in one day, like the hardest thing that I had to face doing a Cheap Trick record was helping them try to finish a song. Because they would show up with song fragments, and we'd use a chorus from one song and a verse from another to create a song in the studio. Or to get Rick to play more serious guitar solos, because he was so intent on being zany, and I think that's because he didn't want to go into the same ring with serious guitarists. But we just had a ball, made their records in four or five weeks, start to finish, no problems. I'd do two, three songs a day with Robin. Bun E. Carlos was the best drummer I worked with in my life. It was phenomenal, the bass playing, I mean everything about it, the songs. That was it, Cheap Trick was the best, and *Heaven Tonight* was the best production job I think I ever did for an entire album.

By the turn of the decade as the 1980s dawned, Werman had become such a master at the craft of transforming hard-rock bands into commercial crossover giants without compromising their integrity with fans that he became typecast as such. In the rise of L.A.-based heavy metal's tidal wave, the producer would continue to surf this surge in trend throughout the 1980s, creating a pop-metal FM radio sound that would define the genre. Where style took priority over substance, Werman did his best to focus on commerciality while respecting whatever artistic vision the bands might have had, along with whatever musical integrity they had mustered with fans. In the case of Mötley Crüe—the band largely credited with founding pop metal in the very early 1980s—where partying was a focal point of the band's sound, style, image, and lifestyle, Werman adopted something of an if-you-can't-beat-'em-join-'em approach in the studio, coupled with good, ole-fashioned record producing to get the job done. As Werman explained,

> Mötley Crüe was the messiest rock band I'd worked with at that time, the band who substituted attitude for musicianship the most. There weren't that many new things I did with them—there were a small group of tried-and-true successful approaches that I brought to that session from other sessions that I had done before that, where I went, "Well, this will work, this will work." It was "Mick, double this guitar, and Tommy, I want you to do this fill. And Mick, when I work with you on the solo." Mick would write the solo to a certain point, and I would help him bring it home. And I think it was just all-around general production approach that helped that album. If you'd really let them run away with it—I tried to clean it up, neaten it up. I tried to make the sound sharp and focused. I always thought *Shout at the Devil* was a very dirty-sounding album, and that's what its appeal is. I didn't do that on purpose. I would have made it cleaner if I could have. It was an accident, a combination accident that was probably foreseen by Tom Zutaut, who said, "You would be the perfect producer for this band."

Ironically, where Werman had been excited by most of the previous bands he'd collaborated with, when he stepped foot in the studio with Mötley Crüe, it was arguably his first real day at work. According to Werman:

> I wasn't that excited about Mötley Crüe, when I heard the Leathur Records *Too Fast for Love*, I said, "Boy, this sure isn't my cup of tea." So you can hear the difference, but I didn't think, again, that—I thought Mötley Crüe arrived sonically with *Girls, Girls,*

Girls, that's always where I wanted to hear them. It would get serious sometimes; Tommy was very serious in the studio, they all were. But they all weren't. In other words, when they were in the studio, they were as serious as they ever were, anywhere. But, it's how they arrived at the studio—sometimes they were high, sometimes they were hungover. Sometimes they were about to get hungover, or about to get high. But they all did take their music seriously, even Vince. But he would come in, and do anything we asked him to do—I would keep him in front of the mic for three hours straight—and he would put out 100 percent. The problem was, he could have been completely trashed the night before. So, he would never take it seriously outside the studio. He'd say, "Okay, that's it for the studio, let's party." And he would go party all night long, and he would show up all night, and he would try, but wouldn't go, "Well shit, I've got to go to the studio and sing tomorrow, I'm going to take very good care of myself, and go to bed." So in a very real way, their lifestyle showed up in the music, on the tapes. Absolutely, yes.

Considering the legendary reputation of Mötley Crüe's excesses, Werman managed to pull off the impossible, by pulling three multiplatinum—and in the context of the genre, groundbreaking—albums with the band that led the pack in terms of debauchery. Ironically, partying was so fundamentally embedded in Mötley Crüe's musical psyche that Werman chose to accept it and work with it, almost to the point where the band were at times functioning addicts.

With Motley, the drugs and boozing and partying didn't really get in the way of recording. Motley would not nod out, they would not come in and lie down and go to sleep, they would not slur their words. They were okay. I mean, I actually had to be informed that they were shooting up. I never noticed it with Tommy, ever. I just noticed it with Nikki. There was really no adapting, because Mötley Crüe was probably more reasonable on heroin than they were when they drank. Because then they weren't rowdy. There were no activities; it's just that they would get a little noisy, and you had to ask people to step outside if they wanted to talk, or tell them to shut up. Things only became messy with *Theatre of Pain*, because Nikki's smack addiction was *way* out of control, which was not good because Sixx was the creative core of that band. He was the creative director where I wasn't. Nikki would do things that were very strange, that didn't have any reason. I remember, there was one song, a ballad, where Nikki came in with a set of lyrics and said, "Here are the lyrics to this song." And I said, "Wait a minute, we finished this song." And he said, "No we didn't, here are the lyrics." And he wrote completely new lyrics, never mentioned anything. I think we'd done the final vocal. And that was when I turned to my engineer, and said, "What's the deal with these guys . . ." And he said, "Dude, he's a junkie!" But I have to hand it to them, they handled it really well. Nikki was a good junkie, he was a practiced junkie. And I later realized that I had spent time with Nikki and Vanity at Nikki's house when they were both shooting up, but I didn't see them. I just knew they were doing something.

By the time of *Girls, Girls, Girls*, Mötley Crüe as musicians had graduated to a level where, even amid their drug-and-booze-induced haze, they were able to create what Werman to this day considers an extremely innovative and groundbreaking album given what the genre had produced up to that point, 1986. This achievement was due in large part to some of the technical innovations that had evolved out of the early 1980s, which gave Werman more room to experiment with the natural limitations of the genre's soundscape.

I think overall the whole hair metal scene necessitated an advancement in technology. I mean, just to put it in context, I had redone all of Lita Ford's vocals on her album using a pitch wheel on a keyboard. Real-time pitch changing, because Lita had a problem with earphones, and could never sing on key when she used earphones. So I had to fix every line, throughout the entire album, I used to come in two or three hours every morning and change that. So we welcomed the newer technologies that became available in the studio given what we had to work with musician wise at the time. That's not something that people think about very often when they consider what the genre lacked in terms of musical substance. Producers saw that firsthand, and really many times gave those records any substance they did have through old-fashioned skill, and sometimes via technical innovations. I think it would have been a much more musically respected generation of rock 'n' roll had we had the assistance of Pro Tools and digital technology. Back then, we worked with what we had available and hoped for the best.

Where technological advances were available, they additionally allowed Werman an easier time in the physical process of recording, so that with the tight deadlines bands had for turning albums in, he could speed up some of the more monotonous and meticulous parts of the process, like comping drum parts. On top of that, because the members of the band had become better players and were accustomed to Werman's production style, they were able to cover more creative ground with the *Girls* record than they'd been able to with previous albums. It would be the band and Werman's greatest and most commercial collaboration up to that time, and their last as a team.

On the *Girls, Girls, Girls* album, first of all, Tommy was doing some really great drum work then with triggers, loops, and things. He had electronic gizmos that he was getting into. Nikki could play the bass by then; he was an accomplished bass player by then, which made things go much more quickly. So it left more time for creative overdubbing. And Mick had a great guitar sound, and a great guitar tech, so the band sounded good. And by the time you're working with a band on their third album, you know them very well, and you know what their weaknesses are, and you can tend to avoid most of them. You don't make mistakes, you don't get into holes. And, I don't know, everything seemed to work really well. There were three or four really good singles, and that's all you needed. "Girls, Girls, Girls" was obviously going to be their biggest hit single to date, and then "Wild Side" was a fantastic, indulgent, sonically wonderful FM cut, which you knew would never be a single. So we fucked around, did some great things with it. Man that was good. I just thought "Wild Side" was one of the best things they ever did. And for the "Girls, Girls, Girls" single, I thought it would be a good idea to get a Harley on the record somewhere, because Harleys were so big in the band, they all had them. And they would ride them to work, and so I decided to put a Harley rhythmically in the front. Which we did in the courtyard of Conway Studios. We brought the mics outside, and I got on it and played it. And since it was on the front, I figured we would take somebody else's Harley and put it on the end. So we went up to Franklin Canyon with a stereo mic, and I drove Vince's Harley back and forth, shifting as quickly as I could. And it turned out to be a great attention-getter, and when that song starts up, you always know which song it is, and it's an unmistakable Harley sound. And in the end, it's just that "See ya, I'm out of here, I'm down the road, off on my next adventure" kind of thing. I just really enjoyed doing that album. I think we really accomplished something on that record that was superior to most of what had come out up to that point in the genre of pop metal.

Still, it was business as usual following the completion of the *Girls, Girls, Girls* record as Werman was recruited to helm production on Poison's sophomore album, hair metal's next big thing.

Werman's ability to churn out platinum records, in general and notably over the course of his collaboration with Poison, amid the incredible artistic fog pop metal's various excesses generated was proof of his preeminence and expertise as a producer in the field. One particularly poignant testament to that came with making the band's *Open Up and Say Ahh* LP, which remains Poison's most successful record in terms of album sales to date. It also remains the producer's least favorite. Most rock historians agree that Poison represented the beginning of the end for 1980s Sunset Strip hard rock, and from the start, Werman was not happy about the assignment. From his very first meeting with the band, he could see that Poison represented everything fundamentally about pop metal that would eventually kill it off. According to Werman:

Meeting that band was funny. Tom Wally was their A&R man, and he called me and said, "I would like you to produce Poison." And I didn't really know them, and didn't really care that much for them. The production on their first album wasn't bad. Rick Rowdy, who used to be the runner for Ted Nugent, produced *Look What the Cat Dragged In*. Anyway, the money was good, so I agreed to meet them, and he arranged a lunch meeting with Tom Muller, their manager, and the band. We met for lunch in Hollywood, and I'll never forget it, because C. C. turned to me at one point during the lunch, and quite seriously said, "We hear you do drugs?" And I said, "Yes I do, I smoke weed, I'll party from time to time. But I don't let it get in the way of my work." And that seemed to be enough for him. Just the idea of having C. C. DeVille look at someone else and say, "I hear you do drugs?" was very funny to me. In today's terms, I don't think people use drugs much anymore in the studio, but I could be naive. They're using different drugs now, probably better drugs, more advanced drugs, I just thought that—I remember the time when liquor was supplanted by fruit juice, and I figured kids were more serious about what they do in the studio now. I just can't see a young band behaving the way Mötley Crüe or Poison did, or getting away with what C. C. or players like that were allowed to in terms of musicianship because of the leniency inherent to the genre at the time. That stuff was just accepted by everyone. Bands got away with a lot more back then than they ever could today with the state of the industry.

For Werman, it was also an omen of things to come, as he would face perhaps his greatest challenge as a producer with Poison, an album that to date he refers to as, "a tinny piece of shit."

Looking back, that was a tough album, maybe my toughest. There were way too many drugs during that album. What made it tough was their inability to play as well as many bands. Rikki Rockett readily admits he's not a great drummer. He worked hard, tried and enjoyed his work, but it was tough. He had to do a lot of what was called "Quantizing," we had to move his foot around, to straighten out a beat that varies, that was not steady. I think overall the whole hair-metal scene necessitated an advancement in technology. And so on the Poison album, C. C. also took hours . . . hours to do his guitar solos. I think we took eight hours to do the solo on "Nothing but a Good Time." Because we'd get somewhere, and we'd have three tracks and be comparing them, and he'd go smoke some crack, and he'd come back and he'd be a different person. That's why people drink a lot and take drugs, I think in part, to get in the mood. Although it still remains quite genuine. You can always replace something if you don't like it. I don't think drugs in the studio are all bad, and can be a positive influence in some instances, but not in C .C.'s. And to deal with it, first of all, you take turns with your engineer. The other thing is I'm very organized with the guitar solos, and long series of notes. A very lengthy sequence of notes. I know where we are, where he screwed up, I know where to go in to record and where to get out. Where to punch in and correct, I'm very good with that, and because I knew what we'd be up against with Poison, that was the only album I ever recorded digitally, so we could facilitate the repair—the punch-in/punch-out—process. And looking back, while I don't like the way the album sounds, I'm not going to blame digital technology on that. It just sounds a little glassy and cheesy. So I remember taking turns, you'd go outside, play a game of horse, of basketball, have a burger—but we started at about noon and went till at least about midnight with C. C. that day, and I think we probably tried it over a few days. It really was a marathon. And he wasn't very open about his drug habit; it was just obvious he had been smoking crack or freebasing. And though Rikki wasn't, Bobbi and C. C. were very druggy. Bret would party as hard as he could, but he was diabetic, so he took better care of himself. He was more serious in the studio, generally. C. C. was the tough one in that band. Bobby was a good player. C. C. just had a terrible confidence problem, and would always bring himself down, be self-effacing, self-denigrating. And with that, you just try to say, "Look, I love this, what you're playing, you're almost there. Let's do this, this is good. Hey, it's another step." You encourage them. When you're being constructively critical with a guitar player, start with something good, cite something good that he's done. "You know that really great solo you did on that song, I think that would be of benefit if you could do that here." It's just common sense, it's politics, it's tact. You just try to encourage people, and build them up, rather than go, "No, you asshole, that's not what I meant."

In 1999, Werman was tapped by Warner Bros. Pictures to produce the soundtrack for the Mark Wahlberg feature film *Rock Star*, a celebration of the height of the 1980s pop-metal scene. The gig was not a comeback shot, but rather a nod of sorts to Werman as the forefather of the genre's soundscape, namely because the studio was seeking a perfect sonic recreation of the '80s heyday. They chose to go to the source, to the man who had been largely responsible for creating the sound itself. Werman oversaw the entire project, hand-picking both the songs and the players, and gave Warner Bros. not just a replica but a reminder of what rock 'n' roll production was missing in modern music. Still, the soundtrack and movie would amount to nothing more than a wistful reminiscence, as both the industry and Werman had, by that time, moved on. Walking back in mind and time through Werman's musical museum of masterpieces, with dozens of platinum records hanging on the walls and the aura of something truly classic in the air, spectators can't help but feel as though they're admiring living snapshots of their most personally treasured and momentous memories, as Tom Werman produced some of the greatest hits from the very soundtrack of our lives . . .

PHOTOGRAPH BY TIMOTHY HERZOG

CHAPTER 16

J. Mascis—The Godfather of Feedback Pop

The history of feedback in rock 'n' roll is as much defined by the artists who pioneered it as a sonic art form as it is a sound itself. Think of Jimi Hendrix with *Electric Ladyland*, Sonic Youth on *Goo*, Neil Young on "Rockin' in the Free World", and '80s alternative rock pioneers Dinosaur Jr., who MTV noted "on their early records, Dinosaur lurched forward, taking weird detours into free-form noise and melodic soloing." *Billboard* called the band an "alternative godfather . . . largely responsible for returning lead guitar to indie rock and, along with their peers the Pixies" and who "injected late-'80s alternative rock with monumental levels of pure guitar noise."

Stylistically, Dinosaur Jr. has always waded through a pool of rock subgenres, with one foot firmly in alternative rock and the other, according to most critics, in folk rock. *Rolling Stone* said that with the band's spin on the latter sound, "*folk rock* starts to take on entirely new dimensions." Viewing the mind of J. Mascis, the brain trust who has fronted Jr. for the past three decades, in dimensions is arguably the only way to see his musical genius, which revealed itself via an evolution MTV explained came "over time [as] . . . Mascis shed his hardcore punk roots and revealed himself to be a disciple of Neil Young, crafting simple songs that were delivered at a crushing volume and spiked with shards of feedback."

Deconstructing his signature feedback sound back down to the roots of its discovery and development thirty years ago, Dinosaur Jr. front man Mascis recalled that "at first, when I started out in the studio, it was just trying to capture the sound I had." Mascis added that that process was made challenging because

> the producers/engineers were really uncooperative—they were just local guys who had studios or ran PA's, and weren't really sympathetic to the kind of music we liked or anything. So it was really hard to get any idea across to them of what we wanted to sound like—so it was more of a battle against the engineer to try and get him to sound any good. So I was always battling with the guy in the studio, just trying to get it to sound decent—get the guitars loud enough and stuff. I was always trying to get them to turn the guitar up louder than it was, so again, kind of a battle.

Frustrated with closed minds and ears he continually ran up against, Mascis said that he began his career as a producer almost by accident, realizing one day following a particularly challenging session working on the band's debut LP, *Dinosaur,* in 1984, that "I found I could make it sound better than they had it, I don't even know what at the time yet. I had a really distinct vision of what I wanted our sound to be. It was necessary."

Over the course of the band's first three albums—1985's *Dinosaur*, 1987's *Your Living All Over Me*, and 1988's *Bug*—all of whose recording budgets were as indie as the label they were signed to, Mascis would prove his production talent a priceless one as he achieved sonic perfection on a shoestring budget, recalling that "for each album, we just tried to make them the best we could at the time. The first record I spent $500 on, the second record, I spent $1,000, the third record $4,000." Recording to two-inch tape in his band's early studio days, Mascis shared that this was his natural preference vs. the digital realm of endless virtual tracks, reasoning that—to his ear—"I feel like analog packages every sound in a more pleasant way for your ear, where with Pro Tools, I feel like my ears got so damaged from everything digitally. There's all this stuff that tape just takes away that digital, makes my ears ring a lot more because there's these weird frequencies it records attacking my ear. And with analog, you don't know about them because tape took them out of your life while you were recording. I feel like everybody's ears just get really tired a lot faster."

By 1991, Mascis and Co.'s unique brand of feedback pop had built enough buzz to land them on a major label, signing with Sire Records in 1990 and catching the ear of *Rolling Stone*, who would announce the band to their rock-reading mainstream at the time as "gifted musicians who can also write alternative-pop hooks with the best of them, Dinosaur

Jr. combined those two skills seamlessly." Speaking specifically to his process as the group's lead songsmith, J. Mascis offered a look behind the proverbial curtain and into the heart of a process that begins with "when I'm writing, I can hear the melody, and the guitar part and the drums, that's as far as my mental way that it all comes together at once. I don't hear a bass part on top of that, but my mind can see the guitar, the melody, the vocal line, and the drum beat. The drums are more a part of a song to me, rather than just to be an afterthought." As elaborate and layered as their finished products become, Mascis prefers a simple approach when writing that consists electronically of "a little one-track recorder at home where I'll put down riffs that I come up with on." Once in the studio, the producer added that he prefers recording in analog, reasoning that "digital makes it harder definitely, because tape helps you to get better sound. It's harder I think for sure. If I can, I still try to track in analog."

Though he concedes that "I'd rather have the song done before recording it," as Mascis entered the studio over the years to work on any of the band's classic LPs—which during the 1990s would include popular staples like *Green Mind* in 1991, *Where You Been* in 1993, 1994's *Without a Sound*, and 1997's *Hand it Over*—he constructed his band's sound largely from the ground up, beginning with drums, which he prioritized: "To me, drums are so much a part of the song, that there's not much room for diversion, so there was no freedom really in how the parts were played or recorded." That typically translated to Mascis playing the album's drum performances himself, reasoning that "I'd rather play drums because the feel of the drums is so important. That's the most important part to me—the drum track— to play on, because the drums are important to the feel of the whole song, and I can't sing if it's off."

Delving deeper into the recording fundamentals that have been staples of his drum-recording technique over the years, Mascis begins with the kit itself, offering that "when producing drums, I think tuning is pretty important." A fan over the years of "a pretty big DW drum set with 28-inch kick drum, and 18-inch toms," Mascis—explaining his process for micing that drum sound live to tape—added in terms of specific microphone preferences:

> Over the years, I have stuck with stuff that works for me. I like Royer Mics for room mics, and I like BMK 4001's for overheads—those are the two main things I really like. For the other things, I still experiment—for instance, like the snare, the toms. I have a kit miced up at my house that has 87's on toms, and one of those Audio-Technica BGM microphones inside my bass drum with both heads on it. Then I have a Phet 47 on the outside, and for snare, I use a Shure Beta 87 condenser mic on the top of the snare, and on the bottom, I have a 414.

Speaking to his earlier point about a poor drum mix throwing off his vocal performances, Mascis elaborated that when setting a drum mix toward the end of the rest of the song's tracking,

> I like to have the hi-hat on the left side of the mix as I'm playing, I hate it when engineers flip it around so you're like looking at the band, I like it from the playing angle. I always—for the way I play—I don't like to not have a bottom snare mic . . . Some people get away with just having a top mic, depending on the snare, but all the snares that I have a bottom mic on them. I like reverb for the room mics, and sometimes on the snare, but I used to use a lot more reverb on the snare than I do now. It just sounded cheesy to me. I don't mind hearing different effects at work in a mix, but I tend to keep drums pretty dry.

Rhythmically, the producer added that "I've never liked drum machines, I guess because I was a drummer, and I'm not a big fan of really steady drums; they more kind of play along to the song in my mind. So drums are definitely part of a song to me, not just a beat you put the song up to."

Broadening the discussion of that approach to the rest of how Dinosaur Jr. is brought to life on record, Mascis confessed that "I always preferred played everything on the basic tracks, and would then layer. I found that to be easier than trying to teach everybody the songs." Turning next to the creation of a guitar sound legendary to the ears of indie rock fans, one where the BBC argued there was a "comfort to be had hearing Mascis's wailing guitar running through a terrace of Marshall stacks," Mascis began foundationally by revealing that "the big muff was my main sound, and we'd either have to keep playing or it will feedback. I kind of stuck with that from the beginning." Taking a technical turn toward the gear he's favored over the years in creating that sound, the guitarist-producer recalled of amplifiers that, historically, "whatever I had in the beginning was whatever the guy had in the studio, then I got a 50 Watt Marshall by the time we did our second album."

As he'd layered his guitar tracks during recording, Mascis said that "in the earlier days of recording, it would be a very fixed amount of time, and you'd just use one amp. On our older albums, I was working with John Agnello, he was really good at capturing the sound of the guitar amp as it was." As his band became more successful and budgets grew, J settled on a core technique wherein

> I usually just like to close-mic the amp with a 57, if it's through the Telefunken D76 mic pre, I like that sound with a 57. Then I'll usually just kind of adjust different things." In the more modern age of recording on the band's newer material, the guitarist next explained that "nowadays, I'd rather just mic up the guitar and use different effects to

tweak with the sound rather than try to capture a specific guitar sound. Now I'm more into just listening to it through the monitors and adjusting different effects to get a sound, rather than getting a sound and then trying to capture it with a mic.

Addressing the question of a signature guitar sound he might have been pursuing over the course of his career, Mascis said that that consideration "depended on the song, but I always liked having really distorted parts and acoustic parts, and quiet and loud. Black Sabbath did that a lot, and I always liked a guitar effect that you could really hear, like 'Badge,' that kind of song." Touching on his preferences for the tracking of acoustic guitars in the studio, Mascis recalled "discovering a ribbon mic, a Cole, that was actually a savior to me, because I'd always hated the sound of the acoustic guitar. But this ribbon mic finally made the acoustic guitar sound normal. When I mic acoustic guitars, I like to place them above the guitars slightly pointing down."

Regarding his electric guitar preferences for tracking, Mascis added that "I'll try different stuff live, but recording I'll use some Gibsons for mixing. I'll never use them live, because for some reason I don't like to play leads on Gibsons, but for recording, I use the P90 Gibson a lot for rhythms." The Dinosaur Jr. front man was less particular on the subject of bass: "I had no ideas and it could be anything. I try to take it seriously but it's hard. I try to enjoy it, but it's such an afterthought usually. I like doing it sort of when I'm doing it, but I'd rather have somebody else do it."

A highlight of Mascis's guitar-playing style has always soloing, which the *L.A. Times* argued was the band's "main attraction and musical exclamation point, an unlikely fusion of Sonic Youth and the Allman Brothers." *Rolling Stone* added that "his solos . . . are as fluid and visceral as those by Sixties dinosaurs like Eric Clapton or Carlos Santana."

Mascis said of his production technique in the studio that "when I'm tracking guitars, I'm kind of listening to see what the song needs, or sometimes going overboard and then pulling back until it sounds like something I want to listen to. For leads, I use a Tele mainly." Turning to his production preferences where effects are concerned, he added that back in the day, "I tended to record my guitars with effects going. I'm not a fan of adding effects afterwards, it's hard to get the sound back. In getting effects, I kind of try out different things and just record different ideas and see which ones stick.

Turning to the production of his lead vocal tracks, Mascis confessed that "when I'm tracking vocals, I'd rather not see anybody" in the studio, adding that when he steps in front of the microphone, "I don't want to record it more than once if I can. I don't really like demos and stuff—if you can't get something in four tries, come back to it another day." When he did succeed in laying down those three or four keeper takes, he said, "I usually record four takes and then comp it." Technically, Mascis added that "the C-12 is a mic that I like for my voice. I've used a lot of different mics over the years and kind of settled on that." As he wound down the production phase on any of the band's nine studio LPs, he added, "I see producing and mixing as one and the same, where mixing is the last step of the recording process. I mix my records, but have worked a lot with engineer John Agnello over the years." Ultimately, Mascis's grander goal in any mix comes down to being "all about getting a mix that you want to listen to."

Mascis also offered the following advice to any up-and-coming artists regarding the one area of the recording process he recommends staying *out* of, the mastering phase:

> I realized you shouldn't really tell the mastering guy anything while he's mastering. Let him do it, then listen to it, and if you don't like it, then say something, but not while he's actually mastering because the mastering guy is the mastering guy for a reason. I'm always more of one who would keep turning everything up. I always hated when the engineer at one point would be like "It's too loud, dude," and turn all the faders down. If you bother him while he's doing it, it can end up ruining the whole thing. I like to sit in, I've just learned over the years not to say anything, because it's ruined stuff before.

In reflecting back on his catalog of then-and-now classics, he says, "I was just trying to amuse myself, that was all I was doing, others just happened to be amused as well," adding on a more serious note that "there's always stuff I'd like to change, but then again I don't care because that was the time when it happened. You have to let go, or it will ruin a lot of about the record you may love." Dinosaur Jr. reunited in 2006, releasing a pair of new studio LPs, 2007's *Beyond* and 2009's *Farm*, the latter inspiring the BBC to say the band was "raising the bar for any alt rock act contemplating hitting the comeback trail." It could be argued Mascis had come back in his own time creatively to a desire to take Dinosaur Jr. back into the studio, but the result reflected that the band had aged as finely as wine, tasting as good to the ear as they ever had, so much so that *Spin* would in 2011 declare Mascis a present-day "eardrum-demolishing guitar hero." ABC News would hail their last studio LP as "not only by far the best album of their twenty-five year career, but it also is quite possibly one of the finest rock albums ever recorded . . . (and) succeeds all around as a flawless exercise in power-chord rockdom." For Mascis, the greatest reward the band's master of creative ceremonies seems to have taken away personally from the last thirty years is his continued feeling that, at the end of the day, "it's cool, because not many people get to make a living doing something they love as long as I have . . ."

CHAPTER 17

Keith Olsen—The Air Hawk

Some producers define themselves as psychologists; others as renaissance men; others still as interpreters; and some as captains. Keith Olsen is the latter, having sailed the storms and sunny sides of every one of pop music's seas, charting hit courses of sonic travel that soothed rough waters, that discovered new lands of listening for his artists and their fans— ultimately anchoring a permanent place for Olsen among the legends of hit record making. Olsen began his journeyman years in the studio in the early 1970s as an engineer, working alongside established rock acts including the Byrds, Dr. John, and the James Gang, as well as a host of up-and-coming artists, perhaps most notably including Buckingham/Nicks. As AOR (album-oriented rock) radio began to take flight on the airwaves in the mid-1970s, those friendly winds would give Olsen wings as a hit producer when he made the career-making decision to recommend to Mick Fleetwood that Lindsay Buckingham and Stevie Nicks join Fleetwood Mac. Olsen recalled: "I did Buckingham/Nicks, and then I put Steve and Lindsay in the band. Bob Welch had quit the band, and Mick Fleetwood called me on New Year's Eve, and asked 'Gee, do you think those two kids would want to join my band. And I said, 'Well, I'll see.' And then it was probably six hours of negotiation trying to convince Stevie and Lindsay to join the band."

Olsen's success in convincing Nicks and Buckingham to join the band secured his spot as lead producer on the first album that would put Fleetwood Mac as a major marker on the pop music map. It was a chemistry that *Rolling Stone* would recognize in its coverage of the band, noting that "Nicks' sultry voice and Buckingham's songwriting knack focused the group's fledgling pop ambitions." In the course of crafting an album that produced several Top 40 hits, Olsen recalled that "it was very hard at first to get Stevie and Christie to work together, because Christie was just very comfortable being the only girl singer in the band. But to get Lindsay, Stevie came along in the package. In the beginning, she wasn't 100 percent into the idea, but then after the first album passed 200,000 copies, and kept going up the charts, she became very happy. The songs that Stevie wrote, she sang, and the songs Christie wrote, she sang."

Describing the creative dynamic between Nicks and Buckingham individually that would produce so many of the group's seminal hits over the next two decades, Olsen explained that

> as a duo, and writing team, Lindsay and Stevie were really amazing. Between Stevie and Lindsay, it was very much an emotional dynamic that spurred on an awful lot of the creativity and writing and everything. What Stevie had was what I call this brute ignorance, and just totally wrote from her hip and from her soul. She had no idea why on a lot of stuff. And Lindsay was the other way—would think through absolutely everything, and for Stevie, made her songs work. Because when you first get a song from Stevie, it has no form at all, it just rambles on and on and on. The melody's intact, and the lyrics are intact, but it just feels so funny to have that part of the melody just roll on and on and on and on for so long, and then it gets to the prechorus, or chorus.

The one exception to the latter process Olsen cites was unique not only in terms of the duo's routine, but also in that it became the group's first breakout pop hit, with Olsen recalling that "one discernible exception to that rule was 'Landslide.' 'Landslide' was very much Stevie just sitting down very depressed, very hurt about a relationship, and sat down with an acoustic guitar and wrote that song almost exactly in that same form. Then Lindsay put that great guitar part on it and fixed the form." In describing some of the technical aspects of tracking Lindsay Buckingham's delicate but forceful acoustic guitar on the smash hit, Olsen explained that "Lindsay had a Mahogany-topped Martin, and it had all this mid-range and clank to it, and his D18 was like glass, with late-gauge bronze strings on the D18, and kind of not-fresh strings on the other guitar, and I just pointed an AKG-451 mic at the guitar after finding the place with my ears, and with any acoustic instrument, what mic you use and the placement of it means nothing to aid the quality of the instrument and how good the part is actually played."

Addressing his approach to tracking the group vocally beginning with Buckingham and Nicks, Olsen explained that "Stevie just has a way of singing and Lindsay has a way of singing with Stevie that just had that incredible blend, and the parts were always unique. Back then, Stevie was very easy to record, I would use a 4-14 mic on her. Later on, after the first couple of records, the first take would be brilliant, and then she would start to think about it, and you'd have to work like crazy to get brilliance again. So make sure you record the first two takes. I record warm-up vocals as a rule." Where vocal recording encompassed the entire group—a harmony blend that would become a signature to their successful sound—Olsen recalled that

> when it came to divvying up harmonies, we would sit out in the studio and keep replaying the track with the lead vocals on it, over and over and over again, and just kept rolling it and rolling it as we would just be coming up with ideas for background parts. And just keep rolling it and rolling it, and these parts would come, and people would take the parts that fit really well with them. It was totally a group effort. I mean it was Christine and Lindsay and Stevie and I, out in the room, just for quite a long period of time.

Regarding the group's namesake, Olsen explained that

> Mick Fleetwood's role in the band was rhythm and spiritual leader. He was a real good drummer, and everything was a little different recording Mick, because he used calf-skin drum heads, and boy does it sound great. A calf-skin kick drum, wow, sounds great, but you have to have a totally different technique to be able to play it. So more than anything, I remember it was his technique. He had calf-skin on everything. I remember his snare drum; he had this piece of plastic puke that he would tape down to the upper-left hand part of the top of his snare drum, and he would tape it about a third of the way into the plastic puke, and when he hit the snare drum, it went up and the snare drum would ring, and it would be a mechanical eighth. And the sound was so cool, so all we had to do was put a 57 mic near the snare drum and it sounded great. Once again, it's about how good the guy hits the snare drum and how good the snare drum sounds, not the mic. It has nothing to do with the mic or what EQ you use, or anything. It's "Gee, that's really clever and sounds really good," and it did.

Upon release, the group's self-titled LP would take the pop charts by storm, producing era-defining classics including "Rhiannon," "Say You Love Me," "Over My Head," and the instantly legendary "Landslide," and prompting mainstream critics like *Rolling Stone* to note that "on Fleetwood Mac's self-titled album of 1975, Nicks and Buckingham not only fit in, but they stimulated the core trio . . . easily outdistancing all the band's previous efforts."

Olsen was next hired by Foreigner in 1977 to work on their *DoubleVision* LP, specifically for the purpose of crafting the group's radio hits—fast becoming a specialty of Olsen's, such that he jokes in retrospect that "I didn't want to sound the same from one album to the next, but in the '70s, '80s, and '90s, they called me 'Air Hawk', because I had so much airtime. It was one after another after another, so AOR and pop-rock radio played me so much they called me 'Air Hawk.'" Elaborating on his knack for crafting hit records in the studio, Olsen attributed his string of successes as his career got bigger to a root belief that "part of my main role as a producer is picking and shaping a great song into a hit. The thing is you get a feeling when you're working with songs, because they impart a really good story. It is all about great songs, followed by that great performance."

Regarding those he captured specifically with Foreigner in the studio in the course of the album's two biggest hits, "Hot Blooded," and "Double Vision," Olsen first recalled the process of recording lead vocalist Lou Gramm's vocal tracks:

> Lou Gramm is a natural, has no idea why he does the things he does. If you ever saw him sing live, he would take his right arm tucked under with a fist, and hold his mic with his left arm, and support his diaphragm so much that he could hit this really wide range, his pitch was great, and what a sound. But he had no idea how he was doing any of it—totally natural, no schooling or idea of why. He just did it because it felt like he should. Well, it's the right way to sing. it's always if you can put the mic just slightly below the person's chin, and the reason why is when somebody sings down, they support their diaphragm more. When they're singing up, and stretching their larynx, the pitch goes away, and the support isn't there of the note. So I could put this mic like six inches below his chin, and he would curl right into it.

Recalling some of the more challenging moments in working with the group, Olsen explains that "within Foreigner, Mick Jones was definitively the leader, and the strengths of Foreigner were the songs and the lead vocals. It wasn't the drum parts or bass parts or guitar parts; they were okay. I mean listen to the guitar solo on "Hot Blooded," it was awful. But did it really matter, no? So once again, the best thing that I could impart to readers is the bottom line is it all starts with the song. If you have a great song that has a great melody and great lyric, you have something that is undeniable. That's it." In further illustrating that point, Olsen cited his next collaboration that resulted in a hit single with Pat Benatar in 1980 on the LP *Crimes of Passion,* "Hit Me with Your Best Shot." As with Foreigner, Olsen had nothing but praise for Benatar as a vocalist, recalling that the she was "just a world-class singer, along with Ann Wilson, and Aretha Franklin, David Coverdale, and Lou Gramm. Just put her in front of a mic and let her go. Her pitch was phenomenal, the depth of each breath she was singing, her breath control was phenomenal. Her control of her vibrato, and her range was three and a half octaves. She was one of the early super-chick rock singers, and tons of attitude. She was a New Yorker!"

In Olsen's next collaboration with Benatar, on 1981's *Precious Time*, he would again deal with the same dynamic, and in spite of it, pull out hits for the singer with "Promises in the Dark," and "Fire and Ice" before turning his attention to a collaboration that would produce among arguably the biggest pop radio and video hits of the first half of the 1980s with Rick Springfield's "Jessie's Girl." Highlighting what would become his signature rock guitar sound, Olsen recalled when they entered the studio together: "I had met Rick before he became an actor, and I remember when Rick and I were recording *Working Class Dog*, I needed a studio to work in because I was sick and tired of renting a studio 300 days a year and paying out the wazoo for it. So I made a deal with Rick's manager, if he gave me a studio next door to Sound City, I would produce two songs for Rick. So Rick came in with two songs, 'Jessie's Girl' and 'I've Done Everything for You,' and I grabbed 'Jessie's Girl' first, and said, 'This is your best song, period.'"

Again showcasing his talent for spotting hit singles, Olsen was banking on that fact when he began working with Springfield:

> Rick's not a world-class singer, but man is he a great writer. He's a very deep writer, one of those guys who writes from his heart, and everything that he writes about has happened to him personally. If I snap the opening riff of that song, "Jessie's Girl," and if you think of that, it's such a hook, and originally, it was just the intro to the song. We already had a hook, with the bass drum hitting on the two and four, it was that lick that made that song's hook really cool. And then the story that was told was accessible to millions upon millions upon millions of guys. So when he was tracking vocals, because he's an actor, he was very precise about the way that he would tell the story in his vocal, and his phrasing and enunciation was really good.

In the course of tracking the album's backing tracks, specifically its signature guitars, Olsen discovered a sound that would become a staple of his production style over the course of countless rock radio hits throughout the later 1980s and 1990s. Describing the genesis of the sound from a technical perspective, Olsen explained that

> the guitar on that intro is a Dean Markley guitar into my Suber amp. I had these amps that Jim Marshall made for me personally, with two EVN ML12s and an open back cabinet that weighed about one hundred pounds, with a 100-watt head built into this little combo-cabinet. And it would rattle the tubes like crazy, and so any time you crunch on the guitar, the chunk would be brilliant and so strong, and the delayed chord that came after it. The poor tubes were just being hammered, because the

sound-pressure level inside that cabinet where those tubes were sitting was 135 DB sound-pressure level. So it added quite a lot to the sound. On "Jessie's Girl," we used 57 and 451 mics with -10 on the cabinets, and ran them straight into the board. Boy, it sounded good. I was in the middle of producing another album, and only had Saturday and Sunday, so we cut both tracks, did overdubs, vocals, and mixed and got them both done in two days by 6:00 p.m. Sunday night. And both songs became hits.

As danceable, rock-driven radio singles dominated jukeboxes and air and video waves across America, the studio soundscape was reshaped in the same time by producers like Olsen, who recorded a variety of artists utilizing the same signature guitar sound, explaining that "I used that guitar setup on the Pat Benatar records, the Whitesnake '87 and '89 albums, all the Hagar stuff. Sammy loved it so much that we tried to get them made for him over in England, and they said they were so behind in production on their 4-12 cabinets that they couldn't build them special. So we hired a cabinetmaker to emulate these cabinets and put red vinyl on them, because Sammy was the Red Rocker."

Focusing specifically on his 1983 collaboration with rock radio veteran Sammy Hagar, Olsen fondly recalled that

he's just a great guy and a really cool artist, and it was just really fun. Everything working with him was fun, but it was also really quick. Remember, Sammy is Mr. Straight Man, so it was all about being at the studio at 10 a.m. and working till 7, a great work ethic. The kid was like me. I usually get to the studio before anybody, and he was already there. I like being set up and ready to go and then I'll wait for the artist, but he was already there, and he said, "Yeah, I like this." So those were the good parts. We used exactly the same amps and mics, and even Les Paul guitar, as "Jessie's Girl." Vocally, he's okay, it would take some punches. After doing a combined, we'd always have some area that just wasn't right, so we'd have to go out and we'd have to hammer that area out and then put it into the composite vocal. Because he strains to hit high notes, and in doing that, his pitch slides up to the note a little bit, so it has to feel just right when you do that. A lot of rock singers do that, you know how you scoop up to the note, especially when it's really high. So that has to feel right. Like every single artist, he was self-critical vocally, and like me, he doesn't like having a lot of people in the studio.

The first album the duo produced together, 1981's *Standing Hampton*, was Hagar's first platinum solo LP, generating the rock smashes "Heavy Metal" and "There's Only One Way to Rock." Two years later, the duo would repeat their musical magic on *Three Lock Box,* which produced hits for Hagar with the album's title track and "Your Love Is Driving Me Crazy."

As astonishing as Olsen's hit-making track record heading into the mid-1980s was the variety of rock subgenres he helped to popularize, a talent amplified via Olsen's long-term collaboration with arena-rockers Whitesnake, which began in 1984 when the producer was brought in to clean-up *Slide It In* for radio. Not surprisingly, the album would become the band's breakout LP, producing hits including "Love Ain't No Stranger," "Slide It In," and "Slow and Easy." In reflecting on his initial involvement in the studio with Whitesnake, Olsen recalled that

> I fixed *Slide It In*, where we had to put on some extra guitar parts and fix stuff. It was already recorded in England, and not up to the quality they wanted for the U.S. market. David Coverdale had first been signed to Geffen Records, and their A&R man John Kalodner said, "I know a guy who can fix this really quickly and won't cost much." So he called me, and I heard the album, met with David, and said, "Sure man, I've loved your voice forever." And I had been a big Deep Purple fan, and so here he was in my house, and I'm talking to him, thinking "Oh God, you're such a star, you know?" I was just overwhelmed, and he was so gracious and such a good guy. So we went in and we fixed the record, and did some new vocal and guitar parts, and mixed it all in about two weeks, and we popped that record out. And *Slide It In* got a ton of chart AOR radio play, then "Slow and Easy" got a ton, but the record didn't sell a ton of albums. It went Gold, which made the record company sit up and pay attention, because at that time, the mantra was "Go Gold or Go Away."

Ironically, even after his work on *Slide It In,* Whitesnake initially hired another producer to craft their follow-up, 1987's seminal *Whitesnake,* which produced the legendary "Here I Go Again," as well as "Is This Love?," and "Still of the Night."

Well prior to the commercial success of Whitesnake's 1987 self-titled masterpiece, Olsen recalls a technical mess in which

> they went up first with another producer to cut the tracks at Little Mountain Studios, and then on that album, and someone had told David he couldn't sing in tune, because all the *guitar* parts were out of tune. What they had done with the harmonizer was a really big deal, and people had found out if you put the harmonizer up .005 on one channel, and the straight one on the other channel, you got a really wide, broad guitar sound. Well, they had twenty-four tracks of just rhythm guitar, and all of them were varying degrees of harmonizing, so the pitch reference that David would hear wasn't anything that was pitched properly. So David was told by this other producer that he was through in the business because he couldn't sing in tune anymore, and this was after spending $200,000 on this album. They couldn't get a vocal. So John

Kalodner pulled the album from this guy, sent it to me, slave after slave after slave reel. Drums that were kind of weak and sometimes not tight, fills that weren't there, bass that was out of tune. So I methodically went through all the guitar tracks and found two unharmonized tracks that were in tune, and put one on the left and one on the right. And John Sykes was playing it, and playing great, so I don't know why they thought they needed to do all this other stuff, because Sykes was just playing phenomenally well.

Once Olsen had figured out what needed to be repaired, and in many cases rerecorded, he elaborated:

We redid most of the bass with a synth. The secret to the way we made it work in the mix as a real bass was the selection of the patches: we used a Profit VS and a DX7, and we Midi'd them together—this was very early in the life of Midi—and it worked really well and we played all those parts on a keyboard. And it was so perfectly in tuned that the guitar then felt so perfectly in tuned that all of a sudden, I got this really in-tuned, really kick-ass track. So now I said to David, "Okay, it's time to do your vocals." Well, this was after he had in his mind that he was through in the business and couldn't sing in tune. So I called him out, said "Come on, let's sing the hardest song in the batch," which was "Still of the Night," and he said, "Okay." And walked into the room, and our first vocal take of "Still of the Night" was David Coverdale testing out a 4-14 microphone, the same one I used for Stevie, Heart. I had my few mics I always carried with me, and David is a world-class singer, but he had a mental issue at the time, because somebody had told him at the time he couldn't sing in tune, so he thought that he had to think about it a lot. So I put him out in the studio with three mics hanging off three mic stands, and I said, "Okay, sing, and we'll test these mics, and you can come in and see which mic you like the best." So then I ran the song three times, and the joke was two of the three mics were *props*! So only one was on, and I only had to do that one time on that first vocal for "Still of the Night" on *Whitesnake* 87, and he said, "My God, I can sing, I can sing in tune!" And I said, "Duh." He didn't know he'd done three passes on one mic, and the first one was the vocal take that is on "Still of the Night."

Continuing on the ever-expansive process as it unfolded, Olsen added that, finally, after days of tweaking,

Everything then became so crunch perfect, in tune. He did "Here I Go Again" and "Is This Love?" each in four takes, just like the vocals on the *Slide It In* album. All the vocals I had to redo and all the backups were such a snap, just bang, bang, bang, bang and it was done. He's a world-class singer. When I mixed David's voice, first off, his voice is so great, you can't get too much of it, because you love it so much as you work with it. Secondly, he's one of those guys that the breath that he takes is as important as the pitch and tone and word that he's singing. He takes those long, labored breaths, but he does it in a way that is so in tune to the passion of the melody and lyric. I used a bit of a delay and a bit of a tape-delay-to-chamber on David's voice. In 1987, I had access to a really good EMG Plate Reverb, the 140, and the EMG plate was tweaked so good and tight. So I used a deep delay feeding to it from the send. From the console I inserted a tape machine with a very old speed-thing on it, and got it till it felt right, and that fit into an EMG Plate, and made the plate sound even better. And that was one of the sounds you heard on David's vocals.

As the 1980s came to a close, change was everywhere. Within rock 'n' roll, one of the decade's giants—the Scorpions—perhaps sensing that the climates were shifting away from sex-driven anthems such as "Rock You Like a Hurricane" to more substance-over-style-oriented rock, chose to shake up their sound, and not surprisingly, brought in Olsen to attain that end. Recalling details of his collaboration with the group, in general, and more specifically in the course of crafting "Winds of Change," Olsen explained that

I got a call from Klaus, the lead singer, in this heavy German accent, calling and saying to me, "Hello Keith, this is the situation here, this is Klaus from ze Scorpions. We have a situation. Matias wants to redo his guitar parts, can we do that? So does Rudolf?" We didn't have time correction back then, we had Germans, and because of it, the Germans like to play very stiff parts. I did everything I could to loosen them up. There's some really cool background effects on "Winds of Change," that made the song. There were so many air hooks going on in that arrangement, those ooh-aahs that happened. That was probably forty tracks of Klaus breathing and singing as soft as humanly possible. I burnt out his throat, and he couldn't sing for a week and half after that. The effects on that vocal came mostly from how we recorded it. We used my level-sensitive, high-frequency expander, and then had him sing so soft, and used none of the direct mic, only return from the high-frequency expander, and then you could hear the whispers, and there's absolutely no bravado. When a singer sings in one area and one pitch over and over again, that part of the vocal muscle is gonna be just fried, and you aren't able to sing for a week. So to get that sound on the background vocals was about forty tracks. Effects-wise, I used a tape-delayed, two chamber with a little bit of delay, and then his vocal recorded with my 4-14 and a Neve compressor. That was the same thing I always used.

Air Hawk," Olsen had successfully sailed across rock's ever-shifting winds of change in terms of trends and popular acts, beginning in the mid-1970s, throughout the 1980s and 1990s, and on into the millennium. He closed with this advice:

The art of record making is being able to be the vehicle to get the artist's creativity onto tape. Some way capturing that performance and getting it out to the market place that you're going after in an accessible way. So over the years, there are songs and albums I really loved and was so happy I was a part of them, from Fleetwood Mac to Foreigner to Pat Benatar to Santana and Whitesnake. They're all really cool and had some great songs and everything else, but I think the thing I was able to do was bring out the artist's creativity in a way that was accessible to the market. As far as advice for today's younger generation of up-and-coming producers and engineers, I would first say once you're in the studio, always remember it's about the artist. There's a lot of producers who will dictate and tell everybody what to do, and will just be an extension of their own artistry. It's just an extension, and because it's the extension of them, the public burns out on them really quick. Longevity in this industry is very, very difficult, and the easiest way to have longevity is to be able to make sure that you impart the artist's creativity out there on the radio waves, not just yours.

PHOTOGRAPH BY ALLAN AMATO

CHAPTER 18

Al Jourgensen–The Ministry of Industrial Rock

The term "legendary" is thrown around a lot in the record business. Sometimes it sticks to the wall, other times it wanes appropriately with an artist's influence. With the genre of industrial rock, which predated all other combinations of dance/hip-hop/electronic beats layered with rock/metal electric guitars, Ministry is without debate or question the genre's godfather, hailed in 2010 by the *L.A. Times* as a "pioneering industrial metal band" and by *Billboard* as "arguably the leaders (and some would say founders) of the industrial metal movement." Also declared "legendary" by *Revolver* magazine in 2012, Ministry has a fan base as devoted as ever, and in spite of his band's longevity, for the band's front man, Al Jourgensen, there has been no formula they followed over the years, other than to run counter to the trends, wherein "Ministry deliberately made music that had weird frequencies, and songs that are way too long to be played on radio, and some people said we shot ourselves in the foot with that, but I don't see it that way. That's the path we wanted to take to make sure the product made us happy, and if it makes anyone else happy it's a bonus."

Though it might have seemed like he had a master plan, Jourgensen revealed that the secret behind his writing science is such that "the modus operandi is there is no modus operandi; everything's thrown out the window, so there really is no set way that we do things." Of the series of landmark albums that were compositionally and studio driven by Jourgensen's vision, *Alternative Press* would muse that "in the short happy history of industrial rock . . . there's absolutely no denying that (Ministry) is year zero." For Jourgensen, his journey toward becoming one of the pioneering producers of industrial rock/metal began years earlier

> studying under Adrian Sherwood, who has worked with every dub act from Lee "Scratch" Perry on down to Depeche Mode, Nine Inch Nails, Skinny Puppy, etc/, doing basically a Luke Skywalker vs. Yoda thing for six months in England while getting my *chi* down, and learning how to use my light saber, so to speak. He taught me you have to have complete confidence in yourself when you're producing, and be willing at the same time to change and adapt if it's not working, but by the same token, have fun finding your own niche and style as a producer without overshadowing the band you're working with's natural, organic sound. He was using techniques I'd never seen before, and that I would use to an *extreme* on *Land of Rape and Honey*, for instance with tape editing. My work with him gave me confidence with my own vision that I had in mind for *Ministry*.

Alternative Press would hail the band beginning with their seminal *The Land of Rape and Honey,* which they called "a seamless collision of musique concrete, dance music, sampling and heavy metal that expresses the semi-articulate anger of this generation better than any slacker handbook." Offering a behind-the-scenes look into how he went about crafting a drum sound that became the foundation for what *Spin* would later s um up as "scene-defining aggro-disco," Jourgensen discussed the making of the song "Stigmata":

> On the *Land of Rape and Honey*, that song was tracked with live drums, but when I say live, it was always a stereo set of a live drummer triggering our own samples—so there's a little bit of live, a little bit of the ambience of the room, and then there's a little bit of samples. So we had a snare sample, a regular snare, then we had an ambient snare, and we combined all three, and we'd do the same thing with toms and kicks and everything. Throughout the album, it would depend on the feeling of the song how those combinations were blended in the drum mix, so some songs you want to sound more live, so you use a little less sample underneath, but it's still there. I just blend, so anything on kick, tom, snare, is basically a combination of three different sounds.

Offering a prime example of Ministry's mastery at bending and blending powerful musical moments from neighboring genres into a rhythmic reinvention, *Billboard* would single out "Scarecrow" from *Psalm 69* for taking "the massive slow pound of Led Zeppelin's 'When the Levee Breaks' and [taking] it to a strung-out, harrowing new location."

Speaking more broadly on his approach to tracking drums for the band's sound in their pioneering heyday of LPs like the latter, *The Mind Is a Terrible Thing to Taste* and *Psalm 69*, Jourgensen shared that

> when I was micing the drums back in those days, I used all the standards, but one thing I did do that was a little bit different was use a Royer 88 on the kick. So along with the standards on the kit, I also have a fourth option for a drum sound, which is I take a couple little cheesy Sony ECM mics that have an input overload, I set them up in the live room, and then I just completely distort them. I slam the input, and mix in a little bit of that with my drums too, so not only do I have an ambient room mic but also these ECM mics I call the "Bacon factor" that I slip a little bit of it in—depending on the song—to build the drum sound. In general, if I'm using live drums, I will mix as I go, because I want to make sure I have the proper sound that I want as I'm going along. It also helps in filling out other ideas you may get later foundationally.

On the programming side of the aisle, Jourgensen recalled that back in the '80s, he favored "Fairlight, and then I got away from that because the sampling time on the Fairlight was just so ridiculously expensive and short."

As the band's lead producer and performer, in the course of crafting Ministry's broader sound over the years, Jourgensen revealed that his collection of playable instruments has included "guitar, bass, piano, a little sax, a little violin, pedal steel, mandolin, banjo, harmonica, organs, and a lot of keyboards," though he avoids the Prince-esque branding of "multi-instrumentalist," preferring to view himself as "a jack of all trades and master of nothing." As a natural part of his progression into eventually producing all aspects of Ministry, Jourgensen as a musician first recalled that "I started out on drums, went from drums to bass and guitar, then keyboards, and then started picking up a little sax, a little trumpet, a little violin, double-steel, banjo, and so on. The instrument I really excelled at was slide guitar, that's my best instrument basically is Delta Blues slide." Still, for as fluent as he became with all of the aforementioned, the singer-songwriter added that "I'm not any good on any of the instruments per se, and so I always preferred to have real professionals doing that stuff in the band—for instance guitar leads."

Turning to the creation of another fundamentally important element of industrial rock sound that Ministry played a key role in creatively incorporating into their own sound—that of sampling—Jourgensen revealed a rich palette of influences at play, recalling that as he dug derivatively back through a deeply diverse array of stylistic eras to inform the band's own album by album,

> you could take Frank Sinatra, for example, and pick up on tendencies that Henry Mancini would do on horn arrangements and with so many great samples at our disposal, I'd pick out the right ones, figure out the timbre of the horn you want, and the arrangements are no problem. I can sit there and spend a whole day playing the stuff, but it's just much easier to take two to three hours, come up with a horn arrangement, and have an entire section going via computer. But it helps to know a little bit about the instrument as a player as well, which is why I dabble in a little bit of everything that I might sample instrumentally.

Emphasizing the importance of arrangement in constructing any of Ministry's PhD-sophisticated soundscapes throughout the years, Jourgensen reasoned that "while you don't have to be a master of any instrument, what you do have to be a master of is arranging, and knowing the practices of people who came before you, and understanding tendencies—things like that. Then if you know just your musical scale and a little bit about the instrument, and you have a sample library at your disposal, you're hooked up." In constructing his sample library, along with previously recorded sounds, Jourgensen introduced and infused an organic approach that broke new ground in terms of the intricacies and authenticities of Ministry's sonic textures. Giving the industrial music genre he was helping to invent a layer of tangible experimentation that was key to its broader evolution, the producer said that "in the beginning, it was all simply me going out to train tracks and steel mills, and renting farm equipment and going to dentist offices and sampling their drills—my uncle was a dentist and would let me sample all his drills. So there was a lot of hands-on organic sampling at the beginning."

Delving further into the complexities that the still-dawning age of digital sampling technology provided—in both artistic inspiration and technical challenge—Jourgensen recalled that "we had the Fairlight, but that was very limited in the sense that it had a 1.6 second sampling time, so we used some Fairlight, but on a lot of those early Ministry albums, I used a Roland Juno 60 and Roland Jupiter 8, and I also had a Prophet 5 I used for some strings, but it was mainly Roland with a little bit of Fairlight thrown in." Past the round critical praise for the album's cutting-edge recording innovations, Jourgensen felt from a production standpoint, "*The Land of Rape and Honey* is one of my favorite Ministry albums, because with *Honey*, I was doing shit with tape that no one else was doing, in the sense of say a William Burroughs, who as a writer would take words, cut 'em up, throw 'em up on the board, rearrange 'em, and then write a book that way—that whole cut-up theory. And on *Rape and Honey*, I *did a lot* of that, and nobody was doing that at that time, so that album changed the paradigm for a lot of different things at the time."

Taking the art form to its literal cutting edge, the producer revealed that, in the studio,

> I was doing real microtape editing, and used to have to wear band-aids on my fingers because I had so many cuts from the razor-blades and shit, so I would be editing quarter-inch tape for literally twenty-four to forty hours for a time without stopping. I would like figure out exactly how long a piece of tape is from one beat to one beat, cut it out, throw it on the floor with a bunch of other ones, and then put it back together. To me, that was really exciting, and really hadn't been done in audio. It'd been done in literature, but it hadn't been done in audio, and those were really heady times because we were going places where a lot of people would not dare to go. That's why that record is really special to me. The production aspect was stuff that would take a half-hour now on Pro Tools, took a week or two weeks back then, but it was worth doing because we knew we were breaking new ground.

As the band spread their creative wings album after album, Jourgensen recalled that, by the time of *The Mind Is a Terrible Thing to Taste*, he had expanded his sampling science to "sampling from some things we felt were cool off of previously recorded albums, so a snare here or there. For instance, by the time of *Mind*, we had sampled a bunch of really early ZZ Top stuff, like off the first three records, and on top of our own live snares, added a little bit of the ZZ top snare in with the ambient snare, the bacon crisp stuff, and that was the album's drum sound." Following the album's release, Jourgensen recalled receiving a call from none other than ZZ Top front man Billy Gibbons: "I got this weird call, and Billy wants to have lunch with me, so he took us out to lunch, and I—at the time—was still trying to figure out why the hell ZZ Top's guitar player is taking us out to lunch, and told me he was a fan of the band. That blew me away, and started a lifelong friendship."

Offering a look at the gear side of a signature guitar sound that *Entertainment Weekly* once characterized as "thrash guitars that . . . sound like Metallica in overdrive," Jourgensen remembered:

> Back then, I was using Yamaha 1500s, which was basically a really weighty SG Gibson, or a Gibson Explorer, and all my amps were Marshalls. I loved Marshalls because they were just no-brainers; you turned them up and it was done. When I was in the studio with all of that, I would always use a micing combo of a 451, a 414, a 57, and a KM 84, and liked four mics per box so I had options. A 57 is kind of a standard, and

I like to get different frequencies out of like the 414, so some mics are right in the speaker, others are an inch or two back, and getting that classic Ministry guitar sound was just a matter of experimenting, depending on the tone, and what you're trying to do. Because obviously the more you pull it back, the more ambience you get, whereas if you close-mic the speaker, you get a direct representation, so I always used four different mics for four different speakers on each cabinet.

Turning to his vocal-recording techniques as a producer and performer, Jourgensen began by sharing that "with any artist I'm producing, including myself with Ministry, I like to get the sound of what we're going to use, as far as effects channels on vocals, as we're going, so I have it in my headphones and know what it's going to sound like at the end of the day. To be safe, I always separate the effects track from the dry vocal so I have an option in case we change our mind later." In terms of specific effects, the producer said, "I'm an Eventide guy, all the way, and have been forever, and will be forever, that's basically all I use. I started out with the Eventide 3000 early in my career and am up to the 8000 now. It's a multieffects processor I know my way around really well, and can pretty much get any effect sound that I want using their template patches and then altering them." Reviewing his traditional micing preferences, Jourgensen said that "mics-wise, I've always used an old 414 or a C-12. I have a vintage C-12, which is basically a precursor to the 414, and I typically track sitting right at the mixing desk wearing headphones, vs. out in the live room. I like recording at the console because that way, there's less time wasted trying to communicate with my engineer in the control room, etc. about the direction I want to go with a vocal. I've always felt uncomfortable as a vocalist sitting out in a room by myself. I want to stay involved in the process."

Contrasting his experience working in the analog vs. Pro Tools medium, Jourgensen volunteers himself as an unabashed fan of digital:

I'm totally sold on Pro Tools. I actually do think analog can sound better. Digital is just a binary reproduction of 1-2-1-2 and doesn't have the entire algorithm of the ambience of the room, because it's too complicated—the signal. So they try manufacturing with binary digits, 1-2-1-2, but digital will *never* be as full-bodied as analog. But for me, what balances it out as a producer, especially with the type of music Ministry makes, are the options you have on Pro Tools used to take me *days* with tape editing, as opposed to the fifteen or twenty minutes it takes me in digital for DSing, balancing out volumes, etc. Now it's a no-brainer and really easy, and so for me, it's a trade-off that is worth it. Back in the day, I used two 24-track 880s. Studer's the only way to go, because you could drop one of those things in a swimming pool, leave it there overnight, bring them out the next day, let them dry off for a day, and they'd still work. So I'd link two of those up and have forty-eight tracks, and be good to go.

When Jourgensen's attention have turned from producing to mixing throughout his thirty-plus-year career, without missing a beat, he shares that "I'm involved in all mixing, everything—there's not a song that goes by in my catalog without me being in the room mixing. I take all the credit and all the blame for it." In terms of his working style, Jourgensen said:

I'm definitely of the Phil Spector school without all the murders and stuff. A lot of people say "Less is more," and I agree in the playing sense, where I think one note can speak for itself, so when we're playing, less is more, but in production terms, *more is more*. I like to fill up everything; I mean every channel, every nook and cranny, I'll put some kind of idea down on a number of different instruments and/or vocals, and then shave it down. So I want to make sure when I'm going into the final mix that I've got every possible idea available, and then I shave it down from there. I like to have those ingredients in hand; then I can pick and choose. So before I even get to the process of selection, I've filled up every possible thing I might need, I have at hand, so having options has always been very important to me throughout the mixing of any of my records.

Nothing can quite sum up Ministry's musical influence across multiple subgenres of rock's broad soundscape because it's still very much a work in progress. To try would be foolish, MTV has argued, because "when you look at the whole aural enchilada that makes up the electro-metal avatar's career, the boomerang effect is simply brutal." In looking past the legacy assessments and back on a more personal level through his broader catalog of some thirty-plus albums that span multiple generations of industrial rock's evolution, Jourgensen reveals that Ministry's landmark *Land of Rape and Honey* will always be his personal favorite as a producer because of the remarkable new ground it broke. "That was like the ultimate in experimentation, trying to blend a bunch of different genres together and make them all talk to each other." Indeed, *Kerrang!* would hail the album as "way ahead of its time, marrying repetitive electronics with ultra heavy music," a marriage of sounds Jourgensen remains fond of for its mystery, recalling that "at the time, nobody knew what the fuck we were doing, we just did it, and that's what made that record exciting. That record was a challenge, just to get it to sound the way it did, and not only that, but it was the first production I'd ever done completely on my own."

For the newer generation of engineers and producers who came up shaped by his influence, Jourgensen gives his thoughts on the most important path to follow:

> If you're an artist and if you're very passionate about your music, don't listen to the producer. Fight for what you think your sound is, because the engineer and producer are coming from a different reference point that is never going to be as good as the band member who's involved 24-7 in knowing how he or she wants their music to sound. So *don't* be intimidated, that's from the band side. From the producer's side, of course use your own imprint, but don't overtake the band, let them have their say and let them have their sound. Having been on both sides of that process for as many years as I have been, I've learned that making records is all about that balance.

CHAPTER 19

Ron Nevison–The Comeback Kid

Ron Nevison as a rock producer operates much like a surgeon, brought in during a critical point in a band's career to bring them back from the commercial brink. Whether kick-starting a stalled hit-maker like Jefferson Airplane back into flight as Jefferson Starship with "Nothing's Gonna Stop Us Now," or breathing a breath of fresh air back into an outdated band's sound—such as was the case with Heart on seminal 1980s FM ballads like "These Dreams" and "Alone"—Nevison has rarely had a patient—metaphorically speaking—that he couldn't heal with his multiplatinum production touch. He kept creative counsel throughout the late 1960s and early–mid-1970s working as a live soundman and engineer alongside many of rock's greatest legends, beginning with his running sound throughout the second half of the former decade with the likes of Eric Clapton, Traffic, and Jefferson Airplane, among others.

Nevison's relocation from the United States to Britain at the dawn of the '70s was con-sistent—in a creative context—with the trend of British rock bands dominating the Ameri-can rock landscape at the time, from Eric Clapton's various incarnations, from Cream to Derek & the Dominos, to bands like the Jimi Hendrix Experience and the Who, all of whom became overnight legends in the late 1960s while Nevison was cutting his teeth on the live touring circuit. Bringing him back home with them to the United Kingdom, Nevison would not only have to adopt different social customs, but also adapt to an entirely foreign way of recording from the studio norms stateside.

> They did things differently, recorded differently. It was the overall ambience of the recording studio, compared with the U.S. And now don't forget, I had never really spent any time working in a recording studio, let alone in the U.S., and went right to England. But I later found out that the U.S. studios, especially rooms in the record plant and places like that, were built for R&B, close micing, and for no big drum sounds, little drum booths that were all padded, and all that kind of stuff, where the studios in England had much more ambience. They tended to mic things differently, use different mic techniques and stuff like that. I think generally listening in the room to acoustic instruments, whether piano, drums, or acoustic guitar, and finding the best place, where they sounded complete.

The irony in Nevison being a U.S. native who'd been raised on American rock sensibilities now sitting in the United Kingdom helping to create the next wave of the British Invasion should not be lost on fans, because it was a subtle first for anyone sitting in that position—and naturally, few were.

Nevison's years in the early 1970s working for Island Studios brought him even closer within the inner circle of the bands that had trusted him with their live performance of songs he was now helping to craft from scratch in the studio. This side-by-side tutelage working with many of the biggest rock bands of the decade—who by that point had decided they were better off self-producing—allowed the engineer to become something of a default coproducer. He worked alongside men like Pete Townshend and Jimmy Page—considered two of the greatest musical minds in masterminding rock's advancement as a studio sound throughout the 1970s. In the case of the Who, with whom Nevison worked especially closely on the recording of both *Tommy* and *Quadrophenia*, the young engineer became an intimate part of creating

> two projects with the Who—beginning in 1975—*Quadrophenia* and the *Tommy* soundtrack, which was recorded before the film was shot. . . . I didn't record 100 percent of it. That was unique, because Pete did a lot of the guitars at his home studio, and I would record everything else. I think *Quadrophenia*, at that time, was the first major engineering job that I got, and the way that I got it was I was working for this company

called Track Plant, and was also an engineer. And Track Plant was a company that Townshend owned that was building studios for people in their homes. We were building a mixer and an 8-track reel-to-reel all in one box, just like a 12-channel mixer. Very primitive stuff, but some of the very first stuff that was built for home recording. And I had been hired to build a studio for Ron Lane in a brand new Airstream Trailer he had bought on tour that was completely naked inside. And so I built a recording studio; first it was 8-track, then 16-track, a mobile, they called them mobile studios. And it had a console I was familiar with, like the one from Island Studios, and this was before SSL. And I think Townshend was so impressed by it, and they were getting ready to start recording *Quadrophenia*, and were building their own studio, and the studio wasn't ready. So they decided to hire Ronnie Lane's mobile to start the record, to cut the tracks, and I was the logical one to get the job to engineer, because I'd built the thing. So, of course if I hadn't done a good job, they wouldn't have kept me. I was originally hired just to cut the basic tracks. And I ended up doing the whole album. And of course, from that, I was hired to do the *Tommy* soundtrack. All the other things came from that.

As Nevison's first big break as an engineer, it was also the training ground on which he would build the foundation for his approach to recording a perfect drum sound on countless multiplatinum albums to come. His guinea pig for perfecting that approach, arguably one of rock's greatest, loudest, and most prolific drummers in terms of kit-size, was the Who's Keith Moon, who Nevison tracked alongside Pete Townshend. Nevison explained that

micing Keith Moon's drum set was presented as a great challenge, because he had so many of them; you couldn't fit any mics in there, because the drums were so tightly grouped. You had to basically get a mic on the snare, and on the toms where you could, and just try to pick up everything else. And he played so fast and so beautifully it was a difficult thing. And also, the other big problem was when I started, the mobile studio was only eight tracks at the time I cut *Quadrophenia*, and it was supposed to be quadraphonic sound; that was the whole idea. So I spread; I premixed the drums to four tracks, I had to, there was no other way to discretely do four tracks. So I spread them out the way I thought they should be spread out, more like you were in a concert situation, and more like you were sitting in the middle of the drum kit though.

Rolling Stone, in its review of *Quadrophenia*, would call it "The Who at their most symmetrical, their most cinematic, ultimately their most maddening," and hailed the album sonically as "beautifully performed and magnificently recorded." The latter credit is shared between Townshend and Nevison as his wingman behind the console. Nevison explained:

Working with all these people, it wasn't like there was a producer; I didn't work any differently than I do now, because in those days, the bands produced themselves, with me. I just didn't get any credit in those days; I was just an engineer. And they asked me my opinion a lot on stuff, but I certainly learned a lot more from them than they learned from me. I was never afraid to give suggestions; my personality is such that I was never afraid to say anything. If they told me to shut up, fine, I would shut up. I think when you're working with a band, where the guitar player or vocalist is producer, they need your help. If Pete Townshend was out there doing a vocal, he wasn't the lead vocalist, but was the harmonizer, and he's out there alone, he needs to know how he's doing. And everything else.

As a mentor, Nevison regarded the opportunity to work alongside Townshend as "just so inspiring, and to have my first engineering project be the follow-up to *Tommy*, and it was highly regarded." One of the first lessons Nevison received from Townshend was the art of preproduction, which for a perfectionist like Townshend, was a recording process all its own. The engineer recalled that

Pete as a producer was prepared; he did demos but didn't do the demos so good that he intimidated the other musicians. He did demos that became tracks in some cases. Some of the stuff he had done so much cool synthesizer stuff, and in those days, he used a big wall of ARP synthesizers. And you didn't push a button to get a sound; you had to work for an hour to get the sound, and you couldn't keep it. I don't know if you realize the amount of work synthesizers were in the mid-'70s. He'd have to get a bunch of Oscillators, and hook them all up and get the sound, tweak the sound, and put it down on tape. And you couldn't keep that sound; if you turned them off, you had to start over from scratch. So basically he did a lot of work on tracks that he would have a click track, and on some things we would basically—like the overture to *Quadrophenia*—we would have John and Keith come in and overdub on that and use that as our master. And Pete would put his own drums on things sometimes, just to show . . . He wouldn't do his drums like Keith Moon would; he would just put a simple drum track on there to give Keith a simple idea. But he had things pretty planned out, and would go home and do synthesizer at home. And then John would take tracks home and do horns on the weekend. So preparation was one thing I learned as a producer from Pete.

In terms of preproduction norms that Nevison would develop in the years to come as a producer in his own right—based in part on his work with rock icons like Pete Townshend—some of the producer's routines include:

With a band, obviously before we started rehearsals, I would be familiar with their music. And I would have tried at some point, I would have a meeting with the band, whether on the phone, or in person, and then what I thought of the music, whether I thought they had what they needed in the way of songs, and if they didn't, I would tell them to go back and write more stuff. Or find songs for them, depending on the situation. And in song terms, that could be a single, or a follow-up single. And in some cases, I would encourage the band to cowrite with people. In other words, I would fill in the slots. And once all the material was gathered, then we would get together right before the recording started, maybe for three or four days, depending on the group, and go in and work on maybe three or four songs a day. And just get them to the point where they were ready to be recorded. In preproduction, the song is the most important thing. And then the vocal performance is the second most important thing, then production, and on down the line. And the way you achieve that, through analog, or digital, is through practice.

Upon entering the studio with the Who to record *Quadrophenia*, the technical complexities of tracking the rock opera covered both conceptual and musical frontiers that were new to the general science of studio recording at the time. Nevison explained some of the specific challenges:

Quadrophenia was about Jimmy, who had four different faces or personalities if you like; he was quadrophrenic, rather than schizophrenic. So he had four sides, and each side was one of the Who. That was the whole idea behind the album. So the whole album was written by Pete beforehand; there was no experimenting with the writing. There was experimenting all along the trail throughout the recording, but he was well prepared. With effects, leading up to my work in the '70s with the Who, you have to think in terms of 1960s effects, where everything was spring reverbs; this was before any digital device. There was, around 70 or 71, Ty Clockworks came out with the Harmonizer and Digital Delay, but it was in its early stages. So even when the Who's *Quadrophenia* came out, it was still very new. Pete always had it all together ahead of time; he knew exactly what he wanted, down to the effect. Because not only was he a good producer and writer, but he was his own engineer at his home studio. So he knew what to do. We also didn't have, when we mixed *Quadrophenia*, we didn't have a console with a computer on it. So what we did was he had these broadcast cartridges, and we loaded the effects, thunder and all that stuff, into the cartridges, which were the kind we used at radio stations. Where you hit a button, and it would play, and cue up to the next one, like you had like eight commercials in a row. So we would just load them as we used them, and as the mix was going on, we would both of us be hitting buttons and cues. So that's how we did a lot of the stuff. There were all sorts of train whistles, and other stuff too.

The success of *Quadrophenia* established Nevison as a sonic puppet master, a technical orchestral conductor of sorts in terms of the multiple musical parts he had to juggle among a limited number of available tracks to record upon given the available technology heading into the middle of the 1970s. Still, the ground the band had broken from purely a technical standpoint would keep Nevison employed as one of the top engineers in the business for the next five years. His follow-up project to *Quadrophenia* would pair Nevison with another of the genre's biggest bands, Led Zeppelin, who hired him halfway through the album's tracking. The engineer/producer recalled that

> I was only involved with recording half of *Physical Graffiti*, because even when they started recording it, they didn't realize it was going to be a double album. And the album prior, *Houses of the Holy*, which was originally going to be a double album, they ended up using about half of the stuff from those sessions that they hadn't used. So it ended up being a double album. We used Ronny Lane's Mobile, the studio I built, again, and Zeppelin had called me up, because they had heard about *Quadrophenia* and the Mobile and were interested in going down and recording at this place called Headley Grange. Now whether or not they had tried to get the Stones' mobile, which was the only other mobile at the time, and couldn't get it because they were on tour or whatever, they just got a good recommendation from Townshend. And I got the call and went down, and the rest is history. I moved the mobile down there and set it up and went to town. Initially, I went down, and John Paul Jones was having some personal problems, and they didn't say, and I didn't ask, so we didn't do—we didn't even rehearse any of the stuff; we spent about a week messing around, just doing old Elvis stuff, honestly. And just having fun down there.

Describing some of the technical aspects of tracking Led Zeppelin to tape, Nevison explained that

> once tracking got underway, in terms of working with Page, I was most fascinated by just the uniqueness of his music, but also just such a unique sound that Bonham had. He could be in a room—for instance, in one case I had wheeled these two microphones on his drum kit, about fifteen or twenty feet away, but—and I say but, because the drum kit was set up in a hallway that was about twenty-five feet square and about thirty-five feet high, and it was a slightly rectangle hallway, in a house where the stairway went around and around and around endlessly. And I put the microphones about

ten feet on the first landing above the drum kit, but it was a place in the room where if you listened, the drum kit sounded even, it mixed itself. And when he played, because of how loud it was, because of the marble floor, the drums, when Bonham played, mixed themselves. And you just put up a couple of mics in a stereo pair and there it was. And I used that same place six months or a year later; I went back with Bad Company to Headley Grange for their first album, and it did not work for Simon; he didn't like it, and I didn't like it. You had to be Bonham. So I ended up doing a different thing with them, in a different room; I put him separately in a different room and put everybody else in another room, where he couldn't see the other players. And it worked.

While working with Led Zeppelin was a dream come true for any rock engineer of the day, Nevison's loyalty to Pete Townshend interfered with that dream coming to full fruition, with Nevison explaining that

one of the reasons I had to leave the Zeppelin project, because I had to start with the *Tommy* thing. What a dilemma for a young guy to have to leave Zeppelin for the Who. But if I'd stayed around to finish up the Zeppelin thing, I would have been replaced for *Tommy*, and I might never have been able to do it. So they weren't very happy with me. And I don't think anyone had ever quit a Zeppelin gig before, but I had told them this scheduling conflict was there, and they had fallen behind. So I had to leave the project before it was done.

While the Who had first recorded the studio version of the rock opera in 1968, the film soundtrack, released in 1975, featured a who's who of guest stars, ranging from Elton John and Tina Turner to and Eric Clapton among others, allowing Nevison to expand his palette of collaborations even further into the upper echelon of rock royalty. In recalling some of the contrasts between the tracking the *Quadrophenia* vs. *Tommy*, Nevison recalled that

there were a couple of different challenges; one was Keith Moon had kind of gone off the deep end at the beginning of this, in terms of alcohol and drugs, and so he wasn't really reliable. And so Pete decided, rather than come in with another drummer, because Pete had so much respect still for Keith and didn't want to hurt his feelings, he decided to have guest people do everything. In other words, Pete would play, but John would only occasionally play, and Eric Clapton would come in, and Kenny Johns from the Faces, Tony Stevens from Foghat, a bunch of different players—and I think Pete did it all to make Keith feel okay, so it wasn't really the Who anymore, even though Townshend was still in control. Pete produced. So it was different, because we had a lot of musicians, so it wasn't much of a band vibe. And with Ken Russell, the whole

soundtrack was recorded before they started filming, so he was always making little changes, edits, etc. And Pete had to come back in and write all sorts of new film
music, like new instrumentals—it was a long process. And it was my first film, it was a
great experience, but totally different from the *Quadrophenia* album.

By the early 1980s, Nevison had transitioned from being one of the most in-demand
engineers in the business to one of its busiest producers. Born in part from the hit album he
had produced for Survivor with *Vital Signs* in 1984, which featured three Top 20 radio hits
with "The Search is Over," "High On You," and "I Can't Hold Back," the true hit that shot
Nevison's stock value into the stratosphere was his 1984 collaboration with Ann and Nancy
Wilson in the course of Heart's self-titled comeback LP. Though the Wilson sisters' brand
of infectiously hooky, radio-friendly hard rock had almost singularly defined women in rock
throughout the latter 1970s, the band had faltered in the early 1980s following a series of
lineup changes and multiple producers over the course of their first few albums in the early
part of the decade. In desperate need of radio reinvention, Nevison recalled,

> The end of '84 is when I got the call to come in and talk about Heart. Don Grierson
> called, I think it was Don, the head of A&R at Capitol. What had happened, as you
> know, was that Heart had come out with one of the biggest debut albums of the
> '70s—I think except for Boston, the Heart girls had one of the biggest debut albums.
> And unfortunately, they basically, unknowingly, they chased a couple of the guys out
> of the band who were boyfriends but who wrote a lot of the songs. And I had always
> thought when I first heard them, this is a cool rock 'n' roll band, a girl with lungs like
> this, and moves like that, that had both sides. The critical elements for rock in those
> days were to have the rockers and the ballads; it happened with all the hits I had,
> even Bad Company. Heart had by this time, 1980 or so, they had nobody to write riffs
> or any of the Barracuda stuff, and they were becoming a little fluff band. And while
> Heart was really adept at the *Dog and Butterfly* type stuff, they really weren't rock-
> ing; they had lost that side of them. And their sales, they had lost their lead single
> potential, and I think by '82 or '83 Epic dropped them. And so Don Grierson saw the
> potential but signed them with a warning that they had to mutually agree on the pro-
> ducer and the songs, that the band had to agree to do outside songs. Which they had
> never been before, so they agreed. And so they had a new manager, Trudy Green, a
> new record label, Capitol, and a new producer, Ron Nevison, and everybody believed
> in them, which is a good foundation.

With Heart's agreement to work with outside songwriters as an iron-clad condition of
not only their being signed to Capitol but also of Nevison's for working with the band, lead

guitarist Howard Leese, for one, felt the decision was pivotal to the success of the album's recording and its commercial results. Lee recalled:

> When we left Epic in 1984 and signed with Capitol, and the band hadn't been doing that well, so we kind of knew this was really going to be our last big shot. If this record tanked, we might not have a record deal, and when things weren't going well, the girls tended to be a lot more interested in listening to other people's ideas and opinions. With that in mind, heading into the Heart record, Ron Nevison had been paying attention and had seen what Jimmy Iovine and Keith had gone through, and the results, and a key clause of the whole deal with him producing us was his saying, "There's a lot of talent here, but I need authority, I need to be able to say no, these songs aren't good enough." And he was right. We went in, on the records we did with Nevison, and would record thirty songs an album, full-on recordings, good enough to be on anyone's record in preproduction. We'd go into a real studio, and just go through tons and tons of material to pick the best songs.

In describing the process by which the album's track listing took shape, Nevison recalled that

> By working with Michael Lippman, who is my manager and also manages Bernie Taupin, Elton John's lyricist, we got some great songs from Bernie, one of which was "These Dreams," which I thought would be great for Nancy, because she's sort of a space cadet in a nice way, dreamy. And Don Grierson sent me this song "What About Love?" which Jim Vallance had written, and they got the girls together with Holly Night. So there were three or four songs they had not written, and like everything else, I had first listened to see what they had, and what was missing, and then started filling in the gaps. I didn't just go out and find songs for them, until I determined what they had. And I liked all their songs, but they needed some solid single material. And the rest is really history.

Prior to beginning principal tracking, the group's confidence in the studio ensemble handling their comeback album's production had shot through the roof, due in part to what Howard Leese described as a dream team of engineers that obviously included Nevison, who, according to the guitarist, "in addition to being a great producer and having a clear idea of what he wanted to get done with the record, was a great engineer—he'd engineered for Led Zeppelin, and the Who, so he was an amazing engineer. On the first record we did with him, he didn't engineer, he produced it and had Mike Clink as the engineer, which was his last record as an engineer before going on to produce Guns N' Roses. So we had two *ridiculous* engineers on that record." Nevison seemed pleased with the team he had assembled, recalling that "it was great working with them. We cut tracks with the band in L.A., and we then mutually agreed to work at the Sausalito Record Plant, because it was equidistant between our homes, mine in L.A., theirs in Seattle, and so we had a lot of fun. So we finished it up in the bay area."

Discussing the album's massively popular hit singles, "These Dreams" was one which Nevison and company took more time with, due in part to his feeling that

> initially I didn't hear "These Dreams" as a hit single. It was the third hit single off the album, and there were other things before it that I had heard as singles. I had maybe envisioned it as a single, but never a number one single. But the way the whole album was set up, with "What About Love?" being a really strong lead-off single, and then "Never" really kicking ass, which set up Nancy's voice with a ballad for the third single, so ultimately the order was perfect. But I don't think the sisters even heard it as a single, until I cut out to the second verse. The original version brought the chorus in fairly quickly, and then all of a sudden, they went, "Wow, that's a single." Initially it was a little bit long, and I wanted Nancy to sing two songs on the record as lead; she had traditionally only done one. And I thought she had way too good a voice to just do one song, and was really happy she had a number one single.

Following the multiplatinum success of Heart, Nevison was the hottest property in Top 40 pop-rock production, and while he stayed that course to some degree by working with Joe Cocker, Nevison also chose to return to his hard-rock and metal roots by collaborating with Ozzy Osbourne on his 1986 album *The Ultimate Sin*, bringing the producer back to Europe. Nevison recalled, "I had flown to England to do some tracks with Joe Cocker, and while I was in London, I got the call to go meet Sharon and Ozzy, and agreed to stay on and do the *Ultimate Sin* album. By this time in 1985, I'd done lots of pop hits, I'd done UFO, and had the history with Zeppelin, and some metal stuff, and so I was a perfect fit, I thought." With one of the most debaucherous reputations in the record business, Ozzy Osbourne's rocker on- and offstage antics were already the stuff of legends, with highlights that included biting a live dove's head off during a meeting with record executives, a live bat's onstage, and being banned from performing in Texas forever after he was arrested for drunkenly urinating on the wall of the historic Alamo. Nevison's first rule with Ozzy during recording sessions that differed from past sessions was: "I wouldn't let him drink. That was a new experience for him. He was sober."

Another change for Osbourne, and a first in his fifteen-year history as a recording artist, was Nevison's approach to tracking the metal legend's vocals:

He was single tracked for that album. He was used to double tracking all his vocals, and I wanted to try and do better vocals with him. Because a lot of times, that's a sign of somebody that's not . . . I wanted him to be proud of his vocals, and if we could do it without double tracking, then I wanted to try to do that. I didn't know if he would; he was never known as a great singer. But he certainly had sold enough records up to that point. So some of the stuff we did worked with that, some of the stuff did not.

Though Nevison categorized Osbourne as a professional when he did show up to record, initially the producer recalled "a little bit of a problem when it came to the vocals, because Ozzy was AWOL a lot. He wouldn't turn up. So I had a word with Sharon, and we agreed to take it to Paris. Sharon didn't go, but I went with Ozzy and his minder—this guy who looked after him. And I booked this studio in Paris, and made sure I took the right microphones with me. And I figured Ozzy would be climbing up the walls to get home, and that's exactly what happened. He didn't miss a day in the studio, he sang every day, didn't miss a day. But it went very smoothly, and we did all the vocals." Aside from the organizational drama of tracking Osbourne's vocals, Nevison painted an environment during the recording of backing instrumental tracks.

Randy Castillo was a great drummer, wonderful guy. Where guitars were concerned, lead guitarist Jake E. Lee was great. When we did track, he was very prepared, got great sounds, and in all was great to work with. There was a little bit of a problem because the guy got up at midnight. And it wasn't drugs or anything; this guy was into martial arts and yoga, and was a very strange character. So my problem with him was I didn't want to start working at three in the morning, and work till eleven, so we had to come to a compromise, and that was worked out. In a band like that, where there's hardly any keyboards, and where there was one guitar player, 90 percent of the over-dubs were with him, except for backgrounds and vocals. So that went great, once we got an understanding. I don't remember specifically what hours we worked out, but we mutually agreed to work those hours, and we got it done.

The *Ultimate Sin* produced another hit single for both Nevison and Osbourne with "Shot in the Dark," and based on its success, the producer decided to stick within the world of hard rock for the moment, opting to next produce Kiss's 1987 *Crazy Nights* LP. In contrast to the challenges of recording with Ozzy, Nevison found his studio experience with Kiss to be

the most fun thing. Not only because I think the musicianship was great in that band over the original lineup, which had some gaps in it, but where the band's new lead guitarist, Bruce Kulick, was just an amazing guitar player. And the drummer, Eric Singer, was a wonderful guy. And of course Paul and Gene were decent players, and they wrote everything. And it's funny, Gene would submit thirty or forty songs to me, and Paul would give me six. And all of Paul's were great, and so I would have to weed through Gene's. Gene would just toss me anything; he once sent me a song called "I'm Going to Put a Log in Your Fire Place." People usually all agree with what the good songs are, and in the end, I don't make people do anything; I back off and just say, "Look, I'm just giving you the result of my experience. You can either take my advice or not." And most people, that scares people. 'Cause they don't want me to say I told you so. And the party was all onstage with Kiss; they were not a party band at all.

Kiss would score a hit with the album's title track as Nevison dived headlong into his sophomore collaboration with Heart for *Bad Animals.* According to the producer: "I had a year between albums to look for material, and started immediately. That's how I came up with 'Alone.'" A smash hit for Heart, it would be the band's fourth number one single, along with "Who Will You Run To?" and "There's the Girl." Recounting the creative genesis of "Alone," lead guitarist Howard Leese recalled that

we knew that would be the first single and that it would be a hit song while we were recording it, and I remember being in my hotel room the night before I had to do the solo, thinking, "This song is going to be number one, so the solo better be pretty good." And so I felt the pressure, but not an intimidating kind of pressure, but a little bit empowering, because I knew I needed to bring my A game. The other thing I wanted to do as a soloist is take the energy from the lead vocal that she hands over to me when the solo starts, and I have to start at the level she's at, and if possible raise it up a little bit, bring the intensity up, and when I hand it back to the lead vocal, she's now higher still. It's your job as the soloist to take over for the lead vocal and bring it up a notch. That was the one case where I knew that song was going to be number one, I could just tell.

In describing some of the technical details of the album's recording, Nevison recalled that "in 1986, I bought a Mitsubishi 32-track, and did the *Bad Animals* album, and was pretty much digital from then on. Except I still recorded most of the basic tracks analog. Digital recording gave me more tracks, it gave me more tracks especially in that I still cut the tracks on analog, and then immediately started going digital, so I saved the analog tracks and then could mix the drums down and use them as guides and have a lot of extra tracks. It gave me a lot more space as a producer, instead of going 48-track with analog." While Nevison had coengineered alongside Mike Clink for his first collaboration with Heart, by 1987, guitarist Howard Leese remembered that "on the next record, *Bad Animals*, Ron did that album himself, and they were just beautiful recordings." With their confidence peaking in the studio, Leese recalled the atmosphere surrounding the album's tracking as being productively paced, in classic Nevison style: "We were just on a roll—everybody knew what they were doing, we had a great producer and had all the best songwriters working for us, so you could feel that we were in high gear. For instance, with 'Who Will You Run To?,' another single off that album, was a Diane Warren song; we learned and tracked that in two days."

Following the massive success of Heart's pair of multiplatinum comeback collaborations, it was the producer's work with rock supergroup the Damn Yankees in 1989 that would produce his next smash single, "High Enough." Featuring a lineup that included Ted Nugent, Night Ranger's Jack Blades, and Styx's Tommy Shaw, Nevison explained that his pairing with the band came via

> my good buddy John Kalodner, who put the idea—and that is what John is best at, ideas—of the Damn Yankees together, because Jack Blades and Tommy Shaw, they were all big schmoozer buddies, and he got them together. They went in, did some demos, and Kalodner took them to Geffen, and Ted Rosenblatt, who was head of A&R, and he said, "No." And so it found its way to Warner Brothers. I'd just done the Chicago albums for Warner's, and had had some hits with them, so Michael Asner called me up, and I came over and listened to the three- or four-song demo, and loved the stuff, and wanted to meet them. And I was supposed to work with Night Ranger previously, and had backed out of the project for personal reasons about a month before the project was set to begin, and I thought that might be a deal breaker. But the guys were gentlemen about it, and we had a great time working together. What had gotten me most excited about working with the band from their demo was "High Enough,"—that was an immediate hit.

Delving into some of the specifics of the album's recording, Nevison recalled that

> in the studio, it was Tommy and Jack's project, really, but when they went on tour, it was Ted's road show. Ted wouldn't agree with that, but the fact was the best part about it was having two guitar players in the band. That left-to-right thing, and Tommy was more than a great guitar player. But Ted presented problems, because he only wanted to fly out from Michigan for five days to do anything. So I never got to have them play together. And Ted played second; he always played after Tommy had finished all his tracks. So I never got to do a trade-off thing that I wanted to do, and that always bugged me about Ted—that he never thought enough about the project to put in the time. The strengths of that project that I tried to bring out was first that Tommy and Jack harmonized so well, and they traded off vocals, and were almost like

one person in a lot of ways. It was great watching them work. And the fact that they complemented each other so well. And we had a great drummer, too; it was just an amazing project to be involved with.

With pop rock alive as ever as a genre almost a decade into the millennium, Nevison notes in addressing the topic of a signature sound that

I think my production style, as a derivative on a new school of producers, is starting to come around because the '70s is making a comeback. And what happens in this cyclical kind of thing, in ten years, the '80s will be coming around again. Fourteen-year-old musicians are forming bands now and listening to Led Zeppelin, and bands like that are going to want me to do them in five years when they make a record. And it's amazing that thirteen-year-old kids right now have gone from Britney two years ago, to hip-hop at thirteen, to fourteen to Led Zeppelin. Talk to me then and I'll probably be more relevant than I am now. Ultimately, I think we will always go back to basic rock 'n' roll fundamentals when we record.

CHAPTER 20

A Grammy nomination for Record Producer of the Year is as rare a thing to come by as a hit record, and for a producer who has racked as up a Top 20 list full of them, Michael Beinhorn has the equally distinguished honor of having done so across more subgenres of alternative rock than most of his producer-peers during the genre's later '80s and '90s heyday. Remember skating in junior high to the Red Hot Chili Peppers' *Uplift Mofo Party Plan* or moshing at your local rock club in 9th grade to *Mother's Milk*? What about getting stoned with your girl or tripping on LSD for the first time in high school to Soundgarden's "Black Hole Sun"? Looking over Beinhorn's resume, one would also find poignant collaborations with legend Herbie Hancock, Soul Asylum, avant-garde bassist/composer Bill Laswell, Violent Femmes, Social Distortion, Hole, Marilyn Manson, Korn, and Ozzy Osbourne among others. Irrespective of the stylistic medley of sounds Beinhorn has navigated throughout his career as a record maker, one of his bedrock principles of production has remained an "attitude from one artist to another that has never changed. To me, it's important to capture the presence of the artist, whatever that is. To me, that's the main thing. If there's any way, technically or otherwise, that you can cause an artist's personality to come out and do their recording, in my mind I feel I've been successful. The ways and means of doing it are always open and subject to change at a moment's notice. It can never be the same, and shouldn't really."

Though they weren't the best-selling of his catalog, Beinhorn's collaboration with the Red Hot Chili Peppers over the course of *The Uplift Mofo Party Plan* and the band's breakout from the underground, *Mother's Milk,* are arguably two of the most successful examples of the producer's talent for helping an artist discover during the making of an album artistic potential they might not have even known they possessed—let alone the fan base that followed. Still, while MTV would indeed later hail *The Uplift Mofo Party Plan* as the Chili Peppers' first album "to make an impression" within the mainstream industry, Beinhorn recalled that prior to signing up to work with the band, an impression was precisely what they had made on the business, such that "at that particular point, no one else wanted to work with them. I felt like I could probably make a record with just around anyone, and I wanted to work with them. They were reviled by their record company at that point."

Heading into the studio with the band, the producer recalled being focused conceptually by the reality that he was facing the headwind of "certain people [at the band's label who] would have been happy to see them languish into invisibility, so I really wanted to try and make a record that would help them survive at that point." Beinhorn's goal would be further handicapped—from a traditional record making model—by the challenge that "in recording that album, we had a very small amount of money to work with." From his own sonic standpoint, Beinhorn said, as the band dove into production on record, something their career was very much riding on at that point, "I was hoping that the recording would sound a certain way, and didn't want to really compromise for the sake of the artist, particularly because I had developed a certain affection for these guys."

Describing some of the technical details of the album's basic tracking, the producer recalled that "the mic setup on that album was fairly rudimentary, like in most cases where people say 'Oh, that drum sound was amazing,' you also have to remember first that you have to start with an amazing drummer." Capitalizing on the band's root rhythmic strength of "always having had the best drummers," Beinhorn added that he regarded then-drummer Jack Irons "as one of my favorite drummers of all time, he was just a remarkable drummer." As the band tracked the album, they did so on "a Neve console in Capitol B studio," where the album's rocket-fueled rhythm section was created. Beinhorn recalled: "I think a lot of the drum sound we got had to do with his playing. I would go so far as to say it's not easy to make Jack sound bad. He knows how to hit. We wound up working with an orange, Ludwig kit, which we didn't have a budget to even rent drums, so we just took the best that we had."

Where with later albums the Chili Peppers would track live together off the floor, at that early point in their recorded career, Beinhorn explained, he preferred an approach where "we didn't track any of the record live. At that point in time, it had to do with wanting to get a certain sound and separation, but I was finding that a lot of bands who were great live bands didn't play well together in the studio. In the case of the Chilis, tracking live didn't work out, so we had to track everything separately." As with most producers, Beinhorn preferred to capture the band at their most comfortable hour of creativity, quipping that "I think most people who have a recording artist's type of job tend to be more oriented toward the evening, and the Chili Peppers were no different.

While the group's broader sound presented a party-up vibe, during its recording, the producer recalled, a key creator of that sound—bassist Flea— maintained a far more serious attitude. "He was there to work. He didn't do a lot of fucking about when it came to recording. He was pretty serious and put his all into whatever he did. He's a great musician and is extremely talented." Elaborating on the fundamentals of Flea's singular brand of melodic funk-punk bass playing, Beinhorn said, "Flea's a stylist, and definitely one of a kind," adding that in terms of pure musicality, "his sense of timing and feel is really, really good. Harmonically, for a bass player, I always found him to be a cut above as well. Flea, he's a very rhythmic bass player, and I think his choice of root notes is always very, very good. He recorded DI (direct input); there was no amp. When we were tracking, he was quite technically proficient."

Turning to the tracking of founding axeman Hillel Slovak's guitar tracks, Beinhorn shared that in the studio, "Hillel played through Marshalls, and as a guitarist he had a very unusual approach to the whole thing. It was Hendrixy, and definitely influenced by a lot of James Brown stuff, but still a whole other thing. He was a stylist as well. I would never characterize him as a songwriter, he was more of a parts writer. Recording Hillel, he had his days. Some days he was more on, other days he was more in the clouds. But he could definitely play, no question about it." Sadly, the producer's cryptic reference to the guitarist's head being sometimes a little too lost in the clouds would play out in a fatal heroin overdose following the release of *Uplift Mofo Party Plan.*

Back in the studio and ahead of the latter tragedy, when attention turned to tracking singer Anthony Kiedis's lead vocals, while producer Beinhorn complimented him as "definitely another stylist, where when you hear his voice, you know it's him, there's no question about it."

As part of this process, Beinhorn also revealed that, from a technical musical standpoint, as tracking got underway and the singer and producer sought to break new ground in taking Kiedis's vocal style in a more melodic direction, "he definitely had a hard time hitting pitch on a lot of stuff." Working without the vocal corrective aids producers and artists enjoy in the digital age, Beinhorn took a hands-on approach to helping Kiedis through his technical difficulties:

> Because we didn't have pitch correction back then, the way we would do it is: if we had a melody line, I would go and sing the melody part, and then go and double-track just to reinforce it. Then when he was in the booth singing, I would go in and kind of sing it to his ear while he was in there singing as well. So it was definitely a process. Anthony worked really hard. I think he knew that he was up against a lot, and when he was challenged, he really rose to the occasion and did his best. We cut vocals at a variety of different studios, and at one point, I remember I tried experimenting with a double-mic array where we used an Eli 251 together with an AKG P-48 414 on a song called "Love Trilogy."

While *Rolling Stone* would later compliment the album as bringing "a modicum of structure" to the band, from outward appearances it looked as if the Chili Peppers were falling apart following the death of their best friend, and quite literally. Along with the loss of their guitarist, drummer Jack Irons also departed the band following Slovak's passing, leaving many wondering if the Chili Peppers would be able to conjure the creative spirit to carry on. That outlook on Kiedis's and Flea's part helped Beinhorn as he headed into the studio with the band in late 1988 to record an album whose expectations were wildly high–internally in terms of the band taking on both a new drummer and arguably most importantly, a new lead guitarist, and externally in terms of a label that was now much more excited about and supportive of the band's potential for a commercial breakthrough given the steady rise of alternative rock. Addressing the biggest change the band was facing heading into their second studio collaboration, the producer recalled new guitarist John Frusciante, "who was his maiden voyage with the band. He was just a little kid at that point, and this was his dream thing to do in the world basically. The Chili Peppers had been his favorite band since he was a little kid, and all of a sudden here he is playing with them. So that was a great big deal for him, and it was definitely quite a contrast between him and Hillel."

Delving into those differences as they aided the band's record-making process, Beinhorn revealed that "John had more of a grasp of the technique of music. I think he could actually read, unlike 90 percent of the guys who are in rock bands. He had a good grasp of music theory, and he just came at it from a completely different standpoint. Aside from being a really good guitarist, he had a pretty good sense of musical structure, which was unusual to the band. I think that was the turning point for the band having those kind of structural elements introduced into what they did, which they'd never ever even come close to before." Turning to how Frusciante's addition to the group altered the Chili's songwriting DNA, the producer shared that "one thing I recall about working with the Chili

Peppers when they had Hillel was they were more of a band that jammed ideas and were able to turn them into songs, whereas with John, he actually brought finished pieces to the table and the band would work them out."

As the Chili Peppers commenced recording in late 1988 at the B Room of Ocean Way Studios, Beinhorn said, part of his production plan was to utilize the band's role changes to push Kiedis in a more traditional direction as a lead vocalist with *Mother's Milk*'s new material. This would prove a requirement for the transition toward their commercial breakout, and one that required airplay. Beinhorn explained that "Anthony *had* to sing more on that record, because John came in with this song 'Knock Me Down,' and it was the first song that the Chili Peppers did that had a real melodic flow to it. It wasn't these pentatonic, blues-based, scaley type things, or that was just shouted. They all liked the song, but when Anthony was recording his vocals, in general, I don't remember that he liked having a lot of people around when we were working, maybe because he was singing more."

Once he was working with Frusciante in the studio, according to Beinhorn, "John came in with these Ibanez guitars, which had these Floyd Rose tremolo systems on them and whatnot, which is completely antithetical to the whole vibe of the Chili Peppers. So they were very, very opposed to that whole thing, which was actually very funny. It took a little while, but eventually John agreed not to use the Ibanez guitars. We hooked him up with a Strat and a Les Paul, which is more their kind of sound. I think he gravitated to Fenders after that. When recording John, I think we used 57s and 421s to mic him."

When attention turned to tracking a bass sound on the album that *Rolling Stone* concluded had evolved to a "mind-melting" level of mastery, Beinhorn seemed most proud of the fact that "on that album, I think Flea showed how good a musician he is, and how talented a creative individual he is by being able to adapt to a completely different element."

Describing what he felt Frusciante's playing brought to the console in upping Flea's game, the producer said:

> John bringing the structural element in is something that involved more harmonic and melodic complexity, which gave Flea the opportunity to go in a different direction. So automatically that mitigated his funk leanings somewhat. I remember one song that he'd actually written the bass line for that was a very fast 6-8 song, and required 16th notes all the way through. It was pretty fast, so he could really only get through a couple bars at a time, so there was a lot of punching in, and he was sweating and cursing up a storm. But what he was doing at that point, considering how he was playing using that Larry Graham style, it was close to impossible anyway. Flea by that album had a Mesa 400 bass rig.

Rounding out a revitalized rhythm section that *Playboy* hailed as "the most dynamic punk funk connection you're likely to hear for a long time," Beinhorn highlighted the contrast between tracking new drummer Chad Smith and former Jack Irons as among the greatest joys of recording the act. This was in spite of the fact that

> Chad and Jack are two completely different drummers. Chad is fun to watch, because he's a real rock guy. Stylistically they are different-type players. Jack always seemed a little more controlled in the studio, and Chad always seemed a little more nutty and like a wild man, which didn't make him harder to record at all. He's technically very adept. It was funny because when they were doing drummer auditions, Chad was the second or third-to-last drummer they saw, and the second he came in and started playing, I said, "Pick this guy, pick this guy." And at first, they didn't like him because he basically looked like he should have been in Poison or something. He had a bandana on and his hair was kind of funny, and they were like "He doesn't fit the image at all." And I was like "Just listen to this fucking guy play! Just pick him." And they waited days, and I was like "You guys have to be kidding me, this fucking guy is perfect! He's the man! Pick him." So finally they were like "Oh, alright" and picked him. Recording Chad, our mic setup for his drums was a 57 on the top, 421s on the toms, 414s for overheads.

Upon *Mother's Milk*'s release in 1989, *Billboard* wrote that the band had succeeded— "with producer Michael Beinhorn again behind the boards" in taking "everything that *The Uplift Mofo Party Plan* hinted at, and brought it fully to bear for this new venture." Beinhorn's talent for coaxing the star out of a reluctant artist—whether from a personal or professional position—was solidified following his success with the Chili Peppers' breakout album, which *Billboard* said "turned the tide and transformed the band from underground funk-rocking rappers to mainstream bad boys with seemingly very little effort." The producer was brought in on the heels of this success to produce Soul Asylum's breakout hit, *Grave Dancers Union*. A collaboration whose recorded results the *Chicago Tribune* would celebrate by way of its "anthemic guitars, desperate vocals and bombastic arrangements" meant the album had "breakthrough" written all over it. Beinhorn recalled that heading into the studio with the band, he was cautious with his approach to steering the band toward the latter direction because "Dave was a little too smart to play like dime-store psychology with."

Often, for a producer tasked by a major label with shepherding an indie band into the mainstream, the greatest challenge can rest in steering them away from their stubborn instinct to avoid that direction at all artistic—and therefore commercial—costs. For Soul Asylum's first album recorded with a major label budget, Beinhorn had to balance the latter considerations on behalf of both artist and record company in his goal of producing a radio-friendly middle ground that passed just enough musical muster with every involved party's ear. Offering an inside look into just how challenging a process that proved, the producer recalled that this struggle began with the fact that the band's lead singer/songwriter, Dave Pirner,

> really didn't seem to have that much interest in the odds and ends details of the re-cording process. On *Grave Dancers Union*, it was more of a challenge than recording Anthony Kiedis because you had a singer, so there was no rapping or shouting that you can kind of hide behind. I don't say that to discredit what Anthony does, because it wouldn't be a fair or accurate representation of my feelings, but Dave had to sing proper melodies on everything. And you really can't hide your feelings or intent about what you're doing when you're trying to sing a song. And if you're not there, and you're not in the frame of mind to be able to be evocative at that point, you're really, really going to fail miserably. So when we got started, Dave's vocal performances were not very inspired at all.

Seemingly as shy behind the vocal microphone in the studio as he projected himself on a music video screen, Beinhorn recalled that as he began working in closer quarters with the band's lead singer-songwriter, he had to navigate the challenge of the vocalist not

> really being the type of guy who could get up on the microphone and just start going. To motivate him, I tried—and try in general—to be somewhat empathetic with the peo-ple I'm working with, and it's sort of unavoidable really. I don't think I'm going to do a good job by them if I'm not. I just try to feel the situation out as carefully as possible, and consider what's going on through this person's mind, almost some new-age type of shit. Usually there's one overriding factor that affects a person's performance, and a lot of times, once that can be breached, everything just kind of starts falling into place. So obviously my first instinct was: I've got to get Dave comfortable.

Building off iTunes' critical observation years later in a review of the album that found "singer/songwriter/vocalist Dave Pirner upfront . . . (in) a role he was built for but always seemed to resist until this clear do-or-die moment for the band," Beinhorn found the pro-cess of bringing Pirner into that light,

> from a recording point of view, to be a question of, "Well, how do you vibe it up for a guy?" Some people—with all due respect—can be condescended to in a way where, basically, the end result is to benefit them anyway. You're not trying to be condescend-ing, it just works out that way; you just play with them until you get them to do what they ultimately will be proudest of. With other people, it's a whole different thing and

tion of making them comfortable. Some people just want to know that you're there with them, and that you're prepared to endure what they seem to feel they need to endure to make the right creative decisions. In Dave's case, it came down to who he was in the room with. So, what happened was, I kind of went "Oh shit, who's the person who's with him right now, who he's been with the longest, who he feels the most comfortable with?" And I looked at Danny Murphy and went "It's Danny," so I was like "Okay, we're gonna try something: Danny's gonna learn how to operate the tape machine, and everyone else is going to get the fuck out— including me." So me and the engineer left the room, and Danny and Dave worked together, and that's where all the vocals came from, with the exception of a song called "99%," and maybe one or two others.

Having made the necessary progress to lay down vocal takes that would later grace radio waves around the world, Beinhorn proudly added that "by that time, Dave felt so comfortable and confident with his singing that it didn't even matter who was in the room. Because he heard his vocals coming back sounding performance-wise the way he wanted them to, and that was all he needed." Still, from a technical vantage point, the producer revealed that

Dave was actually very difficult to record for some reason, partially because his voice is very nasally, so you'd put up the normal run-of-the-mill, go-to type microphones— 67s, M49s, U47s, all the wonderful great names—and we went through probably twenty microphones. And some of them sounded really good, but they all seemed to have this one thing: there was just this horrible peak in his voice, which all these mics tended to really, really amplify a lot. So in the end, I thought to myself, "What is the most neutral mic I can think of?" And at the time, the CU-44 had just come out, and we tried that, and it was the one. That mic is a very neutral, flat microphone that worked.

Upon release, Beinhorn's achievement in helping to steer Pirner and his fellow band-mates in Soul Asylum to a sonic and stylistic synergy would be celebrated by *Entertainment Weekly*: "Mixing up chunky '70s riffola, stirring country balladry, and punky vehemence, Soul Asylum slams its best cards on the table, splashing lyrical wit into 100-proof spirit in *Grave Dancers Union*." *Billboard* would single Beinhorn out for personalized praise as a producer who "knows how to record big, heavy rock," a praise that would soon attract the attention of Seattle grunge-rock stars-on-the-rise Soundgarden, who recruited the producer to helm what would turn out to be the band's best-selling studio album ever with *Superunknown*. Recognizing heading into the studio the opportunity he had before him with the fact that "the band had so much potential," the producer said that his opinion was shared by a chorus of buzz surrounding the band, adding that "everyone in the world were like 'the next record's gonna be huge.'"

Beinhorn did his best to keep that kind of distractive gossip outside the studio, explaining that philosophically as a producer, "I don't really pay attention to that hype, it doesn't matter. A record's gonna be what it's gonna be—either it's gonna be good, or it's gonna be bad. If you've made a record that's middle ground, to me, that's not acceptable. That to me is more sign of the times than anything else, because if a record sells or if it doesn't sell, that's not an indicator of how good it is." Still, the smash success of multiple singles like "Black Hole Sun," "Fell on Black Days," "The Day I Tried to Live," and "Spoonman" off the record motivated the producer to concede that—as a matter of professional habit—he was keeping a certain ear out for the commercial potential of the band's songs throughout the making of the album.

From the perspective of instinct, according to Beinhorn, "I think that a hit song is something that you can just hear, where when you hear it, you know what it is right away." As coincidence would have it, the producer's ear tuned in instantly upon hearing "the two best songs in my opinion that I ever worked on from a song perspective: 'Runaway Train' by Soul Asylum and 'Black Hole Sun' by Soundgarden." Singling both out upon hearing their initial demos as "songs that would stick in a person's mind as classic compositions," Beinhorn added the important detail that "the thing that both these songs have in common is: that the moment that I heard them, I said, 'I've got to do this fucking record! This is amazing, Oh my fucking God!' All I could think about was that piece of music, it was absolutely brilliant."

Honing in more specifically on what he felt was catchy about the compositional heart of each song that allowed him to visualize their full potential as chart-toppers, Beinhorn began with the gentler "Runaway Train," explaining that as he made production notes that would help to shape the hit later on in the studio,

> you want to hear what the guy is singing, you want to understand what he's meaning; it's got a very tangible, melodic flow to it, it's got dynamics. It's a proper piece of music, a classic song that just flows beautifully. It's air-tight, there isn't one moment of wasted space in it anywhere. It's an interesting thing to listen to, and a perfect song. In the case of "Black Hole Sun," I felt as if I'd been taken somewhere else, and someone was trying to shove these crazy ideas and weird images into my brain. I listened to every little bit of what he'd written—every piece of it was essential. The melody, and the way he follows the melody almost like a cannon or ram with the vocal. It all just works together in a really, really air-tight way, and again, there isn't one bit of

that song that's wasted anywhere. It just grabbed me from start to finish. I remember when I first got the demo of that, I listened to it fifteen times, and called Chris up on the way to the airport, because I was going to work with them on preproduction, and I was like "This is fucking amazing, we're ready to start."

Sharing his reflective impressions on working with a singer who was to grunge what Robert Plant was to heavy metal, Beinhorn recalled that during tracking,

Chris's vocal range was just nuts; it was impossible that a person could sing like that, and once he was in the zone, he would literally sing for six to eight hours a day before his head was hurting so bad that he had to stop. I really have never seen anyone do that before and then come back the next day and put it down again. It was just so impressive. We used a variety of mics on him. In the beginning, I had a combo of a modified 67 and a modified U47 Phet that we used on his voice, and a really long signal chain as well, because I was looking to try and get as much of his range as I possibly could. Because there's a lot in his voice, it's not just the tone of it; when he sings there's a lot of grunting going on, and to me, that's a really important part of what he does.

From a production standpoint, the producer shared that his primary focus throughout vocal tracking

was just trying to get as much detail out of his voice as I possibly could, and eventually, we went to a U 87, and I think in the end that's the microphone that worked best on his voice. We went through dozens and dozens of microphones. Because in one vocal take, he would go from low to high, that's why I was using two mics when we started, because there was so much of a disparity between the two ranges that initially I couldn't get it all with one mic. But in the end, the 87 seemed to capture everything I wanted to get, and certainly made him happy, so we were cool all around.

Turning next to the important role one of the band's signature musical assets, drummer Matt Cameron, played in the album's success, Beinhorn said:

I've been pretty lucky to work with some incredible drummers, and Matt Cameron was no exception. At that point, my approach to recording was just to get as much detail out of everything as possible, because I appreciated how well Soundgarden played, and what they sounded like as a band. With all due respect to people who had done their other records prior to that, I hadn't felt that they'd adequately captured in a recording. So that kind of left the field open, and it was a challenge I put to myself: how best can I make it so these guys have a recording that really, really brings them to glory, so to speak, the best way possible. So it was a lot of finagling with mics. I did top and bottom mic the snare with a 57 on the top and a 441 on the bottom. On the kick, I used a 47 fat, and on the overheads, we had a variety of mics, including a pair of 67s that were directly over the kit, and room mics that were 47s. There weren't any other proximity mics, because the 67s were sort of proximity overheads, and we had some B&K 40-11s for cymbals.

Cameron's skin-beating would later be celebrated by *Q* magazine as "depth-charged drumming" that *Spin* added had helped to harness a "pure hormonal energy" that—thanks to Cameron—"thunders" throughout the record.

Of Kim Thayil's guitar sound—one that the *New York Times* would declare throughout the album "bends and stretches Jimmy Page-style guitar riffs, adding Soundgarden's distinctive strategy: odd meters that make the songs heave with unexpected accents"—Beinhorn shared his memory that as they headed into tracking during setup,

Kim had one of the funniest rigs I've ever seen in my life. It was all Peavey stuff, he had this EV VMP 120—I don't even think they make them anymore—with a Peavey cabinet, and he used these old SGs. It was probably the worst-sounding guitar rig I'd ever heard in my life, which I rectified by a lot of talking with him, and asking him to please try something else. He was very, very against the whole thing, and kept going on about how the Les Pauls and Marshalls I wanted him to try were so typical, and everyone used it, and why should he have to do that? Besides, the guy at the guitar store told him this stuff sounded exactly like those amps and guitars anyway. And I was like, "Well, what are your favorite records, Kim?" And he said, "Kiss," and I said, "Well, that's what they used on those records!" And it just kept going around and around until he finally agreed. Chris didn't get involved in that conversation, it was strictly between Kim and myself.

The sound Thayil and Beinhorn creatively channeled into the stunning performances that decorate *Superunknown* would eventually earn the album a ranking at # 5 in *Guitar World*'s Top Ten list of Guitar Albums for 1994.

Throughout tracking, while the band's members individually shined, and maintained the outward presence of a group-driven direction on their inner circle decision-making process where the record's arrangements and broader sonic and stylistic development was concerned, Beinhorn quickly pulled the curtain back on the fact that lead singer-songwriter

Chris Cornell was calling most of those shots. Beinhorn recalled that, indeed, while "Chris tried to play the thing of it being democratic, where everyone was equal band members," ultimately "it didn't really work."

Painting Cornell as diplomatic when "it came down to people's personal choices for instruments and amps"—reasoning that that recording territory "was a different story," in the course of bigger-picture decision making during the record's recording, "there were a couple situations where it was pretty funny to watch Chris just kind of go 'Unuh.' He didn't want to be the bandleader, and he tried really hard not to be, and believe it or not, there was such an immense amount of animosity between everyone in the band, that no one liked it. I think that was one of the reasons why he didn't really want to go down that road, but sometimes there was no choice." Despite the subtext of discord at play among the band's members throughout tracking, ultimately the producer recalled relying on "Chris's talent" as "more than enough to make the things work" as the band recorded.

Beinhorn then stepped away from controversial moments to one he appeared to treasure as one of the album's—and his broader career's—wilder recording moments when the band began work on future live fan favorite and smash rock radio hit/rotation-staple "Spoonman." More sonically defined by its title than any other track off the LP, "Spoonman" spurred Beinhorn to recall the song's biographical roots. He explained that "Spoonman" was about "this guy Artise, who was this maniac street musician who played the spoons." Setting the foundation for a recording session that "wasn't like anything you could ever possibly imagine," the producer next recalled that when tape was ready to roll on the Spoonman's overdubs,

> this guy came in with spoons, a bunch of metal, and he said, "Get a video recorder out, because you're gonna want to tape this." And he wasn't kidding: this guy beat himself so badly with these things that there was blood flying everywhere. We recorded three or four times to make sure the take was right, and he didn't let up for a second. He was out in the main room, and you can kind of hear he's in an open room while it's happening, because some of the stuff rings out a little bit. I used a pair of 67s to mic him up.

On a more disciplined front, Beinhorn recalled that lead singer Chris Cornell had a perfectionist nature as a recording artist that—when it came to getting down what he felt was a perfect vocal take—became

> a real sticking point for him, it was a big, big deal. I was right there with him, because he'd spend the whole day on a couple songs, just rip it up completely. Then I'd come in and do a vocal comp from his various takes, just get the best stuff out of all the

takes, then he'd come, listen to it, look at me, and go, "Un uh. We got to do it again." And what could I say but "Alright, no problem. I'll defer to you." Because he knew exactly what it was lacking at that point, and would come in and do it again.

Remembering Cornell's lion-like prowess when performing behind the mic, Beinhorn highlighted a surprising weakness present in that process : "During the making of *Superunknown*, he didn't seem as if he wanted to perform for anybody. Like the whole idea of performing for people, I think he put it out there in a way where it didn't feel like he felt good about doing it." Acting outside of the box to accommodate Cornell's disposition, the producer recalled feeling confident enough in the singer's vision to turn over the recording reins entirely:

The way it worked was: Chris is one of those people who can record, he can do everything, he doesn't really need the band or me, so I just looked at him and said, "Fuck man, you know how to work a tape machine," and we showed him the rudimentary operation of how to work the console, and I said, "Go to town, cut your own vocal." I wasn't quite sure what the problem was, and I talked to him at some point down the road, and he said that period when he was making the record was one of the worst in his life. He was going through some personal things at that point.

In spite of the singer's personal difficulties, he ultimately managed to sing his way through them to a completed set of vocal performances that—along with the rest of the masterful performances the band pulled out individually and collectively on their fourth studio LP—would inspire Rolling Stone to conclude that "guitarist Kim Thayil, bassist Ben Shepherd and drummer Matt Cameron hammer Chris Cornell's vocal anguish . . . into brilliantly warped power-thump sculpture," while *Billboard* hailed the album as "Soundgarden's finest hour." Fans and critics around the world would concur, moving over five million copies of a collection of songs that *Melody Maker* summed up as "a brilliant, brilliant album," and one that *Rolling Stone* would argue "demonstrates far greater range than many bands manage in an entire career." Recognition of the album's achievement would rise even higher as the band's star continued to as well, reaching another stratosphere for Soundgarden personally and the genre of grunge professionally when, in 2005, the band was honored with two Grammy Awards for "Black Hole Sun," voted the year's Best Hard Rock Performance, and "Spoonman," which took home the award for Best Metal Performance.

Now among the most in-demand producers of his era, Michael Beinhorn's own position as one of rock's mainstream star hit-makers was finally given a legacy stamp with his next gig as producer on metal Godfather Ozzy Osbourne's 1995 studio LP, *Ozzmosis*. A gig he regarded with the same sacred reverence as any of his peers who'd grown up on Ozzy's voice as his first band, Black Sabbath, shaped the heavy metal genre, Beinhorn had been tasked with producing a pivotally important album that would maintain Osbourne's commercial relevance in a metal landscape that had radically altered in the five years since the metal legend's multiplatinum success with hits like "Mama I'm Coming Home," "No More Tears," and "I Don't Want to Change the World."

As artist and producer met during preproduction to discuss how the album's recording would play out, the producer said that, in spite of his eagerness to roll his sleeves up and dig in creatively with the metal legend,

> Ozzy made it very clear to me at the beginning of the record that the recording studio was a place where he just absolutely detested to be. He probably hated being there more than anything, so I was like "Okay, I gotcha." He basically said, "Don't expect me to be around when you're cutting your parts." He let me know he'd give 100 percent when he had to do his vocals, but said "I'm trusting you with everything else, so don't expect me to be around for that." Which is fair enough. It's his record, he's paying someone to do that job for him, so from that perspective, I had to make sure he was pleased.

Beinhorn would discover a much more kindred creative partner in lead guitarist Zakk Wylde, who the producer said

> wrote and cowrote a lot of the music on that record. Zakk just loved music so much, he was just so enamored of it., He could be such a fan of such people's music and at the same time being such a remarkable musician on his own, that he had the chops to back up everything that he did. And he was an absolute riot to be around, he was actually at that point a very, very lighthearted person. We'd go out and get drunk a lot, but he was a lot of fun to be with. We'd make a lot of jokes, and at the end of the night, stand around the studio at 4 in the morning listening to Fleetwood Mac and Led Zeppelin 4, and just stand there in awe of how great that music was, and just be music fans together and just love it together.

Delving into the gear Wylde brought to the studio, in spite of the heavy final sound fans had become accustomed to hearing on Ozzy's finished albums, Beinhorn recalled that

> all that Zakk had in the way of a rig was a 100-watt Marshall, with these bass caps that had PV speakers in them, and this MXR distortion pedal, and MXR phase shifter, and a chorus pedal, and his guitars. I miced him with a combination of a 57, a 421, and a BK5B. Zakk would come in and get his parts done, but would really do it right.

The level of musicianship he was at that point was staggering. He'd be playing these leads, and would say "I want to change that," and would be talking while he was standing there playing these 16th notes, and I'd be going "How can you do that, and what note are you trying to change? I can't even follow where your brain's going." But he'd do it, I'd say "I still can't tell what note you changed, but it sounds great." He'd throw in like perfect harmonies wherever he felt like doing it. All his leads would usually go down one path, and it was just stunning to watch him play. It was the easiest part of recording the album, and I had the most fun working with him.

Once the album's instrumental tracks were completed and Ozzy entered the studio to overdub vocals for a collection of songs that would include the hits "Perry Mason" and "See You on the Other Side," Beinhorn recalled from the technical side that "in terms of mics, I had a C-12 that we used primarily to do Ozzy's vocals." Detailing an approach to recording as unique as the singer's legendary voice itself, the producer added that "Ozzy had a way of working that I've never seen anyone else do. He would sing his parts one line at a time, and insisted on doing it like that. He said, 'Look, I feel more comfortable working like this.' And what are you gonna say to someone who says that, 'Get out of your comfort zone and work the way I want you to work?' If you can prove you're going to get better results, perhaps, but Ozzy wouldn't do it any other way." Ultimately, the album would become a huge and revitalizing hit for Osbourne and add another multiplatinum plaque to Beinhorn's wall as the album moved two million copies throughout 1995 and early 1996, with the producer summing up his studio collaboration with Ozzy as a "combination of entertainment and drudgery."

As the 1990s wound toward their close, Beinhorn would round out his sprawling collection of genre-dominating-and-defining albums by signing up for the challenge of producing Hole, led by perpetually troubled rocker Courtney Love. Paying Love the compliment that "as it is with a lot of people, they had their thing that makes them worthy of a recording contract," Beinhorn set his mind to producing what the *L.A. Times* would eventually deem "the most ambitious and quite possibly the most revealing album Love has made." Heading into production, he found himself a long way from that eventual result, beginning with his revelation that "when Courtney records, she has goals, but I don't think she came in prepared to know how to execute any of them." As he got acquainted with Love's studio style, he comically recalled discovering that "Courtney was a lot of things—but predictable initially wasn't one of them. She's a fantastically talented individual, but it took months to do her vocals."

An investment of time that was also paced by the fact that "everyone on the record wanted to try everything every possible way, so a lot of excess went into making the record," where Beinhorn might have otherwise been sweating one of any producer's greatest fears—bringing a record in over budget—he quickly and pleasantly discovered that "the recording company didn't seem to care, and I kept going to them saying 'Do you know what this is probably costing you right now?' And they all said, 'Just make a great record kid,' which is great, I suppose." Settling for the moment into the rare, label-granted freedom for the first time in his career to—quite literally—take his time making a record, the producer shared that he concentrated a large block of that studio budget building a guitar sound that *NME* would later celebrate as "both monstrous and marvelous."

When his focus was turned to creating Courtney's master vocal performances, Beinhorn soon discovered that the trick to getting the best delivery out of her came "when she was not thinking about what she's doing, then she's perfect, just spot on." Most of those moments, he recalled, came early in their recording process, explaining that after months of recording, "one day I sat down and listened to these guide vocals the first couple of days when we'd cut the drum tracks. She'd done guides for about a day and a half, and there was 70 percent of the record right there. It was all encapsulated right there—all the emotion was there, everything you could want, and everything after that is just a complete waste. For the sake of technique, perhaps you're gonna get something more in tune, but for the most part, it's just not as good as the first takes, which are outstanding."

Coupled with its stellar musical performances, Beinhorn succeeded from the production side in painting Hole's biggest-selling album with a perfectly decadent polish that helped it shine with just the right ragged glory to inspire the *L.A. Times* to conclude that there was a "richness of ambition and passion running through *Celebrity Skin* that makes it one of the few essential pop packages of the year," adding that on a commercial level, the record had the bonus of being "stocked with songs have the delectable spirit and glow that will make you reach over and turn the volume way up every time they come on the radio." Beyond the hits, Rolling Stone paid homage to Beinhorn and Love's journey toward finding her heart as an artist, noting that in the final result they produced, "she knows exactly the kind of rock star she wants to be, and is it."

Now a veteran of thirty-plus years as one of rock's preeminent hitmakers, Beinhorn shared as one of the key secrets to his success avoiding a signature sound: "I prefer not to have one, I prefer not to be pigeonholed. Unfortunately, that's a lot easier said than done, because people ultimately look for a way to be able to make something unfamiliar seem familiar to them, and ultimately rely on some sort of mechanism that looks like pigeonholing. I can't really avoid that, but I don't like to work the same way on each record for many reasons, the most important of which is I think it's highly disrespectful to the artist."

Reflecting on his portfolio of successes as a production artist, Beinhorn—like most of his peers—considers every record in that catalog his babies: "I'm proud of virtually all of my records. There's a signature to each of them that makes them unique, and they are all unique from one another, which is something I've liked about them as well." Offering his closing words in the form of advice to the millennium generation of engineer/producers who were raised on the sonics of his sound in the form of one band or another, Beinhorn urges any modern soundman—whether heading into the studio with an unknown or star with an established style/sound—to "in all matters, rely in your instinct. Even if your instincts lead you to do a record that is not massively successful, it will probably lead to a record that is extraordinarily good, and has your best possible work on it. My preference has always leaned toward what hits me on a gut level, I can work well with it. I think as long as one trusts their gut feeling about stuff, they can't go too far wrong."

CHAPTER 21

Dave Jerden–The X Factor

Perhaps rock's greatest majesty is its mystery—where do the greatest songs and sounds come from? The X factor—as production wizard Dave Jerden, widely considered the god-father of alternative rock production, affectionately calls it—is the seed from which that sound is created and how it is thereafter captured—live and in the studio. Many of rock's greatest historians feel that legendary alt-rockers Jane's Addiction is the closest we've ever come to solving that sonic riddle, or at least approaching its source and soul. Jerden played a central role in translating Jane's Addiction's musical evolution in the studio into the cultural revolution it became in the early 1990s once embraced by rock's last great generation of fans.

By the time Jerden had graduated from engineer to full-time producer in the second half of the 1980s, he was greeted almost immediately with what would become perhaps his grandest professional accomplishment, or at least his most celebrated—a collaboration that would lay the sonic foundation for a new genre of rock, alternative, and a generational movement that would change the face of rock 'n' roll forever, giving way to the advent of grunge. In an academic sense, everything Jerden had accomplished as a producer prior to his collaboration with Jane's Addiction was training, even into the master's level. The day he stepped into the studio with the band was his first day of real class, and his students weren't the members of Jane's, but a generation of disenfranchised listeners starving for a sonic messiah.

In lead singer Perry Farrell, Jerden found his muse. As coproducers of the band's sound, the pair would be unmatched in influence over the eruptive foundation they laid for the next popular wave of rock 'n' roll. In the course of creating the band's debut LP for Warner Bros., the decorously and ironically titled *Nothing's Shocking*, everything about the experience was in fact shocking. Farrell was the first prophet in a generation, his mind a mecca for musical meditation and discovery, his words a sanctuary for solitude and solace from the desolation of life as a teenager. What voices like John Lennon and Bob Dylan had done for their generation in the early 1960s, Farrell with Jane's Addiction would realize largely alone for his era.

Taking the world by storm with *Nothing's Shocking* in 1988, Jane's Addiction's impact on popular rock was "Ocean Size," raising a musical and cultural tidal wave that crashed down on rock 'n' roll like Judgment Day, washing over the disenfranchised like a baptism and giving rise to the next pop counterculture. *Rolling Stone*'s review of *Nothing's Shocking*, produced by Jerden, hailed both the band and their musical epic as

> the latest great hope of the Los Angeles club scene, a product of a city whose often overlooked hard-rock scene has long been every bit as successful and commercially productive as its more heralded punk and post punk scene . . . Jane's Addiction, young and restless, makes music that scrapes against the smooth surfaces of commercial pop. But this perverse, willful, Los Angeles–bred artist . . . straddles the line between the two camps, and several others: the band is indulgent and excessive, adept at typically screeching (but atypically original) hard-rock guitar raveups and at flights into dreamy psychedelia. A classic love 'em or hate 'em outfit, the band is great, and it is also full of shit—often at the same time, a dichotomy that may be the edge that sustains *Nothing's Shocking*. [The songs] are hard-boiled riff rockers, unsettling, lyrically incisive and musically excessive. Best of all is "Jane Says" . . . from the strummed acoustic guitar that carries it along to the song's acid-etched portrait of an addict, the song is a worthy Left Coast successor to "Walk on the Wild Side."

Fusing boundless experimentation with hard-rock convention, Jerden, over the course of his epic two-record collaboration with Jane's Addiction, produced the greatest and most influential pair of art rock albums since the two discs that comprised Pink Floyd's *The Wall*—both revitalizing and reinventing the genre in the process. Ironically, but in a not-so-surprising tendency toward humility, Jerden chooses to view his collaborations with

Jane's as no different from any other project he worked on, when in fact they were radically different from anything the record industry had heard before. As a producer, Jerden must have felt he had enough creative volatility to contend in the moment that he would leave interpretations regarding importance to historians. He explained that while

> there's been a lot of importance put on the two Jane's Addiction albums I did with them, I'm identified with the band through that, but they were just two albums among many. In my mind, every record I do I learn something from. And I learned a lot from doing those records—there were things I tried that worked, and things I tried that maybe didn't work. The important thing is the learning process, and in the grand scheme of things, I don't think those were any more important than any of the other records I've done, because once I'm done with a record, I'm done with the record. It's back to the Brian Eno concept of the process is the important part. The record is a snapshot of my life at that time, just like any other snapshot. It's all part of any ongoing process. Early on, when I started recording, there were guitar sounds that were popular at the time, vocal styles, high-pitched singers, hair bands, that I just hated where rock 'n' roll was going. To me, it just wasn't rock 'n' roll. I grew up listening to and playing rock 'n' roll in the late '60s and early '70s, and to me, those heavy blues voices, and real honest guitar sounds, and all that molded me. To me, there's a certain way a guitar should sound, a certain way drums should sound, certain ways vocals and vocal styles should sound—and all I ever did was just gravitate toward that stuff that appealed to me, that had that sound I identified with. So it might be my more traditional leanings, as we might call them, coupled with Jane's Addiction's experimental rock sound that made it such an innovative collaboration.

Blurring the line between sound science and musical mysticism, Jerden and the band would travel at creative light speeds in the course of their collaboration, as futuristically as the reaches of the band's sound in a time they were truly ahead of. In that context, it was Jerden's willingness to not just push past the boundaries and break the rules, but to shatter them all completely that landed him the gig to begin with:

> Whenever I work, it's just whatever sounded right at the time. Truthfully, at that time, I was going through a lot of personal problems: my marriage was breaking up, my father was dying—and I just said "Fuck it" on that record, I don't care what's happening on the radio, I'm just going to do whatever I want, and that was Perry's contribution to the whole record. He said, "Let's just do whatever we want—fuck everything!" When they were getting signed, they talked to a lot of producers, and every producer wanted to change them. Perry told me this one producer said, "If we do this, this, and this, I can make you sound like U2." And another famous producer wanted to fire Perry

and get a new singer. And when he came and met with me, it was really low-key. He brought the whole band down and said, "Is there something you can play me?" And I was sitting in this office across the hallway from the studio, and it was just a mess, and there was an old acetate laying there of a band I'd worked with that had a bunch of percussion on it, so I said, "I might as well play this." And Perry said what sold him on me was my nonchalance, non-intense like "I gotta have this gig!" I was low-key, just like "This is what I do, and if you like it, great, if you don't like it, I understand. Good luck."

For Farrell's part, he explained in an interview concerning his collaboration with Jerden that "I liked Dave Jerden's work on [the Brian Eno/David Byrne album] *My Life in the Bush of Ghosts*, so I was excited to work with him. He knew how to do a lush production with a hard-rock band."

Traveling back to his years coming up under the creative wing of Eno, Jerden recalled quickly discovering his preference for

thinking outside the box—which goes back to the Brian Eno philosophy of episodic events and trying to see the validity in everything that's being created as a sound. That even mistakes can be valid. And not just doing, always looking for those little things that can make it special, and not just saying, "It has to be this way." You should let the surprises and all that stuff live; that's what outside the box means for me. It doesn't mean you have to go in with an attitude like "I'm going to mic everything with a speaker (you can take a speaker, wire it backwards, and it becomes a microphone), so I'm going to think outside of the box, and do it this way." That's bullshit. But when you're in the recording process, you should let the serendipity of the whole thing be the journey for you.

Brian Eno first taught Jerden about:

what he called "Epi-events," episodic events, so that's what I learned from him—episodic events. It's the mistakes, the unforeseen, the serendipity of recording that's important. The things you discover along the way. And to this day I will work with groups who say, "No, it has to be this way, we have to get rid of that buzz." And I go, "No, let's keep it." For example, on the Jane's Addiction record, on *Ritual*, on "Been Caught Stealing," there's this big bass break, where this sort of sliding roar happens—that was just a mistake on the bass, this "thunk" that was heavily compressed, and I put this little dry reverb on it, and it became a part that people recognize in the song as being really cool, when it was just a mistake. So it's the things you discover along the way.

Art rock by category at the time of its release, *Nothing's Shocking* was a masterpiece of the genre, but arguably more historically consequential because its genesis evolved in real time out of art rock, morphing into the previously nonexistent genre of alt-rock in the process. Because Jane's sound blended elements of virtually all of rock's musical styles without artistic negligence, it was impossible to categorize the band into any other genus than their own. Charting the entire epic as a director might the acts of a play, Jerden explained that

> to tell you how the whole first record was planned out (being kind of concept rock), when I met with the band, the first rehearsal we met together, I said, "How I see this is theatre. It's going to be a dramatic production, and what I want to do is consider having acts, like there's an opening crescendo, which is "On the Beach," and what I want to do is plan the record as far as what songs are going to go in what order," and we rehearsed the songs in that order, and recorded them in that order. And we kept everything in terms of a theatrical, dramatic play. And that was my idea, was that it was going to be, the curtain opens, and the fanfare of the orchestra, and then you go to this trip with Jane's Addiction, and the trip you're going on, what it's about, is an exploration of our culture. It's an exploration of all the things that are happening. There were a lot of things that were starting to happen at that time with computers, and the Internet was in its infancy, the pace was quickening with technology within our society. There was lots of stuff going on, and Jane's Addiction to me was like Jimi Hendrix—who was perfect for his time; his guitar sounded like explosions, Viet Nam was going on at that time, he had an international sound, we were becoming a global community at that time, and Jimi Hendrix captured in sound the feel of society at that time. And for me, Jane's Addiction is the same thing. I once saw them play at Scream, at three o'clock in the morning, and there were like 3,000 kids waiting in line to get in, and what they played was like an old theatre, and the show was very theatrical and dramatic, and this was before we started the record, and was where I got the idea of the record being a dramatic play. The overall feel of that record to me was that it should reflect the culture—be chaotic, and makes sense at some times, and at others, doesn't make any sense at all. Just constant stimuli coming at you from all different angles, as the culture was doing. And that's what I wanted to capture on the record. They're a band for the future; that's the kind of band they are at heart.

As a coproducer, Perry Farrell's method for translating the musical revolution he heard in his head onto tape was as wild and uncharted in terms of convention as the band's direction was for rock 'n' roll itself when the recording process started, such that Jerden decided Farrell was best suited to explore it alone. The practice of artists self-producing or coproducing their debut albums was not entirely unheard of, but industry-wide; it was as rare as the genius that was required to convince the label heads and producers to secure their approval. The accepted standard was generally that the artist had to prove no one else could as effectively, honestly, or accurately transfer what geniuses like Farrell heard in their heads onto tape, that their method could only be pioneered on its own plateau. A handful of artists had achieved it historically—Stevie Wonder and Prince to name a pair of true avant-gardists—but the practice had been truly established by Buddy Holly, who had argued to the president of Decca Records in 1956 at the outset of his recording contract that only he could accurately capture on tape what he heard in his head, becoming the first artist of the genre and time to produce his own music.

The suits at Warner Bros. resoundingly agreed after recognizing what Farrell was onto. To date clearly a fascinated observer. Jerden explained that

> one area I stayed out of, as far as Jane's Addiction went, was Perry's vocals; he even mixed his own vocals. I stayed busy with everything else and let him deal with his vocals. For instance, when he sings and does harmonies, he hears harmonies in his head. So when he sings, he'll sing one line, do one pass, and he may stay on the root note, and then go to a third, and then a fifth, and then the next take, he'll kind of invert the thing—he'll start with the third, and then go to the root note. And maybe he'll do like four, five, maybe six takes; he has all the harmonies going. So it may sound like it was just one track doing a third, and one track doing a fifth, but they're all jumping around. And because I couldn't say to him, "Okay, now let's do a harmony, and do a third on this track." 'Cause like, with most artists, I'll lay down a basic vocal track, then I'll do harmonies. Perry wouldn't know what I was talking about, so what I did was just let him sing it the way he wanted to sing it, and that way, mistakes and all, we'll just deal with it later. And that's what we did, and in the mix, we took out the bad parts. Normally I clean that stuff up as we go along. So what I was doing was working with Dave Navarro on guitars, and working with Steven Perkins and Eric Avery, and then Perry had this delay unit where, when he was doing vocals, he also laid down the delay units as he sang. So I'd let him do any kind of effects he wanted, because I knew that was important to really pull it off. He's not a very technical singer, totally raw. He was always the artist; he never sat there and went, "Dave, I want you to play a certain way." He had complete autonomy over his vocals though.

With the release of the band's sophomore album—and commercial breakthrough— *Ritual De La Habitual* in 1991, Jane's Addiction would crystallize their stature as the Supreme Being in alternative rock like a Greek statue, immortalized in time and worshiped by millions, not just in that generation, but for many to follow—an edict Farrell set forth in "Classic Girl," explaining that "they may say—those were the days, but in a way, for us, you know, for us *these* are the days." The album's anchor, the indeed episodic "Three Days," would quickly become alternative rock's "Stairway to Heaven" upon release. For Jerden's part, as he went about crafting "Three Days" sonically, he was equally aware of the song's episodic nature and social implications:

> On "Three Days"—first of all, when I work on songs like that, that are long, in order to keep them from turning into jams, what I do is chart everything out. What I basically make is a score, like what an orchestra would have. At every point, there should be always focus going on, and setups for the next bit, and resolves from the bit that came before. It's like working out a regular symphonic piece, and so I chart it all out, and then we rehearse it. And I keep an eye to the overdubs, to make sure there's always interest going on, and the feel of the song as it's happening; otherwise it would just turn into a jam. What's interesting about that song is that what you're hearing is an actual take—we went into the studio, ran it down once, and then, just as we were getting ready to record it, Roberta Peterson and Steve Baker from Warner Bros., their A&R people showed up, and they played it for them, and everything you hear there we kept. We filled in a couple things, but mainly that was the performance they played with. The other songs were put together, doing the drums first, etc.—but that was the whole band playing, and that's a real honest representation of Jane's Addiction in the studio, at their best, doing a whole song. And that's significant because, on the first record, they all played together—on the second record, Dave Navarro was on methadone and couldn't come in till later, and Eric and Perry weren't getting along at that point, so it was, for personal reasons, hard to get them in together. The only song I really got them together on was "Three Days." When I started *Ritual*, Perry didn't show up for three weeks, and so I stopped production, and then we halted production for about five months before we started up again, 'cause Perry was using heroin and just couldn't show up. "Three Days" was a highlight, a great performance; on the first record, there were lots of performances that were just great musicianship. Particularly, off of *Nothing's Shocking* was "Pigs in Zen," because everything you hear was done in one take, and that was it. We didn't do any overdubs or anything. The challenging bits and low spots were the fighting of the band, trying to keep the band together to even make a record. But moments like "Three Days" prove why the band remains historic to date.

As the godfather of alt-rock production, Dave Jerden produced much of the theme music for Generation X. In terms of the X factor, he hit the spot by accurately translating the essence of his bands' organic sound—whether their live energy or message in their music—onto tape, at the same time capturing their volatile fan base by providing a seamless continuum through which listeners wouldn't lose harmony with their ethereal lifeline. This is the sum and substance of a producer's devoir—not to bring music to life when it's already alive, but to reincarnate it in a way as powerful as Christ's second coming, at least for a band with a spirituality and following as religious as Jane's Addiction's. The soul of their sound could not lose a generation, or it very well could have lost a generation waiting to follow Jane's into a new frontier of salvation from teenage angst and alienation. Jerden was unafraid to explore the darkness that bands like Jane's Addiction and Alice in Chains spoke for, and the journey would take him deeper into experimentalism than any art-rock producer, with the possible exception of Bob Ezrin, had gone before him. In terms of space, the universe of buttons, dials, and blinking lights on a studio console would be a dizzying circus to most people. Jerden views the process of producing records as just that—a festival of revolutionary creativity.

Most importantly, because serendipity often accounts for the genuinely magic moments of sound, style, and substance committed to tape in the end, Jerden, when producing any record, proceeds as

> the guy in the carnival—I've joined the carnival, I like being around musicians, being in studios, and just the whole camaraderie of working with a band, working with my crew—that's what fun for me. Appreciate the recording part of it, the process—this is what I do. I have a wall in my house with all my platinum records, and people come over and look at them, and they're like, "Wow, I bet you're really proud of them." And every one of those records represents both joy and immense pain. I have really mixed feelings about every record. Every record that I do, there are songs I like, and songs I don't like, like anyone else.

Flipping back privately through his greatest hits collection of favorite highlight collaborations, Jerden noted:

> As far as highlights—probably the number one highlight of my career was working with the Rolling Stones, but other than that, it's sessions that I've done with country musicians come to mind. There are not any monumental moments where I said, "Wow, I have to remember this forever." I think it's important for any producer to learn something from every album they do, we all do. Any artist who says they've got it wired, well they should probably stop doing it then. They're not going to contribute anything new. You gotta make mistakes; it's the reason they put erasers on pencils. You can't be too hard on yourself. It's a brutal business, you get a thick hide after doing it for a while. I don't read reviews anymore, I don't read the press. I'm a producer. That's what I do, that's what like doing, I like the way it smells, I like the way it feels, and when I'm not working is when I feel the most depressed, when I feel lost. And that's sad, to define oneself only by one's work, but it gives me so much joy, ultimately over the years that despite how heartsick I've gotten over a lot of things, I would never stop doing it. I

could never imagine not doing it. So love what you do. I know people who produce one record and they're totally burned out. They say, "I don't know how you do it." And I've produced something like fifty albums. Keep your feet on the ground, realize you're not the star, what you're trying to do is create stars. And of course, people will say, "That's the reason I'm doing it," but I've seen so many producers over the years who fall into the "Where Are They Now?" file because they fell off the face of the earth, and having known some of these people personally, I know what happened to them. They got caught up in being them. All I can say is keep it honest—be honest in your work, and be honest in your relationships with the people you work with; don't try to weasel anybody. I do everything honestly. And not only do I do that for my own personal morality, but also because my father taught me, "If you want to fuck yourself up in the music business, be a shyster." I only ask what's fair for me. And I charge probably less to produce a record than anybody else, especially for what I've done. I know producers who get a million dollars to do a record; I never even come close to that. Get what you have coming to you, and if you're any good, it will all come out in the wash.

CHAPTER 22

Tony Platt—Catch a Fire

In the record business, most producers are known by the company they keep in the studio. For Tony Platt, that company has included creative collaborations that produced legacy hits across multiple musical genres, from Bob Marley ("Stir it Up," "I Shot the Sheriff," and the seminal "Get Up, Stand Up"), Foreigner ("Juke Box Hero," "Waiting for a Girl Like You," and "Urgent"), and a multialbum recording relationship with hard-rock godfathers AC/DC, where Platt found himself sitting in the rare position behind the console working on the band's final album with one lead vocalist who helped shape the '70s, Bon Scott, prior to his tragic passing in 1980. Platt would then take the engineering reins alongside legendary rock producer Robert "Mutt" Lange as he helped the band triumph past their tragedy with a reinvented sound on the seminal *Back in Black*, an album that would years later inspire a BBC reviewer to pose a poignant question to rock fans: "Take a moment, now, and imagine the rock 'n' roll world without AC/DC?" Concluding rightly that "without *Highway to Hell* [and] *Back in Black* . . . it's not a rock 'n' roll world I'd want to live in," Platt described his role in helping the band create some of their greatest hits (including "You Shook Me All Night Long," "Back in Black," "Highway to Hell," "Have a Drink on Me," "Girl's Got Rhythm," "If You Want Blood (You Got It)," "Shot Down in Flames," and "Hells Bells"). The engineer-producer mused that he'd wound up precisely where his instinct had pointed him in his younger childhood.

He first found his way into the world of record making via something "instinctive I think," which he felt was pivotal in "how people find their way into the music industry. Sometimes when you look back on things, it's very easy to read into circumstances, and events that weren't in that particular order." For Platt, the order of his evolution as a sound-man was rooted in a childhood fascination with tape recorders:

> What really happened for me was, I always found tape recorders fascinating, right from an early age, and don't really know how that was, but I managed to save up and buy myself a pretty crap tape recorder to indulge my growing fascination with the whole idea of recording stuff and playing it back. The other thing I do remember from an early age is being fascinated with radio, and specifically music coming out of the radio. I was raised in a very rural village, at an early age in Derbyshire, and later on in Oxfordshire, so we definitely didn't have the local corner record store. The nearest town to me that had a record store was a place called Redding, and even then, the record store was a department in a larger department store. I had to order that tape recorder by mail order.

Coupled with his growing experience in getting familiar with the innate sounds of instruments like the tape recorder—a fundamental tool of a record producer's trade—he added that "at the same time, I was also interested in the electronic side of things and PAs, and so a friend of mine and myself started up a radio station at our secondary school, and we used to play Hendrix, Cream, the Who, and stuff like that via a wired system that the school had for audio/visual transmission around the control room. So we basically made the radio shows up, and then tapped into this wired system that went around the school, and got permission for people to listen in one of the classrooms during lunch hour." While honing his ear for the fundamentals of what made a song work best with the mainstream listening-ear, Platt received an important—and clarifying—boost when

> this same friend of mine, whose father worked in a clinical capacity for the BBC, managed to get us a visit up to BBC Radio, to the broadcasting house, during the holiday. So we went up to visit, at around fifteen or sixteen, and this happened to be just when Radio One was starting, so I remember walking into this radio studio, and seeing all these big tape recorders, and lots of cool equipment, and these guys operating the tape machines and I remember thinking, "WOW, now that's something I might want to do." So that sort of led me into a bit of a hankering for doing something like that,

but of course, I didn't have any comprehension at the time what getting a job in the music industry entailed, how recording studios different from radio studios, anything like that.

That "hankering" was boosted when

I happened to get lucky around that same time because my father, who was a teacher, happened to bump into somebody who knew a guy who was a quite-well-known British engineer with Granada Studios. And as a result of that, I managed to go up to Granada Studios in London, and met with someone at the studio thinking I was possibly in line for a job. As it would turn out, he was just another talking head telling me how difficult it was to get a job in the music industry—how times had not changed! He did wind up the interview by giving me a list of studios I might be able to write off to, and that's what I did—wrote off to every studio on the list about an apprenticeship, and didn't hear back from anyone for a long, long time. I remember I was just about to give up any hope when I finally got two replies—one from Kingsway Studios and the other from Trident Studios. So I fixed up the interviews for the same day, went up to London, and wound up getting offered BOTH jobs!

Making what could be argued was among the most important early decisions in his career—not based on experience but rather instinct—the fledgling soundman recalled that, in the end,

I decided to go with Trident because it felt like a bit more of a professional studio. Malcolm Topp, who is quite legendary in his own right as basically the guy who started building the Trident consoles, and still builds consoles under that name. He was far more welcoming, and the artists working in that studio at that time were amazing: like Elton John, who had just started making the album that catapulted him into recognition, the Beatles had been working in and out of there periodically, Dr. John . . . it was just the place to be at that time.

In spite of the heights of stardom of the artists surrounding him day in and out, Platt started at the very bottom of the rung:

The way it worked back then was: you started off as a tea boy, and slowly but surely, you'd be given a little bit more responsibility, and eventually you'd get to operate the tape machine a bit when they felt you weren't going to screw it up. So when I was working at Trident as a tea boy, it occurred to me at that point in time that it doesn't matter what job you're doing, you should do it the best you can possibly do it, and be the best at it that you can. Rather than taking the attitude, "Well, I'm just a tea boy, it doesn't matter," because you're judged on initiative.

Feeling after a while he needed to go beyond the superstar shadow of Trident in pursuit of bigger opportunities as a lead engineer, Tony's opportunity knocked by way of a happy accident, in what he termed

> one of those strange circumstances where I was in the machine room—which was separate from the control room at Trident—one evening, reading through the *Melody Maker*, and I came upon a very unusual advertisement—the kind I'd never seen before and have never seen since—that read "Experienced Tape Operator for West London Studio." So sitting in there with the tech engineer, I said, "Wow, I wonder what that is? I'm not an experienced tape operator," and he encouraged me to phone up and see where it was at the very least. So I phoned up, and this was in the evening so the security officer for the building answered, and it turned out to be Island Studios, which was part of Island Records. I think they felt I had the right personality to fit in there, and the right enthusiasm—and that landed me the gig.

Elaborating on the lucky chances that came his way in terms of how the system worked in the rock 'n' roll glory days of the early 1970s, Platt explained that I'd been lucky as a tape operator, because the way it worked, you got your first break when an engineer didn't turn up in a session, and the one sort-of unwritten rule was if you were the tape op on the session where an engineer didn't turn up, then the session was yours. I think I got one of my biggest breaks working on one of John Entwistle's solo album, where I got to do quite a heavy amount of engineering on this album, which gave me the opportunity to really learn my way around the desk. Then as you did that, you started to pick up some of the smaller sessions—so I did commercials, we all used to take turns on the pop sessions—and then somewhere along the way you would hope that one of the artists was going to prefer you. So at that point, you sort of moved to having them as a client, and started to pick clients up in that way.

Along with rock royalty like Led Zeppelin, Beck, and the Who, Platt would soon stumble upon his diamond in the rough when he was assigned to engineer a session with a then-still-unknown artist who would as a result of those sessions become a superstar on the level of Elvis Presley and Michael Jackson. That artist, Reggae godfather Bob Marley, who through the albums he created with Platt behind the console, would go on—according to the *New York Times*—to "introduce an . . . international audience to reggae music." Still, back at the start of their collaboration in 1972, Platt explained that "you have to understand that Bob Marley, at that time, had had a couple of forays into the U.K., but was pretty much unknown. So the thing with Bob came about really because I'd been doing a bit of the reggae work at Island, and a bit of the rock work as well, and from what I can gather, the studio owner, Chris Blackwell, basically thought 'Well, if I want to bring rock and reggae together, then I need one of the engineers who'd had experience on both.' So I was specifically asked to go and do those sessions." That instinct on Blackwell's part would pay off handsomely, allowing Marley—in the opinion of *Rolling Stone*—to "hit the white rock audience with the force of revelation."

For as loud an impact as his music would make, as Platt, Marley, and company got underway with principal recording for *Catch a Fire*, Platt described the artist's in-studio demeanor:

> Bob Marley, from the time I first met him onward, was a fairly low-key guy, he had a presence about him no doubt. This was the *Catch a Fire* album, which preceded *Get Up, Stand Up*. The tapes had been sent over from Jamaica, and I'd dubbed them up into 16-track from 8-track, and had the chance to listen through to the songs. He sounded pretty damn good already, so I was quite interested from when he walked through the door, well what's going to happen here? And we also had this completely unknown factor where we were going to be incorporating these rock musicians into the sound. And of course, most of them I knew—guys like Wayne Perkins and Rabbit—who were always hanging around the studios, because we had quite a close relationship with Muscle Shoals, and all these guys were already part of that, and Rabbit knew Bob already. Still, it was fascinating in a lot of ways because all these groups were dealing with a new experience perhaps just slightly outside all of our comfort zones. I absolutely think it's a great thing to be challenged like that, I always went looking for it. I'm one of those sort of people who, when I go to a new town, I'll wander around and try to get lost.

Continuing, Platt recalled that in

> the context of working with Bob Marley in the recording studio, as producers, we'd have to go slowly and surely, and just develop things. One of the things as a producer I definitely took away from it, and this came from working with Chris Blackwell, who produced those records, was he had this idea in his head where he could hear the sound he wanted to achieve with this. And he got it across to me what that was, and I had to kind of work it out for myself and interpret what he wanted. It was a great example of collaboration, and musicians working together toward a common goal, and

it's something I still do now, which is having this sound-picture in your head of where you want to go with something. So after working with Chris, it became cemented in my mind that the whole notion of having something in your head you were aiming at allowed you to map yourself toward that. It also cemented for me something I've never stopped doing since, which was using techniques from one style of music in another style of music.

Detailing some of the technical aspects of bringing Marley's seminal style of Reggae to life during recording, Platt began with Marley's rhythm section, recalling that

the backing tracks for *Catch a Fire* were already recorded on four and eight tracks, so most of the drums were mono or mixed into one track. On a couple of the tracks, the kick drum was separate and mixed with the bass, so what was a big lesson from that was: when you've got a lot of instruments mixed together—and we were still mixing instruments together on 16-track—you learn about making sure you put the instruments together that are actually sonically a little further apart, so you can use the EQ to redress the balance if it's not quite right. The other thing I noticed in those tapes was that the bass sound was pretty crap actually, where there was a lot of bass floating around on the other tracks, so when you put it in with everything else, it really did fill out nicely.

Turning next to the recording of the album's guitar sound, which would subsequently become signature to not only Marley's but also reggae's broader sound, Platt recalled discovering "one thing in particular that I'd not really come across before was the tendency in reggae was to put a slap or repeat echo in, so instead of playing 'dunk-dunk,' he'd just play the first beat, and you'd have a slap echo, which of course gives you a different texture, and that classic Bob Marley rhythm sound." Describing tracking vocal performances that *Billboard* would argue Marley delivered with "sincerity and sense of purpose" and iTunes added "provided a blueprint for his future triumphs," Platt shared from the technical side that "we used a U-67. Unlike the States, where there were far more U-47 tube mics around, and a lot more M-49s around, we didn't have too many of those. We had U-67 tube mics and C-12s, but were moving toward Phet microphones around."

The millions of fans who embraced *Catch a Fire* upon its release found falling in love with Bob Marley's music felt as easy as a Jamaican vacation, and with *Fire*, the singer would introduce the world, according to the BBC, to a style of music that "up until this point, was a niche genre, bought in the UK by ex-pat West Indians (and the occasional skinhead) . . . (and was) even less widespread in the States. *Catch A Fire* changed all that." Returning to the

studio with Marley only six months after the release of *Fire* to record the overnight superstar's second LP, the aptly titled *Burnin*,' Platt was understandably excited to expand on a
sound that Rolling Stone said had a "hypnotic character." Shining the spotlight on Marley's
singularly inspired songwriting gift, which on this LP would produce legendary classics like
"Get Up, Stand Up" and "I Shot the Sheriff," which *Billboard* reported "brought Bob Marley
to world renown,"—Platt recalled feeling amazed by the singer's almost mystical talent
for singing those songs to life, arguing that it worked so magically in a recording context
because "not every singer is capable of making the lyrics come alive, and he was absolutely
brilliant at doing that. When he sang, you just felt like that's what was going on."

Expanding on the maturation of what would become Marley's signature drum sound
over the course of *Burnin*,' Platt touched on both how the sound was created and how that
process shaped his approach to drum micing going forward:

> It wasn't until we came to do the *Burnin'* album that we actually recorded quite a few
> of the tracks, and I was a little bit concerned about "Well, how am I going to get this
> great drum sound that you guys got on the *Catch a Fire* album over here," because it
> was quite different from the sort of drum sounds I'd been used to with rock bands. So
> I just asked Bunny Livingston, the percussionist, "Well, how do you set this up when
> you're in Jamaica?" And he said, "Well, we just put the drummer in the center of the
> room and point everything at him." And it suddenly dawned on me that the leakage
> that came out of the drums was a very important part of the total sound.

Continuing with some of the technical detail of recording that sound, Tony recalled that

> the drum kit was pretty tightly miced—a reggae drum kit is fairly dampened down, to the
> point of putting tea towels under the tom-toms. There's not a lot of resonance coming
> off the drums, apart from the snare, which rings like nobody's business. I would have
> miced the snare with an M160, a small ribbon microphone. The studio's setup for the
> drums would have been two U87s pointing across the kick from the tom-toms, and
> didn't bother even with a snare mic, but other engineers would use the snare mic as
> well. But of course, you see, we were just moving from 8-track to 16-track, which was
> something of a luxury, but you still didn't have a lot of room to spread out.

When he set up the mic to begin the process of creating what the *New York Times* would
later hail as "spellbinding" vocal performances by Marley, Platt said of the singer's technique
that "he was very quick, one to two takes, and Bob tended to have his harmonies worked
out ahead of time. There were a few times where he said 'Run it,' and would try a couple

things, and then it would be fine. There were harmonies that had come on the basic tapes that were already recorded, so a lot of the time we were maybe filling in the gaps or tightening up, or we might have to replace a harmony. It was much the same with the prior album, *Catch a Fire*." The vocal performances Marley delivered on *Catch a Fire* would spark not just a flame but a revolution following the record's international release in 1973, inspiring iTunes to later rank the LP as "one of (Marley and Reggae's) very greatest achievements." Even ahead of that praise, Platt recognized instantly during their recording in the studio that "a song like 'Get Up, Stand Up' was going to be an obvious hit, along with 'Concrete Jungle'—and 'I Shot the Sheriff,' of course." More broadly, the engineer felt that the album played an important role in establishing some of the signatures of Marley—and popular reggae—sound to follow: "Bob was experimenting with music—the innovations that were coming via the use of the clavinet or the rock guitars into his reggae sound made Bob the great adopter of those things. Once he'd done that, and the band had adopted all those little stylistic things we'd incorporated into their sound and made them their own, he was off and running with it."

Following his collaborations with Marley, Platt recalled feeling—temporarily at least—that he'd arrived a stylistic comfort zone in the studio: "After that, I stayed working in reggae, putting together the *Funky Kingston* album, and worked with a pop reggae band in the U.K. called Greyhound, as a freelancer after I left Island, produced the first Aswad album, who were very much following in Bob Marley's footsteps. Then another band called the Cimarons, who were quite a well-known U.K. reggae band, and a white reggae band preceding what the Police did, called GT Moore the Reggae Guitars." The engineer would devote the remainder of the 1970s specializing in the reggae genre before graduating to what would become his mainstay professional specialty as a record producer—rock 'n' roll.

For any sound engineer in Tony Platt's privileged position having coming off of a five-year collaboration with reggae's most influential artist, to walk into the same opportunity with the band who would soon become that for the hard-rock genre would come by way of the same karmic fortune that had landed him in the studio with Marley. Conceding this very happy accident, Platt recalled that

> after I'd left Island Studios, I freelanced and sort of moved around a bit and just really getting a lot more experience. After I returned from Italy back to England, this friend of mine I'd been running a studio for called me up one day and said, "A friend of mine is doing an album with this Australian punk band, and he wants somebody to mix it that knows that kind of Island-rock sound, and I thought of you." So I spoke to Mutt Lange, and went down to Roundhouse Studios, where they were starting to record *Highway to Hell*, and basically they only had enough budget to hire an external engineer for

either the recording or the mix, and they decided to go with the mix. Mark Dearnley, who was the house engineer at Roundhouse at that time, recorded it, then Mutt and I took it over to Basing Street to mix it.

Discussing the album's mixing working on a Helios console, Platt said that the "challenge on mixing *Highway to Hell* was to glue it all together, because it had been recorded a bit separately. Roundhouse is a very dry, dense studio, so to deal with that I just employed a technique I'd used loads of times before and stuck a pair of Altec speakers up in the studio room, and used them as a chamber, and just fed bits and pieces through to kind of correct some ambient glue to glue it all together, and make things sound like they were a bit more in the same room. So that was one of the things that was necessary."

In what would be both a compliment to the band's core sound and a convenience to the mixing team, Platt recalled that "the beauty of mixing in those days was that there was precious little you had available to use for effects anyway, not that AC/DC let many effects go on their stuff. You had Echo Plate, the tape loop, you had compressors, and that was about it. We used just a little bit of slap echo and a little bit of reverb—very, very gingerly, because with AC/DC, if they can hear it they don't like it. So you kind of use it just to push sounds forward, rather than using it as a halo effect." Legendary metal magazine *Kerrang!* would later praise *Highway to Hell* as sounding "impossibly alive." Delving into the nitty-gritty of achieving a mix of Angus and Malcolm's guitars that would allow them to garner such praise, Platt described the creation of what would become a studio blueprint for a generation of hard rock that followed, explaining that the process played naturally to Mutt Lange's production sensibilities:

That's something Mutt's also always been very good at: making sure that the way the song is arranged is fitted together properly, so it actually went together quite quickly and easily. Mutt had this sound in his head he wanted to go for, and he was able to explain that to me, and once I got that in my head too, the two of us just went off and got it. He was using the reference points of where the sound is tight or tough, but where you can still feel the space in between through the economy of faze. Also the openness within his mixes on that album—there's something about a really good balance, and I think you can use the Rolling Stones as an example. When you listen to a mix of a Rolling Stones song, it feels like it could just fall apart at any moment; it's kind of hanging on by its fingertips but is perfectly balanced, which adds an extra little bit of excitement to the mix as well. There's that little bit of ruggedness within the whole thing, and that I think was something we needed to achieve with AC/DC was not to polish it up too much—make it listenable commercially, but not go too far with it.

Another key component to attaining the latter sonic goal came with the pair's mixing of the album's drums, which Platt credits for containing what became mainstay fundamentals of his own mixing norms in albums to come, sharing that "it's no different from anything I do now really, it's just finding the right space for each of the instruments." Honing in on some of the tricks producer Lange pulled out of his magic hat during his creation of a rock sound of which *Billboard* would later conclude, "AC/DC has never sounded so enormous," Platt said:

> One of the things Mutt is particularly good at doing is making sure the instruments are tuned within the chord of the song, so that gives you a lot more possibilities. So for instance, if you have a kick drum and the kick drum has a note in it, and the note that the kick drum has in it is not in the chord of the song, it's going to constantly be interfering with the sound of the bass. Or if you've got a snare drum that's got a note in it that is discordant with the guitar, then it's going to mess with the sound of the guitar. Whereas, if you tune it into the chord, and make sure the drums are ringing in tune with the rest, it just makes everything sound bigger and clearer.

Working alongside the inspired ears and instincts of Lange, who *Rolling Stone* would credit with helping AC/DC "graduate" on *Highway to Hell* "from the back of the bar to the front of the arena on *Highway to Hell* (1979), with a cleaner sound," Platt—as a student of the producer's sound—happily confessed that

> I started off working with Mutt with a great deal of respect for him, and I think one of the things that used to work well with us was: Mutt was and still is something of a perfectionist. And the only time we ever locked horns was when there was a tape of something I thought felt really good, and Mutt was getting concerned because it wasn't as perfect as he wanted it to be. Certainly when we got onto the *Foreigner 4* album, I just used to use my expertise with editing and dropping things in and all those sort of things to make a good-feeling tape perfect so that it actually satisfied all of his criteria. I definitely got practice on that throughout the AC/DC collaborations.

Where Platt had gotten his beak wet working alongside Lange on the mixing of *Highway to Hell*, which would launch AC/DC into global stardom just as their lead singer Bon Scott tragically saw his own star die out from a fatal alcohol overdose, when the engineer was invited by Lange back into the studio to fully engineer the band's next studio LP, the legendary *Back in Black,* he said of the timing, "What happened was, Mutt and I were actually doing another album for another band called Mr. Big, not the U.S. band with Eric Martin, but a U.K. band, and we were doing that at Battery Studios in London, going backwards and forwards with Malcolm and Angus, who were doing the preproduction and sending us tapes. Then one morning on those sessions, Mutt came in and said to me, 'You're not going to believe this, but Bon's died,' so everything was kind of up in the air for a little while."

In spite of heavy hearts, AC/DC decided to celebrate their fallen brother with an even heavier and harder musical ode so moving that *Rolling Stone* would conclude the band had succeeded in "[flipping] off the Reaper and [giving] Scott and his fans the best tribute they ever could have desired." The band's most obvious challenge, from a musical standpoint, was finding a singer with enough musical moxie to fill Scott's shoes authentically in terms of the band's raw, balls-out rock sound, a process that Platt recalled was ongoing while "Mutt and I were still wrapping up the Mr. Big album. AC/DC started auditioning for new singers, so instead of getting preproduction tapes every morning, we were getting audition tapes with different singers, giving the band feedback 'Well, he sounds kind of good, he doesn't sound so great, that one's a definite no.' For me, it was a little bit confusing because I was trying to pay attention to the album we were doing, so we'd listen on Mutt's car stereo on the way into the studio, make our notes, and then get on with the other session."

The band ultimately settled on fellow Aussie Brian Johnson, and as they prepared to brave their way back into the recording studio, Platt recalled that Lange made the wise decision to "return to Nassau to track *Back in Black* at Compass Point Studios," the same studio where they had recorded *Highway to Hell*. Once the band had settled into the recording paradise, Platt shared that the team rolled up their sleeves and began the work of pursuing Lange's ambition to create a record whose sonic perfection would be beyond reproach, becoming what *Rolling Stone* would later deem "the apex of heavy metal art." Looking back at the inner workings of that process as principal tracking began, Platt recalled that it remained a team effort from day one because "there was very much a consensus on *Back in Black* actually between Mutt and the band, in part because I think Mutt—at that point in time—had not become completely a perfectionist, so he was still able to stand back from that a little bit, and the band remained very much a part of the decision-making process throughout. So when we were tracking, we'd do several takes, and some of the songs were edited from more than one take, but Mutt and the band would all sign off together."

Revealing some of his own production priorities in shaping a record that would become the standard in every of its musical elements for the hard-rock genre over decades to come, Platt focused on his ambitions for the album's drum sound: "After *Highway to Hell*, there were certain things I wanted to achieve when I was asked to go and do *Back in Black*. I wanted to start out with more ambience on the drums, and wanted there to be more leakage between the guitars and the drums." Designing the studio's recording blueprint around the latter goal, Platt recalled that "we built booths for the guitars where we could have them open or closed, and open them up to any degree we wanted to, so I could then control the amount of leakage that was going out into the room. So we recorded *Back in Black* much more live I think than *Highway to Hell* was recorded, and I wanted to employ those techniques of allowing controlled leakage between the instruments."

Elaborating on the engineering-related steps he took to arrange the studio for maximum accommodation of the sound Lange and the band were chasing, Platt shared that

> when we got to Compass point—which was sort of a strange place to go off and do a rock record—I might have perhaps, had I been given the choice—chosen a studio with a higher ceiling and a larger floor area. But we were in that studio for reasons that were not necessarily creative, so I had to work out what I was going to do with this room to achieve those aforementioned sonic goals. So what I did was walked around the room with a snare drum, hitting it, to see if there was a part of the room that was going to sound better than another part of the room. And there was this one particular spot right in the middle of the room, where the snare drum sounded bigger and brighter and louder than it did anywhere else, and it turned out the ceiling was a little higher at that point. So we set the drum kit up with the snare right underneath that, and the kick drum just a little a bit in front of that, and just by using natural acoustics, we managed to create a way of controlling the way the sound of the drums leaked onto everybody else.

Detailing the specific micing setup he applied on Phil Rudd's drum kit to capture the latter sound, Platt recalled that

> "I miced the kick drum either with a D-20 or a U-47 Phet, the tom-toms would have been RE-20s or SM-7s, and the snare most certainly was a KM-86 on the top and an SM-57 underneath. The undersnare mic, the SM-57, is a very robust microphone, and you don't need a lot of fidelity from that. I like to use a condenser on top because I want to get the sound of the whole drum, I don't want a narrow dynamic sound field on the top of the snare drum. I prefer to try and come up with a way of controlling the hi-hat on the leakage and have a big sounding snare.

Once the drum sound was just that to the satisfaction of the band and producer Lange, Platt recalled that as drummer Phil Rudd began laying down his tracks, he harnessed a force in his playing that reminded the engineer of legendary Led Zeppelin drummer John Bonham in that "Phil's not necessarily a heavy hitter, he's just a good hitter. In actual fact, it was the same with Bonham; he didn't necessarily hit the drums really hard. Quite often, I've found with drummers that do hit very, very hard, they don't sound nearly as loud, because they're deadening the sound of the drum by hitting it so hard."

Where the sonic underpinnings of Cliff Williams's perfectly steady bass sound was concerned, Platt said of its studio setup that

> there was a DI on the bass, and two microphones, a D-20 and a 47 Phet. I picked up my preference for using two mics on a bass from previous demos I'd recorded with Thin Lizzy, Phil Lynott used to have two stacks—an acoustic 361 and a Hi-Watt 4x12 stack- and a Rickenbacker stereo bass, that actually had been wired so the same signal came out of both sides, and he used to put stuff through the acoustic 361 so he could get the bottom end, and the Hi-Watt to get the overdriven top end. So you have to mic that up with two microphones, which led me to thinking, "Well, this is cool actually, instead of trying to get lots of bottom out of one microphone, and top out of the same, why don't I have a microphone I can lots of nice bottom out of, and another I can get lots of top out of, and put the two mics together. Then I won't have to EQ things nearly as much," and so it became one of those practical techniques that I've kind of taken with me, and one I used on *Back in Black*.

Platt turned next to what many have argued in years since stands out as the album's most profoundly powerful musical statement, the guitar work of brothers Angus and Malcolm Young, who *Billboard* would later conclude "carry on with the song-oriented riffing that made *Highway to Hell* close to divine." In the course of crafting such a heavenly high-powered sound, the engineer recalled that he and Lange paid heavy attention as they tracked to the "combination between Malcolm and Angus's guitars, so as they were playing, Mutt and I were trying to blend the sound in a way that captured the song the best of all. It wasn't so much what I did right in that, but what I didn't do wrong, because when these guys are playing, they play rock music better than anyone else, period—better than any other band on the planet as far as I'm concerned. So really what I had to do was not fuck it up, and I know that sounds very simplistic, but when you've got people like that, it does make you sound good naturally."

Highlighting what individual strengths he and Lange emphasized in recording the collective of Malcolm's rhythms and simultaneously Angus's leads, Platt spoke of the foundational importance of Malcolm Young, whose "sensational rhythm work" Gibson Guitars would later conclude "lies at heart of AC/DC's distinctive sound." Platt agreed:

> The band began with Malcolm playing rhythm guitar, and they needed somebody to play lead guitar, so in fact George taught Angus to play lead guitar before he learned chords and how to play rhythm guitar. And Angus isn't the greatest rhythm guitarist—in some respects—whereas Malcolm's probably one of the best rhythm guitar players known to man. So what makes them play so magically together is: they have a very

simple technique where they basically play in unison but they play in different positions, playing different inversions of the same chords. So you don't get that kind of chorusy effect from the two guitars playing in unison that you would get if they were playing in the same position- it just sounds like one big guitar.

When teamed with brother Angus Young's lead work, the synergy the band channeled throughout *Back in Black* would become a bible of sorts for generations of guitar rock to come, creating a sound that the Rock and Roll Hall of Fame would later declare "rocked with a determined authority that catapulted AC/DC into a class with Led Zeppelin, Deep Purple and the Rolling Stones." This status was cemented for Angus's part via the dizzying and simultaneously dazzling dance his fingers effortlessly performed across his Gibson fretboard on solo after solo, a process that for all its aural sophistication, Platt revealed went down "fairly quick when Angus was recording his solos. We'd do two or three takes and a little comp between them, or drop-ins if necessary, stuff like that, but both he and his brother are very instinctive players. They don't overthink things, they just get on and do it. it's just a good bit of solid Scottish-Australian attitude."

In the course of crafting the Young brothers' sound, Platt recalled that "to record the guitars, we were using amp heads and 4x12s, so quite often the amp head would be outside the booth, and the 4x12 would be inside the booth, but we had lots of combinations— 50-watt heads, 100-watt heads, and different 4x12 cabinets. Over a period of time, you kind of learn which ones do which job best, so I was always choosing the combinations I thought worked best, and I didn't use any compressors at all on the guitars." Utilizing his collaboration with AC/DC as a springboard to touch on some of what became his broader staple techniques to recording guitars in the studio, the engineer added that "my preference on guitars is U-67s or U-87s, and I used two of them, which is based off something that occurred to me a long, long time ago re to get a sound to spread across the stereo, if you've got it recorded in stereo with two microphones, then you can actually spread the sound and don't have to have it quite as loud."

When the production team's focus shifted to newly minted lead vocalist Brian Johnson—who *Rolling Stone* would later praise as "a savage screamer who combines the breast-beating machismo of Led Zep's Robert Plant, the operatic howl of Ian Gillan [ex-Deep Purple] and the tubercular rasp of Slade's Noddy Holder into singular, nerve-racking, Tarzan-type shouts"—Platt recalled feeling an immense amount of respect from the front man from the start, reasoning that "for somebody to walk into that situation under those circumstances and perform like that, you have to take your hat off to him. it's an incredible thing." Addressing the technical pressures Johnson faced, the engineer was equally sympathetic:

You also have to remember it's actually quite difficult in a climate like the Bahamas, because it's an air-conditioned environment. And because you can't turn the air condition off, you've just got pure oxygen, so at times it was too humid, at times it was too dry. And we had to be very careful with Brian coming in and out of the studio, down the corridor and into the control room, because he'd come out of an air-conditioned environment, into a hot corridor, then back into an air conditioned environment, and that's just asking for trouble. So we had to be very considerate to him, and a lot of the time, he just stayed in the studio room, and we just played stuff back down the headphones to him.

As the singer worked through the daunting task of tracking his lead vocal performances, more even than the band, Platt recalled that he remained primarily under the hyper-watchful eye of lead producer Mutt Lange, such that "Angus and Malcolm would wander off and come back in to check on how vocals were going, but it was primarily Brian, Mutt, and I present during tracking." Delving deeper into the work the singer put in reaching for the perfectionist bar Lange had set sonically—on top of the one he was being expected to reach vocally in terms of high notes—Platt recalled that while Johnson walked into the challenge with the strength of

a voice that projects really well, still, it was tough at times tracking his vocals because some of those notes are pretty damn high, and he had to work very, very hard. I gained such an incredible respect for him. That was the point at which Mutt was absolutely a stickler for getting every single note and every single syllable as good as it possibly could be, and it's one of the features of the album. A lot of people focus on the drums and guitars, but let's face it, those vocals absolutely finish it off, top it off to the most incredible extent. Vocally, I remember we used a U-67 and a U-87, depending on the song.

As production wound down and Lange and company prepared to leave Nassau for New York to mix the album, Platt underscored that this phase of the album's recording wound prove in many ways the most important—and the most pressured—part of *Back in Black*'s recording. Explaining that "we mixed *Back in Black* back in the States at Electric Ladyland Studios in New York, which was a *great* place to mix," the engineer added the important technical detail that "we mixed on a Neve, where we'd recorded the record in Nassau on an MCI console and MCI Tape Machines." Though the band had completed the majority of the album's principal tracking back in the Bahamas, "we still had overdubbing to do, some backing vocals, and some bits and pieces to finish up at Electric Lady." For Platt, the overdubbing gave him an opportunity to become familiar with the sonic character of the legendary studio, reflecting a methodical discipline the engineer had refined throughout the course of his collaboration with lead producer Mutt Lange.

Recommending this research process to any engineer or producer as a vital preparatory component to any mix, and critical to his and Lange's forthcoming task, Platt shared that as a result, "I had gotten into the habit working with Mutt of going into the studio the day before and checking the monitors so I knew they were all working, so I went into Electric Lady the day before, and they had this Quad-Amped Westlake system in that room. So I started listening to the tapes in there, and Mutt walked in the room and listened to the monitors, and said, 'Yeah, they sound good.' Normally, he was never satisfied with the monitoring in the room. So we started out from a very, very good place in that respect."

Platt revealed some of the key steps the pair took toward achieving a mix that the *Chicago Tribune* would subsequently say became "Ground Zero for AC/DC fans because it had bigger hooks and cleaner sound, thanks in large measure to the meticulous . . . production of Robert John 'Mutt' Lange." As not just Lange's assistant but his copilot throughout this final leg of their journey toward producing the perfect rock sound, Platt recalled that

> with Mutt, I would spend a bit of time getting the sounds sorted out in the right places, and then the thing we paid most attention to while mixing was getting the blend and the balance right. We mostly achieved that by turning everything down and mixing in mono through an Oratone. Once you know the sounds are the sounds that you want, there's no real point in just impressing yourself every time you play back. What you really want to do is hear how the instruments relate to each other. So you turn the song right down, especially if you put it into mono, and you can hear the interrelationship between the instruments, and make sure you get that balance so no one's covering anyone else up—you can hear everything clearly. What happens when you turn that up is it just gets bigger and bigger and bigger the louder you turn it.

Turning to their work on some of *Back in Black*'s key musical elements, Platt began with the rhythm section, sharing his memory that "in mixing the drums, it was a pretty dry mix. There is a little bit of a slap and a little bit of reverb, and I did have ambience microphones—87s—I'd recorded, so I was able to use a natural room sound. I like 87s for their natural sound; 87s are not great bottom-end microphones, but the top end is always very clear and detailed. You get plenty of detail off them, and their great work-horse microphones." Shifting to the mixing of Angus and Malcolm's guitar tracks while staying loyal to the band's native style, Platt said that he and Lange's approach "was very, very straightforward; there were no double-tracked guitars on those AC/DC albums. There's one track of Malcolm, one track of Angus, and then Angus would continue to play rhythm after he finished his solos so you didn't get a drop in dynamics. So the only time that there was a third guitar playing rhythm was after the solos."

As mixing wrapped and the team handed in *Back in Black* to an understandably eager record label, Platt recounted a humorous story that broke up the tension for he and Lange, one that came

> when we were finished mixing, Mutt and I ended up having to present the album to a room full of marketing people from Atlantic at Rockefeller Plaza. And I wanted to make sure it was absolutely spot-on, so I made a special copy of it on quarter-inch tape, took a Revox in and a really good hi-fi system. So we played it in this boardroom fairly loud, and this assembled gathering of marketing people sat around, didn't really look too impressed. That sort of put it into a real kind of perspective for me. We weren't there to speak up for the song, just to play it. One of the reasons Mutt was so successful was he had an ear for what was going to be good on the radio.

Lange's instinct would be confirmed upon release of the band's legendary hit single, "You Shook Me All Night Long," which became a global and generation-defining hit that *Billboard* would later hail as "the greatest one-night-stand anthem in rock history." Fans found the album as infectious as its first single; *Antimusic.com* would report that "by the second week of August, *Back in Black* had topped the UK charts for two consecutive weeks, and reached the U.S. *Billboard* charts by late August, peaking in January, 1981 at number four. France was also evidently smitten with this golden vein of unadulterated Rock n Roll—by December of 1980, the French had snatched up 2,000,000 copies of *Back in Black*. Love it. By July of 1981, worldwide sales of *Back in Black* had reached 12,000,000 units. There was no apparent force which seemed able to stop this album."

As he ventured on and out from under the wings of Lange to make his name as a producer, Tony Platt would rack up hit collaborations in that role with AC/DC (on 1983's *Flick of the Switch*), Iron Maiden (1981's *Killers*), Motörhead (1983's *Another Perfect Day*), Lillian Axe (1989's *Love + War*), and the Mighty, Mighty Bosstones (1993's *Don't Know How to Party*), along with studio stints working with a who's who of rock and metal, including Cheap Trick, Testament, Krokus, Dio, Buddy Guy, Krokus, and Uriah Heep among others. The one universally applicable role Platt learned across all of these collaborations as vital to the successful helming of any record production was the importance of

> finding the best way to make the artist comfortable. That's really the major role you have, and sometimes you have to jump through hoops to do that, and it's different with every artist you work with. I always recall when I'm talking to students a story I heard about Jimmy Iovine and Shelly Yakis when they were doing the *Damn the*

Torpedoes album with Tom Petty where Tom wasn't singing as well as he had been, and when they asked him why, he said, "I feel more comfortable singing at home in my living room." So they sent the road crew over to his apt., and they brought the contents of his living room over to studio, and set up his sofa, his carpets, his hi-fi, and everything, which translated to his singing in what was a much more familiar environment. They even went from the control room out to the studio and sat on his sofa to listen to the playbacks from each song. To me, that story sums up one of the basic tenets of production, and that is: being an engineer can be a help or a hindrance sometimes, because sometimes you *have* to take the viewpoint as an engineer that "Sound doesn't matter for shit here; actually if I get the environment right, then this artist is going to perform much better than under other circumstances." So finding the right set of circumstances, and getting the artist in the right frame of mind to perform, is by far away the most important thing a producer has to do.

Among the artists he worked with, and the legendary producers he worked alongside as an engineer, Platt, looking back on his charmed career and picking from the artist side of his production catalog, closes not surprisingly with the a trio of history-making/generation- and genre defining albums: "AC/DC's *Back in Black,* Bob Marley's *Catch a Fire*, and *Damn Right I Got the Blues* are up high enough that if I had to pick three albums, those would be the three."

CHAPTER 23

Matt Wallace—The Real Thing

Conceptually, "groundbreaking" as a term for a producer connotes the cracking of some new creative hallowed ground, mining that ground, and coming up with some new mineral of *rock* that is then shaped and polished into a creative, critical, and commercial gem.

Matt Wallace, via his work with Paul Westerberg (the Replacements, Faith No More, and Maroon 5 among others), has helmed many such sonic expeditions. Always with the goal in mind of being adventurous—following the logic that taking great creative risks can uncover greater creative rewards—Wallace explained, "I'm continually working with artists and trying to push the envelope and capturing what I believe to be essential and real. One of my main paradigms of working with bands is I say, 'Look, I want all of us to feel open enough, free enough, and confident enough to fall flat on our faces and fail miserably on a try, because if we're open to doing that, we're also open to doing something absolutely brilliant and stunning.'" With a talent for putting alternative or abstract-to-pop rock artists in a mainstream musical context without comprising their integrity in the recording process, more times than not, Wallace has succeeded in producing that album, as in the case of artists

More, and more notably Replacements front man Paul Westerberg, which sets the bar by which all other catalog pieces are critically and commercially measured.

Westerberg's *14 Songs* is arguably the best example of the latter, wherein the indie legend, according to *Rolling Stone* in its review of the album, "flourishes . . . (through) the colloquial grace at which he excels." *Spin* magazine, at the time the Mecca of alternative rock, had previously concluded that during his Replacements '80s heyday, "Westerberg merged punk ethos with classic rock touches, which made for a gem that both punk and alt. country bands have echoed since then."

The stakes were high for the artist heading into his first solo album. Matt Wallace was chosen as coproducer, based on the pair's work together on the Replacements' 1989 LP *Don't Tell a Soul,* which was critically beloved for its artistic maturity, most notably via *Rolling Stone*'s declaration that the band had "gone out on a new limb, with an audacious album that reclaims its valued independence by confounding audience expectations . . . amid . . . artistic adventurism."

By the dawn of the early 1990s and the rise of grunge into the mainstream, Paul Westerberg could be called the alt-rock John Mellencamp, with *Rolling Stone* arguing that "what distinguishes Westerberg from the misfits populating his songs is his uncanny ability to speak for the tongue-tied, articulating their aspirations and insecurities with intuitive sensitivity, boozy whimsy and straight street talk—leavened with a little poetic license."

Working on Westerberg's first solo LP, Wallace recalled, was as unconventional in its process as the listeners the artist spoke for. While Westerberg had matured as an artist and songwriter by the very nature of his fluid creative genius, the studio climate during recording was as unpredictable as ever. According to Wallace, "Paul's incredibly mercurial, he can certainly be temperamental, and very challenging to work with. The rewards are obvious when you hear the record, but making a record with him, the most difficult aspect is you have to always try to stay a step or two ahead of Paul because the problem is Paul doesn't quite know what his next step is. That album was interesting because it was an incredibly challenging but ultimately very rewarding record to make."

Specifically, Wallace recalled the first week of tracking:

> When we started that record, we had a very talented engineer named Susan Rodgers, and the band, which included Josh Kelly on drums, Rick Price on bass and mando-lin. We rehearsed three or four days in New York and started recording there, and "Knockin' on Mine" was the first song we did. Now I'm a pretty big fan of trying to record with monitor wedges as much as you can, and we certainly did that with the band. We had the drums somewhat isolated in the room, but then I also had monitor wedges for the bass player and Paul so they didn't have to use headphones, because

we were tracking the band live off the floor. So I'm thinking "Great, we have this track," and we'd gotten the song recorded, and Paul sang it—did it quite quickly. The backups on that record were done with three or four of us around a monitor wedge, with no headphones—it was Paul, myself, Rick, and Josh singing in the background. The monitor wedge was blazing, it was insane, and had great spirit, so I thought that recording was really successful. And it was fine, but Paul didn't feel it was working for whatever reason, I guess two or three days into it, so by Thursday of that week, Paul had fired everybody but me, which is typical of Paul.

Though the band's lineup would continue to change, Wallace had nailed down the key step of his strategy for making Westerberg's recording method successful, employing an anti-preparatory, produce-as-you-go method of recording that adapted to Westerberg's musical moods and moments as they so wildly and brilliantly shifted from one song to the next. Because Wallace could not rely on the usual preproduction period to sonically absorb and musically internalize Westerberg's demos, he had to keep a pace—technically and musically—to ensure he didn't miss a beat from his ever-revolving lineup of drummers or guitar solo that the singer, by nature, wouldn't play twice.

Addressing how the latter was accomplished from a technical standpoint, Wallace explained that *14 Songs* was recorded on a 24-track machine.

I did a lot of blending of room mics with the guitar on the track. Because we really couldn't have amps and guitars, and room mics on separate tracks, so you learn to really commit. I started out making records on 8-tracks, and when you've got to combine the drums to one or two tracks, you're basically mixing, you're committing to the mix the moment you start putting music on the tracks. You have to make the commitment then, or if you record on 48 or 96 tracks, you can make the decision later, but in terms of Paul's preference, it worked better to commit in the moment. For the album's general micing, I did this kind of triangulated thing where I put a mic on the kick drum, a really nice tube mic right above the snare, and then off of the toms, I put the same kind of mic basically equidistant, so I could capture most of the general sound, and then you pan left and right and get this really natural sound.

One element of the sound of *14 Songs* that became resonant in rock albums from then on was the guitar sound Wallace and Westerberg created and captured, which so impressed the pair's industry peers that, according to mega-pop producer Don Was, "during the recording of *Voodoo Lounge* with the Rolling Stones, that was the rock record we were aiming in ways to sound like." Capitalizing on his hard-rock foundation via prior work with electric guitar–heavy bands like Faith No More and the Replacements, Wallace returned Westerberg to his own roots from the alt-punk heyday with the latter band, explaining that when the singer did plug in, he still had as wildly emotive a playing style as ever: "Paul, as a guitar player, wrestles the instrument, he grabs onto it for dear life. He's probably not the most trained or articulated player, but what he doesn't have in that regard, he has in emotion, and attitude and vibe in spades. When he grabs the guitar, he really is trying to coax as much emotion, feeling, sound texture, timbre—as much as he can, out of whatever instrument he's playing. With a guitar, he really does do that incredibly well."

Delving into some of his recording norms—in terms both of technique and equipment—for tracking guitars based off the sound he captured for Westerberg on *14 Songs*, Wallace explains that

> in general, the most important concept I try to get across to people is that it's not *how* you record but *what* you record that is most essential. And it's been proven time and time again. You can have an incredibly talented musician pick up the worst guitar, and can make it sing; it's all about the touch—the musician's contact with the instrument. I've also seen people who are very mediocre players pick up an incredible [piece of] equipment and make it sound pretty sketchy. The flipside of that equation, now that I've said that it's really about the musician, is that what can make it better *is* a great piece of gear. Traditionally, Paul always played Les Paul Juniors, but this amplifier was a blonde Vox AC 30 amplifier with original Bulldog speakers in the cabinet; it had a built-in, modified box. It was absolutely fantastic; it's what we used for almost all the songs on that album. It was one of those rare—what I feel to be magical—amps that I used to play my Telecaster through, and it sounded great.

Using *14 Songs* as an example, Wallace explained that the key to producing the album's guitar sound involved the combination of

> a player who's got the intensity, focus, desire, emotion—everything—all going through his fingers onto his guitar into this amplifier in a decent room, and you've got a great sound. Then the trick is to take that sound and capture it on tape, so that's where you get into a producer using his instincts about what you think is gonna work. Because with some artists you can experiment and try different mics, different placement, to get that sound—Paul has absolutely no patience for any of that kind of crap. He's ready to roll when he plugs in, and that's why working with him on that record, and even the Replacements' record some years prior, I learned about instinct. That's where you take all your knowledge of every amplifier you've miced and player you've worked with in the past, and you take every essential piece of information, and go, "Okay, I know Paul is not going to be up for this thing where we go meticulously go through different mics and preamps, so I'm gonna shoot from the hip, put a mic up,

and go with my gut." And that's what I did. On that album, I used a 57 mic, which is always a go-to microphone for guitar amps. It's really easy to do. I also put a 4-14 either somewhere on the cabinet, or I'll back it off there. Usually, a 57 I'll put off next to the cone because it will pick up all the proximity and warmth of it, and then right in the middle of the cone, I'll put the amp turned up without anyone playing, and move my ear around and find that spot where you can hear the hiss really clearly, and that's usually where I put a 4-14.

Still, for all its spontaneous serendipity, some of the album's most inspired songs were among Westerberg's more personal, and commanded a much deeper investment of time to properly capture in the studio. Beginning with "First Glimmer of Light," Wallace remembered the track as

the most produced song on the album, and we were more meticulous about it because it was a much more delicate song. From what I remember, we attempted recording the acoustic guitars in New York soon after Paul fired the band. Then we went to San Francisco and cut it live in the studio at Toast Recording Studios. After that, I believe that we kept trying different approaches and instruments until we got something that Paul and I liked on tape. Everything on that song we had to do, and redo, to the point where I think the version that ended up on the record was the second version of the song we'd recorded. That one took a lot of effort. It was kind of like trying to capture a butterfly, where you're sort of tip-toeing behind it. Vocally we were much more careful, and did the whole headphone approach and did composite takes, and were much more methodical. So we recorded in a bit of a piecemeal fashion in that it took a number of attempts to get it just right. Then, as if that wasn't challenging enough, it was a bit of a challenge to mix it, as Paul was always at my elbows as I attempted to mix it and his impatience never allowed me to spend more than a couple of hours working on it. In the end, my friend and guitarist for Counting Crows, David Bryson, was able to mix it at Sunset Sound Factory while I entertained/distracted Paul.

Among the other mics Wallace utilized in capturing Westerberg's vocals on the album, a favorite for softer vocals involved "having Paul sing into a very delicate, vintage, extremely sensitive Neumann U-47 tube mic . . . while his hands were grabbing it and he was singing in the control room with the monitors extremely loud. Technically that was 'wrong.' However, vibe wise, it was perfect."

Another of the album's more intimate musical moments, among the first songs the two tracked together, and arguably the most personal to Westerberg, was "Runaway Wind," highlighted by the fact that the singer had provided one of the album's rare demos prior to tracking. Wallace spent as much time ahead of recording as he could becoming acquainted with the demo—an action that helped to build a trust between him and Westerberg as the recording process continued. Expanding on the importance of the comfort level between producer and performer, Wallace recalled that

> in trying to figure out how to best help Paul bring his music to fruition, he'd given me a couple of his demos, which was really unlike him, and I spent about an hour or so listening to "Runaway Wind." It was after a day of the two of us in the studio and I was listening over and over to a rough mix of the song, and on my fifth listen, I finally got, I think, where he was at personally, because that song was about his father, and I realized that it was about his father. On my tenth listen, I realized that it was really about Paul and his *perspective* of his father, about getting older, and watching his dad age, but I also got the subtext that it was about Paul. I immediately called him on the hotel phone and said, "Hey, Paul, I have a question. Is 'Runaway Wind' about your father?" He said, "How did you know? Did I tell you about it?" I said, "No, I've been listening to it over and over again and breathing in every aspect about that song and it has gotten under my skin." I then said, "And, it seems to be about you, too, right?" There was a long pause, and I think he knew I got it. That is one of those moments where I realized that sometimes knowing a song really emotionally can help you eventually capture it in a recording setting.

Perhaps with the trust required for the singer to feel comfortable enough to completely wear honesty on his sleeve during recording, Wallace explained that the pair's first attempts to track the song were futile:

> We initially attempted it in New York, but it never quite came together. So we moved from New York to start recording again, and Paul didn't want to go to L.A., so I suggested San Francisco, which was my home base and where I'd done both Faith No More albums. So we moved into this studio called Toad at the time and got it done with the help of Brian MacLeod and John Pierce. After we had a few takes, we had that song—I distinctly remember putting Paul's guitar amp in a hallway for the solo/melody guitar on that song. Once we got that song down right, it was apparent that he could see that I was interested in working with him for the right reasons.

Following his collaboration with the Replacements, and preceding that of the solo record he made with Westerberg, Matt Wallace took on the challenge of capturing the rainbow of musical colors and styles that was Faith No More on tape for *The Real Thing*. Of the band's first collaboration—next to Anthony Kiedis of the Red Hot Chili Peppers— with rap-metal's most stylistically flamboyant front man, Mike Patton, *Rolling Stone* said that

though the band began with "the punk shouting of original singer Chuck Mosley, ı
is on tracks featuring replacement Mike Patton's far more skillful and creative weirdness."

Wallace entered the studio with Faith No More just as Patton was, with an approach that

> as a producer, for better or for worse, has always been very eclectic. To me, everything
> I do is between two bookends— beautiful and brutal. My approach to producing is
> very much like Faith No More's as a band, and that is that I want to take a bite out
> of a lot of different things, and after *The Real Thing* I could have gotten myself into
> a niche where I did rap-metal or heavy metal, but my desires and tendencies kind
> of prohibit that. There are times where I feel brutal and want to get my hands on
> the most heinous and ugly music I can imagine, but then I want to get into the more
> delicate stuff because I think that reflects life. Life is between beautiful and brutal at
> any one point in our lives, and I like to capture that musically as a producer whenever
> I can. The sonic stuff is a means to an end, and if we could bypass it altogether, put
> it on a CD, plug it straight into your brain and get the emotion, we'd do it. To describe
> indescribable emotions, we paint, we write, we sing songs, we dance, we do these
> things to explain the unexplainable, that's always been paramount to anything, even
> if it's to the detriment of the sound. Recording stuff is just a way to get that out and
> on tape. People want to be moved; they want a good beat, a great melody, a good
> lyric, and that's all it takes, that's all that song required. I don't believe that there's
> any signature sound, or one that I consciously go after, but I do believe there's a very
> signature spirit to the records I make.

Ironically, the unexpected hit single "Epic" would prove to be ahead of its time and
that the band's label had been wildly incorrect in assessing the album's commercial ap-
peal. Industry-wise, no one had seen the song coming, just as they hadn't the massive shift
approaching in rock's popular trends as the hair-metal era of the 1980s gave way to the
alt-rock dominance of the 1990s. *Rolling Stone* would qualify the latter in its review of the
band's first LP with Patton, concluding that "the (*Real Thing*) perfectly summed up the era
of discontent that was dawning. That genre-morphing collection seamlessly fused punk,
heavy metal, and progressive rock with soul and rap and was a harbinger of alternative
music to come from the likes of Pearl Jam, the Red Hot Chili Peppers, and Nine Inch Nails."

In illustrating the band's kaleidoscope of stylistic goals for the album heading into
production, Wallace described a climate in the studio wherein

> Faith No More was the most democratic band I've ever worked with, in that it was
> a spiderweb pointing in five equal but opposite directions. During that record, Jim
> Martin was into the heavy stuff, like Sabbath, and the keyboard player was a clas-
> sically trained pianist. Then you had Mike Patton coming from an art-rock band, Mr.

Bungle, where every four bars the music took some weird left turn, and Mike Borden had studied African rhythms, so you had all these guys coming from all these different musical directions. And what made them unique was that you had five distinct, separate elements you throw into this pot, stir it up, and out comes this *The Real Thing*.

Amazingly, for as beautifully and naturally as the band's eclectic circus of styles blended on the LP, Wallace explained that

all the music for that record was written before Mike joined the band, which had gotten rid of the original singer, Chuck Mosley, and the tracks were either in preproduction or being recorded when Mike came in. And when he'd ask if he could make a section longer or different, the band would say "No, this is it, so you have to do it this way." So Mike Patton wrote every lyric and melody to that record over a ten- to twelve-day period. And it is stunning, because he was nineteen or twenty, and pulled all that out of the air, and put together an incredible record. The only thing we did was spend a couple days at this coffee shop in San Francisco, because a lot of the songs were really dark and heavy lyrically, crazily so, and I would sit there and go, "Mike, these are some great lyrics, but we need to at least use some metaphor, or couch some of the concepts, but I think you've got some great ideas here." In the end, they really pulled some great songs together.

Detailing the album's recording from a technical perspective, Wallace recalled that in spite of its conceptually and instrumentally sophisticated compositions and arrangements,

we recorded the album on 24-tracks, and that record was done with one electric guitar, one harmony acoustic guitar we used on one or two songs, one Marshall half stack, one Aria Pro, and a Peavey amp for bass and a crappy SVP Cabinet. That was all we had. It wasn't like "Let's try this amp, or try this guitar . . . No." So out of using absolutely minimal equipment, I think we created some really groundbreaking music, and it was all about attitude, spirit, focus, and desire; all of that was by far more essential than having great gear. I think it's a testament to the fingertips, and hands, and minds of those guys at that time, to make some really inspired stuff. That record was done in two months, from the beginning rehearsal to finished mixes; we didn't have any time to screw around. When tracking Mike Patton's vocals, I double-compressed his vocals to tape through a 166 T-Disc compressor that I happened to have with me. It's nothing great, and we used a 47-Tube mic, and then when I mixed the vocals, I double-compressed his vocals again, trying to control the dynamic, but also wanted every little piece of his voice as up front as possible—the interior stuff—the little breaths, the little cracks. I wanted that so up front, and really pursued it relentlessly. Then, of course, his mind for lyrics. It's also again really about his attitude as a singer. One of the only arguments we had was when we were recording, he would sing really nasally, really snotty, but then off mic, he had a bass voice, he could really sing. And I would ask, "Damn it, why don't you sing like that on this record? You have this full voice, and pitch, and you open your throat, that's amazing." So the only thing we fought about was he had this nasally, snotty-kid vibe he wanted to put on the album, and he was right in the end, but that guy could sing for real. I've never worked with a singer before or since who was built to sing like Mike Patton. He has the throat, the chest, the ability to hit pitch, he can sing a death metal vocal one minute, then swing around to a pop croon the next. He was just phenomenal.

MTV agreed, commenting that the front man "was a more accomplished vocalist, able to change effortlessly between rapping and singing, as well as adding a considerably more bizarre slant to the lyrics. Besides adding a new vocalist, the band had tightened its attack and the result was the genre-bending hit single 'Epic,' which established them as a major hard rock act."

By the time the band entered the studio to record their follow-up to *The Real Thing* in the fall of 1991, the commercial climate in rock was much more native to the alt/art-rock band Faith No More had morphed into with Patton. Expectations within the industry were naturally running high. Still, as Wallace recalled, the band couldn't have been at greater lows personally:

That record was—in my career—one of the most—if not *the most*—difficult records to make because Jim Martin wanted to rehearse in Oakland, and we'd always rehearsed in San Francisco. So we ended up moving all the equipment, everything, to Oakland, and the difficulty of that was Jim Martin didn't really show up much during the rehearsals. His dad was dying, and my first suggestion was that we take a break, but the label was pushing to get the album done, so we were all driving from San Francisco into Oakland for rehearsals, and Jim was hardly there, which wasn't good because he was such an essential part of the group. And what I kept explaining to him was that we needed his guitar sound to be the counterbalance to the heavy brawn, the deep, dark rhythmic underpinnings that are going to balance out the tendency more on Mike's end to go into a real pop vein. And since he wasn't around to do that, Bill Gould and I spent a large amount of time at his home studio in San Francisco working on guitar parts, and on the record. When Jim wasn't around, Bill actually played a lot of what would have been his parts. So everything you'd hear note-wise or noodly parts, that was Jim, but he didn't bring any of the power chords and muscle that he had on *The Real Thing*. Jim and Bill were fighting on the phone all the time from the studio, because what would happen is the band would do the tracks, and then at night, Jim would come in and do his guitar parts, then the next day, the band would come in and not like something, and it would just start this vicious cycle over again.

Conceptually, aside from the aforementioned intrapersonal difficulties, Wallace further revealed that "the band really wanted to get away from the whole hip-hop/metal thing that album had spawned. So they wanted to go for a totally different approach." For the producer personally heading into recording for his second album with the band, Wallace recalled that

> after *The Real Thing*, I almost quit engineering and producing altogether, because it sounded so thin and horrible, and absolutely dismal on my home stereo, sketchy on my car stereo. I still to this day feel it's sonically pretty sketchy, but the spirit is there. Well, fast-forward to *Angel Dust*, we were trying to do a couple things: I wanted to get a much rounder, fuller, fatter, more low-end sounding record. On that record, it was a total and complete contrast from recording the first record I did with the band because of the success of *The Real Thing*. The first album had been recorded without anyone really bugging us because no one expected it to be a success, but for *Angel Dust*, of course, everyone was trying to get their fingers in the pie.

In spite of its plethora of challenges in and out of the studio, the album was hailed by critics, including *Rolling Stone*, who hailed it as "a roiling, musically adventurous record that represents yet another leap forward for a combo that broke through by cramming together rap's vocal cadences, metal's brute force and progressive rock's pompous keyboards on *Epic*." In hindsight, Wallace feels that from the album's challenging recording process, "one positive on that record that I think I really learned from Mike Patton was how to use your voice as an instrument, not just to sing, but as an instrument. He did some spectacular stuff vocally on that album. Still, I was spent at the end of making that record; it was a very tough album to make. But in the end, *Kerrang!* rated it the most influential LP of all time, and so many bands cite that album as the album that really made them want to go pro. *The Real Thing* was a great album, but the one I still get calls about to this day is *Angel Dust*."

By 2002, Wallace was hungry to break new ground, and found just the gamble to make when he entered the studio with a then-unknown Maroon 5. The stakes were high from the moment he laid ears on the group:

> When I got to Maroon 5, I knew that record could go the distance. What's interesting in that Maroon 5 was very similar to Faith No More in that when I made that record, people thought I was out of my mind. I made that record in 2001, and it didn't blow up till 2004. Everyone thought the odds were totally stacked against us; it was the

first album ever for the band's label, Octone Records. At the same time, I was being offered a project for a band called Days of the New that was established, and was paying more money. Maroon 5 was done on such a little budget too that for me personally it was financially devastating. I had done a really cool punky record by a band called Sugarcult that did pretty good, but it was still financially devastating for my family because we weren't making enough money to stay afloat. I knew that it was a great record, and my manager Frank McDonough had always encouraged me to make records that spoke to me, and Maroon 5 really spoke to me. Growing up, I used to listen to Sabbath and Deep Purple, but was also really into funk, like Parliament and the Ohio Players. I had always felt funky ass-shaking music was the kind of music I'd like to make, and Maroon 5 had that. So, first of all, I knew we had a hit record, but didn't know if the band's label would be able to sell it because we had no major label backing. When it was done and they started generating interest, they signed to J Records, but I know for a fact Clive Davis wanted that record six months before Octone finally handed it over. The label wanted to establish some indie credibility, and knew they didn't need J Records until it was time to blow up and become a radio smash. But I knew it was a hit record in my gut, which is why I bet on it.

Continuing, Wallace recalled that

by 2001, the band was so steeped in Missy Elliot and Lauren Hill and Outkast that the record we made is very different from the one that eventually came out. We made a very urban, R&B, loop-savvy, very tight, dry record, and I think it was completely forward thinking and absolutely stunning in the way that Faith No More had taken rap and put it to metal. But the label—and they were correct in retrospect—wanted the band to mix the album more in a rock direction because they explained rightly that five skinny white guys couldn't tour hip-hop markets to break the album. They wanted to pull back and make a rock record, and the guitars on the record were rock, but there were very tight, tweaked, edited, dry drums, which we had to pull back in the loops and go for more of a rock sound. Either way, I felt the whole time the songs were so undeniably catchy, especially "This Love," which was supposed to be the band's second single, ended up being the big smash single off that album.

Once committed to the band, Wallace entered preproduction with the group with a focus almost immediately on developing hit songs he felt at the time were still diamonds in the rough:

In preproduction with Maroon 5. . . I was advocating bridges, where I'd say "You guys have some great songs, but if you want a hit record, you need a bridge." So I was very much an advocate of doing that, so in preproduction it was a lot of arranging, rearranging, trying a key, tempo. Preproduction is really where you can take the song and stretch, and pull, and twist on it to different shapes to see which shape is the right one. I refuse to go into the studio without the songs written and arranged; it's the biggest waste of song. We had very little money, and we had to make every single penny count. We're all taking a huge cut in pay, so in preproduction we were going to write, arrange, and rehearse those songs to the point where when we walked in the studio, we had a very defined road map so we knew where we were heading. That doesn't mean we didn't try a better idea while recording. Of course, I would, but in general, it meant we could relax and focus on the performances, about capturing the vibe, instead of worrying about whether we had the right key. Or spend all day tracking one song, instead of tracking two or three because we weren't trying to figure out what went where in the arrangement. You deplete your energy and that first spark or moment of capturing something special.

Songs about Jane would eventually become a triple-platinum smash, validating Wallace's betting on the band years before it would pay off commercially for anyone.

In closing, Wallace surmises,

I think the most true and precise word that defines me as a producer is I'm the band's consultant. For me, the most important things I could pass along, from my experience, are one, follow your heart, where I've done projects for little money because I loved the band, like Faith No More and Maroon 5. Two, make sure that everyone is open to failing miserably because by being that open, you'll also be open to being brilliantly genius because they're not in their comfort zone, out of a fear of mistakes. Three, when focusing on making a hit record, it has to do with how you arrange the song, the key of the song, how you intend it to be heard by the audience, those elements are essential. And finally four, it's so essential to leave some of the humanity on a track, and not edit out every mistake, because that's sometimes when it sounds like there's a real, living, breathing person playing the music. There's nothing to me that is more boring than a perfect record. I think timing and tuning are vastly overrated, and you can listen to any of the classics, from the Stones to the Beatles to Zeppelin, where you'll hear stuff that's just off time and out of tune, and you know what? It moves people. Record producers are selling emotions, that's all we're doing in the end, so that a listener has a moment where they connect and say "Oh my God, this person has been where I've been, felt what I've felt, made it through the crap, and if they can make it, that gives me a sense I can make it too. The singer singing to me knows my story, and I can keep going another day." There are two bookends to music;

on one end it's entertainment, on the other end, it's absolutely essential pieces of information for people's well-being, and this can happen on any song, and should be the goal. If it cannot change the world, music can definitely change one listener at a time, and give people a lifeline they desperately needed. So those are my words of growth and wisdom.

CHAPTER 24

Andy Johns—When the Levee Breaks

Sometimes capturing a classic guitar riff on tape is like catching lightning in a bottle. A great song can capture the hearts and minds of a generation, and catch a historic wind that carries the band that wrote and popularized the song into rock 'n' roll legend. The same goes for its producer, at least back in the glory days of rock 'n' roll. Looking back from today on the late 1960s, rock 'n' roll was a vintage muscle car that was built to last, and soundmen like Andy Johns were the pioneering mechanics that designed its roaring Corvette engine. Unique to the time frame in which he was earning his wings as an engineer, one where bands often coproduced or produced their own albums with just an engineer acting as a copilot, Johns took some truly amazing training flights, and outright rides in the studio alongside the greatest rock legends at an age when most of his peers were merely fans or listeners.

Under the tutelage of older brother, Glyn Johns, at eighteen, Andy recalled his charmed beginnings:

In the days when I started out, the studio business was completely different from what it is now. There were no independent engineers: engineers were on a salary. And if someone called up and talked to a woman—it was always a woman who ran the phones—"I would like to book some time to work on something orchestral," then they would put some guy who had experience with orchestras on the gig, because that's a tough gig, and you have to be ready, and have to know exactly what you're doing. And the man who ran Olympic Studios was Keith Grant, who was brilliant at orchestras, and also recorded the Troggs' "Wild Thing," so you know, he could do both. If you were what was called a "Tape Operator," you ran the 4-track machine, and you made tea, and you put mics up for the engineer, and you had to know what the mics were, you had to be able to edit things, you had to be able to punch in. The patching and other complicated stuff you would help with, but you were supposed to learn this very quickly. And because it was 4-track, and there was no real outboard gear, you could learn all this fairly quickly. But they would throw you in off the deep end, even though we were all still very young then.

As a tape operator, Johns immediately found himself responsible for managing the recording mechanism through which history-making hits like "Wild Thing" were created. He explained that in his earliest days, rock 'n' roll happened out in the live room, where back behind the boards, as a tape operator, "I soon found myself in a form of indentured servitude, because from that position, then you might become an assistant after six or seven years, but you're never going to get a gig, because the studio isn't going to give you one." Soon finding himself ambitious enough to move out of the shadow of his older brother and the other senior engineers and producers at Olympic, Johns found his lucky break would come, ironically, out of "being fired from Olympic after six months for being tardy. Well, as luck would have it, this friend of my brother who I'd worked with several times, Terry Brown, who'd recorded 'A Little Help From My Friends' and 'Whiter Shade of Pale' by Procol Harum at the young age of twenty-one, had just built a studio called Morgan Sound, in Whiston, England. I remember it was in a very dodgy area, lot of Irish nabbies, but was an opportunity to take on more direct recording responsibility, so I got the gig and was allowed back into work."

Johns reveled in the fact that he'd gotten this second chance "even though I still didn't really know what I was doing; I rolled up my sleeves, opened my ears." And no doubt he opened his eyes even wider after learning that the studio owner had made a lockout deal with Island Records founder Chris Blackwell. Johns recalled that the deal "guaranteed him a certain amount of work per month, and I was doing all the sessions." Overnight, he found he was no longer a bit player but seated front and center behind the console, living out his dream of working "at age nineteen with artists like Traffic, Blind Faith, Free, and Jethro Tull! Those bands swung the world a little bit, and even though I was winging my way through a lot of it, I learned very quickly thereafter that you'd better know what you're doing as an engineer; otherwise you'll look like a bloody idiot."

Whereas his dismissal from his previous position at Olympic for tardiness might have suggested a lack of interest in what he was being assigned to do, Johns revealed that, in fact, he "actually cared very, very much, and wanted to be a part of it, and was lucky to no longer be on the sidelines."

As ambitious as Johns recalled feeling at a time that marked the wonder years for most rock fans his age, rather than tripping out in that spirit on the surrealism of it all, the sound-man instead planted his feet firmly on the ground, keeping his head clear of the clouds despite his feeling "understandably like a kid who if you'd just gone out your bedroom, May 1968, listening to Hendrix and Cream, these people are gods, and then you're thrown in a room with them, and they're actually treating you as if you have meaning and purpose, it made for very heady stuff." Overnight Johns was working in sessions with rock's superstars of the day, including Eric Clapton in Blind Faith on the band's debut LP, *Humble Pie*, and Jethro Tull and Traffic on the seminal *John Barleycorn Must Die* LP in 1970. Johns would soon be swept up into the magic carpet ride that came with the breakout opportunity in 1971 to work with rock 'n' roll's most royal family, the already legendary Rolling Stones, as lead engineer on their seminal *Sticky Fingers* LP. Johns was so stoked at the opportunity to record an album with the band from the ground up—one that would be considered a touchstone for the dawn of 1970s hard rock courtesy of classics like "Brown Sugar," "Wild Horses," and "Dead Flowers"—that he even turned down the chance to work with the Beatles on their final studio LP, *Let it Be*.

Giving fans a front-row seat inside his recollection of the impossible choice he had to make at what would have been a moment of truth for any up-and-coming producer, Johns recalled that

> Paul McCartney came one day, and this is when the Beatles are still the Beatles, and it's hard to recount what the effect of meeting a Beatle at that age would have to a person forty years later, but what it was like for a child of nineteen, it's beyond a schoolboy's dream being in a room with Paul McCartney! This, mind you, is a time when the Beatles basically owned the world of creativity, more than cutting edge, changing the way people thought, or so it seemed, and to have the guy tell you (that) you're doing really well, and ask you if you'd like to come and work for him, it's a hard feeling to describe even now.

Handed the Beatles gig just ahead of the Stones approaching him, Johns's initial clarity about taking the job was soon clouded by the band's internal chaos:

> I went to Apple Studios, and it was just a mess! He gave me a nice tour, "I'm sorry there's so much building going on, look, we're gonna do something great here." So I do the session with McCartney, and it's just a mess. The mixer—there were eight speakers, one for each track, the compressors were permanently put on tracks 1 and 2—and I said to myself, "These guys don't have a clue!" So at the end of the day Paul comes to me and says "So, do you want to come work for us?" And I said, "Well, can I call you on Monday about this?" And he was like "Yeah. Yeah," and I realized that I had just turned the Beatles down, and thank God for that. I'm not going to get involved with this because they were going right out the window—and of course, one's instincts were proven correct, because within a year, there were no more Beatles.

Gambling his own tumbling dice on the ambition of becoming the Stones' mainstay soundman at an axial moment where Johns felt the band had become "the center of this sociological revolution, and all of that was channeled creatively into their music. This was a time when they were saying "Well, we're not going to do 'I Love You' anymore, we're going to go back to kind of blues stuff which was done very well on *Beggar's Banquet*, and on *Let it Bleed*. I mean, 'Gimme Shelter' still to this day stands up. It's as good as 'Like a Rolling Stone,' no pun intended." As the Stones evolved in real time with Johns's own natural tastes as a more ragged glory-oriented rock producer, he found himself instantly drawn to the band's shift toward a rawer channeling of their blues roots: "I set my cap to the Rolling Stones because they were a little bit tougher, and I wanted nothing more or nothing less than [to be] the Rolling Stones' engineer. Because I'd wanted to be a rock star, like everyone else. Or a producer. I wanted the Rolling Stones, and I got them, and it was to be a watershed, seminal moment for me."

Johns revealed that he'd had childhood ties to the band courtesy of the fact he'd known Bill Wyman since he was fourteen. "He'd given me my first electric bass guitar, the one he used to use on Top of the Pops for 'Satisfaction' and 'Get off of My Cloud,' which was more than a Christmas present, for a fourteen-year-old child." That personal history, however, cut him no professional slack once in the studio. Revealing that in contrast to the carefree rock 'n' roll lifestyle portrayed on record and stage, from his first day working with the band, he discovered they were all business, to the extreme that "if you couldn't show up within a half hour's notice for a session, they'd get someone else, and when I met Mick and Keith they sort of frightened me." He discovered quickly that passing his audition for the gig would involve not only facing that fright head on, but more importantly standing up to its source for the sake of the music, even when the source happened to be the band's lead singer.

Underscoring the importance of developing fearlessness as a producer in the face of an intimidating artist, Johns explained that

> when I first got into the studio with the Stones, I remember they were playing very poorly because they hadn't played together for six months, and they were out of tune and couldn't make up their minds up because they were also very stoned. So at that point, only knowing me as this kid they'd met once or twice as a teenager, but Jimmy Miller said I was going to be there, and they come in, and Jagger asks to hear a playback of something I'd just recorded from this sloppy session. As you can imagine, like this is my worst nightmare, and it didn't sound quite right because they were playing so poorly. And they used to have all these hangers-on: drug dealers, groupies, all these fucking losers, intellectual wanna-be groupies. So I had this vocal playback, and Jagger is looking me directly in the eye, from about three feet away and said, "What the fuck in hell do you think that is? I could do better than that on my Sony cassette machine! What are you doing here?" And I remember thinking, "Aah, I've been waiting some years for this," and I said, "Well, excuse me, fuck you! Why don't you get rid of your hangers-on, throw 'em out, because it's a small space, and they're soaking up the sound. Throw them out, and perhaps we'll listen again." And I think looking back, for as scared as I was, if I hadn't been that honest with him, I'd have been history. And then Jagger goes "Well alright then, fair enough. It's not good, but you're worse than your brother, aren't you, fucking ego?" And I said, "Who's got the ego here? I'm not surrounding myself with a bunch of fucking losers." I remember that night I didn't sleep, because the Rolling Stones are more important to me.

Putting himself as far out on the line as it would turn out the band was itself looking to push, and arguably be pushed, as they pioneered into their next creative frontier, Johns recalled that his gamble had paid off. "I'll never forget the next morning sitting on the stairs of this huge mansion, and Mick comes out of his bedroom, and not knowing what to expect, I said: 'Look, I'm really sorry if I'm letting you guys down, the Rolling Stones are more important to me than anything . . . ' And he goes, 'No, no, you're in! That was very good last night, you're in.' He just wanted to check me out, and then we went on to work together for three or four years."

Having successfully gotten past his initial fears due to the thrill that came with riding on the same bolt of radical rock 'n' roll lightning that he heard striking the band, Johns recalled: "At that time, after the pop records—which I still happen to admire tremendously, they were very inventive, it's not straight time, the drum parts were unusual, there were cellos, the lyrical matter—they were at the height of their power in the blues area at this point. So the idea of working with men like that was very intriguing." To that end, while making musical history in real time was not an everyday occurrence for most engineers, in working with the Rolling Stones, Johns would soon discover its rare predictability sewn within the very fabric of the band's creative process, fueled in the moment by the fact, as *Billboard* would later observe, that the record was "a weary, drug-laden album."

Concurring with this observation, Johns noted that as they got down to the business of recording, as an extension of their aforementioned habit, "the Rolling Stones at this time were not a particularly good band, lots of drugs, and trying to find out who they are, so it might take two or three days to get something. Mind you when you'd go over there to work, it's an off planet experience. And the luxury of sitting in there, where you're petrified, 'What's Jagger going to sing?' depending on his mood, was a really wonderful thing. And there's all sorts of weird people coming in and out, and of course, now they're in the throes of—well, Keith was a proper junkie."

Still, rather than becoming lost as most bands would have in their own musical mist, the Stones—as Johns recalled—instead embraced the mystery of the open road their muse was riding at the turn of the decade, one that *Rolling Stone* would later conclude gave the band "a loose, ramshackle ambience that belies . . . its origins." From a production point of view, Johns said, among the greatest lessons he learned from this avant-garde approach to the album's recording was to develop a fisherman's patience where capturing the band's creative lightning in the proverbial bottle was concerned. "I learned from making that record that you just sit and wait for the Rolling Stones' groove to appear, and then when it happens, boy oh boy you better catch it! 'Cause now they're a blues band, not a pop band, but a really clever blues pop band doing tunes like 'Under My Thumb,' which if you listen to that, has a lot of blues, and a lot of fidelity."

Honing in on where he felt the band's greatest secret weapon lay, musically speaking— authentically plugging back into their blues roots from the performance versus songwriting end of the spectrum that Jagger and Richards dominated—Johns shone the spotlight on "Mick Taylor, who, let's not forget, is one of the greatest slide players of all time. Both his sense of melody and melancholy were so evident, that it would draw you in on every take. You'd be sitting on the edge of your seat, what's he going to do next, which blue note will it be? And he would do it time after time."

The Rock and Roll Hall of Fame would later note of the completed *Sticky Fingers* album, "At this point, the Stones had their fingers firmly on the pulse of the fractured mood of the early Seventies . . . The album also reflected the group's internal yin-yang in grainy aural black-and-white: bristling musical energy vs. heavy-lidded world-weariness, love of rock vs. loyalty to the blues, the downward pull of decadence vs. a dogged effort to capture the moment."

The latter focus would remain. Johns as lead engineer throughout the recording of the ambitious double LP, confirmed as much:

> What I learned from all this was, here's what's important; is to catch the moment. With the Rolling Stones, you can be fairly certain they're going to figure it out them- selves. Sometimes I would give them sounds they wouldn't have thought of, and that would seem conducive to making them think or play a little differently. The Stones were fearless in this—if the groove, the pocket, wasn't available to them, after a little while, they would try a bossa nova version, then a reggae version, then if that wasn't working, then they'd always come back to the original idea, which was the one that worked. It just took time.

Seeking to take themselves off the clock that might have paced the traditional record- ing studio session, heading into the creation of *Exile on Main Street,* the Stones made a truly out-of-the-box decision to record in a mansion in the south of France. As foreign as the concept might have seemed to the watching world at the time, within the Stones' universe, Johns recalled the move made sense given the band's desire to have art imitate life in terms of their creative environment. To that end, the producer revealed,

> *Exile on Main Street* was the fruition of *Sticky Fingers*, and so by now, they had kind of grown tired of the whole thing. We go to the South of France, and the Stones had built a mobile unit called, appropriately, the Rolling Stone Mobile, which was the first mobile recording in Europe, probably in America too. Before that, there were things like the Pie unit, which I recorded Led Zeppelin and Ginger Baker on, which was just a bunch of equipment in the back of a van, that you'd take in, set up in a dressing room, and run cables with an 8-track. Now I don't know whose idea this was, but it was a very clever idea. They put the recording unit inside of a Bedford truck, so we could go anywhere and record anywhere.

Convenient to the departure, the band sought on all fronts to head in next with their signature brand of rock. The move was as much a journey for Johns personally, who re- called, "I still couldn't quite believe that I could be part of this, sort of, center of the world team. But Jimmy liked me, so I got the phone call to come to the South of France to work on the *Exile* sessions, and I get there, and I'm twenty-one years old, and it's the South of France. I'd never been anywhere outside of England in me life. And Keith's got this huge house, which is disheveled, but still very elegant."

As Johns and lead producer Jimmy Miller got down to the business of coalescing the Stones' mobile recording control room with the live environment the band would be physically tracking in, the engineer recalled stumbling into his first bout with technical trouble in paradise, which came after "we had the truck run up to the house, and as we'd started working, the band was set up and playing in this basement. Well, the problem with that was this basement had six rooms, none of which were very suitable for recording."

Johns called on another of what he found and continues to believe to be among the most fundamentally important skills for any engineer to develop, that of using his ears to fluidly source out the best sonic backdrop to suit a band's sound in the moment of its creation, which for him at the time meant "moving the band to this other room where the walls were made up of limestone rock, a smattering of carpet, a spectacular iron staircase where Bill Wyman would stand, and another room where I put Nicky Hopkins on headphones." Delving deeper inside this fascinating process of redesigning each individual band member's organic dynamics as players around that of their live recording environment without one getting in the way of the other, Johns recalled, "From there, we set up Charlie's drums in the L-shaped corner, and Keith's amp next to Charlie, and he was using these 300-watt amped combos. So when the time came, he could stand up and look Charlie in the eye, Mick Taylor in the next room."

Even as he and Miller made progress in retuning the room's natural acoustics to better fit the sound the band was after, Johns admitted to feeling "despite the fact that you may have come up with some fabulous ideas that sound good out loud, inside still being slightly unsure of yourself. And in a situation like that, there's an important lesson to be had that you don't get comfortable, you don't see what your work was, what you thought of it, what it meant, what it really means, until later. You go 'Well, that's nice, I'm glad I thought of that, I can accept it.' So they're still very young."

Still, as tape rolled, Johns found himself very encouraged in spite of the experimental nature of the sessions "because in reaction to that, they would do things that were so inspirational, that were so wonderful, they made you feel after you'd done all this waiting around, 'Thank God I was here to experience this.'" An understatement indeed in the context of the broader sound the band was birthing to life as tape continued to roll, that patience Johns expanded past the setup phase to that of the recording process itself, offering the band's methodical creation of the seminal hit "Tumbling Dice" as one such instance where "I think we had eighty reels of tape on that. That's three weeks or maybe twenty days."

Though Jimmy Miller acted as lead producer on the project, in reflecting back on how his day-in-day-out involvement in shepherding the LP's evolution contributed to that of his own growth as a producer, Johns confessed that "in the beginning of *Exile on Main Street*, I was more of an observer. During the tracking, I was still so much in awe of the band itself, I wasn't going to say anything, 'cause you never know. A gem, a world-changing gem might come out in the end, and I was no diamond cutter as of yet. I'm just along for the ride, supplying things, making sure they worked, but not so much making suggestions." His opportunity to wade more deeply into that process came as recording wrapped and attention turned to mixing the double-LP opus that *Exile* had matured into by that point.

That maturation the engineer would luckily discover had also extended to his personal relationships with the band's key members, a breakthrough in trust that would prove pivotal to allowing Johns the opportunity to contribute creatively to shaping the album's final sound. Recalling that "when it came time to mix *Exile*, it was my idea to go to L.A. So anyway, we go to L.A., now I'm feeling a little more power, because the band was tired of working on the record by then, and I could see I was the only one who knew what was on the tape, because they kept forgetting things."

Highlighting with this memory the crucial trust that an artist—no matter their stature—can place in the hands of a producer during the most consequential stages of crafting an album, Johns offered this poignant example:

> By now, Mick and I were becoming somewhat friends, where he would come to my house and drink with me and my wife, make jokes, and on one hand, I thought "What a school boy's dream!" But on the other, there was a great responsibility that came with that trust in the form of his taking my opinion seriously. So, for instance, I remember when we mixed this one song called "On Down the Nine," it was the first thing that was finished, and because it had taken so long and the Stones had never taken this long on a record before, not sort of day after day, they kept asking "Why are you taking so long?" And for that song, it was just Mick and me in the studio and he thought it sounded like a single and asked my opinion. So I said, "Look here, this doesn't compare to "Jumpin' Jack Flash," or "Street Fighting Man." Why are you forcing me to make a hit single out of a great blues song?' And he said, "Do you really think so? Am I wrong?"

Proving for Andy confirmation that he'd understood clearly enough where the Stones were seeking to head with their sound to have earned Jagger's respect by that point as a real contributor to the band's creative process, Johns still regards the memory as among his proudest as a producer:

> At that moment, he's just like me. And I'd known that for some time, but there was the proof. And then he smiled, sat back, and said, "You're having a tough time with the mix, aren't you?" I said, "Yes, I'd really like to hear it on the radio." And he says, "You want to hear it on the radio? Well we can fix that." The power of it all! So he gives the

song to an assistant, Stu, and says, "Stu, take that over to KTLA, and when you get there, call me. And also, I want a limo rented, with a telephone and a decent stereo in it." And I went, "Oh my God, what have I said!" Within like forty-five minutes, Stu calls and says, "Yeah, I'm at the radio station," and of course, they're very excited to have an exclusive on the new Stones album. We get in the limousine—Keith, myself, Charlie, and Jagger, tooling up and down the Sunset Strip no less, and they play it. Now, I cannot be objective, because I'm going this cannot be happening, I'm twenty-one, driving around in a Cadillac limousine, joints being passed around, Keith's falling asleep, Charlie doesn't care, and Mick's looking at me going, "What do you think?" And I said, "I don't know," and he says, "Well you better fucking figure it out!" And so he goes, "Stu, hand me that phone!" And a phone in a car was unheard of in those days, and he has them play it again. So the second play around, I had to say, "Sounds fine to me," and I couldn't tell. And if you listen to the mix, it's not unreasonable.

Johns added that as he, Jagger, and company worked their seemingly tireless way through mixing, understandably,

it was becoming more and more tiresome. Keith was hardly available, Mick was freaking out, and I told them, "I'm going home for Christmas," and I didn't expect to be called back. (I got) a call a few days later from Jagger, who says, "Well, you might have been right, those first five mixes, where I thought you took a lot of time, we haven't been able to beat them. Would you like to come back?" So, of course, I'd love to! "So, when can you come back?" So they said, "Look, you're the only one who knows, here are the tapes, finish the fucking record." And I sat up for three or four days—and this happens sometimes when you're mixing, you haven't been able to get it right at all. It's not lack of vision, lack of desire, it's just the musical goddess isn't being mean enough to you. And on my last day of a thirty-six-hour session, it finally started happening, and I mixed the rest of the *Exile* record all on me own—Bing, bong, done! And that's the record. I was lucky to have been involved.

With the success of the double-LP *Exile on Main Street*, which the Rock and Roll Hall of Fame would call "a sprawling, raucous masterpiece," Andy Johns made his bones—and status—as one of the most sought-after engineers in the business at a point where rock and metal's brightest guiding lights were increasingly taking control of their own crafting of their creative destinies in the studio. Sidelining the traditional control producers had taken of that process in favor of artist-produced albums where A-list engineers like Johns were called upon, in those moments, he took charge of picking up not only the technical side but also that of participating equally in the creative brainstorming of how to capture sounds as epic as John Bonham's drumming throughout the legendary "When the Levee Breaks." Receiving just such a call from Jimmy Page following his work with the Stones, Johns's work with Led Zeppelin in recording *LZ III* and *LZ IV* would elevate his stature to another world entirely from what had already been the creatively unparalleled plateau of working with the Stones.

Heading into the collaboration, Johns recalled that in contrast to the groupthink that dictated the Stones' creative approach to recording,

> in working with Led Zeppelin, I quickly discovered that the point of that band was this—Zeppelin was a band that Pagie had planned on—it was his vision. You have to think about this in a way, like the Beatles. Why have those four guys, Lennon, McCartney, and the others, in a room at the same time? It could have been otherwise. How come they got together to do seven or eight years of work, what are the odds of that? 'Cause you take George Harrison out of the picture, everything changes, the same with the others. Pagie had planned on doing something very important. I don't think he knew how important it would be. But finding those three guys, Plant, John Paul, and Bonzo, it happened. And Pagie and John Paul Jones were the center of it, but Bonzo had this drum feel unlike anyone ever before or since, and they had this singer who could hit any note in creation, and do it on command. So there's serious synchronicity there, and Pagie had these riffs, which to you or I seem so obvious now, "Oh I could have thought of that!" But we didn't, did we now? And I got thrown off the deep end with those guys, and they didn't know that I didn't know, but neither did they, they were unsure. But Pagie had a vision.

In contrast to the drawn-out nature of the Stones' *Exile* sessions, once he was in the studio with Zeppelin, Johns found the band's pace of recording to be quite the opposite:

> Jimmy taught me about mixing, and parts, and magic, and never give in, and this can be done quickly. If you're working with a fabulous band like Led Zeppelin, it's your job to catch, it's also your job to intimate certain things, without stepping on toes. If you're working with Led Zeppelin at their moment of creation, you don't walk over and go, "Excuse me fellows, that's all wrong!" You just sit there and you wait, and you know 'cause you can hear it coming, you know it's just a matter of a half hour or forty-five minutes, and they're going to get there, they don't need help. There's other bands I'd work with, where the format of the song is wrong, they're missing a verse, the melody is incorrect, that stuff that you know, where I'd speak up because it was my role to help get them there. With bands like Zeppelin, you don't say a damn thing, 'cause I knew it would happen, 'cause you could hear it coming. And as far as singers go, my

God, Robert Plant could go "Oh well, time for me to sing? Okay, well, could you play it for me again?" He'd still be there sitting, writing lyrics, and go, "Okay, I'm ready to sing now." Two takes, and he's done. It's a lost fucking art, working with Led Zeppelin!

Johns would also learn a great deal alongside Jimmy Page about the process of capturing a perfect heavy metal guitar sound, as "Black Dog" would indeed become the archetype for in the generations of fans and bands that followed. The producer recalled that

"Black Dog" was another situation in which we really covered some new ground—those are direct injection guitars, and I'd learned this from listening to Buffalo Springfield. I said to Pagie, give me your guitar, I'm going to hook it up through two 11-76s, and distort the fuck out of it, and when I was mixing this thing, the sound I got was so wonderfully level. Normally, when you're mixing the faders are more or less within an inch of a straight line—one for the left, one for the right, one for the middle. On "Black Dog," these guitars, their apparent level was so fabulous, that I had them almost turned off, but you could still hear them. And that makes the record, you see, it's a theory.

In concert with the album's immaculate guitar sound, the equally flawless drum sound on classics like "When the Levee Breaks" were truly historic. Bonham slammed his drums; the effects weren't just groundbreaking, but in fact sonically revolutionary as a breakthrough blueprint for many of the studio micing techniques that would become standard to recording in all rock genres in the years to follow. By working as he had with the Stones recording the record in a house versus the traditional ambient confines of a studio, Johns and company were free to think outside of the box on almost every level, which naturally inspired innovation but also uncovered new recording tricks and techniques with respect to expanding the dynamics of Bonham's power as a drummer. In elaborating on his own ear's evolution along those lines, the producer shared that

by the time I was working on Led Zeppelin IV, that experience allowed me to come up with some serious ideas, inspired by the music. "When the Levee Breaks," for example. Why do you think people use room mics for drums? I would think that "Levee Breaks" has a lot to do with it. Two microphones, two M160s halfway up a set of stairs, at Headley Grange, which is a house, not a recording studio, and much more exciting. We were working there and I come up with the idea to use the Stones' mobile unit, and working in houses like this means you can put the guitar amp in the fireplace, and put a mic in the chimney. Or you can put the boys—they're playing two acoustic guitars, congas, a shaker, and live vocals—in a room with no furniture, in a totally naked room, and it speaks and it sings—and that was called "Sweet Black Angel."

And this is wonderful stuff. So I was telling Pagie we should use the Stones' truck, and he asks how much will that cost, because Pagie is notoriously cheap. And so we record in this house called Headley Grange, which was cheaper than Keith's house on the *Exile* sessions, and we start off in this reception room, you walk in the double doors, cloak room, open the next set of double doors, now you have a nice, sort of lobby effect, like a hotel. Stairs, a landing, another landing, three floors. And I've got them all in this one room, and we do "Rock and Roll" and a couple other things, and they say "We're going down to the pub!" And I go alright, and I've been working on the idea of room mic sound for drums for at least six or eight months, and in those days, that was a long time.

From this point, focusing exclusively on honing in on the ideal sonic arena where placement considerations were concerned with the drum sound they were chasing, Johns recalled that

for this drum sound you hear on "Levee Breaks," I take Bonzo out into this lobby area, and I take two M160s, which came to me during a *Blind Faith* session, and he'd always complained, and was not good at words, but had this one word of his— "Thrutch"—and he used to say "The bass drum doesn't have enough Thrutch!" And I listen to the bass drum, and go, "He's probably bloody right, it doesn't sound in here like it does out there." And so I put him in this big room, and Pagie had bought what in those days was called a Benson Echorec, which was an echo device, which used tape like a whim, a copycat, had a steel drum, with heads on springs, five or six of them, with presets, a gorgeous instrument. And he'd left that, and I hooked it up with those two mics, and now Bonzo goes "Jesus Christ!," cause this is a half-time thing, so there's all this space with the gates, and I compressed the fuck out of it! And there you have the drum sound. And that's not my drum sound, that's what he's supposed to sound like, that's what he sounds like when he plays live! And it was a very wonder-ful moment. And I blew up bunches of speakers just listening to it. And then Pagie puts a 12-string on it, we put some little hand fazer on the guitar, and then, this was clever of Pagie, he says. "Can you faze the vocal?" And this was after I'd put Plant's harmonica through a broken Princeton with Tremolo and a 57, and the harmonica sounds big! And all that is, you don't have to have expertise, you just want to hear it, so you'll do anything to make it happen. It's desire, it's self-love, and "I'll show 'em, fuck 'em!"

Perhaps the pinnacle musical achievement or sonic landmark of Johns's collaboration with Led Zeppelin can be summarized in "Stairway to Heaven," which became the blueprint for virtually all rock 'n' roll power ballads to follow. The song was a baptism for a subgenre still very much in its infancy where the power of acoustic guitars were concerned, and Johns to this day regards the session that marked its inception as a truly inspired and divine experience. Holy indeed in its conception and evolution, and biblical in what was achieved in evolving the heavy metal genre as a whole. Offering his own estimation of this musical miracle's creation, Johns recalled that

> "Stairway to Heaven" was a great session, a wonderful session. I had been working on something, competing with my brother, who had done this Steve Miller record called "Sailing," and Boz Scaggs had ripped off this riff from "Jumpin' Jack Flash," the exact riff, but the way my brother mixed it, it was a building song, it started off loud, and would just get bigger and bigger and bigger. And I wanted to beat that sibling rivalry. And so, I said, "Jimmy, building songs—those that start brilliantly and grow and grow . . ." And he interrupts me and goes, "Oh, we might have something, I'll talk to you about that in two days' time, I'm gonna come in and you're going to like this." So he sits down, he's playing an acoustic, might have been a Guild, and Bonzo was playing drums—and by this point, he would play straight through anything, and John Paul Jones is playing an upright Hono, and that's it. 'Cause Plant ain't singing, he's just watching, or wandering around getting blow jobs upstairs, who knows? And I worked very hard on the left end of the Hono to give it some bottom end, and they play all the way through, and I go, "Wow, this is very nice." And you have to remember, at this point, one expected gorgeousness, 'cause it was happening all the time. And that night I thought "Wow, this is going to be this very incredible thing!" And I worked very hard, and they worked very hard, and then John Paul put a bass on it, and it kept getting better, and I said to Pagie, "Instead of using your 12-string through the box, we do it direct?" And he came back at me with another idea, and when Plant started singing, it became clear that this was more than many other things I had worked on, therefore I wanted to make it greater. And then John Paul comes up with the chords at the beginning and the end, and I was thinking "Wow, this is why I'm here."

Johns's work with Led Zeppelin would represent heavy metal's most divine period of enlightenment in an evolutionary context because the landscape was still being created—and *Led Zeppelin IV* indeed marked a revolutionary step forward, the type of mystical musical trip that *Rolling Stone* would later conclude "made 'Stairway to Heaven' the greatest spell of the 1970s."

In taking a personal inventory of what the song represented in the way of a crowning achievement in terms of astonishing maturation as a producer over the course of the broader decade, while Johns remains eternally proud of metal's greatest musical moment, he said:

With "Stairway," of course, no one was to know it would become an anthem for the redneck, it wasn't designed for that. I mean, I think it's a very nice piece of music, but there's nothing to be seen in it except great work. What it means is that at a certain time, people can create things because they've been given that opportunity, and God bless that opportunity, but it's not a way to live—'cause you don't hear in that song how to live. You might hear it in a Rolling Stones song—"You can't always get what you want, but you find you get what you need." One important life lesson I've learned through music is "you cannot defeat an idea with weapons; you can only defeat an idea with knowledge because music is God." And "Stairway to Heaven" then fits as a part of that, you see? But with the two records I did all the way through with them, *LZ III* and *IV*, there's a lot of history associated with that, and I'm obviously very pleased to be part of it.

CHAPTER 25

Tom Allom—The "Colonel"

Heavy metal's layers aren't defined merely by its signature stacks of guitars, but more substantively by as rich and diverse a history of subgenres as any other mainstream music genre. While the roots of heavy metal go back to the very early 1970s, it wasn't until the end of that decade that—along with Iron Maiden's *Number of the Beast*, metal legends Judas Priest via their seminal LP *British Steel*, would—with pulverizing force—in the highly respected opinion of the BBC, "break the New Wave of British Heavy Metal into the mainstream." Employing a pop sensibility as their secret weapon—set to a hypersonic tempo—*Billboard* would later add that Priest's breakout in the States "kick-started heavy metal's glory days of the 1980s . . . paving the way for countless imitators and innovators alike."

As Priest charted the latter course for their beloved genre with hit album after hit album, the band earned the loyalty of millions of die-hard fans around the globe and in the process—according to *Billboard*—"greatly expanded the possibilities for heavy metal's commercial viability as a whole." Along for this ride in the course of producing a catalog of genre-defining albums including beloved classics like *British Steel*, *Screaming for Vengeance*, and *Defenders of the Faith* was producer Tom "Colonel" Allom, who helped Priest give their genre what *Popmatters.com* would later boldly declare as a previously absent "identity, having been largely responsible for launching the potent twin-guitar attack that would influence many fledgling metal bands to come, while bringing the genre from its seedy underground, skinhead roots to mainstream rock radio on both sides of the Atlantic . . . [making] Judas Priest is one of heavy metal's foundational pillars."

For Allom, while he wound up making his mark with heavy metal, the producer started out years earlier making his bones the old-fashioned way, recalling that

> I did a job after I left school loading the Coke machine, fetching gear, which was straightforwardly a job my father had gotten me because he knew I was interested in sound recording. So it was the people I met there at that studio, one person in particular who was this junior A&R guy, that I got to know, and we went out for a beer one night and he told me about this little 4-track studio he knew of that had just started up in the West End of London, and got me a job there. After a while there, the studio owner got me working with people who were good producers, or who were becoming good producers, and from that, I picked up quite a lot of techniques.

Allom's first lucky break came soon enough, after

> Black Sabbath came through and recorded some demos there, and they wound up doing the first album there and the bulk of the second one too. By then, we had two 4-tracks in studios one and two. I suppose the act that really got me into production, past just engineering, was an prog-rock band called the Strawbs, who came down to the studio there to do some overdubs, and they loved working with me. So for their following album, I started producing them and they loved to experiment in the studio, which is where I really started developing my production skills. From there, I caught my next break through the guys who were managing me at the time, who also managed the Strawbs, and Pat Travers; they also managed Judas Priest, but that would come later. At the time, I got to do a live album with Pat, and that led on to my mixing a live album for Priest, and that's how we started working together.

Allom's charmed studio collaboration with Priest began following *Unleashed in the East* in 1980 with an LP that would announce their presence with an authority that shook metal to its knees on both sides of the Atlantic. With *British Steel*, as the BBC reported, "the band was already 11 years old and onto their second (and most famous) vocalist, Rob Halford, by the time they released this revolutionary album." Heading into the project, the producer began his own preproduction with a field research trip wherein "pretty early on in working with them, I went to see several of their gigs, because I wanted to make sure I captured their live energy on record, and it is hard to capture the power of a heavy metal band playing live." From that launching point, Allom headed into proper production with the overarching sonic goal, "on the *British Steel* record, to record as live as possible, because we really wanted to get into a really live room. One of the things you learn to appreciate is when you turn up a Marshall 4x12 cabinet, there's a hell of a lot of air, and it needs a lot of room to sound right."

From the arrangement side, Allom worked closely with the band to craft an album of which *Billboard* would later say: "Packed with strong melodic hooks, *British Steel* is a deliberate commercial move, forsaking the complexity of the band's early work in favor of a robust, AC/DC-flavored groove. It's a convincing transformation . . . opening up their arrangements to let the rhythms breathe." Breaking the band's science down where achieving the latter was concerned, the producer revealed that "it starts with a relatively simple formula: a heavy rock song with a great guitar riff and a powerful vocal overtop." With lead singer Rob Halford, Allom no doubt had that extremely rich asset to work with, recalling of the singer's considerable vocal skill that "he was brilliant. He and I worked well together. When he was ready to do a song, we would usually put a rough vocal down, a dry vocal, to work from getting comfortable, and Rob would nail the lead in a couple takes, maybe three or four, and we might do some comping. But Rob's got a hell of a strong voice, a big voice."

Along with Halford, the producer quickly found the band a very reliable creative partner during the album's recording, feeling immediately impressed with the fact that "the first Priest studio album I did with the band was written in the studio at that time. Most of the songs start with a guitar riff, so then the three of them would suggest melody ideas to Rob, and the lyrics were left to Rob. So, Priest were very skilled in the studio, the thing I found working with them was they worked so hard on their own sound, rather than just playing and expecting the studio to do the rest." In the course of fully harnessing Priest's metal power, Allom added his memory that "on *British Steel,* we actually laid down some of the rhythm guitar tracks live with the drums."

As the band and producer worked side by side bringing their breakout album to life, in the process, as the BBC would report, they were honing their sound in a direction that "in very loose terms . . . represented a new found maturity and individualism in metal, as it severed the last remaining links to the blues that had informed earlier albums by fellow Black Country bands Sabbath and Led Zeppelin." Though the band's success would be fueled by hit singles including "Breaking the Law" and "Living After Midnight," their producer revealed that, during tracking, "I don't ever think we were consciously recording for radio, they were making songs for their fans, and by the time we got to the *British Steel* album, they had already played in front of big audiences, across Europe and the States, and already knew where they were going."

So too did the band's growing list of crucial fans, both in their homeland of Britain and across the Atlantic in America, where *Billboard* would declare *British Steel* "the first salvo fired in heavy metal's ultimate takeover of the hard rock landscape during the 1980s," arguing that the album "sealed Judas Priest's status as genre icons . . . (and) streamlined and simplified the progressive intricacies of a band fresh off of revolutionizing the entire heavy metal genre; it brought an aggressive, underground metal subgenre crashing into the mainstream." Indeed, upon release, the record would transform metal's landscape forever, to the extreme that *Rolling Stone* would hail the album as a "heavy metal landmark" and *Goldmine* magazine would single it out as "the very best of Judas Priest." As captain behind the console producing the LP, rather than dubbing him with the latter nickname, Allom fondly recalled that during the production, "the band gave me the nickname 'Colonel.' I think it was because of Col. Tom Parker, and they just liked to call me 'Colonel.'" Speaking summarily of the accomplishments he felt the album represented in his own catalog, the producer shared that "*British Steel* will always be a favorite of mine; that album to me was an incredible experience to work on."

Following the massive success of *British Steel*, Allom recalled that the band and producer were eager to branch out, revealing that "we liked to experiment, so we made every album in a different way." Of the album *Point of Entry*, *Billboard* would conclude that when that experimental recording approach worked, "it works well—'Heading out to the Highway,' 'Solar Angels,' and 'Desert Plains,' for example, are great, driving hard rock songs." Delving into some of the technical specifics of the album's creation, the Colonel explained that—in line with *British Steel*—"we did use the same fundamental techniques: the first one being we always started with as live a drum sound as possible. On that, and a lot of the other records, we did wind up using a specific combination of microphones. It was usually two dynamic mics and a close-up mic, and depending on the type of room, maybe a couple of ambient mics. On the toms, I liked to have dynamic mics close on the tom-toms, and I liked 58s on the overheads, pretty high up."

Upon release in February, 1981, *Point of Entry* was well received, with the BBC noting that with live favorites like "Heading out to the Highway" and "Hot Rockin'," "it was Priest's continued ability to pen stone cold classics . . . that saw them move into the 80s at the top of their game," while iTunes years later would offer the opinion that "alongside *British Steel*, 1982's *Screaming for Vengeance* stands as the definitive Judas Priest album." In 1982, Priest would enter the studio to produce their third collaboration and emerge *Screaming for Vengeance*, with Allom recalling of their increasingly ambitious attitude that "as a band, they were always looking for better and bigger, and actually weren't a speed-oriented metal group, they were more of a pop metal group." Still, in spite of the fact that the album would be the band's most successful crossover release yet, the producer revealed that during recording, "they didn't think about radio, with one possible exception being 'You've Got Another Thing Comin'.'"

The smash single would eventually drive the album to multiplatinum sales in both the States and UK, cracking the countries' Top 20 and Top 10 respectively. The Colonel recalled:

> A funny story about that song is the way it was released to radio is actually the way it was recorded in rehearsal one day at the studio. I was working on another song, and they ran that track through, and the guitars were turned way down, and I just happened to record it, and that basic track is what you hear on the final record. It really was one of those things, "Yes that's it!" I remember we added one heavier guitar as an over-dub, and they still didn't have the finished song, the vocal was written around the backing track. It's funny because I can remember thinking after they'd recorded it that that was the track, and they were all saying, "Well, we'll probably do that again in a week," and I said, "I don't think you will," and it was a bit of a fight, because I kept saying, "Look, I think this has just got a fantastic groove, and is something I could absolutely hear on radio, and not necessarily even on rock radio, it's just got that thing that drags you along." And for once in my life I was right.

Turning to one of the most enduringly popular elements of the album's sound, a guitar sound that iTunes would explain by that time had become the band's "patented twin-guitar attack," it would later inspire legendary Guns N' Roses guitarist Slash to identify the album for *Guitar World* as "my all time favorite (Priest LP) . . . it was and still is, one of the best metal records ever produced and the title track is in my humble opinion, still ahead of its time." Delving into the creation of that guitar sound, Allom shared that his job was made easier "first of all, by the two guitar players, K. K. Downing and Glenn Tipton, [who] were two of the best in the business, and really had worked hard to develop their sound, and most of the lightning you hear on record is actually coming out of their hand as they played off each other. It's just the way they actually play, and that's one thing; the other is their placement in the mix. I used to like to use the good old Shure SM 57 on the guitar, and there were a number of Sennheiser dynamic mics that worked well with that."

By that point, Allom and the band had earned via platinum after platinum LP the freedom to take their time working on *Vengeance* courtesy of a lockout at Ibiza Sound Studios in Spain, a luxury the Colonel fondly regarded as one of the great "joys of being in the studio. You're locked in, and not even in the situation that most A&R people find themselves today, which is that they're part of a big corporation where they have to adhere to certain company rules. When you're in the studio, the decisions are left to you and the engineer, and you're not confined to certain rules." Though he moved fearlessly with the band through production on *Vengeance*, the producer would confess years later that when recording wrapped, attention turned to "the most terrifying part of producing," which Allom identified as mixing. He explained that it was daunting for the simple fact that "you're out of time to get everything right. It's your last chance to sort out those moments where you thought, 'That will be alright. We'll deal with that when we mix.'"

Released in July 1982, the album was such an instant smash that *Rolling Stone* reported "*Screaming for Vengeance* (#17, 1982) broke Judas Priest in a big way stateside," eventually earning the band ranking spot in the Top 50 of *Kerrang!*'s "100 Greatest Heavy Metal Albums of All Time" and inspiring *Billboard* to conclude that "along with *British Steel,* it ranks as one of the best and most important mainstream metal albums of the '80s." Offering a peak behind the curtain of mixing the album, the Colonel recalled that "we mixed *Screaming for Vengeance* in Miami, where I was living at the time, and a friend of mine had a studio he'd had to move out of because they were developing the building commercially, so he had all his equipment stored in this warehouse. So we set up a control room in the warehouse office and it took a long time to mix that record. We really liked it there, but that whole record was a bit of a challenge to mix." The legacy status of the album's classic collection of was were celebrated decades later by a new generation of millennium rock fans as part of the wildly popular interactive video game Rockband.com, who at the time announced that "the album's plethora of highlights includes smash radio hit 'You've Got Another Thing ', 'Bloodstone,' title track 'Screaming for Vengeance,' and 'Electric Eye.'"

The Colonel's next collaboration with Priest, on 1984's *Defender's of the Faith*, *Billboard* would report "musically . . . follows the basic blueprint of *Screaming for Vengance*, alternating intricate speed rockers with fist-pumping mid-tempo grooves and balancing moderate musical sophistication with commercial accessibility." Entering the studio to begin work on what iTunes would later compliment as "a craftsman line record," Allom shared his memory of a somewhat challenging technical beginning due to the fact that "the studio we recorded that one at, we had this big room that was so ambient that we had to build a wall halfway across it with concrete blocks cemented together, so we split the room in half, and it was still too light, so we had to start hanging up curtains." From the musical side of the production spectrum, the producer singled out "Freewheel Burning" as "a challenge to record. When I first heard the band demo that song, I thought 'Oh God, this is going to be fast,' and it was a challenge because with the speed of the guitar and everything, we had to capture both the power and attack when we were recording that one."

In spite of moments like the aforementioned, the Colonel painted the broader atmosphere during recording as one where "we used to work pretty hard, but at the same time, I could never be serious, really deadly serious, because after all, you're at a recording studio with a bunch of musicians, so you should be able to enjoy it; otherwise what the hell's the point? Because it's intensely hard work, breaks up marriages, gives people a lack of sleep, and so I think it's very good for your health to have a good time. It keeps you young." In spite of the band's wild worldwide popularity by this point, the producer revealed that throughout his multialbum collaboration with the band, "with Judas Priest, A&R never got involved. I don't think anyone from their label, at least not in senior A&R positions, truly understood why the band was successful. We were making records that we knew Priest fans wanted, and that was the great thing about Judas Priest—along with all other great rock acts—that being that they know inside themselves what they want."

The BBC declared in 2010 that Priest would "always remain the most important of all heavy metal groups," adding that "to their legions of fans . . . they represent the bridging point between the heavy doom rock of Black Sabbath et al. and the myriad forms of extreme metal that came after the late 80s. They basically laid the bedrock for thrash, death, and black metal." Offering his own assessment of the band's long-term impact on shaping metal's mainstream as a legacy music genre, Allom says, "I think Judas Priest were pretty much as influential as any heavy metal band ever was. I would rate them very highly indeed. They certainly influenced a hell of a lot of young rock players from the United States. Wherever I went around the U.S. during the twelve years I lived there, whenever I was around any kind of musicians, they would all want to know about Judas Priest, so they made a big impact." Still, while he enjoys reveling in the past as much as any metal fan, ultimately he finds much more of a thrill in the band's continued relevance thirty years after they first took the metal world by storm, an excitement that— as a producer—makes it "very hard not to want to make another Judas Priest record. When we were in the studio together, we were brothers in arms, we made seven albums together, and after three or four years together and the first couple albums, when we'd start a new record, it was rather like the beginning of a school term when you get back and there are all your buddies again. We were friends, and still are. The band and the music we made will always be timeless to me . . ."

CHAPTER 26

Gil Norton—Alt-Pop Rock's High Priest

If the Velvet Underground are credited with inventing the roots of punk rock, then the Pixies deserve the same distinction for the punk-pop genre they virtually invented throughout
the late 1980s and early 1990s. According to an analysis by VH1.com, the Pixies' "busy,
brief songs, extreme dynamics, and subversion of pop song structures proved one of the
touchstones of '90s alternative rock. From grunge to Britpop, the Pixies' shadow loomed
large—it's hard to imagine Nirvana without the Pixies' signature stop-start dynamics and
lurching, noisy guitar solos . . . [They] laid the groundwork for the alternative explosion of
the early '90s." The band's principal producer, Gil Norton, refers to the band as "the Velvet
Underground of their generation" with good reason, as the latter band in the later 1960s
were widely credited with shaping the roots of both punk rock and new wave. The Pixies
were equally pivotal twenty years later in making both of those genres—as part of the
larger sound of alternative rock—accessible to the mainstream ear.

Rolling Stone, in its review of the band's breakout album, Doolittle, best summarized the
impact the band had via their music in influencing the latter: "Doolittle laid the groundwork
for nineties rock. The album's breathtaking mix of noisy, almost surflike guitars, sweet pop

melodies and primal-scream-therapy vocals inspired a generation of would-be rock stars: Nirvana adopted the Pixies' use of quiet, mumbled verses and loud, crashing choruses, Courtney Love aped their banshee wails, and Beck drew inspiration from their catalog of surrealistic lyrics." *All Music Guide*, meanwhile, concluded: "Combining jagged, roaring guitars and stop-start dynamics with melodic pop hooks, intertwining male-female harmonies and evocative, cryptic lyrics, the Pixies were one of the most influential American alternative rock bands of the late '80s."

Describing his first impression of the band upon seeing them live prior to entering the studio together, producer Gil Norton recalled:

> I had done the first Throwing Muses album, which is how I met the Pixies because Throwing Muse had done a show for me in Boston at the Rat Cellar, which was a local indie bar, and the Pixies were the opening band. That was the first time I'd seen them, and they blew me away. First off, Charles's voice really excited me, and I loved the pop elements in there because I love pop music. I could hear that, and the power within the melodic and quite aggressive vocal presentation. He really went for it, and it was very believable. Kim wasn't with them that night because she had some family emergency, so it was just the three boys. I'd already done quite a lot of work for their record label, 4AD, who had just signed the Pixies. They'd already booked in with Steve Albini to do *Surfer Rosa*, so it wasn't till they'd finished the album that 4AD didn't think the band had a proper single, and so they asked me to go in and redo "Gigantic," which became the first song I did with the Pixies.

In 1986, Norton produced the debut album by Throwing Muses for 4AD, who also had a new Boston-based band signed, the Pixies, who had already completed much of their debut LP, *Surfer Rosa / Come on Pilgrim,* with engineer Steve Albini. Feeling the album lacked a single for college radio, 4AD approached Norton about producing a final track, "Gigantic," which would become the album's hit single and cement Norton's place behind the boards for the group's breakthrough LP, 1989's *Doolittle.* In recalling the specifics of his first experience in the studio with the Pixies, Norton explained that "recording 'Gigantic' with the Pixies was great, and they found it exciting to be working with somebody else. I think we did it at Black Week over two days in the middle of the tour." In what would become a blueprint for Norton's approach to recording the Pixies over the course of future albums, he explained that

> before we started recording the record, I went to Boston, and sat with Charles with just an acoustic guitar, and went through the arrangements with Charles—to see what he liked, and what he didn't like, and what things he was willing to change. A lot of the

songs were very short at that period of time, and so I was trying to lengthen them—if there was a hook, I was trying to double it up, or make the chorus go twice around, just arrangement stuff you're trying out. So at one point he took me out to a used record store around the corner and picked out a copy of Buddy Holly's *Greatest Hits*, and pointed out to me that none of his songs were over two minutes in length. So that made me laugh. In preproduction with the Pixies, the songs were more or less arranged, and so then you're fine-tuning by the time you get to the studio, because it sounds slightly different once you get microphones on everything than when you're in a rehearsal room. But normally, I'd set the whole band up in ISO booths so I could put guitar amps in, or I'll just screen them off and try to get as much separation as I can. Then when they play live you can get a basic impression of what the songs are going to be like, rather than putting the drums down, then the bass, and building it up. Then when it's done, I can go back if I'm doing it to a click, maybe I'll keep the backing track the drummer played if we're still working on a drum part, and get the drummer to play to the backing track, then retrack it, or we just keep everything.

Using the Pixies as an opportunity to expand on his broader approach to preproduction, Norton explains that

preproduction is the most important bit of recording. I can never understand people going into a studio with a producer without doing preproduction. I think it's massively important and should be a priority as far as I'm concerned. It's where you get to know each other, because if you're going to be in the studio together, you've got to get to know what the characters are like, and what people like and don't like. Making sure you've got the right songs—some people think "We'll go in the studio and write another three songs and they'll be great," and now and then, that works, but most times, it's better to know when you go in what the songs are. I mean, it's better for your confidence to know you're going to go into the studio with songs that you actually like, as well, because you're playing with a budget. Especially now where we're up to with budgets in the industry; they're really tight. You've got to go in the studio and be really efficient. I think it makes it more fun for everyone, if you're organized, and everyone knows what they're supposed to do, then it's just a matter of getting the right performances. That's why I think preproduction is really important, a) to make sure you've got the songs sorted out; a) that they're all working together as an album, that they make sense and are coherent; and c) rather than working on drum and rhythm parts in the studio, by the time you've worked them out, the drummer's tired, so that's a whole day wasted. So if you've done that in preproduction and he knows what he's playing, then you've just got to go in and get a nice performance, so it saves a lot of money and time. And d) if preproduction doesn't go well, I don't think you should go into the studio, for both the producer and the band—in case the band doesn't agree with the producer's ideas, or the producer feels like he wouldn't get the right sort of record. If it's not going to work, you'll get more respect for it to walk away. Preproduction is also important for getting to know what the band's influences are in terms of what got them to be where they are.

Once proper recording with the Pixies had gotten underway, Norton recalled that "for *Doolittle*, I recorded the band playing live off the floor, as we did with all the Pixies albums; usually we tracked a song a day. We did the record at Downtown Recorders, and that studio had a fair-sized room; it wasn't massive, but we didn't really have that many room mics on it either, just because everyone was playing together live." Describing his approach to capturing the band's dreamy-while-punky guitar sounds, Norton explained, "We put the guitar amps off in little booths, but there was still spill in the room, so it was probably six foot away with a couple of ambient mics. Charles was very much into Marshalls' middle, and Joey tended to use Peavey Amps at the time, and I always close-miced them with either a 44 or a 57." Addressing Francis Black's fluid style of tracking guitars, Norton explained that

with Charles, what you had to try and do was excite him; he didn't like for things to repeat twice in a song, or do the same thing again within the song. He'd say "Well, we've already done that once." So what you were trying to do was think of ways, if you wanted it to be longer, that it could be more interesting or built or did something different. Like that we might have a different guitar part coming into the second part of the song, or the vocal did something cool. Something had to happen, and he had this thing about everything being plausible—he always liked everything to be plausible, which meant that we didn't do a lot of overdubs. He wanted to be able to play them live, so it was quite nice when you were producing because there was a certain discipline you had to go into in accordance with his preferences. So, for instance, you knew you weren't going to put a lot of overdubs on stuff. If we did, it was in a case like putting some strings on "Monkey Gone to Heaven." We'd done most of the other songs without anything like that. On *Doolittle*, we hardly used any effects, we had to sneak things in there. Things like chorus he didn't like; he liked a little bit of reverb, but there was also a lot of stuff he thought he didn't like until he heard it. On "Hey," which is still one of my favorite songs I did with the Pixies, that song was done completely live. To keep everything separated, Frank was in the cupboard, so imagine him standing up with the guitar up toward his face. He actually sang that vocal live in a closet.

Addressing the effects laden throughout the album's overarching sonics, Norton cited an

AKG spring reverb, which I liked, especially on guitars, I just like the way the spring sparkles, it just gives a nice air around the sound without being too big. Most times it would be that, there wasn't a lot of other types of reverbs we'd use. Or a bit of tape delay; we'd use that too. The effects we used also depended on the studio we were recording at. The first time I used a spring reverb was on *Ocean Rain* by the Bunnymen; it was all over that. The AKG spring is just a fantastic-sounding spring in general, and you can't really get from anything else.

Turning to tracking for the album's vocals, Norton elaborated on the careful line he walked between Frank Black's protectiveness over his role as lead vocalist and the necessity of Kim Deal's voice to balance out the group's dynamics:

Kim was the cool factor in that band to me. She'd be the barometer of the band, she'd give opinions to Charles on songs, or come up with or suggest something. She's a really great singer—that was the shame of the Pixies is, besides "Gigantic." I don't think she did many lead vocals, which is something I really wanted to happen more than it did, especially at the end. Charles was really resistant to that, just because of the dynamic within the band, he didn't want her to do vocals, but back during *Doolittle,* we were trying to get at least a song where she sang the lead vocal. When we were recording, we all threw ideas in, really; if anyone had an idea, we'd try it and see. Some of my ideas to include her vocally might be a backing vocal, "Oh, it'd be cool if we did this," and push Kim to sing it. She's just so great, and just the whole sonic—with her singing, it opened the band up sonically and gave them another dimension. If Charles had done all the backing vocals as well, it would bland itself out really. I just loved the textures that Kim brought to the songs as well. Again, it's so collaborative with these things, so it depended on which song we were talking about, but obviously, you want to give the songs as much variation as you can get. Most of the time recording Kim, it was still pretty light on effects. I always liked a nice plate reverb, that always sounded great, and the other thing I quite liked.

In capturing the album's drum sound, Norton explained his micing setup as one where "I always used a D-12 mic on the kick drum, and I used a top mic, and placed the overheads, which most times were 87s, and a KM84 for a hi-hat."

When principal tracking was complete, Norton explained that

Doolittle was the first album I thought I was more trying to produce than engineer, and at the time, it just needed a fresh pair of ears, because I'd been both producing and engineering it. So Steve Hagler and I mixed *Doolittle* together. It was nice to sort of step back from it and to have Steve help me engineer the mixing. Steve had done some stuff with Throwing Muses, and I'd gotten on well with him, so I invited him to come mix the record with me. So it was good because he put up basic, flat monitor mixes, and then I would come in and we'd do all the levels. *Doolittle* was interesting to mix because we didn't use hardly any effects, but every now and again we'd put a little bit of chorus reverb—which Charles didn't like at all—so we'd use it really subtly in places. It was also nice to have Steve's expertise on stuff like that, because he's a very subtle engineer as well, so he didn't overdue stuff. So I could throw out ideas or suggestions, and it was nice to watch his interpretations of what I was saying. I remember when we finished *Doolittle*, in Connecticut, but we were mixing at the Coach House, and when we finished, it was snowing, before Christmas in December. And it just felt like a classic rock 'n' roll album when we were done mixing. I knew *Ocean Rain* was a great album; those two records, I knew I was working on important albums.

Rolling Stone would agree upon the album's release, with the magazine's five-star review concluding that "when it came out in 1989, the Pixies' abrasive guitars and twisted, nightmarish vision were eclipsed by the bad-boy cool of Guns N' Roses and the frothy pop of Fine Young Cannibals. For angry, punk self-reflection, you had to comb the indie underground. The Pixies changed all that . . . The Pixies . . . represented the new cool . . . [*Doolittle* was] one of 1989's most acclaimed releases; it garnered truckloads of critical hosannas for its disturbing, dizzying variations on alternative-guitar-rock themes."

On his third and final studio collaboration with the group, the producer found that the stress of success had begun to wear on a group who he felt had once thrived creatively under the radar with the freedom from record sales pushing their artistic sails. In validating the latter, Norton explained that heading into production for *Trompe Le Monde*, "the band was imploding at the time—right before we started to record it. And because of that, there was a certain mood about it. In general, it was a hard album, my least favorite Pixies album to record in a way." Elaborating on the interpersonal turmoil in during the recording sessions, Norton recalled that

Charles was just annoyed with Kim most of the album, and that affected their creative interaction, because Kim was supposed to get a song where she was going to sing the lead vocal, and Charles didn't want her to do the lead vocal on that. And I felt it was being a little unfair to her, and again, I just loved what Kim does within the band, so I felt she was a bit choked. I had to fight a little to get her more time, in terms of that record, I think she was getting to the point of "Well, I just don't want to do all backing vocals" kind of vibe, and had an ambition to be a bit more in the front. That's what I was trying to do anyway. You're always trying to get the best out of the musicians you're working with, and play to their talents, and she's very talented vocally, so I was trying to get more for her.

Other musical elements Norton attempted to persuade Francis to incorporate in the third LP's soundscape included

> my talking to Charles about maybe putting some keyboard on it, which he was up for, and that was nice to be able to bring another element into the band. It just sonically broadened it, Alec Eiffel's keyboards on that album just gave it real character, and Eric Feldman—he plays a lot of PJ Harvey, and has done a lot of the Frank Black solo stuff—he's really creative, so it was nice to have him on board as well. Basically, we had most of the backing tracks done, and I drove up to San Francisco one weekend and played him the songs, and we worked out ideas for what he might add on. For instance, "Space I Believe In." We had a backing track, and didn't have lyrics with it, and I had an image in my head, and thought it would be fabulous if we had some tablas, which are Indian drums, and I had gotten Eric Selman in to do some keyboards for the album. And his brother, if you can believe it, was a professor of tablas, so he comes down to the studio, and he did this tabla-singing phrase, and then sat down and played on the drums exactly what he'd sung, and that just freaked Charles out. So that song, in the end, he wrote it about Jeffrey with one F. That was an example of how the process works of making notes from one step, and I thought, "That would sound great with this on it," which turned it into a whole other kind of vibe, and that was great, but then also I always thought I was about space, and it ended up being about the tabla player. "Planet of Sound" I think was a really good song, I think that was really aggressive. "U-Mass" is one of my favorite songs anyway, and "Head On" I thought was a good thing to do because it was the first time we'd done a cover I think.

Summarizing the Pixies' influence over alternative rock is best left to critics, but in Gil Norton's personal assessment:

> Looking back, working with the Pixies was a great time, seeing them grow from playing in a little pub in Boston to seeing them headline Redding in four or five years was major, and being there, and seeing that whole development. It was like being in the band, and was the nearest I've been to being in the band. I did three albums with Feeder as well, but just because the Pixies was the first time I'd done three albums with anyone, I felt like I was in the band. You're as good as your last album, so you can't rest on your laurels, and go, "I did the Pixies so I'm great." I think whatever album you're working on you have to treat as though it's your most important album ever, and if you lose that, you might as well stop recording things. The problem is you're dealing with someone's career, and if I mess it up, they might not get a second chance.

Though the Pixies would break up following *Trompe Le Monde*, much like the artists' albums he produced, Norton's substantial studio talents had never been more in demand. That aspect of Norton's now-signature production sound shined brighter than ever on his next collaboration, 1997's *The Colour and the Shape*, again a high-pressure sophomore studio effort for the Foo Fighters, who had been born out of the death of Kurt Cobain and Nirvana by the band's drummer, Dave Grohl, now lead singer/songwriter and rhythm guitarist in his own band. *Rolling Stone* had artistically validated Grohl in its review of the band's debut LP, bringing the drummer out from Kurt Cobain's shadow by noting that it "turns out Nirvana had *two* great songwriters . . . Talk about beating the odds: The list of great rock drummers who later emerged as substantial singer/songwriters could fit on one side of the tiniest Post-it note . . . Like Nirvana's best work . . . [Grohl's] songs sagely embrace alternative rock's essential contradiction—this is 'popular' music devised by an alienated few."

Where Kurt Cobain had begrudgingly played for the jocks who represented the establishment he was raging against—yet who populated Nirvana's concert crowds—the Foo Fighters seemed to welcome all in with a sound that *Rolling Stone* observed was "not so much about innovation as it is about mining punk for its particularly pleasing aspects. So no matter how fast or damaged the music becomes, those solid and carefully constructed melodies prevail . . . In fact, the main quality Foo Fighters share with Nirvana is making deliriously frisky punk rock seem absolutely effortless."

The pressure was on Grohl to follow up what the magazine had—via the Foo Fighters' first album—identified as the singer/songwriter's potential to become "the '90s punk equivalent of Tom Petty, whose vocal timbre and wry manner he occasionally approximates here. Like Petty, Grohl displays a good-natured humility that belies his talent for nailing the raw emotional substance that lies just beneath the surface of the average rock cliché." Where Norton had made a career out of producing the sophomore albums for breakout acts like the Pixies and the Counting Crows, Grohl clearly felt the producer was the man for the job. Norton recalling:

> They came looking for me. I had gotten a call from Gary Gersh, because Gary was involved with the Counting Crows, and he managed Dave Grohl, and asked me if I was interested. So I went for a meeting in New York with Dave and Pat Smear and Gary, and it wasn't yet about the album specifically, because it's obviously difficult to have that kind of conversation until you hear the songs. They're still getting to know you and putting a face to a name, so we had a nice chat over some tea. I think at the time, normally there's a list of producers, and you're on the list, and I'm sure they met with quite a few producers for that album along with me. The second album was definitely more of a band album, just from the fact Pat was there at the meeting with Dave, and

that the band had been on tour together for a while, and Nirvana were big, big Pixies fans. So from that meeting, it was interesting to hear how influential the Pixies were on that band from a guy in the band.

Norton approached the Foo Fighters assignment strategically in the same way he had his earlier collaborations where a follow-up LP was involved, focusing first on the songwriting by "doing the same thing with Dave Grohl as I'd done with Charles in the Pixies, which was to sit down alone, because to go into a noisy rehearsal room with a full band when you're first starting can be a bit daunting. So I tend to strip it back down, and go, 'Let's get an acoustic guitar, sit in a room, play through the songs,' and I might have some ideas, arrangement ideas, that I throw at the songwriter."

Elaborating on his preproduction sessions with Grohl, Norton explained that

Dave came to my hotel for about two days before we went into the rehearsal with the full band, and I'd gone through the demos he'd sent me and listed them out with the arrangements, and talked to Dave about what I'd like to do with the songs. It's a very similar process. I'd written their arrangements out, depending on which songs were more finished than others. Then we talked about anything new he'd written since then from the demos. Had he been playing them with the band, what were the arrangements they had already, what did he feel were the strengths of the songs, which parts did he like? And he was honest about which parts he thought were weaker, or was still working on, and wasn't happy with. And I'm all about honesty in making music, so if a writer goes, "This bridge or this chorus is just an idea, I think I can write something better," then I can ask what other ideas he's got, and we threw some things around, and picked the best bits, the countermelodies, and so forth, and defined what the parts were that would make the songs work. I think if you come out with an idea to any artist on how to change a song of theirs, you have to have a reason for it, and Dave was very receptive to my suggestions. It's got to be a positive dialogue. I find it's

usually a positive exercise for any writer to explore some different possibilities, and generally find a positive result. Most of Dave's songs come in as songs, so I don't think any of them came into the studio without being finished as songs. We rearranged some of them, but most of the verses and choruses were done before they were presented to anyone—the band or myself. So there wasn't a lot to change—I think the riff on "Monkey Wrench" we didn't have when we first started, and we knew we needed one. And sometimes what happens is you might not have the part, but you know you need the part, so I made a suggestion that we needed an intro riff, and that was a big one because it made the song. Dave came up with that.

With the album's track listing largely intact, Norton headed into a Seattle studio with the band to begin principal tracking. Where Dave Grohl had tracked the first album instrumentally by himself almost in its entirety, Norton explained that "on that album, they play as a band, but it's definitely Dave's show: they were his songs, and his band, and his record label, and I think in the beginning doing the Foo Fighters was kind of an outlet for him. But by that second record, if the band didn't like something, or had an idea, it wasn't a dictatorship, because he would listen, but when the band was playing his songs, they were definitely trying to play something sympathetic to what he had in mind as the writer." Addressing Grohl's process for recording the aforementioned songs, Norton explained that

> as a vocalist, he was a little self-conscious at the time. He always thought he didn't have a very good voice, so he'd track his voice, do two or three tracks, so there was stuff where I was trying to get him away from that in a way. I started doing vocals with him when we were doing preproduction, we did it in a little studio so we could record just some general ideas. And quite a lot of it we'd do in the control room actually, just with a 57 mic and he'd just sing to the monitors. Most of the time, for the rockers, he'd just turn it on, but for things like "Everlong," it was more the lights went down, and we didn't use that in the control room, we used a 47 for that to record because it was more of an intimate vocal. Dave's such a professional in everything he does, and his guitar playing was great, he's such a great rhythm player as well, he's naturally got that, and he locks in with the drum groove easily. They were all good musicians, and the drummer was trying a little too much to sound like Dave, and there's only one Dave Grohl.

The latter observation would showcase itself most prominently where the album's drum tracks were concerned, with the producer recalling that

> when we started, William Goldberg was the drummer who had played live off the first Foo Fighters tour, and he had a little bit of a meltdown during the recording of the second LP, which was a little bit hard for me, because it was one of the few times I haven't gotten a musician through an album. I think the drummer they've had the past few years—Taylor Hawkins—does a good imitation, and those two are like twins that were separated at birth, but Taylor also has his own style. It's similar to Dave, but not the same. And the thing about Dave is he hits the drums hard, but he doesn't over-hit them, and what William was doing was he'd hit really hard, and choke the drums a lot of the time. So when he'd over-hit them, they'd sound flat and dead, and that's sort of what was happening with some of the tracks; they sounded a bit too choked, there was no resonance to them. So he literally just disappeared for a few days, and Dave had no intention of playing drums, and I had no intention of asking him to play

drums. But over Christmas, we'd listened to the backing tracks we'd done for the bulk of the record, and we felt some were good, but that some could be better, and I had a conversation with Dave and said, "Look, I think we're going to have to redo some of these drum tracks. I think they could be better." One of them was "Monkey Wrench," I just didn't think it had the energy it needed, and asked him to have a listen to it on that level, and told him I thought it had to be brilliant, and it was alright, but wasn't great. So he came back in and I was going to do them again with William, and Dave asked "Would you like me to play drums on 'Monkey Wrench'?" And it was only going to be that song at first, and when he set up and played drums, it was just phenomenal, and he did it against the backing tracks in one take, and I was just floored. It was just so much more of what we needed on that level, and was the same song, but had a whole different life to it.

Elaborating on what he felt Grohl as a drummer brought to the tracks, Norton explained that

he's so fantastic as a drummer because he's very musical, and I think musical drummers are the best because he's writing the songs, he also knows exactly what the chorus is going to be. He can feel it, and he knows what type of fill he's going to come in with that won't get in the way of anything; it completely enhances stuff. He's just got a very musical way of playing drums. So from there, we ended up replacing quite a lot of it with Dave. I think William ended up with three songs on the record. We didn't intend to do that, but I think Dave enjoyed playing drums again, and every time he played on a track, it just came to life. Some of them we'd done to clicks, and he just played to the backing track. Others we had to redo the bass and drums. And the drum tracks we recut were just an extension of that. Another example was on "My Hero," where we double-tracked the drums on it. For that song, I had him do it quite a lot of times, and I think it was the only time he got quite annoyed with me. I remember we were on take nine or something, and I said, "Dave that's great! That's nearly it now." And he just looked at me, and said, "Gil, I've never played a drum take more than three times in my entire life. Ever." So I was like, "Well, there's a first time for everything." I think that's a good example of why you have to be as honest as you can with a musician, even if it's unpopular, or else they won't respect you, especially when they're a star. There has to be a reason to make someone do something again, because what you don't want is ambiguity in the studio. You can't ask the musician to do something again, and not have him understand what he's just done wrong. As long as there's an open dialogue, and I'm also trying to look out to avoid it coming back to haunt us in six months time, when the record is out, and it's too annoying to listen to. Better to annoy him a little in the studio and get it right.

Once rerecording on the album's drum tracks was completed, Grohl's perfection-ist nature was still in high season, specifically where commerciality was concerned. Nor-ton explained that, in terms of viable singles, up to that point, "we didn't have 'Everlong.' Dave's just a workaholic, and so we went and had the Christmas break in between recording periods, and Dave demoed 'Everlong,' and it was the type of melodic song Dave and I felt we hadn't yet got on the album. We had gotten most of the rock end of it sorted out, so it was more of the sing-along, melodic songs that he hadn't gotten yet."

Even as principal tracking was still being completed via the unusual circumstance of Grohl's rerecording, Norton to keep on schedule headed into mixing while recording was still underway. With everyone on their creative toes, he again employed an outside-the-box method to finishing the album, enlisting

> Chris Sheldon, who I'd used before on a couple of things, and I thought it'd be bril-liant to bring him in. And we were still recording as we started mixing, because we'd scrapped a lot of the stuff we'd done before Christmas, so we really redid a lot of the tracks over three or four weeks in L.A. It started off with the drums, but then because of the grooves, we had to replay the bass lines, and "Everlong" was a new song, so there was still lots of recording going on. So with Chris Sheldon there, it was easy for him to get a mix up, and then I could come in and have him change different little things. He knew what the job was, and it made my life a lot easier, because I was still recording with Brad as well around the corner at Grand Master Recording.

The Colour and the Shape was a critical and commercial smash, solidifying Grohl's ar-tistic and commercial credentials as a solo artist via the stylistically diverse hit singles 'My Hero,' 'Everlong,' and 'Monkey Wrench,' in the process further validating Norton's produc-tion stylings as being relevant as ever. *Rolling Stone* hailed it as "the classic-rock album Grohl had waiting to come out of him, with as much Queen as Pixies in its bloodline." Comment-ing on the musical performances Norton had captured on tape, the magazine noted that "the band pile-drives everything with maximum force," and further concluded that "*Colour* has a big, radio-ready, modern-rock sound." Perhaps the finest compliment *Rolling Stone* paid the band—in terms of emerging fully from the giant shadow of Nirvana—was the review's observation that "*The Colour and the Shape* is the first proper Foo Fighters album."

In closing, while Norton's production style has been pivotal in shaping an era and genre of pop rock, he always—in terms of a signature to his sound—has tried to keep his focus centered squarely on

> enhancing the band, such that I try not to give them my sound, but try to more en-hance their sound. I don't know if I have a signature sound, but I mean obviously

you're going to influence just being around and expressing your opinion—you're going to influence the parts and the sound, certain guitar sounds I probably go for. One thing I'll ask a band to do is make a CD for reference of their favorite drum sounds and guitars, so there might be an atmosphere to it, or a sonic landscape they're thinking might be nice to adapt for a song we're doing. So I don't have one way to do it, and it all also changes because of the studio you're using. But I'm constantly trying to listen to the band, and know what the bands are about, and most the time, I've been to see them live first; I think that's important, if you can. Then you get an essence of what they're about and how they sound. The next [important thing] is what the song's about, and how that dictates how you go about sonically recording it. The thing I'm trying to do is work within the band's context and what the bands are, and enhance the band, bring out the best in the band. There are no rights and wrongs, that's the beauty, and every time I go into a studio I'll learn something—even to this day.

CHAPTER 27

Richie Zito–Top Gun

By the mid-1980s, Top 40 pop rock had several go-to producers who established classic-rock acts that required radio revitalization routinely enlisted to reformat their former glory in modern commercial terms. Veterans of this club included Keith Olsen, Ron Nevison, and Don Gehman, among others, who had been churning out hits since the mid-1970s. New to the club was veteran Elton John guitarist Richie Zito, who had come up under the tutelage of producers like Gus Dudgeon and Chris Thomas. Zito recalled that

> back in those early days, I worked with Gus Dudgeon, who produced all the early Elton John records, and Chris Thomas, who produced the later Elton John records, as well as the Sex Pistols, the Pretenders, Procol Harum, and some of the Beatles' *White Album*. So I really got to watch the job from a variety of different production perspectives. Also Giorgio Moroder, who was really instrumental in me transitioning from guitar player into producer because during the '80s, for soundtracks like *Flashdance* and *Top Gun*, I was doing a *lot* of guitar playing and arranging on those records. So that really helped me transition. The thing about Giorgio, he wrote and produced virtu-

ally every Donna Summer song and then was the first guy to define the idea of elec- tronic music in film. The first thing I did with him was play on a Donna Summer-Barbra Streisand duo called "Enough Is Enough." From there, we did *American Gigolo*, and then on *Flashdance*, I played on "What a Feeling." I started doing arrangement on a lot of the songs from *Scarface*, and then for *Top Gun*, I arranged and played guitar on "Highway to the Danger Zone." I played almost everything on that song except for the saxophone. I programmed the drums. I played guitar on the *Beverly Hills Cop* soundtrack on "The Heat Is On." So whenever we were doing those soundtracks, instead of having one artist for twelve songs, we had twelve artists for twelve songs, and over the course of three or four soundtracks, you're experiencing forty different performances in the course of a year. So there was an incredible wealth of different talent coming through to learn from working with.

Producer Giorgio Moroder's soundtracks had helped invent a new breed of adren- aline-paced, energetic box-office smashes like *Flashdance, American Gigolo, 9½ Weeks, The Lost Boys,* and *Top Gun*—movies with musical scores that mirrored the social sonics of the booming '80s. In this Don Simpson/Jerry Bruckheimer—dominated genre of moviemak- ing, the success of the aforementioned films often determined that of the accompanying soundtrack. At the same time, the advent of music-video television had inextricably linked the success of most radio singles to an accompanying music video whose rotation on radio was interdependent with its number of plays on MTV. As the industry adjusted, the stock of record producers like Zito, who had a seasoned hit list scoring and producing music themed around a visual backdrop, shot through the roof. The problem was not many had that unique pairing of qualifications and a track record producing hit singles to match.

Having programmed and played the lead guitar on the *Top Gun*—spawned radio smash "Highway to the Danger Zone," Zito was an important driver on that newly paved road; his first assignment out from under Moroder's wing was to produce three demos with Eddie Money, a perfect example of a veteran rock artist in need of some new radio mojo. Money, who had made his bones on album-oriented radio in the latter half of the 1970s, hadn't had a chart hit since 1983's *No Control* LP, which had produced the hit singles "Shakin" and "Think I'm in Love." *Where's the Party* (1985) had been a safe bet in terms of the number of fans it drew to stores—which was to say very few. The worst-selling album of Money's career, it was considered by many to be his last chance to stage a successful comeback. The key to opening that door for Money was a smash radio single, and the stakes couldn't have been higher at the same time for Zito, who required the same result to establish himself as an in-demand hit maker in his own right.

Recounting the genesis of his collaboration with Eddie Money, Zito recalled that

I was starting my career and had only produced a Motels record. I think the biggest hit I'd had at that point was coproducing a Berlin hit called "No More Words." So I was managed by someone named Michael Lippman, and Eddie before that had done some records with Ron Nevison. They had contacted Michael about Ron perhaps producing Eddie. For some reason it didn't work out, and Michael said, "I've got this guy Richie Zito, who's starting his career, and I think you should meet with him." So I went and met with Eddie and his manager, and then had a subsequent meeting with the people at Columbia. We went in the studio and said, "Let's try three songs together and see if it makes sense." And one of those songs was "Take Me Home Tonight." I heard the demo of the song and thought it was a hit. We went into a small demo studio in the Bay Area, and did a demo of that with his live band. We tracked it off the floor live because I'm not sure there was another way to make records back then. I'm not even sure if they'd invented sequencing yet. So we did a demo of the song, and Eddie didn't really like it. He didn't really want to do it. Every singer has his own version of what he goes through, and each tends to be very tortured by the process. With him it was tricky, and a lot of times Eddie and I fought because he didn't really want to sing songs he didn't write. So the trick there for me was kind of knowing that this would be really, really great for him without really having his enthusiastic support. But nevertheless, he was the deciding factor, and if he didn't want to sing it, he wouldn't have sung it. Then it got to that part where it said "just like Ronnie sang, be my little baby," and he thought it was goofy for him to sing it.

Zito's strategy to get around Money's objection to the line proved ultimately to be one of the song's most memorable parts and biggest selling points musically as a single, with a key element, according to the producer, coming courtesy of an omen wherein

there was a girl around the studio who sang some harmonies for us occasionally, and when it got to that part, she sang "be my little baby." The original demo had a male voice singing the whole thing. So the only real allusion to Ronnie Spector was via the lyric, but it became very clear to me that Ronnie Spector should be singing it. After Eddie did the demo with the girl doing Ronnie's part, it was clear to all of us that this was an important song for us to do. So from that point, we went about getting Ronnie. That's an example of, within producing, how important it is to utilize whatever psychology you've got to use to gain the trust of the artist. It gets easier as you have success, and then you can more easily gain the trust of the artist. And legislating some of that stuff is pretty easy, but then again, the more successful you get, the more accomplished the artists are.

With Money's ears and eyes also open to the song's importance to reviving his career, the pair went about crafting a classic, which for Zito seemed in large part to depend on Ronnie Spector's presence as much as any other musical element of the song. Using Spector's classic "Be My Little Baby" as inspiration, Zito mapped out the arrangement of the song's instrumentation:

> My vision was always to try and do, like the *Wizard of Oz*, where it's black and white and then goes to color. When Ronnie came in, I really wanted it to go back to the '50s, and I was very, very conscious of Phil Spector as a producer, and give him credit for being the George Washington of production as I see it. So even when Ronnie came in to record, I did everything I could to try and make it go back thirty years ago and have it sound like it was vintage. That was very much by design ahead of getting in front of a microphone."

With Spector aboard, Zito and Money entered the studio formally to begin tracking the song. The producer recalled that "we tracked the song in the Bay Area and then did Eddie's vocal in Los Angeles. We used a U-47 on Eddie's vocal, and we had the most success most often with old, vintage U-47 tube mics. But to me, performance is way more important than the mic, but those are my first choices.

The presence of keyboards, a staple of Zito's productions to come, made an impressive debut on "Take Me Home Tonight", including using "a Juno 60 and a Jupiter 8 (which was specific to the hit). That was Arthur Barrow playing. I played piano on that track as well, which was a DX7. So some of those keyboards were played before the fact, [and] then we overdubbed the drums and bass and guitars." With the basic instrumental and vocal tracks recorded, the producer next transitioned to recording Ronnie Spector's vocals, which Zito recalled was

> tricky as hell because negotiating the deal took more of my time than anything else. Then finally when she came to L.A. and came to the studio, I had goose bumps. She was a sweetheart—couldn't get any nicer. Still, recording was tricky because the sound of Ronnie Spector singing "Be my little baby" was in my head as if it was recorded three days ago, but quite frankly, she'd recorded it thirty years earlier. So it was odd for me to have to sing to her what I was looking for—to say "Okay Ronnie, here's how I hear it." That was the oddest part. But it was a thoroughly enjoyable afternoon, and that's what it took—about an afternoon.

Zito's emphasis on capturing a specifically choreographed vocal performance from Ronnie Spector of the lyric as it related to selling the broader song stemmed from his own background, with the producer recalling that growing up in the blues era, a lot of it was soulful utterances as opposed to actual lyrics. Then as lead guitarist with Elton John, when I'd stand onstage in front of 12,000 or 13,000 people every night, [people] as far as the eye could see, they all knew the lyrics. It sort of gave me a keen understanding that most of the people are not musical. Although they love and enjoy the music, a lot of times for them the music is a delivery system for the lyrics. So I think I kind of learned that. Oddly enough, as talented musically as Elton is, I learned a lot about how important lyrics are from being in that environment. And that was something I didn't understand until then.

Years later, Zito would reference that experience in practice in the course of coaching Ronnie Spector, whose part was specifically designed for the song's "breakdown, which wasn't really a true bridge. It was more of an instrumental deviation, and then 'just like Ronnie sang' twice, which kicked the song off into *two* breakdowns. One was like a '50s, going back in time to Phil Spector, and the second was a true breakdown, with the guitars doing the chorus of the song— just Eddie and the two guitars. Then Ronnie did her 'Oh, oh, oh, oh' business, so that was a bit more complicated choreography that was peculiar to that particular song arrangement." Elaborating on the popular presence of breakdowns, which became a signature of his singles, Zito explained, "I'm a big fan of what I call breakdowns, which happens usually after a bridge or instrumental or the chorus, when some little aspect of the song is repeated slightly differently—more empty or intimate. I love breakdowns, and always had them every chance I could."

Describing the laborious process by which the signature breakdown in "Take Me Home Tonight" was constructed in the studio, Zito explained that "in terms of that song, half of it was the arrangement in advance, and don't forget—it wasn't so easy to construct. It wasn't modular like with Pro Tools where you just grab this chorus and put it here. If you wanted to move something around in the song after the fact, it was big business. It was hard to do. But the thing with that song [was] half came up in advance, and half came up in the mix." Another element of the production on "Take Me Home Tonight," which would become a popular signature of Zito's style, was his drum sound, which the producer described as conceptually in line with "records that were made in the '80s, where everything was so gigantic, larger than life, and very cartoonlike." Elaborating on that aspect of his creative process in action during recording, the producer shared his memory that, in pursuit of sonic perfection,

we worked very hard, all the time, on our drum sound. I would only work at a studio called One on One or what used to be A&M studios—premier studios. I really, really liked big fucking rooms, so that I could have the benefit of large, ambient snare drums and tom-toms when appropriate. We had this P.A. we would rent, and we'd stick kick drums and sometimes tom-toms into the P.A. and reamplified into the room. Then we'd mic the room with the kick and the tom-toms being amplified through giant P.A. So we went to great lengths to try and make the drum sounds bigger and beefier. Back then, the drum sound was a big, defining aspect of production. In terms of mics, we used 57s a lot over the tom-toms and the snares, and 414s on the overheads. Also, at the time, AMS was a new company, and they came out with nonlinear reverbs, which were all over the snare.

Specific to the drum sound on "Take Me Home Tonight," the producer explained, "Coming originally from the 'organicness' of playing as a session musician, where everyone played together, then working with Giorgio, who used programmed Lynn drum machines, which was before sequencers—so we would use triggers to get synthesizers to trigger, and then play to them. So for 'Take Me Home Tonight,' I actually cut the track originally with a Lynn drum, [and] then built the Lynn drum up with some synthetic stuff."

With the triggers laid overtop the live drums, Zito captured the thunderous snare pounds that drive the song's breakdown, one of several advantages the producer felt the song had working for making it a viable radio hit, in addition to "the intro, which typically is a part of the verse or part of the chorus instrumentally, in that case it was the verse. Then Eddie sang the verse, then we had a B-section, prechorus, which I think was an important tool for setting up the chorus, and then we had that great chorus. That song also had its own choreography with the sax solo and then went to this reprise where Ronnie sang, which set up the breakdown."

Once tracking was completed, Zito entered the mixing stage, which he recalled was a learning experience for him in terms of his approach for future production mixes. He explained that

most of the records I made in that period were very layered, so by the end of the project, the Lynn drum went away, the sequenced bass went away, all the things that were sort of mock-up instruments went away, and the real stuff stayed. So we stripped them back down. So by mixing, I'd put a lot of stuff on tape, and the mix engineer Scott Litt taught me a lot, like "You don't need all this stuff here, and leave this out here." He and Giorgio both taught me to record everything everywhere, and then when you get to the mix, worry about what comes in. That's when you decide which verse has this guitar part. So the combination of me and Scott at the end of the project came from us together, sitting at the console, [and] making those decisions.

The commercial result would relaunch Eddie Money's career and launch Zito's own as a go-to producer for established rock acts seeking another shot at commercial viability. Accordingly, the next rock act Zito revived commercially was Cheap Trick, who scored their first #1 hit in years with "The Flame" off the multiplatinum 1987 *Lapse of Luxury*. Like Money, the band was staunchly opposed to the song upon first hearing its demo, which Zito had already identified as their comeback single based on what he felt was a vocal tailor-made for Robin Zander. Recalling the specific details of the song's recording session, Zito explained that ahead of going into the studio "the album before the one I did hadn't sold well, and like in the case of Eddie Money, the obvious lead single, 'The Flame,' wasn't theirs, and they were very resistant at first. It was a very painful process getting them to record that song, and it was really Robin Zander who made it possible."

Using the same psychology that he had to win Money over, Zito bet on the fact that the magic he envisioned in Zander's vocal delivery would be the selling point, reasoning that "I wasn't going to fight these guys if the song didn't make sense for them, and I knew that Robin was going to be the deciding factor as to whether it would work for Cheap Trick." The band bought into recording the song. Following the same approach he had used scoring countless soundtrack songs and prepping for the proper tracking of "Take Me Home Tonight," Zito explained that "I cut the music for 'The Flame' with me and a keyboard player named Kim. He and I cut that track ourselves with some percussion and some synthesizers." Amazingly, as authentic as the acoustic guitars sound at the introduction to the tune, Zito reveals that in actuality "those guitars in the opening are fake. They're samples put on a keyboard. It was triggered via Midi from a keyboard to a Roland rack mount. We didn't do drums or real bass or guitars, but it was enough for Robin to sing to."

Once he had an instrumental for Zander to sing over, Zito—in spite of his extensive preproduction work for what he expected would be an arduous recording process—stumbled into a creative moment with Zander that beautifully illustrates the inherent serendipity of the recording process. As the producer recalled, "We got Robin to come in the studio and sing a vocal that ended up being the one on the record, except for a couple lines that we changed. That was his first take, and he sang it line by line because he was learning it from a demo. He'd never really listened to it before!" The magic of both the moment and the take won the band over, and further reinforced Zito's instinct that it was the song to bring Cheap Trick back. He felt this so strongly that "once we heard Robin sing it, I was like 'Yeah, I'll fight to the death for this because this is fantastic.' Then one by one, the guys from the band came in and played. The synthesized guitars stayed, and some of the little percussion in the intro and first verse are still there. So one by one, we had Bunnie come in, who begrudgingly just played, then Tom Petersson, and then Rick Nielsen came in last. They didn't want to be there, so they each just came in and knocked it out."

With smash hits for Eddie Money and Cheap Trick under his belt, Zito move on to veteran rock group Heart, who unlike Eddie Money or Cheap Trick, were in the midst of a career high that had begun five years earlier with 1985's self-titled comeback, which had produced the smash hits "These Dreams," "What About Love?," and "Never," and 1987's *Bad Animals*, which produced hits like "Alone," "Who You Gonna Run To," and "There's the Girl." In a nod to the producer's status as a hit-maker, Ann and Nancy Wilson enlisted Zito to produce the band's tenth studio album, the result of which would be their biggest Top 40 hit ever: "All I Wanna Do (Is Make Love to You)." Feeling the pressure with the challenge of following up the band's multiplatinum success, Zito admitted ahead of going into the project that "I worked hard on that record because Nevison and the band had done really well on the prior two albums, so they weren't in trouble when they came to me. Heart was looking to make a change."

Unfortunately, one of the key points of contention motivating the Wilson sisters' decision to change producers involved their desire to record more of their own original music, as opposed to songs written by outside writers, in spite of the fact that the latter approach had given them each of their past six Top 10 hits. Nevertheless, Zito seemed to know better than to toy with the winning formula, explaining that "it became adversarial at times trying to get Heart to record songs they didn't really want to record, and that really cost their last producer his relationship with them because when you fight that hard toe to toe with an artist, it created tension, and at a certain point, they didn't want to make records anymore together. I still had to do the same thing, except perhaps with a different bedside manner."

Contrasting his approach with Nevison's to accomplishing the same end, Zito reasoned that "Ron might have been a tougher guy, and I might have had a softer sell." Either way, Zito was successful enough to produce "All I Wanna Do (Is Make Love to You)," which successfully relaunched Heart as a 1990s radio act, along with the follow-up smash "Stranded." In explaining what had initially attracted him to both demos as potential hits for Heart, the producer recalled that

> we got that song after Mutt Lange had first sent it over to Don Henley, and it didn't make sense for him. I was right at the tail end of the Bad English record, so it didn't make sense to introduce it to them, and the Heart record was coming up, and it made good sense to play it for Ann and Nancy. That song was written from a male perspective, so we had to do some slight adjustments to make it from a female perspective—not many, but slight adjustments lyrically like he to she, and she to he, and there was a surprise in the lyric about a pregnancy, so we had some adjustments to make. The chorus to that song was just so freakin' strong, when I heard it, I went "Jesus." Mutt Lange is one of the best pop songwriters period—forget about it. That songwriting gift doesn't go to a lot of people, but it went to him. "Stranded" I got from a publisher, Wrensongs, and the song just caught my ear, and I thought Nancy sang it really, really well. I think I felt it was clear that Nancy should sing it, and Ann was very supportive. We'd get five or six takes and pick the best parts.

Recalling his excitement at the prospect of recording Ann Wilson vocally, Zito explained, "Ann's voice is just second to none, frankly. There are very few females in rock 'n' roll, and it's not hard to count all the girls that have been forces in rock history in the past fifty years. There haven't been that many. It's been a pretty male-dominated world in the rock business, and I can't think of anyone like Ann. Ann had that voice that you could hear in the back of the arena." For as intense as Wilson's vocals were, Zito recalled a laid-back routine for recording her lead vocal tracks, wherein "like most singers where we'd do late afternoon or early evening, between five and seven, recording sessions, and start the process. And she would just walk in, stand in front of the mic, and just sing. And I'd say "Okay, let's do another take," and then we'd take a little break, for five minutes or maybe not, get a glass of water, and in twenty minutes, I had six performances, and each one better than the next. I didn't know what to do."

A key supportive element to creating the magic that is Heart's vocal blend involved the Wilson sisters' sibling tonality, which Zito explained came from the fact that "brothers and sisters genetically have similarities in the bone structure, and the size of the esophagus, the size of the chin, and all that stuff where the tone reverberates in a similar size. It all leads to vocals coming out sounding similar." The results had been heard on countless Top 10 hits over the past fifteen years and were, as Zito recalled, a enjoyable and touching part of the recording process to watch:

> Nancy was there a lot for Ann's vocal sessions. They came together and had rented a house not far from where I was living. So they came together to the studio most of the time because Nancy would sing a lot of harmonies, and they would certainly suggest things to each other. They were definitely there in the studio for one another's vocal performances. I remember when we were doing vocals, in the control room there was this little alcove right behind the console, and there was this little couch where one or the other would sit when the other was singing. So it wasn't like either of the sisters were sitting next to me pressing the talk-back button. It wasn't really like that. When one came in, the other would have a few words together about the performance, but it was very relaxed.

In elaborating on what made the sisters work well together as a team and in complimenting Ann's strengths vocally, Zito felt

> Nancy had a completeness too. She was a really good acoustic guitar player, and she had her own musical personality that Ron Nevison started to bring out in "These Dreams." I think Ann especially liked that, but I didn't get her to do too much raspiness when I was working with her. I tried to bring out some of the more natural sound

in her voice. But the two of them together were Heart, and it was a magical combination. They each brought something to the relationship. Each of them certainly could have fronted bands that would have been successful for kinds of sounds. Ann definitely had a stronger, more powerful voice, but Nancy was a great singer and great musician. Both are very, very uniquely talented ladies. When recording vocals, they both were very good. They were pros.

Regardless of what's hot in any of pop's ever-changing moments, in a legacy context, Zito's sonic fingerprints have left an indelible touch on a generation of rock 'n' roll and uniquely in both an audio and visual medium. Whether playing "Highway to the Danger Zone," "Take Me Home Tonight," or "All I Wanna Do (Is Make Love to You)," Zito's productions are as timelessly classic as the film, video, and radio eras he helped to shape with his sound. In offering his own assessment of a signature sound, taking all the aforementioned into account, Zito reasons that

everyone making records has his own gauge to judge completion and perfection, and what they want it to be when it's done. By virtue of that, I have to say, I like to have breakdowns in my songs, so you're gonna remember the singles I made for that. To my dying day, I'll always be associated with the '80s, and I'm proud as hell that when you hear those big drums and ambient sounds, I wasn't the only one doing it, but I was certainly one of a few. When the kids know I played guitar on "Danger Zone" from *Top Gun*, it brings a smile to my face. I like to know that I'm living on to some extent by the fact I made that song a hit and that it was due in some part to me. So I don't care what anyone remembers as much as I was happy to have been a part of it.

CHAPTER 28

Butch Walker—The King Of Indie Pop

Butch Walker deserves the crown for keeping alternative pop alive in the mainstream Top 40 in the millennium. Agreeing with that assertion, MTV reported that Walker "has turned into one of the hottest producers/songwriters (Avril Lavigne, Lindsay Lohan, Pink, the Donnas) this side of Linda Perry." *Rolling Stone* reported that "his focused, punchy sound has made him the go-to guy for artists looking for help honing their songs. He's logged producing, mixing or writing credits on albums by Simple Plan, Bowling for Soup, Sevendust, American Hi-Fi, among others." Voted by the magazine Producer of the Year in 2005, Walker was tapped in the summer of 2006 by Mark Burnett and Tommy Lee to produce *Rock Star: Supernova* (a reality TV rock group featuring Mötley Crüe's Tommy Lee, Metallica's Jason Newsted, and Guns N' Roses' Gilby Clarke)'s debut album—a reflection of his importance in shaping the sonically hip as far as teenage rock record buyers were concerned.

For all the hype that has exploded around the Butch Walker sound over the past few years, he takes the praise largely in stride: "I never aspired to be a producer because I never thought it was sexy to be an engineer. I just never wanted to be that. I've always been playing onstage since I was about thirteen, fourteen years old. I was instantly addicted to that and never wanted to quit that, and that's why I spent the rest of my life and all through the '90s basically touring, you know, 200 shows a year." As front man for the Marvelous 3, Walker spent the better part of the 1990s building to the breakout of 1998's "Freak of the Week," which shot his band into the late 1990s punk-pop stratosphere. *Rolling Stone* said of that band, "[After] the Atlanta-based Marvelous 3 . . . spent the better part of a decade struggling to build a grassroots following . . . from the . . . explosion [of the] insidiously catchy radio hit 'Freak of the Week,' . . . what followed was celebrity, modeling contracts [with Calvin Klein and Abercrombie & Fitch] . . . slots on high-profile tours . . . an appearance on the *Late Show with David Letterman* and the opportunity to leave the van behind and get on a real tour bus."

Following another couple of years of tireless touring in support of their newfound success, Walker decided to take some time off, reasoning that "after performing for years, no matter how great it is, you can get burned on one thing. I was just going, 'You know what? I'm going to come off the road for a couple of years. I'm sick of this shit.' So, I think that's what forced the producer element on to myself." As songwriter and producer of Marvelous 3, Walker was no stranger to the recording studio, and as his home away from home he began spending his time off focused on writing songs for what he thought would be a solo album. Little did he know that the influence of his songs and sound had caught up with a new generation of millennium alt/punk-pop stars like Bowling for Soup and SR-71, who suddenly began popping up out of nowhere seeking Walker out as both a producer and cowriter. In reflecting on the timing of his career transition, Walker recalled that "as soon as I decided to take time off, that's when I started, you know, getting all the calls. It was definitely synchronicity. You know, I ended up having so many records come my way over the last couple of years that it was the best two-year hiatus I ever took from performing."

As a different kind of buzz started building in the industry around Walker's chops as a writer and producer, the progression seemed a natural one for him, as he'd spent years learning his way around a recording console and process, beginning with what the producer described as

a $200 4-track I bought as a teenager and learned how to work it myself. So I've always been pretty proactive in the recording process in anything I've done, starting with my little shitty cover band back when I was fifteen years old, and needed a demo to get gigs. My hometown of Cartersville, Georgia, really didn't have any studios and it was too expensive to record in Atlanta, so beginning with that 4-track cassette recorder, I learned how to balance tracks and that kind of thing and do multiple tracks by trial and lots of error. So out of that, I got pretty good at performing and doing my own music and stuff. I ended up over the years spending all my money on whatever

I could get, like an 8-track and a 16-track, all the way up to now where I have, actually now I have my own recording studio. It's a 3,000-square-foot facility in midtown Atlanta. And that's sort of been the Holy Grail for me to feel like I finally did accomplish everything I wanted to accomplish in life just by ending up with a huge console, and a nice room and a lot of mics. That's just, that's kind of always been the big goal for me, not the car or the house.

Offering some insight into what motivated his picking the bands he did to work with over the next few years, Walker explained:

I'm not in the business just for the money or for the opportunity, you know. I passed up some pretty good opportunities recently, which will, you know, go nameless, just because I didn't feel like I would have fun doing it. I'd turn it down if I didn't feel like it would inspire me. As far as how *commercial* it is, I mean, a million people would argue that doing a record with Avril Lavigne wouldn't be inspiring, but it was really fun working with her. I'd never gotten to work with a teen pop princess, and was like, "Maybe I'll try it. It might be fun." And so I did it. And will I ever do it again? I don't know. I just want to say that I tried everything once.

Elaborating on his collaboration with Avril Lavigne, Walker recalled that

the first time we got together, she was still promoting the first album, which was a success but still under three million sold. Nowhere near the eight million mark it was going to hit. And she was like, "I've got some songs that I've been working on with my guitar player that we wrote ourself." She just came out of that Matrix debacle where she was kind of battling them in the press over who wrote what. So in our collaboration, I think she was out to prove something. You know, she was still out promoting the first record and had not even started making that record, but was already writing for it. So during our first meeting, she said, "I love your production work on your solo record you did," as well as some of the other stuff I had done, for SR-71 and others in that genre. She was really into it. And she wanted to see if I would come into the studio with her on a few days off from her tour up in New York and record some demos, basically. And I said, "Yeah, sure, that would be fun." I looked at it like: she's a high profile artist and we'll see what happens. Maybe it'll come out really good, and maybe it'll end up on the next record.

Proceeding creatively even from this demo stage with the commercial end in mind, Walker explained:

I don't ever try to go into something as a demo mindset, so I brought my whole entire rig up to New York and ended up going for real takes. Albeit, we only had three days to do three song ideas, I finished the three songs and kind of rough-mixed them over the course of those three days. The first single off of her new record ended up being one of the demos that we did in New York, "Don't Tell Me." Anyway, sometime after that writing session in New York, she was out in L.A. doing that whole record with all the big established-name guys she wanted to work with, and apparently, everybody was still leaning toward that song, "Don't Tell Me," that we had done in New York as the first single without even rerecording it. So when everybody was leaning toward that after she had recorded somewhere around twenty songs with all those other writers and producers, I think she kind of put two and two together and said, "Well, you know what, maybe, maybe we should do more with Butch." So she called me back out to L.A., and I went out there armed with a couple of ideas because she had no more song ideas—she was sort of burned. And I ended up showing her this one song idea that I had written a few years ago and never wrote a chorus to, and it sounded like it would be really right for her as a piano ballad. So I ended up just sitting down and knocking out a chorus with her and that became the second single, "My Happy Ending."

In spite of the repeat success he achieved in his collaboration with Avril Lavigne, or any of the other projects he has worked on as a producer, Walker believes that his approach is

never a formula. When I'm writing, I don't like doing demos. I hate doing demos because nine times out of ten I'll get really good sounds from the get-go and we'll be kind of be carving it out as we go. Also, everybody gets demo-itis when you do a demo and they try to recreate it. So I just try to go for it from there, you know? I think that it becomes too much of a science project when you have to be aware of it. It should be about the spontaneous spur of the moment. So I like to just take each situation as it comes, but don't be afraid to approach it from any angle, or you're really going to shortchange your opportunity. As far as my writing with the bands I produce, the writing thing will always be weird because I never expected in a million years to get called to write songs for an artist. That's just something I never aspired to get into as a business, and for me, it can't be so contrived as a process. I certainly don't come to the party unless I'm invited. If I'm invited to write, that's when I step in. I certainly don't make it like "Oh, you know, I'm going to have to write on your record."

One steadfast rule Walker observes in preserving his principle that the writing process be collaborative comes from his impulsive feeling that

I'm not going to want to get involved anyway if there's no songs. I don't like to go in and try to write up songs for a record. That's too much pressure. I think it's the band or the artist's responsibility to come in as prepared as possible. Once they have some song ideas, I might feel like offering a little guidance or whatever, and if everybody is mutual to that, then I just start contributing and don't worry about how the song is going to be split up. And I think a song is precious, and a lot of things about a song are personal, so it's hard to just jump in all of a sudden and start writing with somebody because it's personal to you and it's personal to them. So, a lot of times with the writing, it ends up being a song that I already wrote, and we change it around and make it them. Or they have an idea and they're halfway done with it, and I help them try to fine-tune it. But I'm really not good at sitting down and going, "Hey, I've got this, you know, riff." And then, presto, there's a song. It has to be collaborative.

Fortunately for Walker, the majority of the artists he has collaborated with on songwriting have subsequently enlisted him to produce the finished track as well, even when in a one-off capacity with artists such as Avril Lavigne where multiple writer-producers are involved. As stars are typically involved in Walker's collaborations, as a producer, he begins the process by being

both cautious and bold when it comes to managing artist egos. I think the person with the ego has to be relaxed because they're just uptight people and they're intimidated, and often intimidated by producers and record label people. So my approach is just to go in and who it is or what kind of person they are, and give them the benefit try to make everybody feel relaxed from the get-go, which works nine times out of ten. Now, sometimes it doesn't work, and if it doesn't work, and the person is just a straight-up dick, then, you know . . . My dad taught me growing up to always enter the room with a smile no matter of the doubt, but don't back down if they're just impossible to deal with. So when you get hired to do a job, sometimes you've got to say at the end of the day, "You know, trust me on this or we're not going to do this." You do that so you don't end up walking off the project if you can't deal with a band or working with an artist. So a lot of times, I'll just use a little psychology, just to ease up their mind a little bit, and make them feel like it was their idea. And then they're happy. They're so used to being shot down by everybody else their whole life that I guess they're insecure when it's their own project. I get that a lot because I'm not there to say, "Yeah, dude, I totally won this battle today, I'm so psyched." You know? Who cares about that? I don't. I would just rather keep moving. A lot of times with ego, all I find it does is just stifle the process, and makes the record stall out. I'm too impatient for that. If you can conquer ego, a trust forms that makes everything else flow a lot easier.

Attempting to pull the curtain back and offer a peek inside his process for crafting hit singles, Walker is tentative, admitting that

> it really sucks to have to try to put a finger on it. But I can honestly say that if you're trying to get a song on the radio, there's a big difference between a hit song and a really good song. There really is. In the end, it is going to be all about balance. I'll keep doing it as long as producing doesn't get in the way of my going out and touring, playing to my little devout family of fans. So I want to go out every so often, and it doesn't get in the way of me being in the studio and making some great records because I'm relaxed and not burned out. It's also about wanting to have my cake and eat it too, because I don't just want to sit behind a console and get fat, pale, and be antisocial for the rest of my life. I really enjoy performing and making people happy. My fans would probably kill me if I just hung it up and quit performing. So I'm going to keep that balance. My life has always been about balance, and this is the ultimate form of it.

In terms of closing advice he would dispense having succeeded both as a musician and producer commercially, Walker advises that when in the studio in either role,

> don't be scared to ask questions. The whole reason I started producing records for myself was to spite the fact that when I was working with producers back in the day when I was really young, anytime I asked a question, nine times out of ten, I would get shot down because of their insecurity. If I asked a technical question, like "What does this button do? What does that do?" I actually heard the reply come out of one of the producer's mouths one time, "Don't be silly, you're just a musician. You're supposed to fuck girls and do drugs and play rock music. You don't need to worry about this stuff." From that day forward, I learned everything I could about recording and producing. Because I was very pissed that they were so insecure about their role that they wouldn't even lend a hand and share some of the wealth. I always find it cheesy and stupid when someone says, "Oh, I'm not giving away my secrets to my drum sound." It's like, "Get off yourself." Also, it's important to stay humble, whether you have success behind a recording console or on a stage. And that's coming from a guy who's on a mic every night in front of a lot of people singing my songs, so, at the risk of having an ego myself, it's absolutely important to remain as human as the audience you're playing to or the band you're recording with.

CHAPTER 29

Throughout the annals of rock 'n' roll, truly anthemic pop rock has always soared on an indomitable wind of hope. Whether over the radio waves, out of stereo or jukebox speakers, through amplifiers from clubs to arenas and even stadiums, and, perhaps most poignantly, via sing-alongs by a chorus of fans millions-strong, those listeners traditionally expect to be spiritually uplifted and at the same time emotionally comforted by a hit song's kinship to their daily struggles in life. Within that audience, the most embraced of anthems are typically as relevant as family and soak into their listeners as naturally as the buzz of a few beers on a Friday night after work. During the later 1970s—when working-man (whether white- or blue-collared) rock 'n' roll was a major player in Top 40 radio—no group better musically personified this listening base than Journey, who, according to *Rolling Stone*, "may well be the best American band in this idiom." Another band who spoke in mainstream terms for the working-class demographic—specifically the small-town, rural-rock contingent—during the 1970s was Lynyrd Skynyrd. Validating the latter, *Rolling Stone* concluded that "if the Allman Brothers invented Southern rock at the dawn of the '70s, then Lynyrd

Skynyrd perfected it as the decade wore on."What tied Lynyrd Skynyrd and Journey—aside from generically, in terms of the working-class rock theme of their songs and sound—was each band's work respectively with live sound engineer and record producer Kevin Elson.

Beginning with his work as Lynyrd Skynyrd's live sound engineer throughout the majority of the 1970s, as his knowledge and expertise grew in real time with the band's popularity, Elson developed an important set of norms to his style for and approach to capturing live sound that would translate later into the studio. He explained that

> with Skynyrd, I established what became sort of a pattern of mine of working with the same band over a long period of time. I liked the goal of working with one band over a longer period of time, because my general feeling—and this came from my years with Skynyrd—is that the longer you work with one artist or band, the better work you do. There's a trust factor on their side and my side, to where—with Lynyrd Skynyrd, for instance—I basically had the band's ear and had their approval to make whatever decisions needed to be made. If one of them, for instance, was playing too bad from drinking too much, I turned them off. It wasn't like, "Why isn't so-and-so's guitar off?" It was more like, "Use your judgment." In terms of mixing a band live, I think the key is making the sound come across so that the audience is feeling the full power of the band, not in terms of the volume, but in terms of power of the performance. I just try to pick out what's really driving that particular group, and with Skynyrd, it was everything. Three guitars, and they played in such a pocket that once you had your pocket set, it was just really driving the guitar players, and all those little changes and harmonies worked. When you're dealing with the component of an audience in live recording, you'd be surprised how much isolation there is, other than with vocal mics that were up front. It's shocking to be in a 10,000-seater arena and hear presence on all the instruments.

Perhaps his most historic accomplishment in the realm of live recording occurred not in an arena but in a stadium, with Elson capturing Lynyrd Skynyrd at the Open Air Rock Festival in 1976. This was a gig that Elson to date describes as "one of the greatest live recording experiences of my life, and which, of course, produced that very famous live version of 'Free Bird.'" He explained that, regardless of what he brought to the table, "it's all up to the band, most the time;, it's the performance. If you have a great band you're mixing, all you can do is screw it up. I think with them, when they were on, they were impossible to get over. I remember there must have been a couple hundred thousand people at this castle, and the Rolling Stones, who were headlining, just died that day, people just went crazy for Skynyrd." In spite of the professional peak he had achieved with the live version of "Free Bird" a year earlier, Elson's wings were almost fatally clipped before his transition into record producer ever had a chance to take flight, when on October 20, 1977, he went down as a passenger on the plane that took the lives of half of Southern rock's greatest band. He recalls his miraculous survival:

> I remember when we were flying, it all happened very quickly: we were told by the copilot that we were going to be making an emergency landing. Where I was sitting up front, next to Alex and Ronnie, and we were talking about this upcoming TV show we were doing for some Christian rock concert and were really just talking about the set and what we thought would work the best. So we were really still just casually talking when the copilot came back on and updated us that we were going to have to land in this field and to buckle up, because it was going to be a rough landing. So that's what I went away with and the last thing I remember hearing or talking about. Then everything went black, and I woke up in the hospital.

The tragedy was devastating enough for Elson that, in its immediate aftermath, he considered retiring from music altogether, recalling, "I think through the first six months of recovery, it was trying to figure out what I was going to do. I really hadn't done that much studio work other than in Skynyrd's 8-track studio, where I'd cut, for instance, a lot of the demos for *Street Survivors* until they went in to cut the record. So I knew I'd like to do that, but I didn't have any kind of name or anything in that field. So I think initially I wanted to back off of it and stay home."

In spite of his initial hesitations, Elson explained, the most therapeutic route he could follow toward getting over the tragedy was to go back to work: "As I was recovering, I realized I loved what I did and needed to get back to it and go back to a normal life. So my first thing was to go back on the road, while I was still on crutches, for three months with Van Morrison. I've done so many live shows with so many different bands that I take the same approach, whatever fits the building, and some nights it's magic and some nights you just want to be done. It was a mix of both on that tour, and I figured it would be a good way to figure out whether I wanted to stay in the business." Ironically, out of his working with Van Morrison, Elson would wind up transitioning into his first gig as producer, by what he recalled was the pure happenstance of

> working for Van Morrison in San Francisco at a rehearsal studio, where Journey was rehearsing at the same studio. And I was coming in as they were going out one day. So their tour manager and I were talking, along with Neal Schon and Gregg Rolie, and they just came right out and said, "Hey, what are you doing? We're really looking for

somebody to work with us." And they were rehearsing for a tour, and so right after the Van Morrison gig, I went on the road with them for a European tour, and we did some radio shows along the way—which the band really loved the sound of—and it was really Herbie that pushed me into the studio to work with them on the *Departure* album, which I coproduced with Geoff Workman over the course of 1979.

Whether a twist of fate or just serendipity working its musical magic, Elson's collaboration with Journey would send him and the band skyrocketing to the front of 1980's rock royal class, as *Departure* would become the band's highest *Billboard* Album Chart debut to date and produce the #1 smash hit "Any Way You Want It." Ahead of entering the studio, Elson's honesty with the band about what he felt their performances on past productions had lacked in terms of the energy of their live shows helped shape their goals for *Departure*. The producer recalled:

> We'd built up a great relationship touring together, and each guy in the band had a really strong personality, and I think seeing it from the live side they'd gone through ten engineers. So from the tour, they, I think, were happy they'd finally found someone that was delivering and that they trusted. So they started asking me my opinion about this or that, and I'd give it honestly, and it was a just really straight-up dynamic that just carried over into the studio. I was real happy working with them and wasn't really looking to be doing any more than when they approached me. They were a great band, made great music, and I was treated great, I wasn't gunning for, "Man, I need to be doing your studio work." It came from them, and so once I was on board, the first thing I said to them, in terms of my goals for the album, was, "You guys are such great players, as good as the songs are, they sound so sterile on tape?"

Hired to answer that question, and to ensure it didn't happen again, Elson, along with coproducer Workman, set about translating the energy of the band's live concert performances into their studio dynamic, which he recalled began by "establishing what became one of my signatures with Journey, which was recording them live off the floor as a band in the studio. Coming from a live background, and being a musician myself, I sort of—looking at it as a consumer who would go out and buy the record—tried to bring out the life and energy in the band's studio recordings." In terms of the division of duties between him and Workman, who had been the band's engineer on prior albums, Elson explained that "they wanted to maintain their relationship with Geoff engineering—in terms of the vibe and sound they were coming up with—so my role was more to get things loosened up and back more to the band's blues base and away from the stopwatch recording approach they'd had on prior albums. It was a work in progress. I listen back to it, and there's some good moments there—it wasn't a brilliant record, but I think there's some really good songs. That was my first project ever producing, and it was a great thing right off the bat."

Following the success of "Any Way You Want It," an arena tour followed in 1980 on which Elson mixed the band's live sound, resulting in a live album, *Captured*. The tour provided him the best of both worlds in terms of better understanding the technical and musical fundamentals of what had made the band's live performances so superior to their recorded LP counterparts. The latter study would prove crucial to the sound Elson developed with the band—which, live or on record, would become interchangeable to the ear—in the course of their next LP, 1981's *Escape*. Establishing Journey as one of the world's biggest rock bands via the success of three Top 10 singles—"Don't Stop Believing," "Who's Crying Now," and the seminal "Open Arms"—the results proved Elson had done his homework on the *Departure* tour.

Elaborating on his norms for micing and mixing Journey live, the explained that, in spite of his experience,

> I wouldn't say it was easy, because to get things to work the way they should work, they need a lot of headroom and a lot of P.A. There's four or five guys singing, which, with as big as the instrumentation was—twelve keyboard inputs, eight on Neal—and those were coming from single sources, so if you were trying to get all that in the system, it was a challenge. Plus Journey always based around a very interesting drum part, so generally what I would do when I was sound-checking was to listen to the drums and vocals first, then bring keyboards, and guitars and bass in after that, once I've figured out where the pocket was going to be, because drums and vocals were always two very featured parts of each song. Everything else was important, but you're really getting a lot of programming information to deal with, between the instrument inputs, then a bunch of effects, all the little delay settings—it was a busy mix. The great thing was they played great, and that was my heads up.

Using his live approach to micing and mixing Journey as a blueprint for their studio collaboration, in which Elson was now the band's sole producer, he said:

> I think one of the more valuable lessons I took away from my years producing Journey, that built on my live sound background, was the fact that you could record an entire band at the same time, just like you would do a show. In other words, taking live approaches to recording and introducing them into the studio in terms of creating ambient drums and big sounds, so as the band's playing, they don't feel they're

in a studio but rather that they're playing a show. It just really works to enhance the performances we got on tape. With that whole isolated separation that people were doing so much of at the time, our sound and approach was different in that we'd have things going on with the vocals, big ambient things going on with the drums and guitars, and so when you listened, it really sounded like they were playing in a building rather than these headphone situations where everything's so isolated. For instance, we didn't use click tracks, because the drummer and the rest of the band were in such a great live groove when they tracked, and we're talking very early '80s, where the opposite was very much the way things were done in the studio.

Describing some of the specific studio techniques he employed in the course of capturing the latter sound, Elson explained that

some of my tricks in general when trying to capture that kind of sound, I'll record harmonizers on guitars, and ambience on separate tracks, rather than just using an ambient micing. I'll get into different effects to try to create something individually suited to the band's sound and style toward that same end of ambience, or mic the drums through speakers in another room, whatever the studio allows by what equipment and space they have available—I just try to use every part of the studio they have available toward that end. The room is very important in that process for what I do, to where if the room's too small, the drums don't breathe as well generally, and you just can't do a full band like Journey the way you'd like and their sound commands.

Recording in San Francisco, Elson described a routine in which

we generally rehearsed so well that by the time we got into the studio, it was just like, "Okay, let's track it." We'd go in with eighteen to twenty songs done. I don't believe in wasting time in the studio trying to write songs. Aside from the money, everyone is in a completely different vibe in their mind when they go into the studio. I think a band needs to be where they're comfortable in a rehearsal room, where they can let it out and just get their ideas out there. Because it's tense in a studio, and if you don't have arrangements worked out, you can't go in and track three songs a day. Back in the late 1970s and early '80s when we made those records, studios were a lot more expensive, because everything was done on analog, two-inch tape. You had to have it together by then.

Perhaps the most complicated part of preproduction for the band, according to Elson, was song selection:

With Journey albums, we almost always found ourselves in the position where we'd be sitting in rehearsals going, "We've got a lot of material here. How are we gonna weed this down?" So we'd sit there after rehearsal and go, "What are your least favorites? What do we have to do?" And you're trying to get everybody's feeling, because of those changes you get in the studio, where you go, "Oh my God, this is coming out unbelievable," or you go, "Man, this just isn't getting it, what can we do?" And with Journey, we would always record at least eighteen songs for each album, because we always thought we would put at least twelve on, an extra track for Japan, which was always a requirement of the record label, a different track for Europe, that's fourteen. With Journey, where arranging songs was concerned, through the rehearsal process we would run a cassette player with a microphone in the middle of the room, and those were things we really had to sort out first. Because Neal would write five songs in those songs, where there were five sections in each of his songs. That was the biggest thing, really, trying to narrow those songs down. I mean, "Escape" was probably a twelve-minute song in the beginning. It had so many parts, and by tackling it in rehearsal and making it into a workable song, we avoided arguments in the studio, because we were able to get it out of the way, live with it for a week or two, play it in a shorter version, then go, "Oh yeah, that does make sense," rather than make a hasty decision in the studio and go, "Oh man, this isn't working, let's track it again," that kind of stuff.

By the time the band formally entered the studio to record *Escape*, Elson had a formula developed for tracking the band

so that they were generally all in one room. We usually trapped the bass, which was the most critical thing, because it traveled in the drum kit so heavily, to where you'd get notes in the drums, and all of a sudden you'll create these overtones. So we just would isolate what we needed to isolate instrumentally. The biggest thing with that usually came when we were doing live piano in the studio. Getting a good piano sound and being able to trap that piano, because the mic is so hot, and there's tons of drum kit in there. We didn't do that as much on the *Departure* record, because Craig Rally played more organ on the tracking. But by the time of *Escape* and *Frontiers*, at the studio we used, they had a Steinway with one of those quilted covers they build in it, which drapes over the piano but has holes built in where the microphones go through. So you're able to lift the lid up and actually mic the piano, but this thing is like a bulletproof jacket that goes over it. So I would say when they played, Jonathan Cain was fifteen feet from the drums in the room, and Neal had one side of the studio where we had his speakers turned back toward the wall instead of firing out directly into the room. Then we had Steve Perry in a separate room with a glass wall, so he could look through the glass and see everybody, but he would go for vocals full-on during tracking. It wasn't like he did it separately from the band, so when you listen to those records, you'll notice there's very few rhythm guitars—Neal does those solos with a basic track. The overdubs we did, once we had the basic tracks down, generally involved acoustic guitars, or maybe doubling a rhythm here or there. Then, of course, vocal overdubs. We did those records at a time that was before samples and a lot of the available synthesizers, so we made that entire album with a Praha 5, a Jupiter 8, and a grand piano.

Specific to the gorgeous piano sound of the album and the band's biggest commercial hit, "Open Arms," Elson described a micing setup whereby

for the piano on the Journey records, I used an 87 mic on the low strings and a 414 on the high strings. Very simple, a great sounding piano, the Steinway we used. It had a lot of attack to it for an older piano—it had a really bright sound to it. The rest was in the performance. When we recorded "Open Arms," I think the first day I heard it in rehearsal it was done. That song was brilliant, so it was just a matter of saying, "Wow." My job with songs like that, which were just natural, obvious hits, was to make everything work together—to get a great performance from the band, get a great sound, not overdo anything, just make this song come alive.

Elaborating on what he feels should be staples of any hit single, Elson explained:

Whenever I was recording singles for Journey, or anyone, for that matter, I was always listening for great musical and vocal hooks. I want to hear both—as soon as you turn something on, it grabs your attention immediately from the first vocal or note from the guitar or piano. Those brilliant Journey records were great musical hooks and great vocal hooks, sing-along choruses—they were just hits. Speaking in today's terms, it's usually a great musical hook, where I'm not hearing these great singers that used to sell me on it. At the time, you had Lou Gramm or Steve Perry, all these singers who could hook ya—on an okay song, they'd hook ya.

Elson's approach for capturing Perry's singular rock voice was one in which the producer took no chances on missing what came out of Perry—all of it great.

When we recorded Steve Perry's vocals, we recorded everything, from the warm-ups on through the live takes. One unique thing with the dynamic between Steve and

Journey is while we were tracking, there would be certain vocal accents he would be going to that Neal would pick up on in his own playing. Or we'd be listening back to the take, and Steve would go, "Hey, you know what, I'm doing this vocal thing right there, and it would be really cool if there was a cymbal crash right there. Or a tom hit." So things would sort of come up out of him really pouring on the vocal, and so everybody was listening to everybody else, and some things creatively really grow out of that. Especially I would say the ballads, where you're trying dynamically to grow and reach the peak, and I think most times vocally was when we created that, especially with Steve. For instance, we very rarely doubled Steve's lead vocals, but most of the time, getting into maybe a bridge or something is more where we would double or triple his vocals just to create a sound. But lead vocals, it was generally just one track. Generally, we would do some nice flake, and we had this third-octave EQ Steve would want in his headphones, just super bright. Just strictly for his phones, to get him on edge. I think one really unique recording experience with that album was a song called "Mother/ Father." That vocal was a one-take vocal. It was after we'd gotten the track and laid it nice, Steve said, "Well, let me put a vocal on to sit with, and we'll call it a night." That vocal was one take, and pretty much everybody in the room fell on the floor. So as far as recording, it was quite an event.

Delving into his technique for capturing the band's live studio drum sound, Elson recalled that

prior to working with Journey, my studio micing technique was more about the two mics—Shure 57s—on the snare and kick drums. Of course, getting into a good studio, you learned a lot more about microphones, versus the live end, where it was just standard dynamics stuff. When I miced Journey's drums, I used a U47 that went outside the kick and a D12 inside, the toms were all Sennheiser 454s, and on the snare, I always had a 57 on the bottom and a 414 on the top. The drums were all recorded in stereo toms, but the snare top and bottom were recorded separately, and the kick-drum mics were all recorded to one track. With Journey, Steve Smith was a brilliant drummer, and I've worked some projects where you spend a day just getting drum sounds, but with him, it was three hours, and we were ready to record. He knows how to tune his drums, and everything else that you do from there as a producer is enhancing and making things come alive. My key to getting a great drum sound in the studio is just making sure the drums are right from the get-go, just naturally sounding good. "How do these drums sound in this room?" You don't want to put any tape on it, let's get this sounding proper, and then the microphones can only help. You gotta have a good source.

Addressing his process of attaining the same clarity with Schon's guitar sound, Elson revealed that "when we did guitars, Neal had a straight amp, a stereo effects amp, then he was using a synth guitar a lot, so we had that miced separately. At the time he was using a lot of Hiwatts and Marshalls, and then we were using these Roland Jazz Chorus amps that we were running all these synthesizers through, so on average there were four guitar tracks, and each track had four sources. So it was a huge sound, it was Neal's guitar sound, the same way he played at a live show, so he'd go right from a rhythm into a solo live while the band was recording."

The breakout success of "Open Arms" as a single and *Escape* as an album, critically and commercially, was massive, with *Rolling Stone* observing in its review of the album that "now Journey works best as a band. And they've never rocked harder." Building on the success of the pair's second collaboration, Elson and Journey headed back into the studio in 1982 to make *Frontiers*, which generated such smash hits as "Separate Ways," "Send Her My Love," and "Faithfully." Addressing the process by which the legendary latter soft-rock staple was crafted, the producer comically recalled that as the band prepared to track it,

> "Faithfully" was completely written—John had written and demoed it at a small studio, and played that and this other track he'd written, and played them for me coming back toward the end of the Escape tour, and it was done, other than guitar solos and Steve's vocals. We called it "danger of the demo": the demo is so good, how do we play it as a band? When they went into rehearsals, the band went, "It's finished, what the hell do we do?" So they almost felt like, "How do we put our influence on it?" So it was a bit of a battle on that song in rehearsal, where they were almost anti-"Faithfully." It worked out, but it was definitely something the group didn't feel was theirs at first. In Journey, there was very little bickering, and if it did show up in rehearsal, it was almost strictly about how the song was going to be better. It wasn't knock-down, drag-out; it was more like someone saying, "I really think it's going to work better this way."

Although *Rolling Stone* noted in its review of *Frontiers* that the band "takes care to maintain an equally high level of musicianship . . . musical ingenuity and undeniable chops," the album on another level was yet another gorgeous display of vocalist Perry's range and depth. Elson explained that among the other new tricks and techniques he utilized in tracking Perry's leads for the album,

> when I recorded Steve Perry's vocals on *Frontiers*, we did this trick—which actually came from Steve. He learned this thing where we used to take tapes and tape out right into these two old Dolby 301s. And you could put it in, and pull one of the pro-

cessing cards, and it would get all this air about the vocal, this really edgy, airy thing, because it wasn't processing. So we would then take that back into a QV2 compressor and bring it back with depth. A lot of people used it as an effect, almost as an Apex-type thing, but we recorded the vocal right into the thing, so the vocal was real gritty and sounded like a distorted old mic at first, but it worked and gave Steve this certain edge. I think that was the biggest thing we used to do experimentally. We also used to use a lot of delay moves on notes, things like that. We'd have a general effect that would work, but there were definitely little words that would trail and things we would do. Steve just knows how to work a mic, and is a pro, and had been in the studio a lot even prior to being in Journey, and knew how to go about doing what he did.

Describing his approach to mixing Journey albums, Elson offered that "my process for mixing the Journey records was Mike Stone and I would mix until we got it close to done, then we'd have the band come in. With too many opinions in there, it just becomes too much. You have a vision and have been living through these songs, and what you're trying to do at that point in mixing is make it come alive. So near the end, you have the band come in with fresh ears and listen and go, 'You know what, I'm missing this or that,' and then you go about making changes." Offering a glimpse into the band and producer's inner process for settling on final mixes, Elson described a creative democracy wherein, on one end of the spectrum,

I would say "Faithfully" was one of those songs where everybody walked in and went, "That's it." Whereas on "Open Arms," we went back and forth, because it was a great performance, and then they wanted to put some strings on it. We probably had ten different mixes of that song of string levels—for Adult Contemporary, we did one that was a little string heavier, and one that was toned down some for AM radio. We were just having fun with it, but you can run into trouble with a great song like that in the tendency to want to continually do more to it, 'til it becomes too much. That's the danger; that's when a producer has to step in and say, "Okay, that's it, that's enough." Usually it was the rock-driven stuff that was the most time-consuming thing, because everybody's looking to get something out of it. These guys were great about it, because one of them would get upset for a minute, then go, "Okay, how are we going to figure this thing out?" They were very constructive people; that's the beauty of it.

In 1986, following his wildly successfully work with Journey, Elson entered the studio with Europe to produce the band's debut American LP *The Final Countdown*. Recalling the genesis of that collaboration, Elson explained that what initially caught his interest was the fact that the guys in the band were all nineteen and twenty at the time, just kids, so really a new band who had just signed to Epic, so this would be their first worldwide release, which piqued my interest. The band had a very small base in Sweden, and I was called by Epic Records, who had a demo from the band they wanted to send me. So when I went by Epic's offices, they had the demo plus a previous release the band had put out in Scandinavia, and the demos were really just Joey Tempest with an acoustic guitar or piano, very simple arrangements and song structures. So I didn't have any preconceived notions because of the simplicity of one or two instruments and a vocal. One song in particular from those demos, "The Final Countdown," had that lead synthesizer riff originally as a line in it that just sort of occurred, but it wasn't prominent. So there were things in the songs I thought were really interesting. So a week later, I ended up flying to Stockholm in Sweden to meet everybody and ended up staying for a few days, and we started working on songs right away. We liked each other right away and started working on songs that same week. I had their previous record to go by to get a sense of the band musically, but meeting them in person was really the first time I got a true idea of where I wanted to go with their sound.

Following the mutual decision to record an album together, Elson began, as usual, with a preproduction process that included a special focus on what would later become the band's biggest hit, "The Final Countdown." The producer recalled

heading into a rehearsal space, and I got an idea of how they played together, which is key to the way I produce. At the time, for instance, I remember that the only thing the keyboard player owned was a Fender Rhodes piano, so there really wasn't anything to hear at that time in terms of what I thought we could do with "The Final Countdown," but as we started working on things, the songs really started coming around. Anyway, there were so many personal distractions within the band that made recording in Stockholm almost impossible, so I booked a studio in Switzerland that I'd worked at before. The way I explained it to the band was simply that I wanted to get them all together in a spot where they were thinking about music and not about all the other things going on. And they were excited about it, to get away.

From the preproduction sessions, Elson had identified the album's title track as the obvious hit and explained that he went about

first starting work on "The Final Countdown," because I felt it had the most potential as a lead-off single for the album. So with the whole keyboard line, I decided if we're going to make it stand out, I'd brought a Yamaha DX7 rack-mount sound module and a controller, and I found a guy outside of Zurich that was a jazz keyboard player but had all the latest synthesizers. So he had an EBG Wave Synthesizer and a ton of keyboards, and I told him, "We'll take everything you have," and set up everything in the control room. And the first tracks we cut were bass, drums, and guitar live together and then tracked the keyboards separately, because our process was more experimental, playing with sounds, and again starting to create tracks using effects on different keyboards, and I didn't go into it thinking it would be a synthesizer-driven rock record—that's just the way it ended up working. When we recorded Joey's vocals, we used a lot of effects, which was the popular sound of the time, but my feeling was if you listened to any of those songs dry, you'd go, "Well, what happened?" So it felt appropriate creatively anyway.

Europe's U.S. debut *The Final Countdown* would go on to sell three million copies and establish the band as an international hair-metal favorite. His first foray into the hair-metal arena, Elson's work with the band more resembled his radio rock roots with Journey in terms of what *Rolling Stone* described as a "sensibility [that] has more in common with . . . Boston. Like Boston's Tom Scholz, Europe's Joey Tempest sees no point in innovation for its own sake, preferring instead the proven pleasures of accessibility. So Tempest doesn't invent—he distills, taking this bit from Asia, that bit from Foreigner." In spite of a predict-able dismissal of the band's lyrical content and image, critical praise across the board for the album's accomplished production and performance delivery validated Elson's success in establishing the band's credibility with critics, leading *Rolling Stone* to conclude that "the vocal harmonies and instrumental arrangements say far more than either the lyrics or the titles, and maybe that's the point."

Elson's success with Europe helped establish his credibility within the broader hard-rock/glam-metal scene that dominated MTV and the airwaves in the latter half of the 1980s. His next collaboration in that genre would come via his work with Mr. Big, a super-group composed of Talas/David Lee Roth bassist Billy Sheehan and Racer X shred guitar-ist Paul Gilbert, beginning in 1989 with the band's self-titled debut as well as their 1991 double-platinum follow-up, *Lean into It*, which produced the worldwide smash ballad "To Be with You."

Almost forty years into his career, in examining the full landscape of his considerable catalog, Elson seems to feel proudest of the long-term creative relationships he has culti-vated with bands in the studio and out on the road, whether Journey, Lynyrd Skynyrd, or Mr. Big. In Elson's opinion, the longevity he has established with each of those bands was rooted in a more general philosophy that kept the producer working constantly to

have the relationship to where the band trusts my opinion, and I'm able to add some-thing. There's nothing worse than sitting out in the studio or mixing live where there's a problem you hear every night, or there's something that needs fixing, and the artist doesn't want to know about it. Having that bond makes it easier in that they trust you. Generally, the repeat situation bodes well for both parties. I love that a group wants to work with me again. I just feel like each thing I did in the next phase with a band always got better, because there was so much openness about it in the songs and sounds, and in the relationship, just being able to throw the music aside for a second and talk about something about music.

In terms of an overarching signature to his production sound and style, Elson has always striven for a sonic consistency, wherein

my records tended to sound less studio than most. It's a hard thing to pin down, because on certain songs I go for the whole lush production—the ballads and things where I've gone for strings. I would say I go for more of a live feel, and I would never use the stuff that people wanted to hear the perfect records with. I didn't care, I just wanted a great feel, and for it to feel like the band was performing. I think I produced records from a reverse thinking, where I recorded bands in the studio as though we were making a playing live, but without trying to fool anybody. Generally, following my blueprint for Journey, I took that approach with every project I produced from then on, where I try to create band atmosphere in the studio that is akin to how they would play live, when bands like Journey are usually in their prime. One other validation I thought the band gave to that approach was when I went in later years to see them live, Journey played the songs we'd tracked in the same arrangement and tempo, and a lot of times, you see a band live where the tempo is all over the place in terms of the recording, and they're already changing parts of the song up, which signals to me that they really didn't get what they were happy with in the studio.

Despite a legacy that spans more than four decades and millions of records sold, Elson's approach to producing bands hasn't changed fundamentally since he got his start in the business in the late 1960s. "One thing I can say from my work with Lynyrd Skynyrd—who I did sound for from the club days up through to the arenas—all the way through my years working with Journey, from Michael Jackson to Aerosmith, is this: there really isn't that much difference if you're after the right things, like ambience, energy, and so on." In offering some closing words of wisdom to the newest generation of Pro Tools babies, Elson emphasizes a focus on capturing performance, an art he feels has become lost

because too many times it's an easy way out, as far as I'm concerned. That's my problem with it, is really lack of performance. So if you're going in to work with a band, first go see them in clubs and work with them live. Even if they're in writing mode or rehearsing, try to get them to go play a club with new material. Then watch people react, get an idea, and see what people are reacting to before you commit. Because if a band's willing—from playing—they can experiment and maybe see a song grow in a different direction, or I think really capture the right feel. I'd say that's probably the biggest thing that helps me, to hear raw material in a club where an audience hasn't heard it on the radio. Once you are in the studio working with them, use Pro Tools as a tool but not as a talent.

CHAPTER 30

Eddie Kramer—The Rear Admiral

The legend of Jimi Hendrix looms as supernaturally over rock today as it did in the late 1960s when he first walked and played among us, prophesying the future of guitar rock. Hendrix showed us that guitar players could walk on water, pulling musical revelations out of his axe that could only have been divinely inspired. His longtime sound engineer Eddie Kramer confirmed *Rolling Stone*'s designation of Hendrix as "the greatest guitarist of all time" with his memory that "the first thing I learned working with Jimi in the studio was to be very flexible, because of the fact that you had an artist who was considered—even in the early days—to be an absolute genius, a fact that was confirmed as the years went on, and reconfirmed after his death."

Preceding his coveted role as Hendrix's copilot in the studio, Kramer earned his wings coming up in the early 1960s in London, working at the legendary Olympic Studios. Kramer recalled of his early years learning the engineering trade:

> I came to England and basically started there as a tape operator, because back then there were no such things as recording schools. You learned by trial and error, becom-

ing a tea boy, and working your way from the bottom up through the ranks from great engineers. So I wound up landing a job at Olympic Studios and from there was very fortunate to be in the right place at the right time, and was able to carve out a career as an engineer. In those days, one was able to learn from the masters, and the masters there were Keith Grant, who was the chief engineer at Olympic, and prior to that, a particular engineer named Bob Auger trained me and many engineers, and was an absolute genius. So I learned from them both how to record symphonic orchestras with three microphones, and that was normal. That was what you were expected to do, shut up and learn, and training was really wonderful in the sense that you got to work with great engineers and big orchestras. Then you would come back the next day and be doing the Kinks, or one day you'd do a jingle, and the next day you'd be doing the Rolling Stones. So there was a continual shuffling in and out of musicians who were amazing, and of the best quality and highest standards, and that's what one responded to. So one learned how to record everything—whether it was pop music, film music, or classical music, which I did a lot of, obviously with my training, and I was always given the weird stuff.

Kramer came from a classical music background, and his interest in engineering began during his childhood growing up "in South Africa, where I was very fortunate to come from a very musical family, and grew up studying piano and was scheduled to be a concert pianist, and studied classical music pretty much all my life, which was a great experience. Cape Town was a beautiful city, and I had good teachers, and my father was very open-minded about the music I was listening to, even though I pissed him off eventually by getting into jazz. After jazz I got into rock 'n' roll, and from rock 'n' roll, here I am." Ironically, it was Hendrix's uncategorizable approach as a recording artist at the time that gave Kramer his first foot inside the studio door, working on what he recalled was "again, the weird stuff that came through Olympic, and in fact, that's how I met Hendrix. I got a call one day from the studio manager, who said 'There's this American chap with big hair named Hendrix, and you do all the weird shit anyway, so why don't you do this session?' That was my introduction to Jimi."

Lucky two times over as a sound engineer to be working in the presence of greatness from both the artist side and the producer side, Kramer recalled that on his early Hendrix sessions, "I was working alongside a *very* good producer named Chas Chandler, and my function there was as engineer." Detailing the essence of his function as tape began rolling on what would become Hendrix's— and arguably psychedelic and experimental guitar rock's—most influential album, *Are You Experienced*, Kramer recalled as a bottom line that "anything that Jimi came up with, I had to make sound better; that was my job: to make the sounds that would make him happy. Since I approach everything from a very musical standpoint, rather than a technical standpoint, I was able to manipulate the sounds to his satisfaction, and to Chas's, and certainly to mine."

Crafting an album that was as far ahead of its time as Hendrix was himself as a musician, Kramer quickly discovered the importance of exercising the skill of staying on his toes and keeping as close a pace as possible with the guitarist, emphasizing the importance of "not falling behind—you *cannot* fall behind. That is the tragedy right there, if you lose track of what's going on, because you might miss some great musical moment, so you have to be up there with them and stay with them. I found that same rule applied later on in my career to Jimmy Page, or Pete Townshend, or to any great artist who really has a vision for what they want to do. You have to think like him, and that's a technique and a trick that you learn when you're working with someone of that caliber." Along with bringing the skill of working fast on the technical end of capturing that vision on record, Kramer found it equally crucial, "using Jimi's genius as a baseline, to be flexible, in the sense that whatever sound he's trying to create, you have to be there 24/7 and three steps ahead of the game. So that begins with *anything* the guy does in the studio you've got to be paying attention to, no matter whether he's breathing or picking a guitar, you have to pay attention, and learn as much as you can about his creative habits as he works so I didn't miss a single moment of his musical magic when it happened."

For as bold as his guitar playing spoke and his voice boomed through the speakers, in the studio, Kramer revealed that Hendrix's vulnerable space came with the vocal recording: "Jimi felt his weak spot was his voice. He thought he had the worst voice in the world, and thought he sucked at vocals. He was very shy, as a human being he was shy, and as a vocalist he was *terribly* shy. He was very insecure about his vocal abilities." Underscoring the importance of both resourcefulness and adaptability for any engineer or producer in helping artists work around their insecurities, to build Jimi's confidence during vocal tracking, Kramer recalled, "We constructed a three-sided vocal booth for him with a little light, and it was turned around so that it was facing away from the control room, and we couldn't see him. This was his little house where he could feel more secure, happy, and comfortable. The whole idea of working with artists is to build up their strengths and try to make them feel comfortable and confident, and I think we did that with Jimi."

Once Hendrix was comfortable enough to get vocal recording underway, Kramer cited another vital norm to his recording process with Hendrix: "The tape never stops, absolutely. The singing actually gets better as they go on, as they warm up, and the singer becomes more confident like Jimi would of his own voice. He always sounded better as he went along, but as a rule, I recorded everything that came out of him."

Clicking with Hendrix enough for the guitarist to invite Kramer to continue their musical journey in the U.S. following its British beginnings, the producer recalled that move came when he came to America in '68, which is when I went over to continue working with him after Chas left. We'd actually started working on *Electric Ladyland* in England, and then I continued working with him at the Record Plant. After Chas left in the middle of 1968, it was up to Jimi and me to continue the process, and from there my role changed from being just the engineer to being a bit more than that: I would be the de facto producer, even though I wasn't listed as producer, because it was Jimi that was producing; there was no doubt in my mind about that. I was engineering, but was the person he would rely on to ask questions of: "Was this good enough?" And so my engineering job covered a tremendous amount of ground and sort of went right into the production area.

As he did in his Hendrix heyday, Kramer has maintained his preference for "tracking in analog; everything I've done in my career has been analog and continues to be to this day. I still use 24-track 15 IPS Dolby SR, or 16-track, for cutting the basics. I always use a Neve board, and use vintage gear to get a record's basic sounds, and working in a *great* sounding room." To ensure that the records he makes in the digital age maintain their analog dexterity, the producer shares two tricks. The first is

being sure to use a really good work plug, and I use something called Big Bend, made by Apogee, which assures that the transfer from the analog world into the digital world is really good. Now there's also a method where you can bypass the Pro Tools A-to-B converters, and use outboard A-to-B converters, and that is very critical in preserving the sound of analog. I still love analog, and will continue working with it as long as tape is available for cutting basic tracks. My big rule with digital is *not* to abuse the technology, but to *use* the technology of Pro Tools as a tool, as part of a palette of colors that you use, but analog has always been my canvas, if you will.

Emphasizing just as firmly and forcefully today as he did thirty years ago the vitally important role Kramer has felt throughout his career preproduction plays in making the best possible album, Eddie reasons that

I make the record not in the studio; I make the record in preproduction. To me, if you go into a situation with a band, and you start preproduction, you should do your homework diligently as a producer so the band members understand their songs in terms of their chord sequences, the progressions, the lyrics, the dynamics, or a certain change that you're going to make, so everybody in the group knows what's going on, and the songs are well-rehearsed. To that end, preproduction should take as long as you need, be it three weeks or three months, whatever it takes, to really get that material finely honed. Not to the point of it being too polished, because you've got to leave work for improvement and spontaneity, but when you walk into the studio, you should be fully armed and prepared. This is the crunch time: so when you walk into that studio, and put up mics, it should be easy. Recording a band ain't rocket science; it's easy, because what you're trying to do is capture a performance; that's all you're trying to do.

Leading Kramer to touch on another of his bedrock fundamentals for recording any album, he reasons that, in the grand scheme of record making,

the mic you put on a drum on a singer is immaterial, simply because microphones are just a tool; it's all in the song and the delivery. For instance, I have a standing rule: if my drum sound is not together in twenty minutes, I walk out. I know I can get a drum sound in ten minutes that is very close to what it's supposed to be, and in twenty minutes it's very close to the final thing. The first thing you have to realize is it's the song, and I don't care if the song is recorded on a cassette machine; that can become a hit. It's the song first: song, song, song, song. After the song, what's next? It's the performance and the delivery of that song. I think when a producer is too rigid in choice of gear, a record can sound sterile. For me, anything that sounds cool and is appropriate for that particular song and particular mood, we'll use.

Reflecting briefly on other highlights from his superstar catalog in terms of what within the artistic heart of each of those acts inspired his ear toward or throughout the collaboration, beginning with Led Zeppelin, Kramer recalled that group producer Jimmy Page

always knew what he wanted. He's a genius, and has an amazing concept about what's cool and what's not, and has great ideas that he pursues to the very end. They were the greatest rock band I ever worked with, and certainly the best rock drummer I've ever worked with, and certainly that the world has ever known. And John Paul Jones is the unsung hero of the band. He's on par with Page in terms of his musical genius. I think if it wasn't for John Paul Jones, Zeppelin never would have become what it did. They all complement each other.

Turning to the style-over-substance end of the artistic spectrum, Kramer offered Kiss as an example of a band that he recognized early on, "though they couldn't play worth a shit," had the potential

to become very good artists. The whole point about Kiss in the beginning was they were an attraction. I produced the demo that got them their record deal, and then got a phone call about a year later to produce a proper album. At the time, I had to choose between working with Boston and Kiss, and I chose Kiss because it was a challenge. How the hell do I make them sound as great on a record as they looked up onstage?

They had a very clear direction, very clear vision, and a lot of drive and enthusiasm that makes up for a lot. Well, we did it.

With the Rolling Stones, Kramer said that, as a recording experience, "the best section of my work with the Stones was working in the studio alongside Jimmy Miller, who was a genius and the best producer they ever had. He taught me how to produce, and I was fortunate to have him as my mentor as far as record production. Getting to work on *Beggars Banquet*, I learned from Jimmy Miller how to get a band like the Stones off their asses and get them inspired—it was an amazing transformation to watch him work with them. I owe him a tremendous debt of gratitude."

Commenting next on his recommended bedside manner to maintain throughout the process of coaching the best performance with any artist or band on record—in spite of how closely acquainted he became over his career through multialbum collaborations with the norms of his bands' artistic processes in the studio, Kramer was quick to hammer home the importance of "drawing a line in the sand when it comes to how close you allow yourself to get to an artist that you're working with—you have to be circumspect. There's a little bit of a distance you should put up, I think, as a producer, because once you become so personal and friendly with the band that they can manipulate you—which happens—then you're in the wrong business. They have to look up to you with a certain amount of respect, because that's what they're paying you for."

Translating that broader concept into specific advice for engineers/producers, Kramer said:

> You have to be right up in your artists' faces, understanding exactly where they're coming from, where you think they're heading, and how you can help them. Your job there, as a producer or engineer, is to help; you're not there to hinder, you're there to help make the record sound better. That's my job, and I still do that today, and if I can do that, then I've done my job. You have to find a place where you're comfortable, and where he or she as an artist is comfortable, and you establish that early on in the sense that you're a sounding board. You're the objective viewer, and the person the artist will turn to with "Did I do this okay? Did it sound okay?" And if the answer is "No," then you go on trying other ideas. You've got to keep trying ideas; that's the whole thing, to constantly and consistently keep your mind open to whatever the artist wants to try.

Kramer added the caution that

with any artist, you have to be very careful about how you raise the bar—sometimes you have to do it gently, and sometimes you have to beat the artist upside the head with the equivalent of a 2x4 with a nail in it. It's a constant adjustment, and you're also very aware of how fragile the artist's ego is. The most important piece of advice I can give to any engineer or producer coming up in today's world of record making is, more important than knowing all of the technical side of things, you *have* to know music. If you don't know music, don't even bother. You have to understand music, and know what the hell you're talking about. It's better, and preferable, if you can play music, but you can get by in understanding music.

Looking back over the entirety of his forty-plus-year career as a creator of touchstone records for multiple generations of rock fans, for Kramer, the greatest personal impact he felt he made on those years as a producer came—not surprisingly—via his work with Jimi Hendrix, simply because "any of his albums are stamped into the memory banks of any musician who has every picked up a guitar." His judgment is confirmed by *Rolling Stone*'s conclusion that "Hendrix pioneered the use of the instrument as an electronic sound source . . . (whose) studio craft and virtuosity with both conventional and unconventional guitar sounds have been widely imitated . . . Players before Hendrix had experimented with feedback and distortion, but he turned those effects and others into a controlled, fluid vocabulary."

As the studio interpreter of that language when translating it to tape, Kramer is most proud of the fact that the records he made with Jimi Hendrix throughout countless ages have remained

timeless as classics, and I'm thrilled and honored to have been involved with a genius like that. Those albums right there—*Are You Experienced?, Electric Ladyland, Axis: Bold of Love*, and so on——it doesn't get much better than that. You can take the best Zeppelins and the Stones and Traffics and just go on and on and on through all the records that I've been really fortunate throughout my career to be involved with, and take the best out of each, and you just have to say, "You know, they were all really great albums, except for this one guy who was just that one step above anybody and everybody else."

CHAPTER 31

Daniel Lanois—The Gift of Greatness

Daniel Lanois is one of those names that rolls right off the tongue when speaking of true legends. Much like a divinely gifted athlete—Michael Jordan, Mickey Mantle, Muhammad Ali, Jim Brown, Nadia Comaneci, Carl Lewis, Wayne Gretzky— who have made the kind of plays in their career that are not only remembered, but still revered decades after they were made. The same could be said for the records Lanois has made throughout his career; they play timelessly to our ears. Consider U2's most beloved hits: "Pride (In the Name of Love)," "Where the Streets Have No Name," "With or Without You," "I Still Haven't Found What I'm Looking For," "Bullet the Blue Sky," "Mysterious Ways," "One," "Stuck in a Moment You Can't Get Out Of" or "Beautiful Day." Or Peter Gabriel's epic "Sledgehammer," "In Your Eyes," or "Big Time"; or Bob Dylan's *Time out of Mind*, to name just a few from that class. A master of atmosphere irrespective of subgenre, rock has been a happy lab rat for Lanois's sound-making science for the better part of thirty years, as the producer went about tuning sound to its perfect texture; bringing the precise essence out of a band's performances that make them Greatest Hits collection cuts; and perhaps most importantly, reminding music fans with his productions of precisely why the art of record making is just that—an art. And in that context, Daniel Lanois is arguably akin to Andy Warhol, as the "avant-*guard*" of pop producers.

Much like the athlete who had a basketball, baseball or football first put in his hands as a toddler, for Lanois, his introduction to music "came pretty early on in Quebec, back when I was a kid—mostly people playing violins at family gatherings. In regards to records, I just heard some things on the radio that sounded great to me as a kid. I kind of caught that wave of late '50s/early '60s rock 'n' roll being played on radio, so I caught some of that. Then I bought a little tape recorder—kind of an all-inclusive tabletop model that had microphones, speakers, and everything in it, a little reel-to-reel flea market machine probably from the '50s—and that's where the recording started." As his ears fast became fascinated with the creative possibilities of recorded sound, he recalled graduating to the more sophisticated

> Roberts, which was a 4-track machine that was a quarter-track 2-track, where you could flip the tape over, so it had a skinner head, and I thought didn't sound as good. The flea market machine had been a quarter-inch mono model, which I preferred, but wanted a more sophisticated machine. So shortly after the Roberts, I got my hands on a Sony TC-630, which came with speakers on board, and had a little sound-on-sound feature on it that was really cool because it allowed me to record a lot of stuff on the left channel and then transfer that to the right channel while adding overdubs, and I would just ping-pong back and forth. That's how it started . . .

Lanois would team up with another of rock production's most astonishing sonic pioneers, Brian Eno—who *Billboard* would recognize as an "ambient pioneer, glam rocker, hit producer, multimedia artist, technological innovator, and world beat proponent"—in the early 1980s. The arguably fated collaboration came ironically via

> a chance encounter, because we were both making instrumental music initially, and Brian was looking at New York City and had started a project with a piano player named Harold Budd, and had done these 2-track recordings in New York already, and wanted to find someplace where he could add to and modify them. So Eno had heard some music I'd worked on in New York City, even though I worked on it in Hamilton in Canada, but the band was visiting New York, ran into Brian and played him the album, and that's how he got hip to my sound. So he asked the girls in the band for my number, called me up and booked a session.

Detailing their charmed first studio collaboration, Lanois recalled that "he waltzed in with those Harold Budd tapes, I transferred them to my 16-track, I had a 2-inch 16-track at that time, and we just went on and worked on this beautiful instrumental music for weeks on end." Out of that first collaboration on *The Pearl,* Lanois and Eno would discover they both heard endless possibilities with ambient music, motivating them to "keep making instrumental music for about the next three years together, and we got better and better at it, and worked in that time on some very specific and special music. It was kind of the beginning of this ambient sound Brian was very fond of." Eno was among the pioneering founders of the genre that was blooming into existence during the early 1980s out of collaborations that included what some consider the bible of ambient sound—*Apollo: Atmospheres and Soundtracks.*

The process of transitioning beyond the ambient genre and into that of rock 'n' roll would come in 1984 when Eno called Lanois, inviting him to coproduce U2's third studio LP, *The Unforgettable Fire*, recalling heading into the production, "When we went to Dublin after that, that was the sound we brought with us, because we were very excited about our technique and had spent years building this sound." Using their collaboration with U2 to describe his and Eno's preproduction norms, Lanois revealed that

> heading into preproduction with a band like that, Brian and I always have sounds and some technical ideas that we're excited about, and it's good to keep the laboratory alive that way. And to this day I do that: every day I go in the studio and fiddle around in the hopes of bumping into something, an original angle, sonically, and that's just part of my menu, if you will, as a dedicated studio artist. When it's time to make a record with U2, or anyone else, the first thing we do with them is we hang out and talk, and through those conversations we find out how people tick, what's going on with them philosophically, what their hopes and dreams are all about, and probably more importantly where they're at in their own lives. That's the part that's hard to write about, or even talk about, because it changes from season to season, person to person, but without any doubt, there was an awful lot to read in the people of U2. So we hung out with them just listening to a bunch of demos, leaning in the back seat of the car with the music up driving around Dublin, having a drink, stuff like that. Because there's no vision to be had if you're not hanging—you might think you know an artist by having heard their last record or something, but not really; you really have to get in there and get to know people.

U2 felt so comfortable with the production team of Eno and Lanois that from 1984 on the pair would become a permanent part of the band's signature production sound in the decades and generation-defining hits to follow. Via their collaboration with U2 from the mid-1980s on, Lanois and Eno would help the band realize what the L.A. *Times* recognized as "rock on a grand scale," producing music that "established U2 in the '80s as the first band in years to offer the ambition, craft and leadership that characterized the Beatles, the Who and other great rock bands of the '60s." Of the pair's impact on shaping the band's sound over the course of later-'80s albums like *The Unforgettable Fire* and the landmark *The Joshua Tree,* the *New York Times* would add that their "new direction . . . was toward more elusive, fragmentary songs, potent and unusual instrumental textures, loads of busy detail and washes of synthesizer sound."

Giving fans an exclusive VIP Pass inside U2's songwriting process, a very experimental one by nature of the fact that it's ongoing throughout production, Lanois shared that

> specifically with U2, we're lucky because they very much welcome any kind of ideas in the studio, so they're not so somber that they don't just walk in and say "Alright, Eno, Lanois, here's the song now, what are you guys gonna do with it?" That's not how it works, so we set up sounds and we set up stations, and they're terrific little stations—the drum station obviously for Larry; Edge has always got a vast array of experiments on the go. We like all this stuff because we're very innovatively driven, so oftentimes, something will just start, like Eno will start with a little beat box of some kind that he's processing, and he pipes it into everybody's monitors, and they start playing along with that. There's an awful lot that comes out of exorcism, to exorcise whatever you've got bottled up inside to the point of expression in a band room. That's a very powerful energy, because it doesn't belong to just one person, it belongs to everybody as a collective. So you're forced to communicate, and whatever baggage you're carrying on that day you can somewhat leave it at the door, and off you go, and you hope that the thing gets off the ground, that you get "liftoff" as we call it. Because once you've got liftoff, then you've got the bedrock to work with, and we can build something fantastic—so that's what we hope to bump into, and that happens in the U2 environment because we are allowed to provide people with surprises.

For all of the bravery of the band's writing process, producer Lanois recommends maintaining the safety net of recording everything as a vital underpinning to developing the band's broader sound on any album, such that "we keep the machines going at all times, because you never know when you're going to get something rising up—even if it's not a finished take, it might be like fifteen bars of something really special within a jam." Working side by side as a band with producers who *Rolling Stone* has said "lent discipline and nuance" to the group's broader sound, as the collective moved creatively through preproduction on any record, Lanois shared that we earmark things as we go along, and at the end of the day, I might have twenty or thirty different markings to come back to, and I come back to those. The band doesn't even have to be around for this. I'm happy to stay on a little later after school, and I listen to the many earmarks of the day; sure enough, they'll be some good ones—even if it's only two or three. I'll then fiddle with those, extend them, chop them up and edit them, and maybe even do some overdubs on them to then play for the band at a later time of listening. So quite a few things start that way, and then songs build from those established magic moments.

Recommending the habit to any working producer as a tool that has remained at the top of his chest of production gems of wisdom over the years, the producer concedes that while "the note-keeping is a big project," it remained a vital reference source "throughout the '80s and '90s, when I kept very elaborate notes in a book about projects at hand, so if there's any mystery about a sound and a couple of weeks go by and you're scratching your head wondering what about a particular guitar or vocal sound, I would have the notes on that, and I insist that my assistants also keep notes for their little domains relative to how to find things and so on. Eno is a master of the pen, and he keeps very sophisticated journals, so I picked up the habit from him. So that never changes."

As it developed into one of his key production aids over the years, Lanois discovered another advantage to the practice of note-taking as he headed into production on any record as it related to

writing out an arrangement, which is a very big part of what I do as a producer. I use graph paper for that; sometimes I use very big books, like a 14 x 18 graph page, and I start on the lefts and rights of the pad—the long part of which is horizontal— and I just write out the arrangement, and everything gets included on that page: all lyrics, all tempo shifts, all rises and falls and dynamics, notations about what to be reminded of at the next meeting. So by this one page, you see a complete graphic display of the song—the way it's structured. So when you get in the band room, you can speak and connect it well because you know what you're talking about relative to a beautiful sculptured image.

Using this visual aid to address the smaller idiosyncrasies within any song's arrange-ment/production, the producer excitedly adds that "because it's graph paper, you can *really* get in there and pinpoint why one kick drum is a little bit off; you're built to see it on the page of graph. So that's the secret weapon really right there. And that idea does not only belong to those of us who are in the heat of it, it belongs to any student whose interested in studying song and structure." As much as he brings a song to life on paper, Lanois—shedding light on his internal creative wheels as they turn throughout this process—reveals that "in my head, I can also do the thing I just described, I don't need to have a piece of paper because of my training. I've been doing this for so long that when I listen, I have kind of a very instant memory of the arrangement, so by being good at that way of doing things, I can talk to the room, and people will respect my position because I know what I'm talking about."

Sharing his memories of production bringing to life U2's breakout albums like *The Unforgettable Fire* and *The Joshua Tree*, beginning with what the *Washington Post* would later refer to as "Larry Mullen's rolling thunder drums," Daniel recalled that

> in micing Larry, there was not a great deal of mystery and nothing terribly unique about the micing. We always used dynamic mics mostly, maybe an old U-47 or 67 would creep into the picture as an overhead, but it was pretty much dynamics because we couldn't afford any breakdown, so we didn't want to start using too many fancy mics with power supply and all that; you just get more trouble with that stuff. So it was always a relatively tight mic technique, and we'd use Shure mics all around and a D-12 on the kick, but we were always fiddling around a little. Sometimes we'd change the drum, but I think the best drum sound we got was in Adam Clayton's house, the one he lives in now, that's the one we were renting at that time. It was kind of a country estate, and the main large room in the house was a beauty. It had a big old wood-plank floor with a rug in the middle of it, and was a very live room but sounded fantastic. The drums were amazing in there, so to me, it's hard to talk about Larry's drum sound in terms of sound because you could say "What drum and what mic . . . ," but these rooms had so much to add, and that particular room was a monster. You'd touch the bass drum and it sounded like a cannon, and though that would get a little noisy as a room to be in sometimes, I'd rather start with a room that's got a little too much than not enough. So that's what was happening room-wise.

Speaking beyond the room's sound, the producer shared that

> the rest of how we capture U2's drum sound is always changing relative to the part that Larry plays, because sometimes the floor tom will be a big part of the beat for him, like if you listen to "I Still Haven't Found What I'm Looking For." That song is kind of an odd example, because those drums were from another song, and I'll always love the beat and didn't want to see it go mixing. So in regard to what I spoke about with keeping notes and building your own sort of menu for a project, that beat certainly went on the menu very early for me, and was something I wanted the band to come

back to. So I kept fighting for it, and sure enough, it came from that early jam that was not a song and evolved into "I Still Haven't Found What I'm Looking For." Lucky for us, the bar markings were such that we got real lucky and Larry was putting a drum roll right where we wanted him to. That drum beat is a very odd drum beat with a big floor tom skip in it; it's terrific, and really celebrates Larry's innovative tendency. That's how he shines, because he can really come up with very unique, identifiable parts that become part of the hook of a song, like the backbone, the personality of the song. It's quite striking, and I think he gets that by following Bono's singing—he's very song driven, so the little flicks and details of his work are all placed there relative to the vocal. He's a rare bird that way, and that's part of what we're hearing on U2 records.

Aside from Larry Mullins's voluminous drum sound, Lanois recalled that for the album's vocal tracks the drummer played to, as Bono recorded them, "on all our albums with U2, we used the control room as a recording environment in a big way." He treated the room as a lab of sorts: "We spend most of our time there, and that's where the ideas are tried out." In getting Bono psyched up for the energetic performances the singer delivered on *The Joshua Tree* and beyond, Lanois said of his and Eno's strategy for helping to conjure the record's epic vocal performances that

you have to give them a sound, you've got to juice them up. So I just make sure that we're putting up a track that's happening when we play it back, and hope to develop enthusiasm around the room. We always have a surround sound, and have stage wedges as monitors plus the console sound, and usually another few speakers around the room. So you can make a lot of noise in the U2 control room, and Bono loves that, so you gotta juice him up, give him a nice big sound, and make him feel like a somebody and you'll get something out of him because he's an incredible improv artist. I think some of his best melodies and so on have come from these moments of inspiration out of nowhere, where we're just blasting the track and we get a vocal of sorts.

When attention turned to the recording of "Bono's soulful, grandiose cry," as *Rolling Stone* put it, the producer recalled when recording

Bono, pretty much all roads have always led to the Beta 58, because if you're in the band room, you can't use too fancy a mic because you're gonna get a crazy amount of bleeding, and in the studio, we just keep a couple 58s going at all times in the control room, and Bono's on the couch and he picks up the 58—that's usually what happens. We have used a Sony C-500 on him, which I thought was really beautiful on his voice, because the C-500 has a silkiness in the top that you can't get with an EQ—it just comes with the design of that mic. I used that on a song called "MLK" on *The Unforgettable Fire*, and you can really hear all the little whisperings in his voice, it's a very beautiful sound. A couple times we tried some big, fancy mics on Bono, the usual U-47 or Telefunken 251. I brought all those mics from my collection when I went to Dublin to work with those guys. I don't really think it matters much in the end; if you're a rocker, they always sound best on a 58.

Taking fans inside the creation of some of the signature effects chains that often lace Bono's rich, soaring vocal performances throughout *The Joshua Tree* and beyond, Lanois recalled that

we always have quite a complicated chain of effects, and that's just what happens with it naturally—a project will find what it likes in effects, and then you just kind of roughly leave it set up. So everything you put up from your multitrack source ends up going through your chain of effects. The AMS Harmonizer was something I used on Bono that I use to this day; that was our main echo machine on a vocal. With Bono, I always hit a slap verse, like an AMS, and then send that to something else. On *The Joshua Tree*, the PCM 70 was a big one for us, because it had a lot of tuned echoes—they're a lot of work because a tuned echo will not likely work through the entire song, so you have to repitch and keep printing. So in the case of those types of effects, you have to lay them down on your multitracks.

Another of the band's signature sounds that would firm up stylistically on *The Joshua Tree* was one of which the *New York Times* would say, "The Edge's fixation on obsessive, repetitive guitar textures is allied with Mr. Eno's eerie synthesizer coloration." Lanois singled out the album's opening song, the hit single "Where the Streets Have No Name," as an example of the latter sound in the making during recording, recalling that

the symphonic intro to "Where the Streets Have No Name" Edge made at home. He had been fiddling around with this symphonic thing that made a little jewel of an intro production. We didn't know what we were going to use it for when he first brought it in, and it sounded so beautiful we decided we needed to try and work it in somehow. I think it was relatively free time initially and then goes into the repetitive part, so I remember we had to merge that intro with the rest of the song. So every time we did a take, we'd pipe that into people's headphones with a time-keeper because we were cutting that to fixed time to a click. So we prepared this whole thing based on that lovely intro Edge built at home.

Speaking more broadly on the guitarist's favorite go-to effects on that album and beyond, Lanois revealed that "the Edge always had a lot of delays in his rig, he always had his own delay in his rigs, so when you recorded him, you automatically got that stuff. We might add something after, and there were some boxes at the time that had really good delays—the Korg STD 3000 that we use to this day, and Roland made a similar box, and then there was the Lexicon PCM 41. We used mostly echo repeats and not that much reverb, but right off the floor Edge has his sound down." Offering insights as a player in his own right into what natural skills as a guitar player the Edge brought to the fore in creating the signature rhythmically repetitive sound, the producer said, "Edge is very gifted musically, and lucky for him, he's very rhythmic, so I always say that if he'd been born earlier, he would have been playing for James Brown. He has a lovely sense of timing, and a very delicate right hand, which makes me jealous because I have a very heavy right hand, and consequently I play fat strings to stay in tune. So he's got a great touch, and an interesting finger-picking angle on the flat pick, because he arpeggiates quite a bit, or he'll find a little riff within two or three strings." *Billboard* would say of *The Joshua Tree*'s blending of those elements of the band's sound with the atmospheric, ambient attributes of their producers: "Working with producers Brian Eno and Daniel Lanois, U2 created a dark, near-hallucinatory series of interlocking soundscapes."

Those evolutions in the band's sound won fans over to the tune of twenty-five million copies sold upon release, launching U2 into a realm of superstardom reserved only for the greats. Scoring their first #1 hits on *Billboard*'s Top 200 Album Chart with "With or Without You" and "I Still Haven't Found What I'm Looking For," and following up *The Joshua Tree* with the concert film and soundtrack *Rattle and Hum*—where *Entertainment Weekly* concluded that "with the one-two punch of their 1987 multiplatinum album *The Joshua Tree* and 1988's *Rattle and Hum*, U2 parlayed college-radio respect into a reverent cult, and thence into superduperstardom"—the band returned with Eno and Lanois to the studio in 1991 to record *Achtung Baby*. *Rolling Stone* would reveal that on this album, "Daniel Lanois oversees the entire album, with Brian Eno and Steve Lillywhite assisting on a number of songs," adding that musically, this time around, U2 set out "to experiment rather than pay homage. In doing so, the band is able to draw confidently and consistently on its own native strengths."

Highlighting the method behind the musical mastery that was the Edge's axe work throughout the groundbreaking transition/evolution in the band's sound—one the *L.A. Times* would praise for the Edge's "arty, guitar-driven textures" as among the band's most confident and vigorous ever"—Lanois revealed of the technical side of its creation that "there's usually a few boxes that we collectively embrace. Oftentimes, Edge is playing in the control room, so we'd have a couple of amps in there we just kind of put behind the couch. It was on that album and still is amazing how much gets done right in there in the heat of the moment." Using one of the album—and decade's—biggest hits to illustrate that creative process in action, the producer highlighted a memorable moment in "Mysterious Ways" involving "a part toward the end of that song where Edge breaks down into something funky sounding, and I believe that was a setting on a PCM 70, the box that Edge was excited about at that time. It had kind of an auto-wah setting built in, and normally that equipment is meant to be used in plus-4 environment, like in a pro-level studio environment. But somehow we had rigged it so it was part of his guitar rig, so the intro to that song was coming out of those amps barking like dogs, it was amazing." The results he and Edge achieved together would be celebrated by *Rolling Stone* as the "boldness on *Achtung* [that] . . . is key to the album's adventurous spirit. His plangent, minimalist guitar style—among the most distinctive and imitated in modern rock—has always made inspired use of devices like echo and reverb."

When Lanois, Eno, and company's attention turned from recording to the mixing the album—which with a band for whom the mixing process was one of blending their individual elements into one final aural gallery of portraits that would be revisited for decades to come with the loyal admiration Picasso's works still command around the world—the producer recalled that

> what usually happens is rough mixes along the way will have very dynamic personalities, because you'll be excited about a certain blend at a certain time. And band members end up pushing CDs they pull out of the bag come mixing time where they might say, "Oh, it sounded really great on this mix," and that's usually true because maybe there was a particular sound on a particular day. So that's where we keep notes, and where my assistants are very good, because as we record, I can say, "Please, let's make a note of this vocal sound, this drum sound," again as we go, so we have our sonic menu. That gets back to the journal—whether it be my journal, Eno's, or my assistant's, so they can say, "Oh yeah, it was the Eventides," or this or that, so it's very important to write a few details down as you go along before you start drinking the whiskey.

That toast would later come critically in the form of the *New York Times'* high praise that in the "production by Daniel Lanois and Brian Eno . . . the band creates noisy, vertiginous arrangements, mostly layers of guitar, that eddy around the melody or tear at its edges . . . yet the band has maintained its pop skills; just when a song might turn into a noisy vamp, a melodic interlude chimes in. Stripped-down and defying its old formulas, U2 has given itself a fighting chance for the 1990s." That fighting chance became a victory for the band on the level of winning a Championship Boxing Belt, with Lanois and Eno the trainers successful in guiding the band toward a Grammy win in 1993 for Best Rock Performance by a Duo or Group with Vocal and spawning Top 10 hits with "Mysterious Ways," "One," "Even Better Than the Real Thing," "Who's Gonna Ride Your Wild Horses," and "The Fly." The fourth Lanois/Eno collaboration with the band would sell a record eighteen million copies worldwide, reaffirming the team's success. *Entertainment Weekly* would observe that, due to "the band's longtime collaborators Daniel Lanois and Brian Eno, the album is refreshingly personal—deeper and denser than any of the band's previous releases—and a musical consolidation as well."

As they kicked off the millennium with their eleventh studio LP, the *BBC* would report, not surprisingly, the group in choosing the production team best suited to ensure their creative transition into the next decade, had as with the 1990s, once again recruited "the old dream team of Brian Eno and Daniel Lanois." Later hailed by *Billboard* as the band's "best anthem in years," as the producers and band began the process of crafting the smash hit "Beautiful Day," Lanois recalled quickly discovering what he felt would

> become one of the big driving forces behind the U2 sonics and tendencies is loyalty to the room. I think the support within, and the power in a team, really applies to them, because we're not about to outsource anything. Maybe we'll bring in an orchestra if we have to, but I think that that loyalty to the room is a big part of the U2 sound. So to get back to the background singing thing, if we're all singers out there, and I sing okay, Eno's got his thing, and the Edge sings pretty good, are we the greatest singers in the world? Probably not, but we don't want to bring in the greatest singers in the world, we want to use the people in the room, and ask them to sing, because they're involved in the tapestry of the work, and obviously dedicated to trying to make a masterpiece.

Playing heavily into the band's success, as always, in the studio in crafting an album that would go on to achievements critical and commercial including winning seven Grammy Awards over two years—a record—for Song of the Year and Record of the Year in 2001 for "Beautiful Day" and Record of the Year and Best Rock Album for "Stuck in a Moment You Can't Get Out Of" in 2002, was the majesty and mystery of lead guitarist the Edge's artwork throughout the album. Coupled with his performance abilities, producer Lanois pinpointed the guitarist's songwriting talents as a key complement to Bono's vocals. Lanois says of the Edge:

> This is a guy who came up at a time when a part was everything, and not necessarily the ad-lib expression. Ad-lib was not a part of Edge's education, it's not what he grew up with as a player—he came up learning parts, and it really suits him because he's

a brilliant mind. So he can study the structure of his work against Bono's vocals, and one is chasing the other, and because he arpeggiates a lot, it's almost like a four-part Bach or any great arrangement of four parts. So though the Edge doesn't have a formal education in music, I think instinctively he understands the placement of parts and their roles, so he for instance never recklessly strums through a verse. He pinpoints details within the chordal structure to support Bono's melody and so, so he's a very sophisticated dude.

Turning to another of the musical colors that shined bright as a highlight of the song's broader musical beauty within the ears of U2's fans, the producer revealed that—on that hit and countless others dating back twenty-five years—

we always did our own background singing, so it was always Eno, the Edge and my-self. On "Beautiful Day," for instance, there's this monosonic voice, no vibrato, and Edge can sing way up there; he has a lovely falsetto. I'm a pretty good harmony singer myself because I have a lot of experience at it—so I can learn parts real quick. So I'm usually the conductor of the little background singing team, from "I Still Haven't Found What I'm Looking For" to "Beautiful Day"—that's me, and then Edge is up there singing the five up above me, the really high up there. We're just trying to copy the line "Sleeps tonight," then we stacked up about four tracks of those, me and Edge, because it was just the two of us on "Beautiful Day," and Eno processed us and got us sounding like a choir.

Taking fans behind the scenes of Bono's spacey vocal soundscapes as they were laid in organic, collaborative layers with the Edge and the rest of team U2, Lanois recalled that he and coproducer, along with Bono, all

had our own little station on *All That You Can't Leave Behind* which, for Brian Eno, meant in fact he had an entire 24-channel mixer at his station which was just a piggy-back on the main console. So in the corner of the room with the headphones, he had access to all the ingredients of the multitrack, so he'd put up his hand when he hit on something cool. Then we'd just raise up his faders and see what he was up to, and he had processed those backgrounds to the point of it sounding very or-chestral, very beautiful. We never use just straight-out-of-the-box sounds, and I don't remember exactly what Eno was using on that, but he's a very good VCO man. He really understands you can't just leave a voltage control oscillator with one setting, or it's going to sound like a machine, so by performing the VCO, as I do, Eno puts a lot of personality in his work. So if we're printing, you have to print as you go if it's a very complex chain of processing equipment and you're doing a manual VCO, and there may be a graphic equalizer that's also performed on. That's not something to save for a mixing day; if you hit on the sound on a day of processing, then it's very important to print it on the multitrack. So if I remember right, that vocal sound was printed onto the multitrack, so come mixing time, one fader up and you get this whole orchestra of people singing it.

Famously known for working alongside Brian Eno, Lanois would step out on his own with several collaborations that became touchstones of his legacy. One of them, his role as coproducer on Peter Gabriel's landmark *So* solo LP, helped define the art-rock genre commercially in the 1980s. A Grammy committee's wet dream, the album helped Gabriel not only succeed in retaining ownership of his own galaxy within the art-rock genre, but would more importantly it made the case for its permanence with the album's success, which the L.A. *Times* called "a great album" and "possibly Gabriel's best." Lanois recalled—not surprising in terms of the serendipitous nature of their future collaborations—that his invitation to work with Gabriel came out of the blue one day "when I got a call from Peter to fly to England and meet with him about working on a film soundtrack together. He'd heard the Harold Budd ambient records, and loved the sounds of those records, and recognized a lot of thought had gone into them, and a lot of devotion. So our first collaboration began with producing a soundtrack for an Alan Parker film, *Birdy*."

Confessing that "I always get a little stage fright getting on the plane to a new project; that's what happened with Peter," Lanois's initial jitters would be calmed by how *Birdy* went over with fans, so successfully that it would win Gabriel the Grand Jury Prize at Cannes, with a proud producer recalling that, as a catalyst for the next elevation in their collaboration, "following that, Peter next said, 'Okay, I want to do a singing record; do you want to do it with me?' So we already had a nice relationship and were excited about sonics and so on, so I think he just recognized we had the team right here and didn't need to go anywhere."

Relying heavily on Gabriel's musical imagination heading into preproduction on the album, Lanois opted to begin the adventure that was settling Gabriel's next level of musical territory and terrain naked enough that

the record started with no band—there was nobody in the building except me and Peter. David Rhodes lived down the street, who had played guitar for Peter for a long time. So because the songs weren't finished, and there were just some rough beginnings of others that were beautiful but not fleshed out yet, I said to Peter, "Let's just keep using the beat boxes," which he'd been using to lay things down for himself, "and we'll ask David Rhodes to come in every other day or so." So we had a little team, and so preproduction on that album was either me and Peter or the three of us. So we showed up for work every morning, and in a little bit of office humor, would wear these yellow construction hard hats, where you had to wear your hard hat to come into the dangerous workplace.

Those risks would lead in short time to the construction of one of the album's—and genre's—biggest radio hits with "Sledgehammer," an achievement that *Billboard* would argue was "easily his catchiest, happiest single to date. Needless to say, it was also his most accessible, and, in that sense it was a good introduction to *So*, the catchiest, happiest record he ever cut. 'Sledgehammer' propelled the record toward blockbuster status, and Gabriel had enough songs with single potential to keep it there." Of the diamond that was discovered in the rough of the record's first days of recording, Lanois recalled, "I remember I'd walk in every day and say 'Okay, let's have the sledgehammer,' which kind of became a slogan for the song we were working on at the time that eventually made Peter decide 'Well, I guess that's what the song should be called.'"

From that conceptual infancy, Gabriel and Lanois began writing the album within and based upon the singer's synthesizer universe, wherein, as the producer recalled, "Peter had all his own keyboards; he had a Fairlight, which was pretty cool, and had just gotten an Emulator, and had his Prophet 5, and got lovely sounds on that. He was responsible creatively for everything you hear in the way of keyboards on that record. He wrote and played everything; we didn't have anyone come in. He had a vibe in there, and I didn't want to bring in a stranger. Peter's a great, great musician, and I like his touch." Playing those keys that contributed to the creation of "Sledgehammer," Lanois said of the album's signature introduction that "it was the Emulator that produced that sound that opens 'Sledgehammer.' It's a stock sound, but the nature of the sound made it so the tracking of notes was a little irregular, so Peter's playing a little kind of arpeggiating hook, and then the machine's trying to catch up to it, so it's sort of tripping over itself. I've never been interested in external forces, I'd rather use the forces of the room."

Delving into the album's construction, Lanois touched on some of his own norms for that progress, recalling that

we built the whole record without drums and bass, and stuck to one of my preproduction principles of: never proceed without magic. That meant I wanted to make sure the songs, that the tracks, had magic in them, and fun in them, and so once the songs had clarified themselves, and we really had structures, we brought in drums. Ultimately, we favored Manu Katche, who had been recommended to us by a friend of Peter's from Senegal, and Manu was already quite a well-known drummer in Paris at that time. Prior to that, I had experimented briefly with another drummer, and it had fallen flat on its face; that was not a good day. I was trying to get a drummer who could shuffle, and at that time, that was not happening; drummers were putting mics in ceilings and gating snares and so on. So it was hard to find a drummer who had a lot of speed in the tops, or jazz drumming. And I said to Peter, "Listen man, I know you've left out the cymbals and the hi-hats on your previous few records here, but enough of that, let's get somebody who can make something sound sexy and has some fun with it." And that comes from getting a guy who's a great hi-hat player, so when Manu came in, the first thing I asked him was to go out into the live room and give a shuffle, and make it sound sexy. So he listened to the track, said "Yeah, I can do that," and went and knocked it out in one take. He had a really great foot too, a top-notch foot, there's no better man on the foot, which was great because you can struggle in the studio trying to get a bass drum sound. So I got hooked on him, and thought, "Okay, we've got somebody here," and that was it. He played on the whole record as an overall.

Turning to the technical side of building a rhythmic soundscape that fused the elements of Gabriel's eclectic palette of tastes—which ranged from pop to R&B, world to experimental, art rock to psychedelic, and well beyond—Lanois revealed a methodical research method he employed in the course of mapping that sound out loud whereby

I had already miced everything on the kit and had been working on the drum sounds for weeks on end. I don't just drag mics out of the closet when the drummer turns up at the door, so we made sure we'd done our homework. My process with that is to just keep moving mics around till I find the best one. Sometimes the RE 20 worked pretty good, or even a 57 or 58. Along with the live drums, we were working mostly with the Linn drum machine on *So*, but in some cases, we might have had a little sample of something we built on top. For example, for the song "Don't Give Up" had a little Linn drum pattern Peter had programmed, and it had this key figure rhythmically established, and when Tony Levin came in, he mimicked the phrasing of that, and added some notes that made sense with the chords.

Rolling Stone would celebrate *So* as "a record of considerable emotional complexity and musical sophistication," and *Entertainment Weekly* took note its achievement in sharpening the singer's "writing and expanding his sonic scope." Lanois recalled that many of the album's greatest musical moments came

out of jams. Usually, the beginning of everything had eccentricity written in it. We take it for granted in the studio, but that's what had Peter excited at the time. So I always extended our arrangements so that we had a nice patch of bars on the back end to jam onto, so we always stayed on the grid rhythmically, so—for instance—the back end of "Sledgehammer" went on for ten minutes. So a lot of what you're hearing in the back end of "Sledgehammer" is from those ad-libs where Peter'd just lose his mind and go off. Then I'd come through those ad-libs after work and make a little best-of and present them to Peter. They were usually somewhat blurry to Peter because he'd been shouting them, so the next day we'd go in and mimic the phrasing of the ad-libs and refine the lyrics. So that was a way of presenting a mate with some of his best melodies that might go missing if you didn't take the time to listen back—it's like archeological work, or mining for gold.

Detailing his process for settling on an always-important tool in the creation of such magic vocal tracks, Lanois recalled that ultimately selected the microphone used to capture Gabriel's vocals based on the sonic baseline of liking

the air in Peter's voice, and I wanted to find a microphone that captured that, and he had a beautiful old Neumann 47 from the '50s that had a fault in it, and so when you plugged it in, the only thing that came out was the top end. I didn't know what was going on with it, but the top end sounded really beautiful, so I said to the tech, "Could you fix this mic, but don't change what I'm hearing. Keep the broken mic sound, but then do a side-chain with the full sound, so when you repair it, don't change the broken sound because I like it." So he delivers this thing back to me that has two SLRs coming out of it, and he said, "This XLR is your broken sound, and this other SLR is the stock sound." So from there on, as we were tracking, I could put up the full-bodied all-natural sound, and then bring up the other fader and add the top end. And I never knew what it was. I always would commit to one track as the lead, and was just treating it like an equalizer but from the source. The mic had a little bit of that sound that you get from recording with Dolby when you take the buttons out; it had a bit of that vibe in the silkiness, a little bit of that C500 Sony sound.

With the release and smash success of *So*, *Rolling Stone* would argue that Lanois had helped Gabriel "finally figure out how to play these new tools as pop. Amazingly, he does so without compromising the ambition or adventurousness of his previous efforts." The *L.A. Times* would concur with its conclusion that, following the artist's "first four brilliant solo albums . . . Gabriel stands out as never before," hitting home on a broader general commentary that could be made of the producer who has faithfully dedicated himself over decades of hit albums to the same great ends. Recognized by *Rolling Stone* for his talent at achieving "flawless high-tech production" across a multiplatinum universe of star-styles, subgenres, and generations, as he passes his legacy in terms of experience along to the next generation, Lanois emphasizes his love for the game: "I never went into it as a business. I went into it because I loved it, and still there's a part of me that has that fire, and lucky for me, I was alive at a time where there was a paradigm in the culture where music was a big part of who people were. Though times have changed, I don't think that means there isn't another frontier for somebody to invent or pursue. So if you love it, man, go after it . . ."

ABOUT THE AUTHOR

Music biographer Jake Brown has written thirty-three published books in his decade-long career, including fourteen in his trademarked In the Studio series, highlights of which include authorized collaborations with legendary female rock band Heart, metal pioneers Motörhead, late hip-hop legend Tupac Shakur, and living guitar legend Joe Satriani (due in spring 2013), along with forthcoming anthologies including *Nashville Songwriter: The Inside Story Behind Country Music's Greatest Hits* and *Beyond the Beats: Hip Hop's Greatest Producers Profiled*, both due in 2013. He was also a coauthor of late funk pioneer Rick James's authorized memoir, and his broader catalog includes books on Tori Amos, Lady Gaga, Iron Maiden, AC/DC, Biggie Smalls, Jay Z, R. Kelly, Tom Waits, Amy Winehouse, Dr. Dre, Kanye West, Rick Rubin, Jane's Addiction, Death Row Records founder Suge Knight, Nikki Sixx, Prince, Lil Wayne, and a host of others. Brown has received major media coverage in *USA Today*, MTV, *Billboard*, *Publishers Weekly*, and *Classic Rock* magazine among others, has been published by multiple publishers in North America and internationally in UK and broader Europe, Japan/the broader Pacific Rim, South America, the Former Soviet Bloc, etc. He has appeared as the featured biographer of record on Fuse TV's *Live Through This* series and Bloomberg TV's *Game Changers* series, and recently was nominated alongside Motörhead founder Lemmy Kilmister for a 2010 Association for Recorded Sound Collections Award for Excellence in Historical Recorded Sound Research. Brown is also owner/operator of Nashville-based Versailles Records, in business eleven years and distributed nationally by MVD Music Distribution.